Man Music

THE EARLY
ROMANTIC
ERA

Man & Music

THE EARLY ROMANTIC ERA

Between Revolutions: 1789 and 1848

EDITED BY ALEXANDER RINGER

M

First published in the United Kingdom 1990 by
The Macmillan Press Limited
Houndmills, Basingstoke, Hampshire RG21 2XS
and London

Associated companies in Auckland, Delhi, Dublin, Gaborone,
Hamburg, Harare, Hong Kong, Johannesburg, Kuala Lumpur,
Lagos, Manzini, Melbourne, Mexico City, Nairobi, New York,
Singapore and Tokyo.

ISBN 0-333-51601-X (hardback)

British Library Cataloguing in Publication Data
Man and Music
    Vol.6, The early Romantic era
    1. Music, history
    I. Ringer, Alexander L.
    780.9

Typeset by Florencetype Ltd, Kewstoke, Avon
Printed in Hong Kong

Contents

Illustration Acknowledgments   vi

Abbreviations   vii

Preface   ix

I   The Rise of Urban Musical Life between
the Revolutions, 1789–1848
Alexander L. Ringer   1

II   Paris: Centre of Intellectual Ferment
Ralph P. Locke   32

III   Vienna: Bastion of Conservatism
Sigrid Wiesmann   84

IV   Berlin: 'Music in the Air'
Christoph-Hellmut Mahling   109

V   Dresden and Leipzig: Two Bourgeois Centres
Sieghart Döhring   141

VI   Italy: the Centrality of Opera
John Rosselli   160

VII   London: the Professionalization of Music
Joel Sachs   201

VIII   Moscow and St Petersburg
Gerald R. Seaman   236

IX   The USA: a Quest for Improvement
Kathryn Bumpass   259

X   Latin America: Independence and Nationalism
Gerard Béhague   280

Chronology   294

Index   308

Illustration
Acknowledgments

The publisher would like to thank the following institutions and individuals who have kindly provided material for use in this book:
Oxford Illustrators: 1; Österreichische Nationalbibliothek: 2, 3, 28, 38; Städelsches Kunstinstitut, Frankfurt am Main: 4; Bibliothèque Royale Albert Ier, Brussels: 5; Museum für Hamburgische Geschichte: 6; Kurpfälisches Museum der Stadt Heidelberg: 7; Bibliothèque de l'Opéra, Paris: 8, 24, 25; Artephoto/Ziolo, Paris: 9; Musée des Beaux Arts, Strasbourg: 10; Museum der Stadt Wien: 11, 36; Private Collections: 12, 69(b), 70; Haags Gemeentemuseum, The Hague: 13; Frans Halsmuseum, Haarlem: 14; Mary Evans Picture Library, London: 15, 32, 53, 75; Bodleian Library, Oxford: 16 (Ms M.D. Mendelssohn c.21, f.123), 81, 84; Kunsthalle, Hamburg: 17; H. Baron: 18; Musée Carnavalet, Paris/photo Lauros-Giraudon: 19, 20; Trustees of the British Museum, London: 21; Bulloz, Paris: 22; Bibliothèque Nationale, Paris: 26, 27 (from *Musique et Caricature en France au XIX Siècle* by Yane Fromich, Editions Minkoff, Geneva, 1973), 31; Musée du Louvre, Paris/photo Réunion des Musees Nationaux: 29; Trustees of the Wallace Collection, London: 33(a); Dover Publications Inc, New York (1981) in association with the Lilly Library, Indiana University, Bloomington: 33(b); Österreichische Galerie, Vienna/Fotostudio Otto: 34; Beethoven-Haus, Bonn: 35; Bärenreiter Bildarchiv, Kassel: 37; Stadtbibliothek, Vienna: 39; Gesellschaft der Musikfreunde, Vienna: 40; Bildarchiv Preussischer Kulturbesitz, Berlin: 41, 45 (Staatsbibliothek), 54 (Mendelssohn-Archiv); Opera Rara, London: 42, 65; Archiv für Kunst und Geschichte, Berlin: 44, 46, 47, 49, 50; Märkisches Museum, East Berlin: 48; Sächsische Landesbibliothek/Deutsches Fotothek Dresden: 51, 52 (Carl-Maria-von-Weber-Gedenkstätte, Dresden-Hosterwitz); Museum für Geschichte der Stadt Leipzig: 55, 57; Richard Macnutt, Withyham, Sussex: 56, 64; Museo Teatrale alla Scala, Milan: 58 (photo Giancarlo Costa), 59, 62 (photo Giancarlo Costa), 63, 67; Board of Trustees of the Victoria and Albert Museum, London: 60, 68, 73, 76; Museo Correr, Venice/photo Giacomelli: 61(a); Civica Raccolta Stampe 'A. Bertarelli', Castello Sforzesco, Milan: 61(b); Museo del Risorgimento, Milan/photo Giancarlo Costa: 66; Mander and Mitchenson Theatre Collection, Beckenham: 69; Oxford University Press: 71; Royal College of Music, London: 72, 74; Robert Harding Picture Library, London/photos Victor Kennett: 77; Society for Cultural Relations with the USSR, London: 79, 80; facsimile by Da Capo Press Inc, New York: 82; Moravian Music Foundation Inc, Winston-Salem: 83; Henry Madden Library, California State University, Fresno: 85

Abbreviations

AMZ	Allgemeine musikalische Zeitung
AnMc	Analecta Musicologica
CMc	Current Musicology
EMH	Early Music History
Grove6	The New Grove Dictionary of Music and Musicians
GroveA	The New Grove Dictionary of American Music
IMSCR	International Musicological Society Congress Report
JAMS	Journal of the American Musicological Society
MGG	Die Musik in Geschichte und Gegenwart
ML	Music and Letters
MMR	Monthly Musical Record
MQ	The Music Quarterly
MT	The Musical Times
NOHM	New Oxford History of Music
PRMA	Proceedings of the Royal Musical Association
RdM	Revue de musicologie
RIM	Rivista italiana di musicologia
RMARC	R[oyal] M[usical] A[ssociation] Research Chronicle

Preface

The *Man and Music* series of books – eight in number, chronologically organized – were originally conceived in conjunction with the television programmes of the same name, of which the first was shown by Channel 4 in 1986 and distributed worldwide by Granada Television International. These programmes were designed to examine the development of music in particular places during particular periods in the history of Western civilization.

The books have the same objective. Each is designed to cover a segment of Western musical history; the breaks between them are planned to correspond with significant historical junctures. Since historical junctures, or indeed junctures in stylistic change, rarely happen with the neat simultaneity that the historian's or the editor's orderly mind might wish for, most volumes have 'ragged' ends and beginnings: for example, the Renaissance volume terminates, in Italy, in the 1570s and 80s, but continues well into the seventeenth century in parts of northern Europe.

These books do not, however, make up a history of music in the traditional sense. The reader will not find technical, stylistic discussion in them; anyone wanting to trace the detailed development of the texture of the madrigal or the rise and fall of sonata form should look elsewhere. Rather, it is the intention in these volumes to show in what context, and as a result of what forces – social, cultural, intellectual – the madrigal or sonata form came into being and took its particular shape. The intention is to view musical history not as a series of developments in some hermetic world of its own but rather as a series of responses to social, economic and political circumstances and to religious and intellectual stimuli. We want to explain not simply *what* happened, but *why* it happened, and why it happened when and where it did.

We have chosen to follow what might be called a geographical, or perhaps a topographical, approach: to focus, in each chapter, on a particular place and to examine its music in the light of its particular situation. Thus, in most of these volumes, the chapters – once past the introductory one, contributed by the volume editor – are each devoted to a city or a region. This system has inevitably needed some modification when dealing with very early or very recent times, for reasons (opposite ones, of course) to do with communication and cultural spread.

These books do not attempt to treat musical history comprehensively. Their editors have chosen for discussion the musical centres that they see as the most significant and the most interesting; many lesser ones inevitably escape individual discussion, though the patterns of their musical life may be discernible by analogy with others or may be separately referred to in the opening, editorial chapter. We hope, however, that a new kind of picture of musical history may begin to emerge from these volumes, and that this picture may be more accessible to the general reader, responsive to music but untrained in its techniques, than others arising from more traditional approaches. In spite of the large number of lovers of music, musical histories have never enjoyed the appeal to a broad, intelligent general readership in the way that histories of art, architecture or literature have done: these books represent an attempt to reach such a readership and explain music in terms that may quicken their interest.

★

The television programmes and books were initially planned in close collaboration with Sir Denis Forman, then Chairman of Granada Television International. The approach was worked out in more detail with several of the volume editors, among whom I am particularly grateful to Iain Fenlon for the time he has generously given to discussion of the problems raised by this approach to musical history, and also to Alexander Ringer and James McKinnon for their valuable advice and support. Discussion with Bamber Gascoigne and Tony Cash, in the course of the making of the initial television programmes, also proved of value. I am grateful to Celia Thomson for drafting the chronologies that appear in each volume and to Elisabeth Agate for her invaluable work as picture editor in bringing the volumes to visual life.

London, 1990   STANLEY SADIE

Chapter I

The Rise of Urban Musical Life between the Revolutions, 1789–1848

ALEXANDER L. RINGER

The six decades that elapsed between the storming of the Paris Bastille on 14 July 1789 and the ultimate defeat of the Hungarian revolutionary forces at Villagos on 13 August 1849 witnessed a virtually continuous series of rapid changes not only in the political realm but also in the arts and sciences. Indeed, the very word 'revolution' was used in connection with music (specifically with the operas of Gluck) well before it gained political currency, conceivably because drastic changes of an aesthetic nature tend to entail considerably less personal risk than public violence. Indeed, as integral aspects of the quiet intellectual revolution that often precedes its public political counterpart, artistic manifestations may in their distinct ways anticipate socio-political cataclysms.

Beaumarchais, in his preface to the opera *Tarare* composed in 1787 by Antonio Salieri, postulated a new art geared to the general commitment to progress which, he felt, was the hallmark of his age:

> [it] will be instanced as one of deep science and philosophy, rich in discoveries, full of energy and reason. The mind of the nation seems to be in a happy kind of crisis: a bright light over all things makes each one feel that everything could be better . . . everything grows, prospers, and improves. Let us, if possible, see if we can improve a great type of entertainment.[1]

But in the end it was an overriding philosophical concern that motivated men and women of Beaumarchais' ilk – the concern for human dignity and the rights of individuals irrespective of their ancestry or inherited social status. *Tarare*, Beaumarchais declared,

> is the title of my opera, but it is not the subject. The subject is that of the following maxim, which is at once severe and comforting:

1

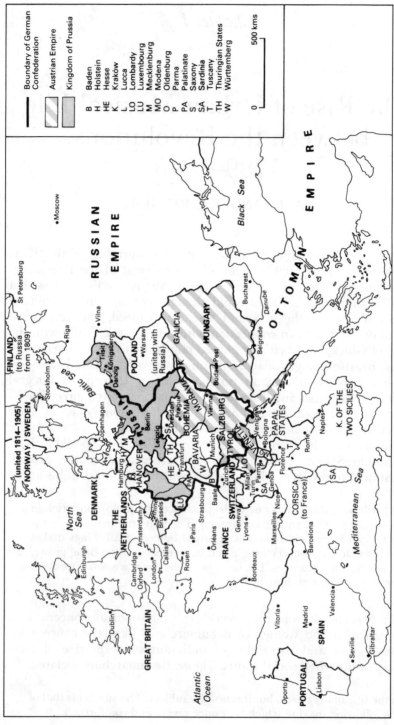

1. *Map of Europe after the Congress of Vienna in 1815*

Man! Thy merit on the earth
Does not depend upon thy birth:
It springs from character alone.[2]

It was clearly a new spirit that spoke from this 'severe' yet to an
emerging middle-class audience understandably 'comforting' maxim,
the spirit of a bourgeoisie that owed its forthcoming victories over the
entrenched interests of the traditionally privileged to its self-generated
sense of personal enterprise and its contingent devotion to the idea of
inexorable human progress. When Beethoven nearly four decades
later identified himself proudly as a 'brain owner' in response to his
brother's rather grotesque 'land owner', he did so as a true child of
'the revolution that occurred before it actually took place' (Chateaubriand); it in fact 'took place' over a period of nearly a century and
reached its apogee during the era explored in this book.

In his lifetime (1770–1827) Beethoven witnessed not merely the
French Revolution and the rise and fall of Napoleon Bonaparte but

2. A scene from Beet-
hoven's opera 'Fidelio' as
illustrated in the 'Wiener
Hoftheater Almanach'
(1815) after the success-
ful 1814 revival at
the Kärntnertortheater,
Vienna

3

also the reforms instituted by Joseph II, which included the abolition of serfdom, the granting of freedom of religion and the suppression of the monasteries in the Austrian Empire. As a boy of thirteen he heard of Montgolfier's first balloon flight, and five years later he could ponder the democratic rights embodied in the American constitution. In 1792, the year he decided to settle permanently in Vienna, Londoners marvelled at their first gas lights; and a short time later Eli Whitney's cotton gin transformed an entire industry, just as his invention of the rifle with interchangeable parts revolutionized warfare at the crucial moment of Napoleon's ascendance to unlimited power. Meanwhile, in 1796, Jenner had produced the original smallpox vaccine, a medical breakthrough of momentous proportions, and Laplace's *Exposition du système du monde* drastically changed basic conceptions of the cosmos. Of more direct musical interest was Senefelder's invention of lithography in Vienna the year after. In 1800, when Beethoven's grand Akademie offered proof to all and sundry that music could boast of its own Napoleon, Volta produced the first electric element, while Paris reached the 'astronomic' number of 550,000 inhabitants. Beethoven had barely completed his Eroica Symphony when Napoleon signed the *Code civile* that was to have such far-reaching socio-political consequences for all of Europe. Ironically, he was at work on *Fidelio*, the last of the great 'rescue operas' in a line with similar works by Méhul, Cherubini and other French revolutionary colleagues, when Napoleon crowned himself Emperor of France.

Mälzel's metronome of 1815, which so intrigued Beethoven, was but a minor link in the scientific-technological chain that stretched tightly across the first quarter of a new century intrigued by Fulton navigating his steamboat up the Hudson river and Stephenson manning the first steam locomotive. A year after Beethoven composed his Hammerklavier Sonata op.106, the *SS Savannah* reached Europe from America in an astonishing 26 days. Yet, while individual inventiveness as well as commerce and industry could boast one major achievement after another, Hegel in 1807 quietly wrote his *Phenomenology of Spirit*, the *chef d'oeuvre* of idealistic philosophy, and his exact contemporary Beethoven composed his Fifth Symphony. Meanwhile Napoleon, flushed with his victory at Jena, dismantled parts of Prussia and created the new state of Westphalia for his brother Jérôme. The latter, in turn, anxious to enhance his new court's cultural prestige, made Beethoven a lucrative offer that was difficult to refuse. In view of the political situation, it may thus have been as much a sense of patriotic duty as genuine admiration for the greatest musician of their time that impelled a consortium of reigning Viennese aristocrats to come up with a counter-offer generous enough to keep Beethoven in the Austrian capital.

3. Beethoven's 'Wellingtons Sieg oder Die Schlacht bei Vittoria' ('Battle Symphony') op.91; title-page of the first edition for piano (Vienna: Steiner, 1816)

Barely two years later, with Napoleon at the zenith of his power, Vienna came under French occupation for the third time. But popular resistance 'presaging important events', as Reichardt speculated in his 'Confidential Letters', was on the upsurge. Anyone capable of carrying a rifle, he reported, 'wants to join the war, insists . . . Even the nobility of the greatest and richest of families reveal themselves as true citizens'.[3] Beethoven responded in his inimitable way with his E♭ Piano Concerto, the 'Emperor', and the music to Goethe's heroic drama *Egmont*. Nothing less than a symphonic poem *avant la lettre*, the *Egmont* overture ends with a 'victory symphony' in miniature, so rousing in its highly charged conciseness that it puts to shame the empty noisiness of *Wellingtons Sieg oder Die Schlacht bei Vittoria*, the official, hugely successful 'Battle Symphony' with which the great composer celebrated the eventual defeat of his erstwhile idol. Typically, though, the 'Battle Symphony' brought with it what unparalleled years of creative work had failed to achieve: widespread fame and considerable fortune. Nor did this windfall come a moment too early for Beethoven. For the financially as well as politically troubled times ruined his principal benefactor, Prince Lobkowitz, in 1811 and a year later Prince Kinsky was killed in a riding accident.

5

Notwithstanding the sensationalism associated with a technically brilliant piece that appealed to the passions of the moment, 'serious' music was well on its way to becoming the symbol – if not the fetish – of 'high' bourgeois culture that it has remained to this day. Consequently, publishers were not only multiplying but doing reasonably well. Beethoven, who around the turn of the century had advocated 'a single Art exchange in the world', where the artist would send his works 'to be given as much as he needs',[4] in his later years dealt extensively and often shrewdly with Breitkopf, Schott, Diabelli, Clementi, Schlesinger or whoever else might be ready to pay him adequately. If anything, his by and large successful negotiations, though replete with complaints on his part, marked a new era: music now functioned as an autonomous art form, developing more or less freely, uninhibited by constraints of the sort that came with steady employment (whether in a religious or worldly context) or with restrictive commissions handed out by opera directors, court officials and others beholden to established custom or hallowed regulations. By the same token, however, where market forces governed musical life, anyone determined to defy them did so strictly at his own risk.

In purely aesthetic terms, the new-found artistic freedom was a corollary of the Romantic discovery of music as the 'language of feeling'. It was this, its much heralded affective appeal, which turned

4. Goethe in the Roman Campagna: portrait by Johann Heinrich Wilhelm Tischbein (1751–1829)

music into 'the favourite art of the middle class, the form in which it can express its emotional life more directly and with less hindrance than in any other'.[5] With 'imitation of nature' no longer touted as a universal aesthetic ideal, the weight of musical production inevitably shifted from vocal to instrumental genres free of 'concrete' verbal implications. Ties to literature persisted, though, and in some instances became stronger, not only in France with its entrenched literary tradition but also in Germany, where the music-loving bourgeoisie constituted the new reading public as well. Poetry flourished as never before: Klopstock, Lessing, Schiller and Goethe had managed to transform a rather unsystematic, unwieldy eighteenth-century means of verbal communication into that remarkably flexible language that underlies some of the nineteenth century's most intense lyricism. Among the leading authors of Romantic prose, E. T. A. Hoffmann may have been one of the few who tried their professional hand at musical composition, performance and criticism; but most were at the very least enthusiastic amateur musicians who drew much of their literary inspiration from musical experiences. The natural union of music and literature was something Romantic artists of the most diverse persuasions took for granted. But the pre-eminence of the language of feeling over the daily language of fact was never in question. As Felix Mendelssohn told a correspondent who inquired about the 'meaning' of some of his *Songs Without Words*: 'The thoughts that are expressed to me by music that I love are not too indefinite to be put into words, but on the contrary, too definite'.[6]

Especially in the German-speaking lands, music rapidly assumed metaphysical qualities which in the past had been associated primarily with religion. And as the moral dilemmas of their new, essentially materialistic clientèle continued to grow, most of the leading composers rose to the challenge. As early as 1817 Carl Maria von Weber declared that music was:

> to the arts and to mankind. . .what love is to man. . ., for it is actually love itself, the purest, most ethereal language of the emotions, containing all their changing colors in every variety of shading and in thousands of aspects; *true only once*, but to be understood simultaneously by thousands of differently constituted listeners.[7]

So considered, music represents far more than a mere aesthetic exercise, since it shoulders not merely social but also significant socializing functions akin to those of traditional organized religion. And it was this novel aspect of musical art in an ostensibly secular context that was quickly institutionalized, at first characteristically in the shape of large-scale music festivals and then by means of more or less permanent concert organizations like those presided over in Paris by Habeneck and in Leipzig by Mendelssohn. Under these changed and continuously changing conditions, the new breed of generally independent musicians interacted with their environments in any number of ways. As the young Robert Schumann, hardly a typical 'man of the world', confided to Clara Wieck in 1838: 'I am affected by everything that goes on in the world, and think it all over in my own way, politics, literature, and people, and then I long to express my feelings and find an outlet for them in music'.[8]

By then Schumann had made a name for himself as founder-editor of the *Neue Zeitschrift für Musik*, the progressive music journal committed to 'a stern attitude toward foreign trash' and, conversely, 'benevolence towards aspiring younger artists, enthusiasm for everything masterly that the past has bequeathed'.[9] Sheer virtuosity and unadulterated showmanship were the main targets of Schumann's journalistic arrows: 'On the stage Rossini still ruled', he remarked looking back in 1854; 'at the piano, with few rivals, Herz and Hünten'.[10] A prominent positive aspect was a budding sense of nationhood, at least in cultural terms, harking back to those heady days of the wars of liberation against Napoleon, when a Beethoven no less than a Weber had lent the patriotic forces their creative support. While it is true that the Metternich era that followed had given the word 'censorship' a new meaning, as it were, the revolutionary fires of individual freedom and national independence continued to smoulder.

The extent to which music and musicians were sharing in the rapidly changing course of historical events was demonstrated one summer night of 1830 in Brussels: after a performance of Auber's *La muette de Portici* the audience, deeply aroused by the musical élan of this spectacular grand opera based on a true story of political oppression and natural catastrophe, streamed into the square in front of the opera house and in open rebellion declared Belgium's independence from Dutch rule. As for the plight of Poland, in all likelihood Chopin and his music did far more for French popular support of its national aspirations than any single political force. In Italy Giuseppe Verdi's contributions to the cause of the Risorgimento eventually secured a seat in the new nation's senate for the composer whose chorus from *Nabucco*, 'Va pensiero', had served for a while as its provisional national anthem.

In short, music, which had so long been the handmaiden of religion and provided entertainment for royalty and nobility, now addressed a largely self-made bourgeoisie and its ever-widening interests and aspirations, whether aesthetic, ethical, political or strictly material. In keeping with the business spirit, it was increasingly treated as an admittedly valuable commodity available for purchase without restrictions and promoted and marketed accordingly. Well before the

5. *Riot following the performance of Auber's 'La muette de Portici' at the Théâtre de la Monnaie, Brussels (25 August 1830), which helped spark off the rebellion leading to Belgium's independence*

turn of the century Muzio Clementi in England, where commerce and industry reigned much earlier than on the Continent, had banked on his reputation as a keyboard player and built an enterprise which in its heyday manufactured and sold pianos, published piano music from beginners' études to Beethoven sonatas and provided live advertising for its merchandise with the help of leading artists like the young John Field who travelled as far as Russia on its behalf. In 1798 the Leipzig publishers Breitkopf & Härtel founded a house magazine, the *Allgemeine musikalische Zeitung*, that set the highest standards for music journalism; instead of succumbing to the temptation of promoting only their own immediate interests, Breitkopf and his associates ranged widely over the entire subject, confident that a well-informed public would ultimately also be to their benefit. E. T. A. Hoffmann was but one outstanding contributor who vigorously furthered the cause of Beethoven in this model journal, which has remained virtually unmatched in its breadth of coverage, literary excellence and catholicity of taste.

In the past, when music had been composed primarily for specific individuals or occasions, or both, a single public hearing was often all that might reasonably be expected. Bourgeois concert life, by contrast, depended more and more on repeat performances. For one, Beethoven's works made intellectual and emotional demands on musicians and audiences alike that no single performance was likely to satisfy. Conversely, once repeat performances became standard practice, composers felt free to require even greater efforts on the part of all concerned. The result was an expanding repertory of concert works written for large paying audiences whose members were not necessarily as well informed as their noble predecessors. Beethoven initiated the trend, but others followed: Berlioz in France, Schumann and Mendelssohn in Germany and – at least indirectly thanks to Schumann's discovery of his great C major Symphony – Schubert in Austria, to mention only a few whose combined instrumental output far outlived its authors. Not only did their large-scale compositions invite repeated hearings for the sake of better 'musical understanding'; in a spirit of competition previously limited to the operatic world, concert establishments all over Europe soon vied for the same pieces by prominent musicians whose names were becoming household words and who, therefore, attracted the merely curious or desperately fashionable as much as the truly interested and informed.

In a society in which wealth was rarely the lot of those who produced it, much attention focussed on the expert performer, the appealingly re-creative rather than uniquely creative individual; except that ideally the two qualities were united in one extraordinary artist, as in the celebrated case of Franz Liszt. By the middle of the century the kind of empty virtuosity that Schumann so despised threatened to get out of hand. Even Paganini, whose 'devilish' feats on the violin trapeze had paved the way for an era of unprecedented technical achievement in both vocal and instrumental performance, could not have imagined the gimmicks used by clever promoters ever ready to cash in on the well-nigh universal fascination with musical stars whose often crude mannerisms caused young ladies to swoon and their companions to stand in awe before some male idol or to kiss the feet of an adored female singer. The newspapers, for their part, were quick to catch on with musical *feuilletons* that became widely read, especially in France where Berlioz regularly added his authoritative voice to that of Heine, Liszt and many other well-known artist-writers.

From the essentially moral perspective of a Schumann and his imaginary *Davidsbündler*, the musical 'philistinism' he perceived all round him was bound to precipitate the doom of music as a 'pure' language of feeling. During his student years in Heidelberg, Schumann had listened attentively to the scholarly pronouncements of the venerable Professor Thibaut, a persuasive advocate of 'purity in music' as embodied in the sacred *a cappella* art of the High Renaissance. What concerned the God-fearing jurist Thibaut was less a matter of aesthetics than of ethics. And that was pretty much the way a young Romantic like Schumann approached the artistic problems of his time. Thibaut's influential esay on the subject appeared in 1826. But even

6. Enthusiastic audience at a public concert given by Jenny Lind in Hamburg, 1845 ('We are lucky! We are delighted! The Lind has turned our heads'); anonymous lithograph

7. A group of singers performing Renaissance music at the Heidelberg home of Professor Thibaut; watercolour by Jakob Götzenburger (1800–66)

back in 1814, E. T. A. Hoffmann had taken a similar stand with an essay on 'Old and New Church Music' in the *Allgemeine musikalische Zeitung*. By 1828, when Giuseppe Baini published his fundamental Palestrina study, the *a cappella* movement was also well on its way in France, where Alexandre Choron presided over the Institut de Musique Religieuse Classique until the revolution of 1830 closed its doors for good. The Bach revival, meanwhile, received an unprecedented boost in 1829 when the twenty-year-old Felix Mendelssohn revived the *St Matthew Passion* on the supposed 100th anniversary of its first, and until then its last, performance. That year the Dutch Academy awarded prizes to the Austrian Raphael Georg Kiesewetter and the Belgian François Fétis for their respective pioneering studies of old Netherlands music. Thus musical scholarship too, though not yet an academic discipline, proceeded directly from the Romantic fascination with distant realms in time as well as in space.

Those characteristic concerns found their most immediate expression in operatic subject matter that ranged historically from medieval lore to British 'Gothic' novels and geographically from Mongolia to Latin America. Nor was the music immune to what came to be known as *couleur locale*, exotic flavour which in the eighteenth century had remained limited to an occasional 'à la turca' or 'chinoiserie'. In 1811 Beethoven gave an amazingly accurate account of whirling dervishes in his incidental music for Kotzebue's *Die Ruinen von Athen* without the advantage enjoyed by Félicien David who in his 'symphonic ode' *Le désert* (1844) could draw upon Egyptian melodies collected by Villoteau during Napoleon's north African campaign, though published only in 1826.

Opera, of course, had always relied on colourful displays, not only vocally, but by way of lavish scenery and costumes as well as the wonders produced by elaborate stage machinery. The traditional reliance on classical subject matter, however, imposed considerable emotional constraints especially with regard to stage deportment. The lively action that typified eighteenth-century Italian *opera buffa* and its French counterpart, *opéra comique*, did meet some of the rising bourgeoisie's objections to the staticism of *opera seria* and *tragédie lyrique*. But it took nineteenth-century grand opera to turn the opera stage into a mirror of public concerns and private passions to the point where a realistic production of an Auber opera could precipitate a political upheaval. Six years after that remarkable event, in 1836, Eugène Scribe and Giacomo Meyerbeer managed to infuse their most famous work, *Les Huguenots*, with such well-measured doses of history, politics and religion that their timely and theatrically effective version of the perennial Romeo and Juliet theme virtually by itself brought the long-unchallenged reign of Gioacchino Rossini over the European opera stage to an abrupt end. At any rate, the highly popular composer of *Il barbiere di Siviglia* henceforth confined his artistry to strictly culinary delights.

To Schumann *cum suis*, Meyerbeer's sensational successes offered

8. *Costumes designed by F.-G. Menageot for the first production of Spontini's 'Fernand Cortez, ou La conquète du Mexique' at the Paris Opéra (28 November 1809)*

irrefutable evidence of the pernicious spread of materialism in the arts no less than in society at large. Admittedly Meyerbeer's brilliant orchestration, though following in the footsteps of Weber (his erstwhile fellow student in Abbé Vogler's Tonschule), reflected in opera some of the preoccupation with instrumental colour that distinguished the concert works of a Berlioz. But then Meyerbeer wrote *Les Huguenots* for Paris, not Leipzig or Berlin. Scribe's highly effective mass scenes, on the other hand, brought a measure of realism to the opera stage exceeded only by Wagner at his most Meyerbeerian. Surely Meyerbeer's musically identified groups of soldiers, gypsies, nuns and Sunday strollers in the third act of *Les Huguenots* inspired similar scenes in both *Rienzi* (1842) and *Die Meistersinger* (given its première in 1868).

That any such conception of the nature and function of musical drama was by definition incompatible with the convention of the 'marvellous' in earlier opera and, for that matter, the fairy-tale atmosphere of its German Romantic offshoots goes without saying. In comparison with Mozart's *Don Giovanni*, Meyerbeer's *Robert le diable* (1831) unquestionably appealed more openly and directly to the cruder instincts of its mixed audiences. And so Schumann 'began to waver' in his opinion of Meyerbeer even before *Les Huguenots* prompted him 'unhesitantly' to 'rank him among the performers in Franconi's circus'.[11] One as sensitive – indeed uncompromising – in matters of

9. *The coronation scene from Meyerbeer's opera 'Le prophète', first performed at the Paris Opéra (16 April 1849): painting by Louis-Gabriel-Eugène Isabey (1803–86)*

10. Don Juan and the Commendatore's Statue (c1829): painting by Alexandre Evariste Fragonard. In Romantic art the fantastic is often emphasized by the juxtaposition of figures of different scales

morality and taste, both real and imagined, as Schumann was bound to think of the mature Meyerbeer as a kind of operatic Herz or Hünten, if not Paganini: 'to strike dumb or to titillate' seemed to be his principal goal; 'nor does he fail to do both to the rabble'.[12] Schumann did not deny that 'Marcel's battle song is impressive, the page's song charming'; he acknowledged that 'the first part of the duet between Valentine and Marcel is effective through its characterization', but wondered, before proceeding to review 'something nobler', – the oratorio *St Paul* of his friend Mendelssohn – 'what does this amount to compared with the vulgarity, distortion, unnaturalness, indecency, unmusicality of the whole?'[13]

Thus the musical battle-lines were clearly and ominously drawn decades before the Wagner–Hanslick controversy erupted along well-defined party-lines and with tragic historical consequences well beyond the relatively benign realm of music journalism. Hardly by coincidence, it was Meyerbeer whose name was most often invoked later as the very symbol of 'Jewish internationalism' in music, corrupting the innocent in a typically unfair competition for the pure at heart. 'And you respectable German girls', the disheartened Schumann had asked himself, 'is it possible you do not hide your eyes?' Unlike Wagner and the demagogues acting falsely in his name,

Schumann singled out Mendelssohn as the perfect counterweight: '*His* road leads to happiness, the other, to evil'.[14]

The operatic wars of the eighteenth century had rarely, if ever, exceeded the verbal boundaries set by polite society. In nineteenth-century Germany, by contrast, aesthetic controversies were often marred by intractible rancour and, occasionally, outright viciousness. Inevitably, the German idealistic tradition found itself on a collision course with a musical market economy which, though not necessarily profit-orientated, reflected the capitalist mentality of both the new public of urban middle-class consumers and large numbers of musicians ever ready to cater to its simpler tastes. Richard Wagner's notorious essay on 'Judaism in Music', published at first anonymously in the middle of the century, was but the most recklessly irresponsible product of that deep-seated conflict which has never been satisfactorily resolved – because it is no doubt insoluble. The Romantic hero of W. H. Wackenroder's semi-autobiographical novel *The Remarkable Musical Life of the Musician Joseph Berglinger* (1797) 'thought himself made purer and more noble' after listening to a concert which, it should be noted, took place in a church.[15] But wherever he went to hear a concert, Joseph 'seated himself in a corner, without so much as glancing at the brilliant assembly of listeners, and listened with precisely the same reverence as if he had been in church'.[16] Half a century later Wagner referred to harmony as a sea into which 'man dives to yield himself again, radiant and refreshed, to the light of day'.[17]

As German Romanticism conceived of him, the musician of genius was honour-bound in an irreversibly secular world to assume his sacred duties as the priestly guardian of an irreproachably 'pure' musical grail. Hence, with some attending the concert hall much as though it were a house of prayer and others after a hard day's work looking simply for a pleasant evening's entertainment, there appeared to be little hope for common ground. Yet in the end, the twain did find two mutually acceptable and enjoyable meeting-places: the opera house and the ballroom, a combination so powerful that it penetrated even the hallowed walls of the traditional church. As the little Viennese seamstress told her mother in the late 1820s, the organist had played with such fervour during Sunday Mass that the entire congregation felt like dancing.[18] Schubert, for his part, could hardly stay away from the inn where Joseph Lanner performed with his orchestra.[19] Beethoven, Weber, Berlioz, Schumann, Chopin, virtually all 'serious' composers made their voluntary sacrifices to the waltz frenzy that seized the Continent during the early nineteenth century. In 1838 Ignaz Moscheles, one of Beethoven's most successful pupils, noted that even staid Londoners had fallen prey to Johann Strauss the elder: 'Where he fiddles, all dance – dance they must. In the concerts

11. *'Wiener Faschings Lust': lithograph from the supplement to the 'Wiener Theaterzeitung, Satirische Bilder' (1854) caricaturing, in descending social order, some Viennese dance halls*

which he gives with his small orchestra, people dance as they sit; at Almack's, the most fashionable of all subscription ballrooms, aristocratic feet tap in time with his tunes'.[20]

Such a wide range of creative and re-creative activities was obviously not sustainable in the long run unless proper provisions were made for the musical training of first-rate professionals, if only because technical facility of the highest order was now expected in every walk of musical life. Singers could point to a long history of professional instruction of one kind or another, given the essentially vocal base of European music from medieval chant through the operatic seventeenth and eighteenth centuries. Instrumental training, on the other hand, had been patchy at best since the days when ambulant minstrels introduced their young apprentices to the anything but hidden secrets of their limited instrumentarium. That relatively little changed in this respect over a long period is evident from the autobiographical accounts of several eighteenth-century musicians, including Johann Joachim Quantz. Even so, the trend in favour of specialization in a world convinced of the benefits of the division of labour affected music well before instrumental virtuosity became all the rage. Quantz's principal medium was the flute, Leopold Mozart's the violin.

Good wind players were badly needed, especially for the numerous military bands that sprang up in the wake of the Turkish campaigns when many a European prince heard and saw for the first time what such a band could do for military morale and discipline. By the time Captain Bernard Sarrette founded the Ecole de Musique de la Garde Nationale in revolutionary Paris (1793), the constant flow of large-scale outdoor festivities, not to mention the wars fought soon afterwards by *la patrie en danger*, required thousands of players to intone hymns to freedom and to lead the people's singing during endless patriotic processions through the streets of Paris. Quickly transformed into a 'national institute of music', Sarrette's school absorbed the Ecole Royale de Chant, which Gossec had directed since 1784, and in 1795 became the comprehensive Conservatoire National Supérieur de Musique that inspired the array of conservatories established in rapid succession throughout nineteenth-century Europe. Sarrette, meanwhile, saw to it that virtually every prominent local musician joined his staff. They devised systematic curricula for an unprecedented variety of musical pursuits, instituted competitions and commissioned the first modern music textbooks from the best specialists. Thus it was in revolutionary Paris that a distinguished group of musicians, including composers of the rank of Méhul, Le Sueur, Gossec, Catel and Reicha, laid the foundations of professional musical education.

Thanks to Napoleon, the Paris example found speedy emulation wherever the emperor's long military arm reached. In 1807 his son-in-law Eugène de Beauharnais founded the Milan Conservatory, while in Naples Joseph Bonaparte abolished several existing schools that went back to the sixteenth century in favour of a single institution in tune with the times. In view of Italy's special vocal propensities, the emphasis on singing was nevertheless retained, unfortunately to the continued detriment of orchestral standards. Louis Spohr, the German violinist-composer whose memoirs cover the entire period under consideration here, found on a visit to Milan in 1816 that little had changed in this respect:

> As in most Italian operas with from six to eight contra-basses there is one violoncello, and usually not even a good one, they as yet know nothing here of the (since *Mozart's* day) frequent use of the violoncello for middle voices, which, skilfully brought in, has such splendid effect; and they are far behind the Germans in the knowledge of how to get the best effect from the wind instruments.[21]

Spohr's criticism pertained ostensibly to several Rossini performances he attended, but Mendelssohn and Berlioz registered similar complaints decades later. That Germany was not really that much better off follows from Wagner's oft-cited statement that he grasped Beethoven's Ninth Symphony in all its complexity only when he heard it conducted by Habeneck in Paris.

Proper leadership was a large problem as long as various eighteenth-century habits persisted without due regard to the inherent requirements of quite different musical structures and textures. Again Spohr serves as an excellent witness. It was in 1820 that he had occasion to work with the Philharmonic Society orchestra in London, at that time one of the best anywhere. He had been invited by Ferdinand Ries, Beethoven's pupil, who in accordance with established custom sat at the piano with

> the score before him, not exactly to conduct from it, but only to read after and to play in with the orchestra at pleasure, which when it was heard, had a very bad effect. The real conductor was the first violin, who gave the *tempi*, and now and then when the orchestra began to falter gave the beat with the bow of his violin.

Spohr went on to explain that the ensemble was far too large and its members seated too far apart to be able to play properly together under these circumstances, the excellent qualities of its individuals notwithstanding: 'I had therefore resolved when my turn came to direct, to make an attempt to remedy this defective system'. Ries graciously gave up his score, and, Spohr recalled, 'I then took my stand with the score at a separate music desk in front of the orchestra, drew my baton from my coat pocket and gave the signal to begin'.[22]

Not only that: '[I] indicated also to the wind instruments and horns all their entries' and at this first modern rehearsal in London 'took the liberty, when the execution did not satisfy me, to stop, and in a very polite but earnest manner to remark upon the manner of execution, which remarks Mr. *Ries* at my request interpreted to the orchestra ... Surprised and inspired by this result the orchestra immediately after the first part of the symphony, expressed aloud its collective assent to the new mode of conducting, and thereby overruled all further opposition on the part of the directors'.[23] London music was never to be the same again.

Before long things musical changed everywhere – and drastically. 1836 was not only the year of *Les Huguenots* and Mendelssohn's *St Paul* but also of Glinka's *A Life for the Tsar*, the first 'national' opera produced by a native Russian composer of genius. Across the Atlantic Stephen Foster responded in his hardly less individual ways to the deep-seated populism of a new world which, in the judgment of Ralph Waldo Emerson, had already 'listened too long to the courtly muses of Europe'.[24] There, however, in old Europe the courtly muses had long since begun to yield to 'a muse for the masses'.[25] The year Emerson made his characteristic statement, 1837, Berlioz produced his Requiem with 400 instrumentalists and singers, not to mention an additional four brass bands for the 'Tuba mirum'. But while Berlioz in the French revolutionary tradition, according to his own words, un-leashed a veritable deluge upon those gathered to commemorate the revolution of 1830, Albert Lortzing's *Zar und Zimmermann* at that very moment successfully introduced German audiences to a far more intimate new genre, the Spieloper, an expanded, Romantic version of the eighteenth-century Singspiel which retained considerable middle-class appeal for generations.

Generally, however, the tendency to write for 'bigger and better' performing forces was unmistakable. Instruments previously reserved for special situations in opera (such as trombones in 'ombra' scenes projecting awe of the supernatural) were increasingly called for in symphonic scores. And chamber ensembles, too, gradually absorbed the new sound ideals. Many composers, German ones in particular, started their careers as pianists and hence favoured the piano not only as the pre-eminent solo instrument but also as the lead in chamber music. Schubert, Mendelssohn and Schumann wrote distinguished piano trios, quartets or quintets. Occasionally additional strings or wind were called for, as in Schubert's and Mendelssohn's quintets and octets. As for the orchestra, Beethoven, who required a third horn in his Eroica score, added three trombones, contrabassoon and a piccolo in his Fifth Symphony and in his Ninth expanded the apparatus further with a total of four horns and various percussion instruments for the 'Turkish music' in the finale. Moreover, instru-

12. *Chamber music: Anthony (the artist's husband, facing centre) and friends playing a string quartet at his Frankfurt home: watercolour (c1843) by Mary Ellen Best*

ments previously limited to supporting roles were assigned more prominent tasks, as in the Trio of the Fifth Symphony's Scherzo, where the double basses join the cellos in rapid passage-work that few would have dared to assign at that time to orchestral cellists, let alone double-bass players. Schubert in his last two symphonies used the trombone in unprecedented thematic ways. Similarly, in his superb string quintet the second cello ensures both a dense texture in general and solid bass sonorities in particular. The growing stress on bass lines, too, had come to the fore with Beethoven's Eroica, which owes virtually all its thematic material to a pre-existing bass subject.[26] Schubert, in his 'Trout' Quintet, went so far as to omit the second violin in favour of a double bass.

All that bass heaviness was, of course, the natural corollary of the overriding structural significance of functional harmony in the nineteenth century, truly the age of harmony. Since triadic harmony is literally based on the bass, a strong bass line was bound to enhance the effectiveness of the principal chords formed by the three lowest overtones of its constituent pitches. It is this historically inescapable phenomenon of nature, by the way, which must account for a good deal of the enormous popularity of the nineteenth-century piano and its virtuoso practitioners. Typically, the flute, a favourite instrument in the eighteenth century, suffered a rapid decline when it proved incapable, in spite of various improvements, of matching the clarinet's full, well-rounded tone, produced by the lower spectrum of the

Der General Bass wird durch List in seinen festen Linien überrumpelt u. überwunden.

13. 'The general bass, in its fixed lines, is taken by surprise and overwhelmed by List [Liszt]' (List = cunning); anonymous lithograph (c1842)

harmonic series. The piano, of course, became the ideal harmonic medium by virtue of its technology which, thanks to the fierce competition among British, French and German manufacturers, experienced virtually continuous upgrading: before long it could render credible two-handed approximations of entire orchestras. Chopin, for one, though justly famous for his 'singing tone' in his lyrical nocturnes, turned to the orchestra for inspiration when it came to scherzos and, above all, sonatas in which an orchestrally conceived funeral march was by no means out of place. Much the same holds for Liszt, whose B minor Sonata (1854) has all the hallmarks of a symphonic poem idiomatically written for the piano.

Orchestral instruments, too, improved rapidly, upgraded in terms of both sonority and flexibility. Horns and trumpets received valves or pistons, enabling players to perform with relative ease in any key, while changes and additions put the woodwind almost on an equal footing with the strings, which themselves were altered to allow for more speed as well as volume. And newly invented instruments further enriched an ever-expanding body of sonorous resources. By 1844, the year his compatriot Jean-George Kastner first demanded a saxophone in an orchestral score, Berlioz completed a *Traité de l'instrumentation et d'orchestration moderne* that has lost little of its practical validity, let alone its historical importance for a better understanding of the musical thinking of one of the greatest masters of the orchestra of any time.

The sophistication that typified the instrumentation of Berlioz or Meyerbeer, was not merely a matter of exquisite timbres for their own purely sensory sake. Rather, musical colour, like that of the english horn, the lowest member of the oboe family, took on powers of characterization which, especially in association with particular keys, permitted composers to convey more or less definite meanings, at least for the benefit of adequately informed listeners. Neither the notion of key characteristics nor that of concrete attributes of instruments was new in itself. Both were rooted in the early eighteenth-century theory of musical affects and had influenced vocal music for generations, as almost any aria with an obbligato solo instrument will demonstrate. And that particular practice persisted well into the era of Bellini and Donizetti. But these early nineteenth-century Italian opera composers were still steeped in eighteenth-century traditions. Nineteenth-century instrumental music, on the other hand, devoid of any text, had to rely on a set of strictly musical codes to convey 'meaning'. And it is in this

14. Interior with a clarinettist: painting (1813) by Johannes Reekers. The clarinet found favour among early nineteenth-century composers for its wide range and variety of tone colour

15. *The instrument factory of Adolphe Sax in Paris: engraving from 'L'illustration' (5 February 1848) showing a completed baritone saxophone (right) and 'Berliner-Pumpen' valves which are being assembled (centre foreground)*

context that specific mental associations assumed an entirely new significance, not only in so-called 'programme' symphonies that purported to tell a story or relate a series of events.

Exterior motivations of this sort may or may not be compatible with classical musical patterns like those of the rondo, the sonata-allegro or three-part song forms. Hence, anyone endeavouring to follow a composer's narrative outline faithfully may have to go beyond such traditional structural confines, let alone their conventional combinations into various multi-movement types. Neither, however, as Liszt pointed out in his review of Berlioz's *Harold en Italie*, is it likely that a composer concerned exclusively with 'the consumption of the material alone' will be 'deriving new forms from it, breathing into it new strength, for no intellectual necessity urges him'.[27] In other words, a composer who wishes to avoid conventional patterns had better find an appropriate 'programme'.

Such considerations in fact accounted for much of Berlioz's work, beginning with his *Symphonie fantastique*, and later steered Liszt himself in the direction of the symphonic poem. In 1849 both he and a young César Franck tried their hands at orchestral renditions of what they each independently regarded as the essence of Victor Hugo's *Ce qu'on entend sur la montagne*. The symphonic poem, or tone poem, descended directly from the Berliozian programme symphony on one hand and, on the other, the concert overture; the latter, following the Beethovenian model, survived quite well for a while within the liberal constraints of the Classical sonata-allegro form with or without a slow introduction. Mendelssohn's descriptive masterpiece of 1830, his *Fingal's Cave* overture, is an outstanding case in point. Interestingly, Liszt's arguably most famous symphonic poem, *Les préludes* (1854), retained the sonata pattern in apparent violation of its alleged programme. However, it was not conceived in terms of any such programme, but as an overture for a series of male choruses dealing with the four elements, composed at the latest in 1848. This curious case aptly demonstrates the tenuous relationship between musical works and their true or imagined sources of inspiration.

Romantic poetry did find its ideal musical realization, however, in the most genuinely Romantic of all nineteenth-century genres, the German lied. Schubert was by no means the first to set late eighteenth-century German ballads or love poems to music; Mozart, Zumsteeg and Reichardt, among others, had done so before him. Nor did he initiate the practice of stringing them together in a *Liederkreis* or song cycle. Beethoven's *An die ferne Geliebte*, written in 1816 to texts by the minor poet Jeitteles, was not only the first genuine song cycle in purely poetic terms; to assure perfect musical continuity, the composer went so far as to eliminate breaks between the six constituent songs. But it was Schubert who first told a continuous story in an extensive,

16. View of Amalfi: watercolour by Felix Mendelssohn painted in May 1831 on a tour of Italy during which he began work on his Italian Symphony

yet tightly structured grouping of a total of twenty songs. *Die schöne Müllerin* projects a drama of unrequited love more dramatically than many an opera of its time (1823). However, the decisive events occur between, rather than in, the songs which focus on the narrator's reactions and anticipations, much like arias in eighteenth-century opera. Schubert's was an intensely lyrical disposition. Like Schumann, Chopin and indeed much of the German Romantic generation after him, he made up generously in melodiousness, harmonic imagination, sonority and colour for what he lacked in dramatic instincts and theatrical flair.

The powerful generation and often heroic resolution of conflict with purely musical means that had been the glory of Beethoven was not for those who put feelings far ahead of ideas. Nor did Romantic composers generally possess the polyphonic wherewithal that enabled Beethoven to engage in the kind of dialectical discourses that are at the heart of his extended thematic developments. Lyrically in- clined composers repeatedly ran into rhythmic problems too. When Schumann in the first movement of his First Symphony, with its countless repetitions of the initial dotted-note pattern, moves from key to key in a starkly homophonic development, that pattern assumes well-nigh obsessive qualities, the more so as his bland orchestration does little to avert the very real danger of ultimate tedium. By contrast, Schubert wisely decided to let the two beautifully lyrical movements of his B minor Symphony stand by themselves, even if the result was in conventional terms 'unfinished'. In aesthetic terms more would have been too much, in spite of the fact that Schubert resolved his first-movement problem with a stroke of genius: instead of belabouring the extensive lyrical themes of his exposition he based his development on the introductory bass motif which, though short, is imbued (unlike Schumann's pattern) with the requisite melodic-harmonic qualities. Along somewhat different but equally brilliant lines *Die schöne Müllerin* follows a carefully laid-out key scheme with due regard to poetic as well as musico-structural considerations. And both receive reinforcement from motivic links that make for a remarkably tight overall design on a par with that of any early Beethoven sonata. Considering, moreover, that all twenty songs remain well within the vocal reach of any good amateur singer, Schubert, to all historical intents and purposes, initiated a genre that was to offer subsequent composers from Schumann to Mahler to Schoenberg a wide range of opportunities for expressing their most intimate musico-poetic ruminations.

Such an unprecedentedly personal, often highly emotional relation-

17. Wanderer above the Mists: painting (c1818) by Caspar David Friedrich. The isolation of the individual was a recurring Romantic theme

ship of nineteenth-century creative – and, for that matter, re-creative – musicians to their work was, of course, typical of Romantic artists and largely determined the very nature and quantity of their output. Berlioz characteristically sublimated his infatuation with the British actress Harriet Smithson in the 'fantastic' apparitions of his first great orchestral work, while Schumann's much-delayed marriage to Clara Wieck in 1840 turned that beacon year into the song year of the century. The reverse side of this particular Romantic coin, however, was the drastically reduced productivity of individuals struggling for 'inspiration' from quarters that most of their predecessors would have considered of little aesthetic import. The more the 'language of feeling' sought to fathom the human psyche, especially the composer's own, the more tortured and extended, it seems, was the creative process. Whatever results it yielded, moreover, frequently underwent periodic revisions, as if, at a time when performers began to insist on 'highly idiosyncratic 'interpretations', at least some composers felt they ought to contribute their share. This Romantic trend reached its apogee only later in the century. But the young Brahms was by no means the first to experiment with different versions of what were in essence semi-autobiographical musical essays which, as in his case, might end up as a piano concerto, quartet or symphony.

Scruples of this sort rarely affected opera. With two centuries of

18. Two scenes from Weber's opera 'Der Freischütz' from the Leipzig 'Orphea-Taschenbuch' (1824): (a) Agathe's cavatina in Act 3

(b) Wolf's Glen scene in Act 2

evolving theatrical conventions behind it, an entrenched form of public entertainment like opera, by virtue of its eventful history, collective nature and social function, was ill-suited for personal confessions of any kind. And, for all we know, that is at least one reason why, with all the great symphonies, sonatas, string quartets and other products of a growing concert repertory, it remained a favourite of bourgeois audiences which, politically, had little use for its erstwhile aristocratic patrons. From Spontini's *La vestale* (1807) and Weber's *Der Freischütz* (1821), Bellini's *Norma* and Meyerbeer's *Robert le diable* of 1831, Donizetti's *Lucia di Lammermoor* and Halévy's *La juive* of 1835, to Wagner's *Tannhäuser* (1845) and *Lohengrin* (1850), opera was the talk of German towns as much as of Paris, Vienna, Naples or Milan, where Bellini, Donizetti and Meyerbeer held sway. Character-istically, too, nearly all the new works retained some form of *le merveilleux* – some element of magic, the supernatural or at the very least an inexplicable psychological occurrence. There are magic bullets and midsummer-night spirits in Weber's operas, sprouting walking-sticks and mysterious swans in Wagner's and the ubiquitous sleepwalkers in Bellini's and Donizetti's. And their musical character-izations or contexts, or both, added greatly to the ever-expanding list of orchestral devices. Moreover, virtually every area of musical activity reflected operatic practices, church music by no means excluded. Berlioz's 'dramatic symphony' *Roméo et Juliette* (1839) in fact seems more Shakespearean in spirit at given moments than Gounod's opera of the same title composed nearly three decades later. And much the same could be said of the former's admittedly hybrid *La damnation de Faust* in relation to the latter's *Faust*.

Whether on the operatic or the concert stage, however, the singer, especially the female singer, still reigned supreme. That this was so, continuous advances in orchestral sonority notwithstanding, must be attributed at least in part to the new vocal techniques taught by a few dedicated individuals like the members of the García family; they improved voice control to the point at which their best pupils easily held their own against the ever-larger forces in the orchestra pit. The great French tenor Adolphe Nourrit, for example, owed his triumph as the original Marcel in *Les Huguenots* in large measure to the elder Manuel García, possibly the first to insist on proper use of the head voice. 'The singular strength he was able to give to the sounds in this register', explained one authoritative eyewitness, allowed him to 'sing without that excess of fatigue he would have experienced if he had made constant use of the chest voice'.[28] A second-generation García pupil, the 'Swedish nightingale' Jenny Lind, appeared in New York in 1850 in Bellini's *Norma* with a full orchestra under Julius Benedict (at the time Britain's leading conductor); at her rendition of 'Casta diva' 'the audience were so completely carried away by their feelings that the remainder of the air was drowned in a perfect tempest of acclamation'.[29]

That year, in his Swiss exile, Wagner completed his vision of 'the artwork of the future'. Like Schumann before him, he abhorred the more circus-like aspects of musical life in general and their operatic manifestations in particular. Taking his cues from Greek drama, as had the originators of the *dramma per musica* and virtually every opera reformer thereafter, Wagner looked for the perfect union of all the constituent elements of musical drama in a collective work of art admittedly inspired by, yet going well beyond, what Beethoven had wrought in his Ninth Symphony, the Choral. To Wagner's admiring mind, Beethoven remained in essence a musical Columbus who 'discovered America only for the fulsome petty profiteering of our time'.[30] Whether Wagner in his singlemindedness would acknowledge it or not, 'our time', the time of emerging public concerts as part of a growing appreciation of 'the finer things' in middle-class life, the age of revolution in every realm of human existence, also laid the foundations for his own radical achievement and thus for most of what has happened since in music.

NOTES

¹ *The Pleasures of Music*, ed. J. Barzun (New York, 1951), 229.
² Ibid, 233.
³ K. Schönewolf, *Beethoven in der Zeitwende*, i (Halle, 1953), 457–8.
⁴ See Beethoven's letter of Jan 1801 to the publisher Franz Hoffmeister, in *Beethoven: Letters, Journals and Conversations*, ed. M. Hamburger (London, 1951), 17.
⁵ A. Hauser, *The Social History of Art*, iii (New York, 1958), 82.
⁶ Mendelssohn to Marc-André Souchay, 15 Oct 1841; see *Letters of Composers*, ed. G. Norman and L. Shrifte (New York, 1946), 146.
⁷ *Source Readings in Music History*, ed. O. Strunk (New York, 1950/R1965), 146.
⁸ *Letters of Composers*, 157.
⁹ Schumann, in his 1839 'speech from the throne'; in *Source Readings*, 827.
¹⁰ Ibid, 828.
¹¹ R. Schumann, *On Music and Musicians*, ed. K. Wolf (New York, 1969), 194.
¹² Ibid, 195.
¹³ Ibid, 196–7.
¹⁴ Ibid, 199.
¹⁵ *Source Readings*, 753.
¹⁶ Ibid.
¹⁷ Ibid, 884.
¹⁸ J. Mainzer, 'Vienne et la synagogue juive', *Gazette musicale de Paris*, i (1834), 144.
¹⁹ See E. Reeser, *The History of the Dance* (Stockholm, n.d.), 48.
²⁰ *The Pleasures of Music*, 327.
²¹ *L. Spohr's Autobiography*, ed. E. Schmitz (London, 1865/R1969), i, 288.
²² Ibid, ii, 81.
²³ Ibid, 82. The accuracy of Spohr's recollection in this matter has been seriously questioned. But even A. Jacobs, in his well-documented 'Spohr and the Baton', *ML*, xxxi (1950), 317, confirms that Spohr did use the baton at least at one of his London rehearsals.
²⁴ *American Scholar*, i (1837), 113.
²⁵ For a general discussion, see C. L. Donakowski, *A Muse for the Masses: Ritual and Music in an Age of Democratic Revolution, 1770–1870* (Chicago and London, 1977).
²⁶ See A. L. Ringer, 'Clementi and the *Eroica*', *MQ*, xlvii (1961), 462–3.
²⁷ *Source Readings*, 863.
²⁸ François Fétis in his *Biographie universelle des musiciens*, as translated by J. Stratton in 'Operatic Singing Style and the Gramophone', *Recorded Sound*, xxii/3 (1966), 49.
²⁹ As reported by her American tour manager, P. T. Barnum, later of circus fame; see *The Pleasures of Music*, 404.
³⁰ *Source Readings*, 896.

Chapter II

Paris: Centre of Intellectual Ferment

RALPH P. LOCKE

The history of modern France – and of the modern world – begins, in many ways, with the storming of the Bastille on 14 July 1789. This uprising of the people of Paris against the monarchical state initiated a series of experiments in government that followed one another with startling rapidity over several decades. Outside France, too, the challenging of the Bourbons' long supremacy sent waves of fear through the ruling élites, at the same time giving inspiration and encouragement to people of humbler class suffering under conservative dynasties, from Spain and Italy to Germany, Poland and Russia, everywhere redefining the terms of political and cultural debate.

The variety of governments that France experienced in the 60 years under consideration – ranging from the anti-aristocratic extremism of the Jacobin dictatorship to the harshly repressive Bourbon Restoration – had wide-ranging ramifications for the basic structures and institutions of musical life, as also for musicians and their lives. These ramifications will be surveyed in the first two sections of this chapter; the third and fourth sections focus on the ways in which the music written and performed in Paris reflected these larger structural and institutional changes. The various strands are then brought together in the revealing story of how one musician of genius and integrity, Hector Berlioz, lived, worked and suffered in Paris, a city unsurpassed in its musical resources yet deeply resistant to the demands of true musical originality.

MUSIC AND REVOLUTION, 1789–99
The essential question raised by the French Revolution was at once subversive and liberating: by whom and for whose benefit should society be ruled? Like government, literature and the visual arts, music was called to account during the early years of the Revolution and, as practised under the Bourbons, found wanting. The most advanced or cultivated forms of music-making in France had been the elaborate *grands motets* performed at the Chapelle Royale and Notre

Dame, the *tragédies lyriques* of Jean-Philippe Rameau and Christoph Willibald Gluck at the Opéra, and the performances of symphonies by Franz Joseph Haydn, Johann Stamitz and François-Joseph Gossec at the Concert Spirituel. On a purely aesthetic level, none of these fitted the needs of a society in which mass action, rather than aristocratic privilege and connoisseurship, was now the guiding criterion. On a more practical level, the Chapelle Royale had been shut down in the early 1790s, the Concert Spirituel ceased in late 1791, and many of the nobility fled, leaving the opera houses without much of their usual audience (though opera and concerts did continue – in altered and sometimes novel forms discussed below).

The Chapelle Royale had employed nearly a hundred instrumentalists and singers, and there were hundreds of musicians in the Grande Ecurie, the Garde Royale and other ensembles attached to the king's household, and yet more who made their living in cathedrals and choir schools across the nation. With the collapse of the monarchy and the outlawing of the church, many of these musicians were forced to subsist on private lessons or find other kinds of work.[1] Fortunately for some, a number of bands were formed for use by the National Guard, thanks to the initiative and diplomacy of a young officer named Bernard Sarrette. These ensembles tended to be heavier in clarinets, brass and drums than the dozen-member, oboe-led bands of the *ancien régime*, and larger, too – sometimes more than 45 players strong. In 1793, a school was founded to train recruits for Sarrette's bands;[2] in 1795 it took the name Conservatoire National Supérieur de Musique and incorporated many professors from the former Ecole Royale de Chant (founded in 1784), giving it a total of 115 teachers (though few, if any, taught 'full-time' in the modern sense), including such composers as Luigi Cherubini, Charles Catel and Jean-François Le Sueur, the violinists Pierre Baillot and Pierre Rode, and such leading wind and brass players as the bassoonist Etienne Ozi and the horn virtuoso Frédéric Nicolas Duvernoy.

It may seem odd that the National Convention, at a time of great instability, with armies of exiled aristocrats and Austrian troops threatening at the borders, would agree to establish and subsidize an institution that envisaged offering over 800 students free training in, of all things, music. But music had succeeded in proving its value to the government, in the form of propaganda songs and choral 'hymns'. Between 1789 and 1803, over 1300 such pieces were written for performance, by voices, band instruments or both, at patriotic gatherings of all kinds, whether in schools, army barracks or open-air festivals. Of the songs, relatively simple pieces intended to be sung by a single person or in unison, many were set to well-known tunes; others, and nearly all the choral hymns, were newly composed by musicians who were, in varying degrees, sympathetic to the ideals

19. Citizens singing 'La marseillaise', at the refrain 'Aux armes, citoyens!': gouache by Lesueur

of the Revolution, most notably Gossec, but also Etienne-Nicolas Méhul, Le Sueur, Cherubini, Catel, Rodolphe Kreutzer, Henri-Montan Berton, Ignace Pleyel and others.

Several of the most successful revolutionary songs – including *Ah, ça ira!* (1790) and *La Carmagnole* (1792) – used existing dance tunes that, like the repeated cheap printings in which the songs were issued, facilitated their distribution and penetration. As for the newly composed songs (and the simpler of the choral hymns), Claude-Joseph Rouget de Lisle's *La marseillaise* (1792) is typical in many respects: rapid march character, recurrent use of triadic and upbeat dotted-rhythm figures reminiscent of military fanfares, spare texture (the first publication simply gives melody and words over an instrumental bass line) and a touch of minor mode just before the refrain (at the reminder that the enemies of revolutionary France were crossing the Rhine and coming 'right into our arms, to cut the throats of our sons and wives'). Also typical is the song's absorption of ideas and even specific words and images from government propaganda. The official proclamation of war against Prussia and Austria had included the words 'Aux armes, citoyens! l'étendard de la guerre est déployé! ... Marchons!', and indeed had repeated the call 'Aux armes, citoyens' several times. Rouget de Lisle echoed this rhetorical gesture by placing the same phrase at the head of his refrain.[3]

Although Rouget de Lisle's song had been written in Strasbourg under the title 'Chant de guerre pour l'armée du Rhin', Paris learnt it from a battalion arriving from Marseilles, hence its accepted name. Songs such as *La marseillaise* became prime weapons in the revolutionary arsenal and, like other weapons, could be wielded in spontaneous and unpredictable ways. During the three years in which France was ruled by the National Convention (1792–5, including the so-called 'Terror' and the Thermidorean reaction), theatre audiences battled verbally over which politically loaded chanson to sing next, showered the auditorium with printed songsheets and threw messages, verses and yet more songs – including some that were distinctly pro-royalist – on to the stage for the actors to pronounce.[4] The decree in 1796 that 'songs dear to republicans' be performed by all theatre orchestras 'before the rising of the curtain' was clearly an attempt to control this potentially explosive singing mania.[5] In 1794 Danton had already felt the need to request that petitioners addressing the Convention, in the hall of the Tuileries, do so 'in reason, in prose only'.[6]

The most popular of the songs were given various new texts reflecting current events and ideological shifts, or the varied concerns of different audiences. The standard version (1790) of *Ah, ça ira!*, for example, spoke confidently of the inevitable victory of 'the people' and good-humouredly of the capitulation of the aristocrats ('L'aristocratie dit: "Mea culpa" '); another version put it more bluntly: 'Les aristocrates on les pendra' ('We'll string up the aristocrats'); and yet others praised General Lafayette, or accused the Sorbonne professors of being smug.[7] In reactionary Brittany, the *Marseillaise* was even turned for a time into a counter-revolutionary tract ('Allons, armées catholiques . . .').[8] More dangerously popular – the government's decree of 1796 expressly forbade its performance – was *Le réveil du peuple*, in which, to a march tune by Pierre Gaveaux, the Jacobins were branded 'a fierce horde of assassins and brigands . . . those drinkers of human blood'.[9]

The more elaborate revolutionary works performed their own specialized functions with distinction. Most of these hymns were written for specific occasions determined by the government: not Christian holidays but rather the political and civic celebrations that took their place, in what has been called a 'transfer of sacrality' on to the secular sphere.[10] These might commemorate non-recurring events, such as recent military victories or the reburial of Voltaire in the former church of Ste-Geneviève, renamed the Panthéon (11 July 1791),[11] or annual celebrations of praiseworthy activities and social groups (e.g. agriculture and the aged) or of a proud historical moment such as the storming of the royal palace (10 August 1792) or the founding of the Republic (22 September 1792). Like the songs, many of the hymns consist of alternating verses and refrains, but their refrains are usually set for three- or four-part chorus; some begin with an instrumental march (e.g. Méhul's widely sung *Chant du départ* of 1794) or with recitatives in the manner of a cantata.

20. Festival of the Supreme Being on the Champ de Mars, 1794, showing the specially erected mountain, Tree of Liberty, statue of Hercules (on the pillar) and a goddess representing fertility pulled on a chariot: painting attributed to P. A. Demachy (1723–1807)

The largest and most important of the ceremonies were held out of doors, mainly at a specially constructed parade ground on the Champ de Mars, hence the preference for band instruments and choral forces numbering in the thousands at times. Thus amplified and physically embodied, music became the voice of the Revolution, the aural equivalent of the tricoloured flag, the Tree of Liberty, the enormous statues of Hercules and the Goddess of Reason, and the Phrygian cap and other revolutionary garb. The instruments even carried a visual symbolism of their own. The wind and brass, previously associated with the monarch, were now publicly extolling the government of the people. Furthermore, they were at times (as in the ceremony for Voltaire) reinforced by newly constructed instruments modelled after depictions from Ancient Rome: the *buccin*, a kind of straight trumpet, and the lower-pitched *tuba curva*, said to make the sound of six serpents. These 'antique' instruments, like the Phrygian caps and the archaizing language favoured by many of the leaders, reflected the desire of the revolutionary leaders to seek justification by nostalgically evoking a golden age of democracy that preceded the more 'decadent' centuries of monarchical feudalism.[12]

The emphasis on music with words permitted the crowd to take part as well. Thus, on 7 July 1794, the night before Robespierre's Festival of the Supreme Being, musicians from the Conservatoire went out with their instruments to teach 'the people' the 'songs of liberty' that would be performed the next day.[13] On the day itself, Robespierre addressed the crowd at the Tuileries and a Gossec hymn written for the occasion, *Père de l'univers*, was performed by personnel from the theatres and the Conservatoire, joined by many members of the public. A carefully planned march to the Champ de Mars followed; among the thousands participating were groups of cavalry and firemen, the members of the National Convention, hundreds of drummers (who signalled with thunderous drumrolls the main events of the day's ceremonies), several bands or choruses associated with different groups of marchers (including a group of blind children performing a Hymn to the Divinity, by Antonio Bruni, on a rolling platform) and a *corps de musique* – Sarrette and Gossec's large band – that performed 'patriotic tunes' during the march. At the Champ de Mars a 'great symphony' for band was followed by the climactic mass singing of the *Marseillaise* with new text. The singing was led by a trained chorus and symbolic groups of old people, adolescents and seven- to ten-year-olds with their mothers, all arrayed on the slopes of an artificial mountain, just below the government leaders and the band.[14] In such grand outdoor festivals as this, many Parisians of simple means must have experienced for the first time the thrill of hearing and participating in large-scale music-making.

Music's new public function demanded a new language: simple,

21. *Fountain of Regeneration on the site of the Bastille, part of the festival held on 10 August 1793, the anniversary of the overthrow of the monarchy: engraving (detail) by Helman after Monnet (the newly constructed brass instruments can just be seen back right)*

direct, striking, memorable, and – most of all – flexible. The tunes of Méhul's revolutionary pieces, in particular, are marked by a slow harmonic rhythm that suited them to a variety of performing conditions: without accompaniment, by large forces widely spaced, or in excessively resonant surroundings (such as church buildings) or entirely unresonant ones (as in the open air). The best of the revolutionary repertory breathes the spirit of a new age, in that it is frankly directed to large audiences, to simple, communal sentiments and to a taste for sobriety rather than frivolity, individual amusement or reflection. Its broad dimensions and forthright grandeur relate it plainly to certain sacred and ceremonial works of the *ancien régime*, such as the aforementioned *grands motets*. But, no doubt for symbolic not just for practical reasons, it rejects all elegance of vocal line and artful texture, thus participating in what has been called the revolutionary 'purge' of aristocratic luxuries and of the 'excessive ornamentation and superfluous regulations' of Catholic worship.[15] Many of these hymns (and the band pieces associated with them) would, in their very bareness, sound out of place in a modern concert hall, but they had a major effect on the French operas of Cherubini, Gaspare Spontini and Giacomo Meyerbeer, on the symphonic works of Beethoven and Berlioz and even, via Meyerbeer, on Richard Wagner's *Rienzi* and *Tannhäuser*.[16]

It would be misleading to suggest that the shift in French music from religious to civic themes was entirely a product of the Revolution. Like so much else, it had been anticipated in part by the Enlightenment. In 1745 Voltaire and Rameau had produced *Le temple de la gloire*, an *opéra-ballet*, to celebrate a military victory; in 1779 François-André Danican Philidor had written his *Carmen saeculare*, an oratorio in praise of civic virtue, and six years later the essayist Nicolas-Bricaire de la Dixmerie had called for concert works 'in which would be recalled certain events glorious to the nation and dear to its memory'.[17] In a more general way, the direct and accessible style of mid-century *opéra comique* proved a helpful point of reference for the composers of revolutionary hymns; indeed, the tune of Dalayrac's *Hymne à la liberté*, also known as 'Veillons au salut de l'Empire' (1792), was originally composed for his opera *Renaud d'Ast* (1787).

None the less, the influence of the Revolution on the music of the 1790s is undeniable, and not just on music written for political ceremonies. In the theatres, especially, works sprang up in abundance responding to the ideals of liberty, or even dealing with particular events and issues of the day (see below). New mixed theatrical forms, involving pantomime, melodrama (declaimed speech over instrumental 'mood' or 'action' music), spectacular feats of stage machinery, well-researched and eye-catching sets and costumes, in addition to more traditional elements such as ballet and topical songs, flourished to satisfy the tastes of the new and more diverse audiences that filled the theatres; such diversity and experimentation was further encouraged by the abolition (in 1791–2) of longstanding restrictions on the number of theatres and the kinds of repertory they were permitted to pursue. The new freedom was tempered and at times undermined by censorship: old royalist operas were shelved by government order, new librettos lacking sufficient references to 'liberté' were scuttled or sent back for overhaul, and even anti-clerical parodies, however desirable from an ideological point of view, were suppressed if they seemed too likely, by their inflammatory language, to stir up the reactionaries in the audience.

The highpoint of musical activity during the Revolution coincided with the two years of Jacobin rule, when the emphasis on producing art for 'the people' was greatest. It was during this turbulent time that the bulk of the revolutionary songs and hymns were composed and that the people of Paris were most heavily involved in performing and listening to the hymns at outdoor festivals. This contrasts greatly with the first three years of the Revolution, when Louis XVI was still on the throne, though dependent on the National Assembly, and when official public celebrations still retained traditional religious texts such as the 'Te deum' and 'De profundis' and 'the people' were expected to listen but not participate. (To some extent 'the people' created their own, more modest patriotic celebrations, including 'fraternal suppers' in the streets and singing and dancing round symbolic 'trees of liberty'.) During the later, post-Jacobin years of the decade, in turn, the larger patriotic works – notably hymns by Méhul and Le Sueur involving multiple choruses and orchestras – tended increasingly to be performed indoors, in theatres and former churches, before a limited and even hand-picked audience, thus lessening the risk of popular uprising. The government had learnt the lesson of 1792, when 20,000 National Guard members from across the country gathered in Paris for the Bastille Day Festival and possible shipment to battle against the invading Prussian and Austrian troops; charged up with revolutionary fervour by the festival, they proceeded to agitate against the monarchy for several weeks and, on 10 August, helped lead the attack on the Tuileries Palace that resulted in the imprisonment and execution of the king.

THE CAPITAL OF THE NINETEENTH CENTURY, 1800–1850

Napoleon's accession to power, as first consul in 1799, then as emperor in 1804, moved France into a new phase of stability and prosperity. His startling string of military victories spread across the Continent certain achievements of the Revolution, including a legal code based on civil equality (for men) and an efficient centralized administrative system, simultaneously opening up new markets to French manufacturers and financiers.

Napoleon's offer of amnesty brought back from exile many aristocrats whose taste for elegance and virtuosity in the arts – visible and audible symbols of luxury and privilege – was shared by the growing entrepreneurial class, as well as by the new Napoleonic nobility: supporters and marshals of Napoleon to whom he awarded hereditary titles and, often, lucrative positions in the judiciary and bureaucracy.

Napoleon fostered this renewed emphasis on music as decoration and display. During his Italian campaign he had become fond of Italy's tuneful and often extravagantly florid operas; now he took advantage of his prerogatives to help form and nurture a company, the Théâtre-Italien, devoted to performing works by such composers as Domenico Cimarosa and Giovanni Paisiello. And some of the French operas commissioned by Napoleon were barely disguised pageants in honour of the emperor and his foreign conquests, in the vein of Lully's homages to the 'Sun King' but – especially at the Opéra – done up with the bombast and brass developed for the revolutionary festivals.

If Napoleon used certain revolutionary traditions when they suited him, he did not hesitate to undo others. He shut down all but nine of the city's theatres and imposed strict repertory guidelines on those that remained. His Concordat with the pope of 1801 led to the reinstatement of the Chapelle, under the direction of Paisiello and, soon afterwards, Ferdinando Paer; by 1810, under Le Sueur, the choir numbered 34 and the orchestra 50. Throughout the country, church music had suffered greatly during the revolutionary decade, and Napoleon encouraged the work of Alexandre Choron, a forceful, well-informed spokesman for the Catholic musical heritage, including Gregorian chant and Renaissance polyphony.

Napoleon's empire, seemingly so stable about 1810, was already beginning to crumble under its own weight; in particular, his ever-expanding campaigns required him to exact money and fighting men from his satellite states, creating resentment and occasionally open rebellion, as in the guerrilla war in Spain. His foolhardy decision in 1812 to invade Russia was the beginning of the end, in part because it threw the major European powers into alliance against him; two years later, after hundreds of thousands of lives had been lost in battles and starvation, he agreed to abdicate.

The early days of the Bourbon Restoration were dogged by the shadow of the former emperor. To many Frenchmen, Napoleon represented at once the social ideals of the Revolution and the spirit of national glory. (In 1815 he escaped from Elba and with a small army sent the court scurrying into exile until he was finally overwhelmed at Waterloo. Such turbulent shifts in politics naturally led, that year, to another wave of 'song battles' on the stages of the nation's largest cities.)[18]

Throughout the Restoration the Bourbons' lack of a clear mandate resulted in wavering and insecure cultural policies defined mainly by a desire to return to the practices of the *ancien régime*. At the Conservatoire, Sarrette and Gossec were dismissed from their positions, salaries and budgets were drastically cut and the emphasis in the curriculum was tilted back from instrumental music to opera (thus reversing, in a way, the Conservatoire's absorption of the Ecole Royale de Chant during the Revolution). Cherubini, who had not always got on with Napoleon, was invited to serve as co-director with Le Sueur of the ever-growing Chapelle and (from 1822) as director of the restructured Conservatoire. With government support, Choron now formed a school for church musicians, the Institut de Musique Religieuse Classique. The taste for Italian opera, officially encouraged during the Napoleonic era, now blossomed into a widespread rage for the operas of Gioacchino Rossini. Censorship with a royalist slant was imposed, limiting the situations and issues that could be presented on stage or in the political songs that made the rounds of the city's many singing-clubs.

None the less, the Restoration contributed substantially to the growth of musical Paris. The return of ever-greater numbers of émigrés led to a flourishing of amateur music-making. This in turn led to a striking growth in music publishing (especially of simple *romances* and arrangements of operatic airs) and in the manufacture of musical instruments. Virtuoso singers and pianists appeared frequently at court, in the salons of the wealthy and in concerts at the Théâtre-Italien and the Opéra. Certain far-sighted officials proved especially helpful: the Vicomte Sosthène de la Rochefoucauld, at the Ministry of the Interior, assisted François-Antoine Habeneck's efforts to bring Beethoven's symphonies to Parisian ears. Similarly, the rapid building of a major new theatre for the Opéra in 1821 and the decision to invite Rossini to create or rework pieces for the company may be seen, in retrospect, as important steps towards French grand opera, the genre that would typify Paris to the world for half a century or more.

During the 1820s, the Bourbons gradually destroyed themselves, in large part by refusing to respond to the need for agrarian reform, by failing to provide capital for industrial development and by subjecting journalists and other writers to increasingly repressive and offensive censorship. The Bourbons' failure to win the support of the middle classes (much less the urban workers) can be glimpsed in the phenomenon of the songwriter Pierre-Jean de Béranger, a well-educated clerk at the Sorbonne who regaled the nation with songs, set to well-known tunes, attacking privilege and censorship and summoning up visions of Napoleonic glory and the noble sufferings – and engaging good fellowship – of the lower classes. Though he was imprisoned twice, his message travelled through city and town on cheap songsheets and in collections, some authorized by him, others pirated, with combined press runs in the tens of thousands.[19]

The Bourbons' lack of a power base led in July 1830 to a swift (three-day), almost painless revolution, supported by the bankers and liberal businessmen. The outcome of this 'July Revolution' was a perfect political compromise: a king (Louis-Philippe, of the Orléans line) who would be limited in his constitutional powers by the will of the two Chambers, consisting of representatives elected by the landholding aristocrats and the *haute bourgeoisie*. (In a country with a population of over 30 million, only 170,000 males were eligible to vote during the July Monarchy.) Now, led by a 'King of the French' rather than a 'King of France', the nation could begin its process of modernization and become 'the capital of the nineteenth century'.[20]

Louis-Philippe knew that a monarch, even a constitutional one, was unwelcome to many of those who had fought in the July days and that there would be political as well as financial advantages in terminating the most obvious of the royal prerogatives in the arts: he made a point of shutting down Choron's school, to the distress of such musicians as Berlioz who appreciated the high standards inculcated there, and he dismantled the Chapelle, the Musique du Roi and the royal bands (though he eventually restored all of them at a more modest level). The new royal family preferred a different way of encouraging the arts: contributing money to 'benefit concerts' put on by one or more musicians, the beneficiaries being occasionally 'the poor' or 'the wounded' (of the July Revolution) but more often the artist performing. The royal award was rarely based on financial need: the great opera star Giuditta Pasta received 1000 francs for each of two concerts in 1831 compared with the meagre 50 or 60 francs bestowed on many a lesser-known and poorer artist.[21]

This policy may reflect the regime's desire to encourage the entrepreneurial spirit in France: the organizers of a benefit concert had to write to the king requesting his patronage, much as today one would apply for a foundation or government grant. More frankly entrepreneurial was Louis-Philippe's solution to the vexing problem of containing costs at the Opéra: he leased the franchise for running the theatre for one or more years at a time to a series of willing investor-administrators. The first and most influential was Dr Louis Véron, a businessman who had assured himself of an annual income of 40,000 francs by marketing, through the newspapers, a chest balm that he had not even invented. Véron was easily able to put up 50,000 francs towards the 250,000 demanded by the government: the rest came from Alexandre Marie Aguado, a fabulously wealthy financier and merchant from Spain who in 1810 had served in Napoleon's army of occupation there.[22]

The government must have felt some qualms about handing such an important showcase over entirely to market forces, for it continued to provide a subsidy, albeit reduced, and to insist that all plots and librettos be cleared with a government-run commission. Similarly, though some ticket prices seemed to suggest that the lower classes were finally welcome in the nation's grandest theatre (the cheapest seats were 2 francs and 2.50), in practice the Opéra remained nearly as exclusive as the Théâtre-Italien: boxes of four to six seats were usually rented only in their entirety and the bench seats in the parterre and uppermost level could not be reserved in advance, a serious inconvenience except to students (male students: the parterre was out of bounds to women).[23] Véron and the commission actually argued against lowering the prices of the least desirable boxes, since 'one would risk attracting to the Opéra the lower classes, whom one might hold in high esteem, but with whom good society does not like to have contact'.[24]

The Paris of Louis-Philippe was widely recognized as the musical capital of Europe. Instrumental virtuosos flocked there in ever greater numbers; now they played regularly in public halls and their triumphs were reported in the relatively inexpensive, widely read daily newspapers of the new bourgeois age. Foreign composers who were not primarily performers – Gaetano Donizetti, the young Wagner – also came hoping to make their fortune, as Paer and Rossini had done under the Bourbons. The splendour of the Opéra, the brilliance of the concerts – from Beethoven's symphonies to appearances by the violinist Nicolò Paganini – and rapid growth in music publishing, instrument manufacture and journalism made musical life in Paris as lively and striking a manifestation of Romanticism as Delacroix's paintings or Hugo's *Hernani* and *Les misérables*.

As Hugo's plays and novels may remind us, French Romanticism had a rather large component of social criticism and concern, and musicians responded accordingly, especially during the early 1830s. Berlioz actually took to the streets with revolver in hand during the July Revolution (though he arrived too late to use it: he had been sequestered in the Prix de Rome examinations during most of the fighting). Berlioz, Franz Liszt, Félicien David and Béranger were among the musicians who paid eager attention to the teachings of the Saint-Simonians or other social and religious reformers such as the Abbé Félicité de Lamennais. David became a Saint-Simonian and composed choruses for the movement's communal settlement outside Paris.[25] Liszt, Béranger, Giacomo Meyerbeer, Fromental Halévy and numerous others encouraged and assisted Wilhem (pseudonym of Guillaume Bocquillon) in his plans to build choruses of school pupils and members of the working classes.

This participation of workers and bourgeois in a common effort was not as easy to achieve on the political front. In 1831 and again in 1834 the silk weavers of Lyons and other workers rose in protest against inadequate pay and working conditions and were brutally suppressed by the government. In late 1835 censorship was restored, and in 1840 the conservative François Guizot was installed as prime minister, a clear signal of the government's resolve to squash dissent. Middle-class supporters of the workers' cause, including Béranger and Liszt, now tended to keep their political opinions to themselves.

In February 1848 a coalition of students, workers and the middle class overthrew the government and established a republic that promised to take seriously the problems of hunger and unemployment that had been hidden under the surface of Louis-Philippe's elegant Paris. Quickly, though, the demands of the more radical republicans (for example, the establishment of cooperatives and the nationalization

22. *Wild reaction to the first performance of Hugo's play 'Hernani' on 21 February 1830: engraving by J. J. Granville*

of railways and insurance companies) came into conflict with the more limited goals of the moderates, who allowed only a limited and ill-thought-out version of the cooperatives plan, the so-called 'national workshops', to be set up. In April national elections, based on universal manhood suffrage, revealed that the provinces were still far more conservative than Paris. In June the government abolished the national workshops. Protesters filled the streets and built barricades, only to be gunned down by the army; at least 1500 died and 11,000 were arrested (many were shipped off to Algeria).

After this episode, bloodier than any in the original French Revolution, the way was open for an opportunist. Louis-Napoleon Bonaparte, the nephew of Napoleon, used his magic name and much shrewdness to win the December 1848 election and to lead France in the direction of a new empire, which he proclaimed in 1852, taking the name Napoleon III. (Hugo, in self-imposed exile, dubbed him 'Napoléon le petit'.) With the Second Empire came eighteen years of steady economic growth, and eighteen years of hedonism and cultural ostentation. The giddy whirl of Offenbach's can-cans marks the reign of Napoleon III as an age determined to drown all memory of the bloodbath that had given it birth.

THE DOMINANCE OF THE VOICE
For centuries French composers as well as audiences and bureaucrats

thought of music primarily as an art linked to words, to stage action and to public and religious ceremony, rather than as one of independent stature. Though instrumental music grew in importance over the 60-year period under discussion, vocal music in its various manifestations, and opera in particular, still reflected more accurately the competing interests and unspoken forces within French society.

Many of the best composers of the day were drawn to write operas for Paris, and for good reasons. The high status that the French traditionally granted to spoken theatre carried over to the 'théâtre lyrique'; during the nineteenth century nearly all the musicians elected to the Académie des Beaux-Arts were opera composers, as were three of the four long-term directors of the Conservatoire: Cherubini, Auber and Ambroise Thomas (the one exception, Théodore Dubois, was best known for another large-scale vocal genre, sacred oratorio). The leading houses could offer a composer, as one of them admiringly put it, 'immense means' for writing 'truly dramatic music',[26] namely the best singers, orchestral players, designers and technicians of France and, to a large extent, of Europe generally. A successful opera at a major theatre could also bring the composer substantial income in the form of royalties for each performance and a large lump sum from a publisher willing to secure the right to produce and market a complete piano-vocal score and separate vocal excerpts.

The opera houses were the most distinguished venues for musical theatre – but far from the only ones. In 1830–31, for example, no fewer than sixteen stages made regular use of music in their productions.[27] Satirical comedies at the boulevard theatres generally contained songs made up of new words set to well-known tunes, sung (or half-sung) to the accompaniment of a few players. Theatres specializing in melodrama and pantomime, such as the Théâtre de la Porte-St-Martin, often employed elaborate and original musical accompaniments, and the more established of the boulevard theatres specializing in spoken drama and comedy similarly used a sizable orchestra and incorporated songs that commented on character or even helped advance the plot. These lighter forms of music theatre constituted an important testing-ground and vehicle of popularization for a wide range of musico-dramatic techniques.[28] They also served as a valuable barometer of public sentiment: within months of the storming of the Bastille, one performer in a small theatre in the Palais-Royal was singing to any aristocrats in the audience: 'the little guy is not so stupid; he turned that world of yours upside down'.[29]

*

Pre-revolutionary traditions did not entirely disappear during the 1790s. Despite objections from republican journalists and government censors, certain older operas were still mounted at the Opéra and, one assumes, applauded. Gluck's *Iphigénie en Tauride*, an opera whose heroine reviles the 'hateful monster who would dare raise his hand against the king', was given on 20 January 1793, the day Louis XVI was sentenced to death (perhaps, though, the line in question was changed). Similarly, in spite of M.-J. Chénier's eloquent argument in 1790 that 'little arias' (*ariettes*) would hardly be adequate to the task of 'moulding citizens' of 'a free country',[30] many of the *ariette*-laden comic operas of Grétry – though not the too plainly royalist *Richard Coeur-de-lion* – continued to hold the stage right through the Jacobin years.[31]

Increasingly, though, operas of a new kind were created, dealing explicitly with heroic events of the Revolution, such as the widely praised self-sacrifice of thirteen-year-old Agricola Viala, who died in 1793 trying to loosen the cables on a pontoon bridge in Provence that royalist forces were about to cross. Operas also made political points indirectly, through tales of civic virtue from ancient history: in Méhul's *Horatius Coclès* (1794), which the librettist Antoine-Vincent Arnault wrote in part to prove his patriotism, the hero of the title (much like young Viala) destroys a bridge, thereby halting the invasion of Rome by foreign troops.[32] Hymns of the Revolution were sometimes absorbed into the body of an opera to make explicit the composer's and librettist's support for the new social order; indeed, the borderline between opera and scenic cantata was often crossed, as in Gossec's *Offrande à la liberté* (1792), which contains the earliest fully scored setting of the *Marseillaise*.

Much of this new operatic repertory was written to order and was quickly forgotten. At its best, though, revolutionary opera formed an innovatory and durable genre that managed to combine the democratic directness of pre-revolutionary *opéra comique* with a high moral tone, musical sophistication and imposing grandeur. This flowering owed much to the persistence of a talented batch of young composers – Cherubini, Méhul, Kreutzer, Daniel Steibelt, Le Sueur, Catel – and to the open-mindedness of two theatres that welcomed their efforts. One, the Opéra-Comique, was in a building in the Rue Favart also known, misleadingly, as the 'Salle des Italiens' (since the company had arisen out of a merger of two theatres, one of them the Comédie-Italienne, in 1762). The other had been created in 1789, only months before the outbreak of the Revolution, under the protection of the Count of Provence (brother of Louis XVI) and hence originally named Théâtre de Monsieur. Its mixed repertory consisted of comedies, vaudevilles and comic operas in French and Italian, but it gradually limited itself to *opéra comique*, especially after 1791 when it settled in the large, new Salle Feydeau (with some 1800 seats). Whereas the Opéra-Comique produced patriotic operas and cantata-like tableaux, the Théâtre Feydeau tended to draw aristocrats and other royalists, many of whom, seated in their boxes, hissed the required revolutionary songs, thereby inciting anger in the parterre.[33]

The Favart, thanks to its longer tradition, had a more extensive repertory and 'a large roster of [singing] actors who excelled in the art of making people laugh',[34] including the tenor Jean Elleviou, handsome in appearance and elegant in stage manner. The Feydeau offered a quite different star, Mme Julie-Angélique Scio, a grippingly dramatic singer. Accordingly it was the Feydeau that produced some of the most serious operas of the day, such as Cherubini's *Lodoïska* (1791) and *Médée* (1797) and Le Sueur's *La caverne* (1793), though the Favart tried its best to offer a similar product, even commissioning works on the same subjects, for example Kreutzer's *Lodoïska* (1791) and Méhul's *La caverne* (1795). These might all, in later terminology, be described as 'opéras comiques', for they use a certain amount of spoken dialogue and *mélodrame* (dialogue over orchestral music) whereas works performed at the Opéra relied entirely on recitative between numbers. But these 'opéras comiques' are not primarily

23. Cherubini's 'Médée': title-page of the full score, published by Imbault (1797), with the date of the first performance at the Théâtre Feydeau according to the revolutionary calendar, 23 ventose [windy month] year 5 (13 March old style). The scene shows Medea begging the nursemaid to hide her children from her lest she kill them in her rage against Jason

comic or even sweetly touching. Rather, they deal with disturbing issues, such as sexual vindictiveness or the abuse of political power, and they regularly invoke the turbulence of nature in ways that clearly echo the forces of social upheaval then at work in France.

Particularly characteristic, at both theatres, were plots centred on the rescue of a captive hero or heroine. Beethoven's *Fidelio* (1805, revised 1814), a rare German example of such a 'rescue opera', is based on the libretto of Gaveaux's *Léonore, ou L'amour conjugal* (1798) and shows the influence of Cherubini's *Lodoïska*.[35] The captor in these operas is often a corrupt official and the rescue is delayed by onstage battles, tropical storms, exploding castles and the like. Musically these operas are shot through with novel features: evocative instrumentation, powerful reminiscence motifs, unconventional harmonies, an imposing use of symphonic form and accompanimental motifs, and a feeling for dramatic coherence and flow that often turns the mandated use of spoken dialogue to good effect, as in the passage in Cherubini's *Médée* in which Medea scorchingly curses the bride during the wedding chorus for Jason and Dirce.[36] (Unfortunately, the opera is often performed now in an inauthentic Italian version that replaces these spoken interjections with much less effective singing.)

During the early years of Napoleon's reign, Cherubini and Méhul tried, with some success, to continue writing serious *opéra comique*. Cherubini's *Les deux journées* (1800) takes a stand against the class-hatred of the revolutionary decade by relating the story (with dignified music for all parties) of a poor seventeenth-century water carrier who, during the oppressive reign of Cardinal Mazarin, concealed a fugitive aristocratic couple (the husband had dared to speak up against the government's policies). Méhul's *Uthal* (1806) and *Joseph* (1807) anticipate, respectively, the nature-painting in Weber's *Der Freischütz* (1821) and the biblical austerity of Berlioz's *L'enfance du Christ* (1854), and *Joseph* was rightly praised for its sober simplicity by Berlioz, Weber and Wagner. By 1807, though, Méhul found himself going against the tide of fashion: the merging of the two rival theatres in 1801 had resulted in a move back to a more traditional, light-hearted type of *opéra comique*. Le Sueur, equally committed to serious work, turned to the Opéra, and Cherubini began to shift his energies towards sacred and instrumental music.

The interest in light opera had never entirely disappeared during the Revolution, but it had increased again about 1798–1802, with major successes by three young composers, Pierre Della Maria, François-Adrien Boieldieu and Nicolas Isouard (whose pseudonym was Nicolò). The public during the Consulate and Empire was interested in diversion again (one critic in 1802 argued that, after all, 'opéra-comique is not made for weeping').[37] Boïeldieu went on to gratify their taste, in simple but artful manner, and continued to do so during the Restoration, providing, in the fabulously popular *La dame blanche* (1825), a tuneful, sometimes wistful link between the delicate Grétry tradition and the hardier varieties that would be produced by Daniel-François-Esprit Auber and Ferdinand Hérold in the 1830s.

*

While theatrical and musical experiment flourished fairly freely at the *opéra comique* theatres during the revolutionary decade, the Opéra proper became the focus of much political conflict. It was severely criticized in the revolutionary press and by the secret police for its outspokenly royalist audiences and its outdated repertory; in autumn 1792 the Commune of Paris under Robespierre appropriated the Opéra, reduced its budget and appointed new directors, who promised to mount patriotic cantatas. In September 1793 the company undertook a public burning of certain papers bearing the royal *fleur-de-lys*; it had already given substantial sums of money and some 30 of its young men to the government's armies. Gradually placated, the government began subsidizing free performances at the Opéra of *Le siège de Thionville*, a pageant in which revolutionary soldiers proclaimed 'we have a king no more'. The audience joined in when the costumed commander sang the *Marseillaise* and patriotically hissed rather than applauded the singer of the villain's part.[38] The Opéra, in short, had become in just a few years the 'people's' theatre. But the attempt to serve the republic's needs on a limited budget forced the company to fill the schedule with new ballets on traditional mythological subjects and the least offensive repertory staples from the *ancien régime* (mainly French operas of Gluck, Piccinni, Sacchini and Salieri).

With Napoleon's arrival the Opéra gradually resumed its traditional role and prestige. Spurred on by increased funding (Napoleon restored the traditional tax on the lesser theatres to generate the subvention for the Opéra) and by the arrival in 1801 of a brilliant dramatic soprano, Caroline Branchu, the house welcomed a series of new productions that either struck out on new paths (Le Sueur's austere *Ossian*, 1804, and his grandiose opera-oratorio *La mort d'Adam*, 1809) or revived much of the Opéra's traditional monarchical grandeur but applied it now to the glory of Emperor Napoleon. *Le triomphe de Trajan* (1807, with music by Le Sueur and Louis-Luc Loiseau de Persuis) responded to Napoleon's taste for neo-classical pomp (triumphal arches, horse-drawn chariots, 432 new costumes). The emphasis on a purely external splendour allowed the opera to stay in the repertory even after the emperor's defeat; as one Restoration official noted, the work 'is so well known and so devoid of interest that one can regard it as, in a sense, nothing more than a beautiful spectacle'.[39]

During the first years of the century, Napoleon tried to impose Paisiello and then, with more success, Paer on the city's musicians and audiences. But it was another Italian, Spontini, who, supported in part by the Empress Joséphine, found just the right mixture of features to restore the Opéra to its pre-eminence in Europe. *La vestale* (1807) and *Olympie* (1819) reached back past the Cherubini generation to the *tragédies lyriques* of Gluck but enriched them with arias that look forward to the fluent melodic style of Vincenzo Bellini. And *Fernand Cortez* (1809, revised 1817), with its overloaded sets, massive choruses, carefully studied stage movement and blustering marches for full brass band (clearly inspired by revolutionary traditions), pointed the way to Meyerbeer and, beyond, to Verdi's *Aida*. Spontini succeeded in endearing himself to the Bourbons after Napoleon's fall, but his autocratic ways and penchant for intrigue elicited increasing resistance from the city's musicians; in 1820 he accepted a court position in Berlin.

The Opéra-Comique produced a string of elegantly turned pieces by Auber throughout the 1820s and 30s (*Le maçon*, 1825; *Fra Diavolo*, 1830; *Le cheval de bronze*, 1835) and by Hérold (*Marie*, 1826; *Zampa*, 1831; *Le pré aux clercs*, 1832), most of them, in their alternation of lyrical arias and jaunty ensembles (the latter often using dotted rhythms to excess), betraying the influence of Rossini, whose works were mounted with increasing success at the Théâtre-Italien, beginning in 1817.

The Théâtre-Italien, from the moment it was restored in 1801, was the favoured theatre of Paris's social élites, and it quickly won the hearts of the city's early Romantic authors, such as Stendhal and Chateaubriand. During Spontini's brief directorship (1810–12), the theatre gave the first decent Paris performances of Mozart's *Don Giovanni*, and over the next few decades it proved itself increasingly able to attract and hold some of Europe's best singers: Giuditta Pasta, Giulia Grisi, Maria Malibran, Manuel García, Giovanni Battista Rubini and Luigi Lablache. It took its greatest single leap forward in 1824, when Rossini, who had settled in Paris the year before, became its director and brought its repertory up to date by mounting operas of his own (among them *La donna del lago* and *Semiramide* as well as *Il viaggio a Reims*, a celebratory work for the coronation of Charles X) and *Il crociato in Egitto*, a work by Giacomo Meyerbeer (whose real name was Jakob Liebmann Beer), a German Jew who had lived in Italy for nine years. Thereafter Rossini conquered the Opéra, first with heavily reworked versions of three of his Italian operas (including *Le comte Ory*, a brilliant comic work based in part on music from *Il viaggio a Reims*) and then with *Guillaume Tell* (1829), an entirely new five-act work that not only revived with astonishing ease many of the best features of Cherubinian opera (Tell and the Swiss people

24. *Interior of the Paris Opéra during a performance of Meyerbeer's 'Le prophète' (1849): engraving by G. Janet. John of Leyden forces his mother Fidès to deny she recognizes him in order to preserve the fiction that he is the 'Son of God' whose coming has been announced by the Anabaptists*

are portrayed as active, admirable fighters for liberty) but also evinced a truly Romantic feeling for colour and mood, as in the pastoral section of the overture, the scene of the gathering of the cantons and Mathilde's pity-wrenching *romance*, 'Sombre forêt'.

*

In spite of this artistic rejuvenation in the last years of the Restoration, the Opéra remained in a sorry financial state, partly because the list of people entitled to free tickets had grown to a burdensome 502.[40] In the early years of the July Monarchy, Véron swept the house clean of many such obligations and brought a keen sense of marketing to the task, as well as a taste for the grandiose and sentimental that matched that of the audiences he wished to attract. Almost in the manner of a Hollywood film producer, Véron and his able successors brought together creative talents that had elsewhere (or earlier at the Opéra) demonstrated stage sense and willingness to compromise: Eugène Scribe, a prolific playwright and Auber's librettist on many comic operas and on *La muette de Portici* (Opéra, 1828); Pierre-Luc-Charles Cicéri, a stage designer experienced at building volcanos and the like for the boulevard theatres; Meyerbeer; and French singers, including the dramatic soprano Cornélie Falcon and the great tenor Adolphe Nourrit, who combined to varying degrees the pathos and word-sensitivity of the Gluckian tradition with the elegant virtuosity of the Italian. The result was a distinctive new genre, French grand opera, consisting of works – among them Meyerbeer's *Robert le diable* (1831) and *Les Huguenots* (1836) and Halévy's *La juive* (1835) – that were long and brilliantly produced (and painstakingly rehearsed), that assigned a major dramatic and musical function to the chorus, that made imaginative use of the new chromatic brass instruments (including those developed by Adolphe Sax) and that offered not three but five or more major singing roles: *Robert* and *Huguenots* both feature two sopranos, one more soulful or suffering (e.g. Valentine in *Huguenots*), the other richer in coloratura, more playful or imperious (Queen Marguerite de Valois in the same opera). Even Wagner admired the adroit musico-dramatic construction of Act 4 of *Les Huguenots*, and in many other passages Meyerbeer's handling of harmony and orchestral colour are keenly apposite to the dramatic action.

Other examples of grand opera before 1850 included, besides Auber's *Muette* and Rossini's *Guillaume Tell*, three major works by Donizetti: *Les martyrs* and *La favorite* (both 1840) and *Dom Sébastien* (1843). In 1841 Carl Maria von Weber's *Der Freischütz* finally received the production it deserved (unlike the horrendous 1825 travesty by Castil-Blaze, in which the plot was rewritten to tell the story of Robin

Hood). Berlioz, who provided the necessary recitatives for the 1841 production and who later assisted in some Gluck revivals, succeeded in getting only one of his own works, *Benvenuto Cellini* (1838), performed at the Opéra. As for Rossini, having made his fortune in Paris as he had hoped, he wrote no further operas after *Tell*, though he lived until 1868. His own explanation was that vocal technique had declined too much.

Indeed, the elegant *passaggi* of Rossini's youth were giving way to more strenuous melodic lines, featuring long-held high notes and much singing over a loud orchestra. Nourrit could sing florid passages up to high D because, like Mozart's and Grétry's tenors, he took the highest notes in falsetto. The practice of singing with the full voice throughout the range (as is usually done today, even in the eighteenth-century repertory) arose in Italy in the mid-1830s, no doubt a manifestation of the 'heroic' side of Romanticism, as well as of a bourgeois public's taste for startling and impressive, if crude, feats of skill. When the tenor Gilbert Duprez returned to Paris from Italy with his new-found 'C from the chest' and was engaged to perform Nourrit's roles at certain performances, Nourrit resigned and two years later threw himself out of a window.

The obvious emphasis on display, on conspicuous consumption, on the coordination of high individual achievement into a greater enterprise – or at least a more impressive 'product' – clearly marks French grand opera as a prime cultural expression of the entrepreneurial and professional classes that profited so much from the July Monarchy. The ambitious proportions and episodic construction typical of five-act grand opera also owe much to the model of the historical novels of Sir Walter Scott, Victor Hugo and Eugène Süe. (A more intimate, diaphanous side of French literary Romanticism is apparent in the ballets that flourished during the same years, notably *La sylphide* (1832, original music lost) and *Giselle* (1841, music by Adolphe Adam), in both of which the central character is a girl who either 'vanishes with the illusion of flight' or, in *Giselle*, dies and reappears as a weightless shade.)[41]

But there is more to grand opera than just size and spectacle: the scenarios, which had to be approved by the government's representatives before the composer could be named and authorized to begin writing, dramatize essential tenets of liberal and *juste milieu* political doctrine by portraying individuals trapped in the self-serving schemes of religious fanatics or political extremists. In *Robert le diable* human happiness is nearly dashed by Robert's obsessive participation in Bertram's unholy machinations, and in *Les Huguenots* the loving couple is doomed by the unrelenting antagonisms of Catholics and Protestants around them. *Le prophète* (1849, but largely completed before the 1848 revolution) makes the political point even more

25. The ballet 'La Péri' (music Frederick Burgmüller, choreography by Jean Coralli) first performed at the Opéra in 1843: lithograph after a drawing by Alophe. The scene shows Carlotta Grisi's leap into the arms of Lucien Petipa in Act 1

explicit: John of Leyden naively agrees to join efforts with the conniving and false-pious Anabaptists – socialists slightly disguised by the sixteenth-century setting of Scribe's libretto – only to bring grief to his devoted mother and death to himself and his beloved. The workers of Paris, if they knew these operas, did not heed their warnings. As 1848 approached, ever more songs of protest were written stressing that brotherly harmony could indeed be achieved if the 'immoral' upper classes (*les aristos*) were thrown out of power.[42] Neither Meyerbeer's operas nor *La juive*, with its related if less cynical message of the dignity of the individual in spite of religious differences and accidents of birth, could do anything to halt this renewed groundswell of revolutionary fervour or the predictably violent response from the ruling classes. Grand opera could enhance Paris's reputation as the city for luxury and opulence; as a means of political control, it proved to be useless, unlike the political pageants and resonant operas of the 1789 Revolution.

*

During the July Monarchy, the two other 'subventioned' opera theatres tried less hard to influence the life of the nation and, perhaps for that reason, produced works that were more diverting and stylistically coherent. Auber, at the Opéra-Comique, continued into the 1860s to turn out trimly proportioned pieces of great theatrical vitality: nothing in Meyerbeer is more effective than the moment in Auber's *Manon Lescaut* (1856) when the dressmaker heroine scandalizes the party-goers with her risqué 'Bourbonnaise' or when, after the duet with her neighbour Marguerite earlier in the act, she turns inward (thanks to a skilfully modulated transition) to reflect on her own situation and feelings. The achievements of Gounod, Bizet and Massenet owe much to the often underrated expertise of the mid-century *opéra comique* composers, both those at the Opéra-Comique itself and those at the new house established in 1847, the Opéra-National (which was succeeded, to some extent, by the Théâtre-Lyrique in 1852).

As for the Théâtre-Italien, it now served as a showcase for a new generation of composers and as the ultimate place of diversion for the moneyed classes; it even shut down for a long spring and summer vacation, when its patrons repaired to their country homes. Successful recent works from Italy, such as Donizetti's *Anna Bolena* and Bellini's *La sonnambula*, made an enormous impression on such audiences, attuned as they were to the charms of fine vocalizing; the square-cut yet mellifluous themes reached a wider public too, since they lent themselves well to the manufacture of arrangements, variation sets and quadrilles. In addition, Bellini, Mercadante and Donizetti all came to Paris in the 1830s or 40s in order to write new operas or rework old ones specifically for the Théâtre-Italien, and in Donizetti's case for the Opéra and two other Paris theatres as well. Bellini, in *I puritani* (1835), and Donizetti, in his works for the Opéra, give striking evidence of the impress of Parisian taste: large ensembles are prominently featured, scenes are organized more fluidly, cabalettas are fewer and the orchestration is richer. Many of these traits continued to show in Donizetti's and Mercadante's works written for Italy after their first Paris commissions.[43]

*

The prominence of opera in Paris was evident wherever music was made. Arias and duets from stage works were performed in public concerts and more frequently still in private homes, in arrangements for voice and piano. This love of singing in the parlour naturally gave rise to pieces composed for the purpose. Throughout the Revolution, Empire and Restoration, large numbers of technically undemanding *romances* were published. These songs, for one or, less often, two voices, with accompaniment of piano (or guitar or harp: the published scores often propose several options), were composed by a wide range of musicians from the established composers Cherubini, Méhul, Boieldieu and Berton to the now-forgotten Joseph Blangini (an Italian singing-teacher who maintained an exclusive salon during the Napoleonic period) and Joseph Doche (a *vaudeville* composer), as well as singers such as Sophie Gail and Pierre-Jean Garat, and dozens – thousands during the Restoration, according to one complaint – of rank amateurs.[44] Most *romances* were simple in melody and accompaniment, unambitious in harmony, strophic in form and anodyne in text. The accompaniment, though, tended to be fully written out, a fact that distinguished these songs from most *pastourelles* and *bergerettes* of the pre-revolutionary decades and that allowed at least the possibility of a more artful interaction of voice and instrument. Indeed, a more thoughtful approach to the genre can occasionally be seen in a small number of exploratory songs from the 1790s, such as Louis Jadin's through-composed *La mort de Werther*. The neo-classical fashion, similarly, prompted carefully considered settings of odes of Anacreon, sometimes in the original Greek, by Méhul and others.

During the 1820s and 30s, the traditional *romance* found an increasingly comfortable niche in commercial musical life. Publishers such as Jean-Antoine Meissonnier discovered a ready market for single songs, especially if issued with exquisitely illustrated title-pages, as well as for vocal 'albums' each containing a half-dozen or so *romances*. Music magazines vied for the chance to offer the latest waltz-like vocal number from the workshop of Loïsa Puget or Antoine Romagnési as a supplement or New Year 'bonus' to their faithful subscribers. Pauline Duchambge, a student of Auber, turned out some 400 such songs, and Puget produced five albums between 1834 and her marriage in 1845 to the dramatist (and poet of her songs) Gustave Lemoine.[45] The chanson texts of Béranger were treated to new settings by many of the same composers; in place of the folksongs and quick duple-metre dance-tunes that Béranger used, Meissonnier, Wilhem (in the choral realm) and Auguste Panseron (a future singing teacher at the Conservatoire) provided elegant vehicles that matched the accents of Béranger's verse better than had his chosen tunes but sacrificed much of the sturdy confidence and ironic glint that made his songs so powerful as political and social commentary.

The traditional *romance*, however successful commercially, began to be challenged about 1830 by an artistically more demanding type of accompanied song. Hippolyte Monpou, an imaginative and experimental but wildly inconsistent composer, and the more disciplined Berlioz created songs that mark the maturity of the genre, its transformation from *romance* to the more substantial *mélodie* (the French equivalent of Schubert's lieder, many of which were published

– in dreadful translations but to great acclaim – during the July Monarchy). Berlioz's *Les nuits d'été*, a cycle of six songs to texts by Théophile Gautier, shows a wide range in style and mood, from the light, strophic pleasantries of the opening 'Villanelle' to the quasi-operatic 'Le spectre de la rose' and the haunted grief of 'Sur les lagunes'. (Berlioz later orchestrated the songs for use in his many concerts in France and abroad.) In this cycle, especially, Berlioz broke the path for composers still unborn, notably Gabriel Fauré, Henri Duparc and Claude Debussy.

*

Choral and sacred music during this period underwent drastic shifts and changes. During the Revolution, sacred music as such all but disappeared, though we have noted the use of certain styles and conventions of sacred music in the festival hymns. After Napoleon restored Christian worship in 1801, some of the best composers welcomed the chance to cultivate again genres that until the Revolution had been among the most highly valued and the most serious. Occasionally the resemblance to ceremonial works of the revolutionary years is particularly striking: the moving *Marche religieuse* that Cherubini wrote for the moment during Charles X's coronation when the monarch took Communion could easily be mistaken for one of the solemn marches of the Revolution. Yet there can be little doubt that Cherubini was sincerely devoted to writing religious music; the masses for chorus and orchestra that he composed during the Restoration are finely worked and deeply felt, offering grandeur without vulgarity and a reflectiveness that never cloys. Le Sueur, a less conventional composer in every way, produced for the Chapelle a series of quirky but dramatic and imaginative Latin oratorios on biblical heroines (Ruth, Deborah, Rachel) as well as other oratorios using a diverse and personal assemblage of texts, for instance the three he wrote for the aforementioned coronation of Charles X in 1825. Le Sueur's church works are filled with stage directions (largely unrealizable) and marginal comments to the performers, the result of his leanings towards opera and also of his wide-ranging curiosity and restless intellect. The harmonic style is often extremely simple, suggesting a conscious desire to exploit the large resonant spaces of a cathedral such as Notre Dame and recalling the effective bareness of many revolutionary hymns.

At the very beginning of his career, Berlioz thought to make his mark with an imposing sacred work, a mass, from which the 'Resurrexit' was finally absorbed into his Requiem (*Grande messe des morts*) of 1837. If the vividness and blazing originality of the Requiem testify to his composition lessons with Le Sueur, the solid mastery of texture and proportion can fully stand comparison with the best of

Cherubini; indeed, the work beat Cherubini's own second Requiem (in D minor) in a competition for a government-sponsored première to celebrate Louis-Philippe's escape from an assassination attempt on the anniversary of the July Revolution. One passage, the 'Tuba mirum' (with four brass bands and sixteen kettledrums, based on the early 'Resurrexit'), is reminiscent of the revolutionary festivals of the 1790s. (Berlioz made his admiration for those traditions even plainer in a full-length *Symphonie funèbre et triomphale* for band (1840), commissioned by the government for performance in a parade celebrating the tenth anniversary of the July Revolution.)

The sacred works of Le Sueur, Cherubini and Berlioz were in every way exceptional. In most of the country's churches the music was less than dignified. Plainchant, including the undistinguished seventeenth-century chants of Henri Du Mont, was most often sung lethargically, to the accompaniment of a raucous, ill-tuned serpent. Hardly better were the choral motets of the day, which often included arrangements of light-hearted opera tunes; even at Notre Dame the music, in the words of the music theorist Jérôme-Joseph de Momigny, was 'dry, insignificant and poorly performed'.[46] People who took up the fight for higher standards in church music, notably Choron and Berlioz's friend Joseph d'Ortigue, tended to favour a tasteful and scholarly revival of Gregorian chant, interspersed with *a cappella* performances of Renaissance polyphony or new works in a Renaissance-inspired style. One organist-composer, Alexandre Boëly, similarly looked to the past for guidance, to the best traditions of the French Baroque (in his own *alternatim* versets) and to J. S. Bach (in his Fantasy and Fugue in Bb), at a time when other organists, such as Edouard Batiste, were regaling congregations with depictions of storms, and 'wistful love song[s]' for the Elevation of the Host.[47]

Unfortunately, the pitiful condition of the country's organs (many had been attacked or destroyed during the French Revolution) combined with Louis-Philippe's termination of Choron's subvention to cripple most attempts at church music reform. It is surely no accident that some of the most important large-scale works for chorus and orchestra during the 1830s and 40s – such as Berlioz's *La damnation de Faust* (1845–6) and Félicien David's enormously popular *Le désert* (1844), a kind of travelogue based on his two years' stay in Turkey, Palestine and Egypt – were entirely secular in aim and effect. The task of rebuilding church music was not addressed in a coordinated and lasting fashion until after 1850, but then by leading talents, including the organ builder Aristide Cavaillé-Coll, the German-trained organist Jacques-Nicolas Lemmens, the choral conductor and teacher Louis Niedermeyer and a diverse group of composers, from Charles Gounod and César Franck to Alexandre Guilmant, Louis Vierne, Gabriel Fauré and Vincent d'Indy.

INSTRUMENTAL MUSIC, HIGH AND LOW

In spite of the dominant influence of vocal music, especially opera, on Parisian musical taste, the city was also a centre for the composition and performance of instrumental works, ranging from the most demanding symphonic masterpieces (not always appreciated by Paris audiences) to ephemeral, if often tuneful, piano pieces for domestic diversion.

In the late eighteenth century, there were already 'more instrumental composers, performers, and publishers operating in Paris than in any other city in Europe', and the city's two major and artistically invigorating public concert series, the Concert Spirituel (so called because the bulk of its performances were originally devoted to oratorio and other sacred choral music) and the Concert de la Loge Olympique, were 'without peer in size and brilliance'.[48] Though both series died out during the first two years of the Revolution, as did private concerts previously mounted by wealthy patrons, other series sprang up to fill the gap. Some of these offered new repertory and rested on a very different social base, yet all followed the eighteenth-century tradition of juxtaposing in a single concert works for different performing forces: one or more overtures or symphonies, a concerto, opera arias and duets, perhaps even some chamber music.

Of the new concert series, the most distinguished took place at the Salle Feydeau, beginning in 1791 and continuing, on and off, until the theatre merged with the Opéra-Comique in 1801. Besides the obligatory Haydn symphony (Parisians were as fond of the Austrian master during the Revolution and Empire as they had been before) and concertos for one or more instruments (often with the composer performing, for example Giovanni Viotti, the flautist François Devienne or the horn player Frédéric Nicolas Duvernoy), the Feydeau concerts featured a singer or two. At first Anna Morichelli was the star, but after the political events of August 1792 forced the Italian contingent of the Théâtre Feydeau to decamp (Morichelli soon was captivating London audiences instead), her place was filled by Mme Barbier-Walbonne (wife of the well-known painter Jacques Luc Barbier-Walbonne) and the widely adored Garat. These brilliant performers helped to attract and hold a glittering audience; indeed, two satirical plays – with songs – from 1795 suggest that the Feydeau concert audiences laid great store on being fashionably dressed and came more to be seen than to listen.

HE: I cannot enjoy myself, I do not exist, except at a concert.
SHE: But you do not know anything about music?
HE: Well, I can hear perfectly well. Besides, I admire; I do as the
        others do.

The political satire here is admittedly rather mild, but when talk – or, rather, song – turns to certain republicans (the play calls them 'terrorists') who had dared to criticize the snobbism of the Feydeau concerts, the tone becomes more vicious:

> The horrid art of giving birth to crimes
> Is the only one that can attract their heart.
> The pleading cries of their victims
> Is the only concert that pleases their ears.

(The song is sung, with obvious irony, to the tune of 'Les Montagnards', the latter being a longstanding nickname for the Jacobins.)[49]

Less disputed, because less redolent of the *ancien régime*, were the concerts (or 'public exercises') of the Conservatoire. In 1793 the Institut National de Musique (as it was called until 1795) offered a concert and invited all deputies of the National Convention to attend. The programme, which included an overture by Catel, *symphonies concertantes* by François Devienne and Gossec, as well as the latter's stirring *Marche lugubre*, must have been intended as a republican counterpart to the more cosmopolitan diversions of the Feydeau concerts. The event was an enormous success and concerts became more frequent, reaching six a year in 1797–8 and eventually twelve. The orchestra consisted of the strongest students and was thus entirely French, whereas German players filled many of the wood-wind chairs in other French orchestras, and the concerts were held at a sober time of the week: Sunday afternoon. It was the custom for Méhul and Cherubini to coach the orchestra in rehearsals but to hand over the direction at performances to a gifted student, who would lead by playing his violin, gesturing, or tapping his bow on a music stand. In the early nineteenth century François-Antoine Habeneck was given the job on a regular basis. He took advantage of his position to perform (sometimes on more than one occasion) Beethoven's Symphonies nos.1, 3 and 5 and Mozart's nos.39–41. Though Habeneck was criticized by German observers for his rapid tempos, and though the local critics found the new works dissonant ('barbaric chords') and incoherent ('doves and crocodiles caged together'), Habeneck would not give up his campaign to bring the German masterworks to France.[50]

The Conservatoire concerts, like those of the Salle Feydeau, had the advantage of a ready-made orchestra. More difficult was the task of creating an orchestra expressly for giving symphonic concerts. The most successful such attempt in the early nineteenth century, the 'Concerts de la rue de Cléry', attracted 600 subscribers in its first year (1799) but closed six years later, for reasons not now known.

26. *Concert in the hall of the Paris Conservatoire: engraving from 'L'illustration' (15 April 1843)*

Habeneck, too, suffered reverses. When the Bourbons reduced the Conservatoire budget, the 'public exercises' were essentially eliminated as an important source of serious music for the city (only 19 concerts in 1815–30, compared with 144 in 1800–15).[51]

*

The repertory at all these concert series was remarkably consistent, allowing for certain shifts in emphasis, for example more French music at the Conservatoire (at least in the 1790s) and more Haydn at the rue de Cléry. Though it is tempting to think of the music in national terms – Haydn as Austrian, Viotti as Italian, Gossec as French – it would be more accurate to say that these composers, perhaps especially the minor masters such as Duvernoy, Rodolphe Kreutzer and Xavier Lefèvre, wrote in a more or less international musical language that we today, knowing our Haydn and Mozart, associate with Vienna but that actually derives much of its character and many of its procedures from the bustling overtures and finales of Italian *opera buffa*. The composers active in France spoke this language with their own accents, it is true: Boieldieu's harp concerto contains episodes in pure *opéra comique* style. And the more serious among them, such as Viotti, in his influential series of violin concertos, did not merely keep repeating a watered-down Italo-Viennese Classicism, but found ways to add a personal element; Brahms called Viotti's concerto no.22 'a glorious piece . . ., sounding as if improvised, and yet everything so well planned'.[52]

This Italianate and international style did not express itself, oddly, in large numbers of new symphonies: 785 French symphonies, more than thirteen a year, have been counted for the years 1730–89, but the number drops to three or four a year after 1789 and less than one a year between 1800 and 1830.[53] This genre, in which Gossec had triumphed during the *ancien régime*, was being practised during the revolutionary period mainly by several foreign-born composers, such as the melodious and skilful Pleyel. (The only post-1789 symphony of Gossec, as well as Cherubini's sole but marvellous symphony, written for London, and five of Méhul's six completed symphonies, all date from 1809 or later.) In contrast, certain overtures to recent French operas broke loose from the theatre and established an independent life as concert pieces: this was no doubt partly because of their large and colourful instrumentation, but also because of their frequent use of pastoralisms and local colour or even extended programmatic writing, as in Méhul's much loved overture to *Le jeune Henri*, a musical description of a hunt that 'offers the first satisfactory compromise between the sonata outline and the expressive demands of the underlying topic' and thus seems to point the way to Berlioz.[54]

The *symphonie concertante*, a French speciality since the 1770s, maintained its attraction for Parisian composers and audiences during the revolutionary decade, tapering off only gradually and disappearing about 1830. *Symphonies concertantes*, in essence concertos for two or more instruments (e.g. two violins; clarinet and bassoon; flute, oboe, horn and cello), tend to avoid darker shades: almost all are in the major mode and many consist of only two rather cheery movements without an intervening slow one (the traditional locus of introspection and touching turns of phrase and harmony). Odd though it may seem, this essentially *galant* genre continued to flourish during the stormy 1790s, not only in formal concerts but also as ballet or entr'acte music in theatrical productions. It may be that audiences saw in the alternately chattering and cantabile interplay between the soloists – the orchestra did little more than set the stage and reinforce the sonority – something similar to the conversation between characters in a play or opera. (In 1785 Etienne de Lacépède had described the various instruments in orchestral music as joining to produce 'scenes for several characters'.)[55] One suspects, too, that listeners appreciated the refuge of diverting sounds and elegant performances: sweet music for rough times. Most of all, leading performers of the day – the horn player Duvernoy, the clarinettist Lefèvre, the bassoonist Ozi – helped keep the genre alive, reviving older *symphonies concertantes* and composing new ones; clearly they relished the opportunity of displaying the variety of their talents and those of one or more friends in a setting of relaxed yet visibly captivating interplay.

*

Whatever the combination of factors that encouraged the soloistic element in the orchestral repertory, a similar focus can be seen in chamber music, even in that clearly intended for performance by amateurs at home. Though Haydn had shown the way, in his op.33, towards a truly organic string-quartet texture, with all the instruments sharing in the musical argument, the French preferred the *quatuor brillant*, in which the first violinist performed a more or less self-contained solo part, replete with flowing melodies and busy passage-work, while the other three instruments supported their colleague. The more modest *quatuor concertant* featured not one soloist but several, each carrying the melodic line for a time before passing it on, in a musical dialogue analogous to the exchanges between solo parts in many *symphonies concertantes*.[56] At least one serious composer of chamber music was frustrated by the limitations the French market imposed on him. Luigi Boccherini, writing from Madrid, complained to his publisher Pleyel that the latter's insistence that he keep his quartets short and orientated towards tunes would mean 'farewell to modulations and to the working out of themes . . . In few words one can say but few things, much less meditate on them'. He finally agreed to protect his 'reputation' by writing, in every set of six, 'two according to my desire and four according to yours'.[57] (Pleyel, after offering Boccherini plentiful assurances, instead published – as if they were new works – a disorganized collection of twelve quartets, some composed eighteen years earlier.)[58] Cherubini, even less inclined to compromise, delayed publication of his first string quartet (1814) for 22 years; the last three (quite experimental works) still lay unpublished when he died in 1842.

Not surprisingly, the most popular categories of chamber music were straightforward arrangements of opera overtures and arias – for string quartet, for two flutes, for two bassoons and so on. One of the most active arrangers about 1800 was a certain Abraham (whose full name is unknown), described by Fétis as 'a sort of musician-labourer on the payroll of the music publishers'; through his work many an opera became known, without words, to families in Paris and the provinces that played chamber music at home but rarely if ever stepped inside a concert hall or opera house.[59] Not until 1814 did a professional series, with Pierre Baillot as first violin, attempt to establish serious credentials for chamber music, as had been done 30 or more years earlier for orchestral music. Baillot played standing up, in the spirit of the *quatuor brillant*, whereas his three colleagues remained seated.[60]

In the realm of piano music, too, the French were slow to accept serious work – and this in spite of the profound impression the Bohemian-born Jan Ladislav Dussek had made as court pianist in 1786–9 (before fleeing to London) and renewed when he settled in Paris at the end of his life (1807–12). Few sonatas of importance were written in France during the 60 years under discussion. Instead, French taste brought about characteristic ways of using the instrument: melodically, colouristically, even programmatically, as in Louis Jadin's *La grande bataille d'Austerlitz, surnommée La bataille des trois empereurs, fait historique arrangé pour le piano-forte*. Straightforward opera arrangements of the Abraham type were also created for keyboard, and it was not long before these were being elaborated with slow introductions, modulatory passage-work and glittering variations, the result being the operatic fantasy, also known by such titles as 'caprice', 'reminiscences' and 'souvenirs'. The earliest such fantasies (e.g. those of Jadin and the German-born Daniel Steibelt) are technically easy and aesthetically modest, in apparent continuation of the eighteenth-century tradition of writing keyboard variations on Christmas carols or, during the Revolution, on such tunes as *Ah, ça ira!* But the arrival of an increasing number of central European (mainly German-speaking) pianist-composers raised the level of the genre and brought it, and piano music generally, into the concert hall.[61]

*

Dussek, Steibelt, Johann Nepomuk Hummel (who made a six-month visit in 1830), Friedrich Kalkbrenner, Henri Herz, Johann Peter Pixis, Franz Liszt, Sigismond Thalberg, Ferdinand Hiller, Stephen Heller, Léopold de Meyer, Fryderyk Chopin – many of these names must at first have seemed foreign indeed to Parisian music-lovers. But the technical skills these men brought to Parisian concert life, skills they were able to hone further on the pianos of the Erard and Pleyel firms, overwhelmed any resistance. All these pianist-composers tended to play mainly their own music, and most of that is never heard today, for in it musical substance was usually outweighed by superficial feats of technique, especially involving rapid finger-work in the glittery high register. But all of them contributed mightily towards the goal – about which Liszt, for one, was quite explicit – of gaining for instrumental music the kind of attention and respect that vocal music had long enjoyed and of establishing the piano as the central instrument of the Romantic age. True, the piano had a close competitor in the violin; the already legendary Paganini conquered Paris in 1831. But even the greatest violinist still depended on a pianist or orchestra. A solo keyboard artist, in contrast, would play entirely unaided and give with two hands (and judicious use of the sustaining pedal) the impression of being at once orchestra, conductor and, in operatic arrangements, singers as well.

Three pianist-composers stood out from the rest by virtue of their youth and their unique creative gifts: Thalberg, Liszt and Chopin. All three had trained or made important early débuts in Vienna, and all three settled in Paris between 1824 and 1835. Each took the pianist's art to undreamt-of heights – but in his own way. They also differed so strikingly in their attitudes towards public acclaim and the concert stage that a sketch of their Parisian careers amounts almost to a panorama of the options and limitations that the city presented to the serious instrumentalist.

Thalberg was born in 1812 to German parents of modest class but, because of his extraordinary talents, he was sent to Vienna, where he prepared for both a career in music (studying with Carl Czerny) and one in diplomacy (at the Polytechnic School, beside Napoleon's son, the Duke of Reichstadt). His pianistic gifts won out and, by the early

27. *Caricature of the pianist Sigismond Thalberg: woodcut (c1835)*

1830s, he had played for Metternich, given concerts in many European capitals and been appointed court pianist to the Austrian emperor. Fétis and Schumann, among others, hailed him as the greatest of Europe's many pianist-composers, for to the classical dexterity of Herz, Pixis and Kalkbrenner (he also studied with the latter two in Paris) he added a number of archetypally Romantic traits: surging melody, mysterious or veiled textures (often based on widely sweeping arpeggios) and more than a touch of bombast. Schumann singled out for praise several of his short pieces as well as the Fantasy and Variations on Themes from Bellini's *Norma* op.12; operatic fantasies were the main source of his fame, in part because of his use of the crowd-pleasing 'three hands' trick, in which the melody is assigned to the middle of the keyboard (struck alternately by the thumb of one or other hand, the necessary legato being provided by the sustaining pedal), while florid passage-work and contrapuntal lines swirl above and below it in the remaining fingers. The effect in performance was all the more impressive in that Thalberg maintained an unruffled demeanour, viewed at the time as 'aristocratic' or 'patrician'; indeed, many of his friends were aristocrats, and rumour had it that Thalberg was himself the illegitimate son of a count and a baroness.

Thalberg arrived in Paris in 1835, aged 23, and Liszt (his elder by only a year) could not resist feeling challenged. Liszt arranged to give several recitals consisting pointedly of music worthier than opera fantasies (notably Beethoven's Hammerklavier Sonata, a Paris première); for one of these he rented the Opéra, a spacious and public venue that seated nearly 2000 listeners, six times as many as the hall that Thalberg favoured (the Conservatoire). Liszt's short-lived but violent resentment of Thalberg was clearly tinged by issues of social class. Indeed, he made this explicit when he published an article attacking Thalberg – and, quite unnecessarily, the latter's connections to the rich and powerful – in the *Revue et gazette musicale*. (The article, like many others bearing his name, was actually written for him, at least in large part, by the Countess Marie d'Agoult, and reveals a keen sense of the power of publicity in the modern age.)

Unlike Thalberg, Liszt had been obliged to fight for respect and dignified treatment from the social élites of the city. (In 1828, when he fell in love with the daughter of the Minister of Commerce, her father reminded Liszt of his social station and terminated the relationship, sending him into a nervous breakdown.) By the mid-1830s Liszt had come to resent much of what passed for social propriety among the upper classes. He openly maintained a lengthy relationship with the Countess d'Agoult, a married woman, and they produced three children (one of whom, Cosima, later married Wagner). Furthermore, he willingly allied himself with large public audiences, with the labouring classes (his piano piece *Lyon* was inspired by weavers'

28. Liszt at the piano: painting (1840) by Josef Danhauser, said to have been made in Liszt's Paris apartment, with (left to right) Alexandre Dumas (the elder), Victor Hugo, George Sand, Paganini, Rossini and, at Liszt's feet, Marie d'Agoult (the central portrait is of Byron, and the bust on the piano is of Beethoven)

uprisings in 1831 and 1834)[62] and with other musicians, writers and painters (his series of articles 'On the Situation of Artists and their Condition in Society', written largely on his own, proposes that musicians, far from being menial servants, are capable of 'uniting mankind in brotherhood by means of rapturous wonders').[63] Though fully Thalberg's equal in keyboard technique, and even more willing than he to pile up a raging storm of sound, he was a serious composer at heart and particularly interested in extending the emotional and depictive boundaries of instrumental music (as in *La vallée d'Obermann*, later incorporated in his *Années de pèlerinage*, Book 1, 'Switzerland') and in experimenting with the most basic musical elements (as in the rhythmically and harmonically audacious *Harmonies poétiques et religieuses* of 1834).

This was apparently what nettled Liszt most about Thalberg: to be challenged in the public eye by a rival whose works could not compare with those that Liszt knew he had in him. The difference can already be seen in Liszt's operatic fantasies of the 1830s. His paraphrase on themes from Bellini's *Norma* (1838) transcends Thalberg's (1835) in conception and execution alike. Whereas Thalberg's themes are drawn seemingly at random from the opera, Liszt's are carefully selected to encompass the work's dramatic and atmospheric range and are ordered in a cunning tonal scheme of ascending major 3rds and minor–major alternations that helps to give musical coherence to the series of tableaux.[64] Liszt here uses the three-handed technique to poetic rather than acrobatic or merely sensuous effect, creating for Norma's sorrowful 'Qual cor tradisti' a pianistic analogue to Bellini's layering of solo voice, chordal accompaniment and ominous triplets in the timpani. This respect for the integrity of another composer's music became an ever more important part of Liszt's work as arranger and adapter; he created solo piano versions of the symphonies of Beethoven and Berlioz, thus helping audiences to get to know them. In 1847 Liszt's insistence on using his talents to benefit the art of music ('génie oblige', as he put it) finally led him to abandon public concert-giving and to redirect his efforts towards original composition and promoting the works of others. He settled in Weimar, where he served as a valuable conduit for the best and most searching works to come out of Paris: those of Chopin and Berlioz.

Chopin was less well suited than either Liszt or Thalberg to the showman's life that Paris demanded of a virtuoso musician, yet, paradoxically, this forced him to find his own novel and highly principled way of surviving and interacting creatively with the city's musical and social life. Chopin arrived in 1831, at 19, from his native Poland, by way of début concerts in Vienna, and Paris remained his home (except for an ill-fated trip to the British Isles to escape the 1848 revolution) until his death in 1849. During his two decades in Paris he appeared in fewer than 40 public concerts, and in many of those he performed but one or two pieces, as a favour to a musician-friend such as Liszt or Charles-Valentin Alkan (another astonishingly gifted and original composer-pianist). He supported himself primarily by giving piano lessons to daughters of the wealthy, some of them quite talented, destined by social custom however not to take up a professional career. He was a generous, attentive teacher and a demanding one, technically, musically and financially: his fee of 20 francs a lesson (30 if he went to the pupil's house) was roughly equal to two weeks' salary of a manual labourer. Chopin's decision to live from teaching rather than performing, though regretted by many of his contemporaries, anticipates the teaching-orientated careers of many twentieth-century musicians. He also learnt to manipulate the complex details of publishing contracts (there was as yet no international copyright) in such a way as to maximize his income and protect his work from appearing in inauthentic and error-ridden 'pirate' editions.[65]

Several of his earliest Parisian compositions were designed to meet local taste: fantasies on operas by Halévy (op.12) and Meyerbeer (op.16). Quickly, though, he found his own voice, writing original piano pieces ranging from lyricism (e.g. in the nocturnes) and

29. Fryderyk Chopin: portrait (1838) by Eugène Delacroix (once the right-hand side of a double portrait that included the novelist George Sand, listening while Chopin played the piano)

elegance (waltzes) to concise evocation (preludes, studies) and epic grandeur (ballades, scherzos and polonaises). His natural adventurousness in harmony was reinforced, in the mazurkas especially, by modal features from Polish folk music, notably the raised or Lydian 4th. The passages of intense chromatic modulation that appear in many of his pieces seem to speak of personal anguish and occasionally unbridled rage. Even at its most turbulent and idiosyncratic, though, his music retains something of the sheen, suppleness and poise typical of much French music, thereby creating a delicate and often disturbing tension of mood; his slow melodies, in particular, reveal in their ecstatic coloratura embellishments a love of the kind of singing heard at the fashionable Théâtre-Italien, yet suggest in their chromaticism and asymmetry some unspoken sadness.

*

The struggle between surface glamour and inner seriousness, exemplified in different ways in the works of the pianist-composers, can be seen in every other aspect of Parisian concert life. In the chamber-music repertory, for example, a more substantial sort of music became important from the 1820s, thanks in large part to the continuing efforts of Baillot, whose quartet concerts introduced to Paris audiences many of the chamber works of Haydn, Mozart and Boccherini, and, among the moderns, Mendelssohn, Georges Onslow (a native-born – though his father was English – composer of Viennese-style string quartets and quintets) and Cherubini, all six of whose quartets received their first performances at the Baillot concerts. Beethoven was less appreciated by Baillot's highly conservative subscribers, who were mainly aristocrats (many of them amateur musicians) and well-heeled officials, financiers or businessmen. Fortunately a number of younger musicians, many attending with free tickets from Baillot, later formed chamber concert series of their own and succeeded where Baillot had not.

The 'brilliant' style of chamber music continued to flourish, especially in concerts devoted otherwise to orchestral music or soloistic virtuosity; examples include Charles Dancla's string quartets, with their frilly first violin parts, Kalkbrenner's quintet for piano, clarinet, horn, cello and bass (the four instruments often forming a miniature orchestral accompaniment to the highly soloistic piano part) and many piano trios. As for music for a single instrument – violin, flute or cello – with piano, most of it lacked the interplay of instruments typical of the duet sonatas of the Austro-German

30. Concert in the Salle Pleyel, where Chopin and other leading performers appeared: engraving from 'L'illustration' (9 June 1855). The intimate, informal nature of the occasion (with some of the audience seated round the stage) suggests an expanded private salon concert

tradition: rather, the tunes – again largely operatic – and their variations are allotted almost entirely to the featured instrument, the piano being relegated to a supporting role, much like that of the male dancer in a *pas de deux*.

The battle for a serious approach to instrumental music was perhaps most successful in the orchestral realm, and much of that was Habeneck's doing. Even in 1817–24, when he was occupied primarily by his duties as principal violinist and then director of the Opéra, he seized what opportunities he could, for instance at the Opéra's *concerts spirituels*, to perform orchestral music by Beethoven. In 1824 he became chief conductor at the Opéra (jointly with Valentino, then alone from 1831 to 1846), a position that allowed him not only to rebuild the orchestra there into what an English critic called 'a machine . . . in perfect order',[66] but to begin assembling a band of hand-picked players from the Opéra and other theatres and from the Conservatoire (where he taught violin), with the aim of giving regular, professional performances of the German classics. In 1826 the Eroica was tried out, and in 1828 the first formal concert was given, in the Conservatoire's concert hall (hence the name Société des Concerts du Conservatoire).

The orchestra was organized along democratic principles, each member receiving an equal share of the year's profits except Habeneck himself, who received a double share,[67] a striking contrast to the extreme disparities at the Opéra, where the leader was paid 3000 francs a year compared to a back-desk violinist's 1000 and a bass-drum player's 600 (and, in the other direction, to a prima donna's 16,000).[68] Though the society's players numbered many a famed soloist – Baillot, the flautist Jean-Louis Tulou, the horn player Louis François Dauprat – and though they performed only a dozen or so concerts a year together, Habeneck managed to forge them into a true ensemble, partly because the string players had almost all studied with the same few teachers.

From 1828 until Habeneck's death in 1849, one Beethoven symphony followed another, to the astonishment and delight of French audiences as well as professional musicians from home and abroad. The Ninth Symphony received its Paris première in 1831; Habeneck, in anticipation, had rehearsed its individual movements during the three previous years to assure the work a fair hearing. He also performed much music of other composers who could be considered 'classical' – Haydn, Mozart, Cherubini – and won the ear and pen of respected writers in the city and the subscriptions of prominent members of the business and professional classes. The solemnity of mood that prevailed at the society's concerts, the prevailing serious-ness of the repertory and the continued devotion of the subscribing families (seats were handed down as precious heirlooms) led one critic in 1856 to snipe: 'Will one perhaps soon need to prove that one is dead in order to add one's name to the list of subscribers?'[69]

Orchestral music of more modest sorts, requiring neither proselytizing efforts nor rehearsals, was given most nights of the year at the concerts or 'balls' of Musard and Valentino, where people socialized, ate, drank and danced while the music played. Tickets were less expensive than those for Habeneck's concerts and, by virtue of the frequent performances, more easily available, making these concerts accessible to members of the lower-middle and even working classes. Occasionally a work of some pretension by a young composer would be performed (e.g. Félicien David's early Symphony in F and his Nonetto for brass), perhaps just for novelty's sake, or at the instigation of a player, tired perhaps of quadrilles and galops.

Such an opportunity occurred all too rarely – certainly not at Habeneck's concerts. It was accepted that a truly serious French composer, young or old, would avoid the major orchestral genres and would stick instead to writing conventional sacred music or finding a way of adapting to Paris's more diverse but equally convention-ridden world of opera. The most demanding and most visionary musician of the age was drawn to all three realms – symphony, sacred music and opera – and was uninterested in adapting to anyone's conventions. The story of Berlioz and his love–hate relationship with Paris encapsulates all that was nourishing, and confining, about Parisian musical life during the first half of the century.

BERLIOZ AND THE DECLINE OF PARIS

Berlioz had been given a traditional classical education (he adored Virgil) by his father, an accomplished provincial physician. In contrast, the music in his early environment was lightweight and somewhat sentimental: mainly *romances* and *opéra comique* airs, which Berlioz liked to accompany on the guitar. When he moved to Paris in 1821, ostensibly to study medicine, he encountered a diversity of music great and grand that, within a year, decided him instead on the career of a composer. His determination to keep his sights set high was reinforced by Le Sueur, his composition teacher at the Conservatoire, by his eye-opening exposure to whole bodies of modern literature (Goethe's *Faust*, in Nerval's published translation, and, on stage, the tragedies of Shakespeare), but most of all by the power and elegance of the music he could now hear performed – often splendidly so – almost nightly: operas by Gluck, Boieldieu, Spontini, Rossini and Weber, and symphonies by Beethoven. (He would pay lifelong homage to Parisian standards of instrumental execution in his own works and in his orchestration treatise of 1843, revised in 1855.) His first mature works were highly dramatic, even explicitly programmatic, for example the *Symphonie fantastique* (1830), which illustrates

31. 'One-man orchestra', a caricature of Berlioz that appeared at the time of the failure of his opera 'Benvenuto Cellini' in 1838 (the harlequinade taking place is based on the pantomime in Act 1 of the opera): lithograph by B. Roubaud from 'Caricature provisoire' (1 November 1838)

'episodes' in a love-affair, from the first stirrings of passion to distant admiration, daydreams amid nature, rejection and wild opium-inspired visions of death and revulsion.

Berlioz's originality and the outspoken opinions in his music criticism (and in the belligerent spoken text of his *Lélio*) mostly won him enemies among the established composers and critics who controlled the paths to a career. He had to try for four years to win the coveted Prix de Rome, and he won it only by forcing himself to write the examination cantata in as conventional a manner as he could manage without seeming to be parodying the judges' own works. His trip to Italy gave him the opportunity to deepen his distaste for the predictable harmonies and conventional florid vocalises of post-Rossinian *opera seria* but also to explore on foot the Italian countryside and admire its still-flourishing traditions of folk music-making. Back in Paris in 1832, he began a campaign to get an opera accepted by one of the major houses; finally, in 1838, *Benvenuto Cellini* (originally intended for the Opéra-Comique) was put on, half-heartedly, by the Opéra under Habeneck and then allowed to drop from the repertory after a handful of disaster-ridden performances. For the rest of his career, Berlioz – the greatest French opera composer of his day – was forced to look to much less distinguished theatres, or indeed to the concert stage, to produce his various dramatic vocal works.

Concerts were in many ways his artistic, if not always financial, salvation. His second symphony, *Harold en Italie* (inspired by Byron's *Childe Harold* and by his own Italian memories), was as deeply inspired by Beethoven as the *Symphonie fantastique*, and similarly well received, not least by Paganini, who publicly rewarded him with 20,000 francs, thereby freeing him to bring to fruition a work that would unite and give form to several of his abiding passions: a 'dramatic symphony' – part Beethoven, part Meyerbeer – based on Shakespeare's *Romeo and Juliet* (1839). The work made a deep impression on many musicians and literary figures, including Hugo and the young Wagner; along with the government commissions of the Requiem and the *Symphonie funèbre*, *Roméo et Juliette* strengthened his stature as the leading young composer of France. For a brief moment in late 1844, Berlioz even thought he found an ally in Félicien David, whose 'symphonic ode' *Le désert*, with its mixture of spoken narration, choral movements, tenor arias and exotic dances for orchestra alone, also inhabits the border territory between opera and

32. *Berlioz conducting David's 'Le désert' at the Cirque Olympique, Champs-Elysées, in the presence of several Arab chiefs: engraving from 'L'illustration' (25 January 1845)*

concert music. But David's was a limited talent that after 1850 found its natural home in conventional if still exotically tinged *opéras comiques* such as *La perle du Brésil* (1851) and *Lalla-Roukh* (1862).[70]

Meyerbeer, Auber and David were, by the very fact of their lower musical temperatures, more acceptable to those who ran the opera houses – managers, singers, government commissions – than hot-headed Berlioz. Fortunately, to mount concerts one did not have to please as many powerful people, but one did have to have a lot of initiative and be willing to risk financial disaster. The main steps included renting a hall (the Conservatoire's was usually denied to anyone but Habeneck or foreign virtuosos in the 1840s), engaging the musicians, negotiating with sometimes temperamental soloists (often needed if one wished to draw an audience), paying a copyist to prepare the performing parts, arranging for posters and newspaper advertising, working with a conductor (or conducting the music oneself, as Berlioz nearly always did), and covering various obligatory expenses, such as the 'tax for the poor' to which all entertainments were subject. Berlioz supported his habit of concert-giving by writing music criticism for the *Revue et gazette musicale* and for an important, politically conservative newspaper, the *Journal des débats*; and in 1838 he managed to gain a lifelong sinecure as assistant librarian (eventually librarian) of the Conservatoire, where by rights he should have been a professor of composition, orchestration or conducting.

Concerts, whatever their miseries, were a psychological necessity for Berlioz; if he could not get the response he wanted in Paris, he would try other cities and lands. In the 1840s, after his unhappy marriage to Harriet Smithson finally collapsed (she was the English actress who in 1827 had helped reveal Shakespeare to Paris and to Berlioz), he took to the road several times with baton and with heavy trunks full of performing parts, in the double hope of conquering Marseilles, Lyons, Belgium, Germany and the Austro-Hungarian Empire with his music, and of making a profit. He regularly returned with financial losses (the freight costs were killing) but also with the knowledge that audiences and musicians in Vienna, Prague and other cities grasped what he had to say more fully than the Parisians had ever done.

On his second big tour (1845–6) he managed to compose portions of a long-percolating work that would do for *Faust* what his 'dramatic symphony' had done for *Romeo and Juliet*. The resulting *La damnation de Faust* is a 'dramatic legend': more opera than symphony but intended for concert performance rather than the stage. The Paris critics were lukewarm and, as Berlioz recalled, 'the fashionable Paris audiences . . . stayed comfortably at home . . . Nothing in my career as an artist wounded me more deeply than this unexpected indifference'.[71] Berlioz took this as proof that the philistinism of Parisian taste that he had often bewailed ('I regard [the mass of the Paris public] as children or half-wits')[72] was growing steadily more pervasive. He embarked now on conducting tours of Russia and England, which again, thanks partly to his now finely honed stick technique and rehearsal methods, gained him further adherents; the Russian trip also netted him a good profit and the English trip permitted him to ride out the 1848 revolution. He finally returned to Paris, hoping to set up an alternative to the Conservatoire concerts. His Nouvelle Société Philharmonique lasted a year and a few months and allowed much of his own music to be heard in Paris again, but the recipe was still not right. Not until twenty years later would a new generation of conductors (Jules Pasdeloup, Charles Lamoureux, Edouard Colonne) find the special balance needed for concerts to succeed in the French capital – between classics and moderns, between the symphonic repertory and music featuring soloists, between musical complexity and the public's love of tunes and splash.

Berlioz lived the twenty years until his death in 1869 in a state of resignation and increasing bitterness, though not inactivity, for the tours continued (until his health declined), as did the masterpieces, notably *L'enfance du Christ* (1854), *Les troyens* (1858) and *Béatrice et Bénédict* (1862). Unfortunately, these works too were not welcomed according to their true merits; *Les troyens* was given only in a mutilated

33. Two illustrations of Goethe's 'Faust' by Eugène Delacroix: (a) Faust and Mephistopheles, painting (1826–7)

version (the first two acts were removed entirely) and at the Théâtre-Lyrique rather than the better-equipped Opéra. Few could have realized then what is so obvious now: that Berlioz represents in many ways the second flowering of a characteristic French musical Romanticism that had been adumbrated many decades earlier. His various debts – in *Les troyens* to Gluck and Spontini, in his evocations of nature to Cherubini and Méhul, in his public works to the *style énorme* of the French Revolution – were there for all to hear, but few wished to do so.

Berlioz's inability to gain recognition and support in Paris, beginning about 1842, can be seen as one symptom of a wider problem: the dominance of Paris that in the 1820s and 1830s had seemed so apparent to all musical Europe was coming to an end. Even Meyerbeer had more than his usual trouble finishing *Le prophète* during the 1840s and never put *L'africaine* into final form, preferring instead to abandon Paris for Berlin and, when back in Paris, to write, less persuasively, for the Opéra-Comique. Berlioz's tours in Germany, like Liszt's decision to settle in Weimar (also in the 1840s), marked a shift in European musical life that would be consolidated in the second half of the century. As Paris became more and more confirmed in its position as the capital of pleasure, fashion and luxury, even the best of its music tended to be light-hearted or gracious, or – in its most incisive manifestations (Offenbach, Bizet) – to invert ironically or seek to

(b) The Ride to the Abyss, lithograph from the set of 17 published in 1828 to accompany Albert Stapfer's French translation of 'Faust'

extend those same characteristics, increasingly viewed both at home and abroad as being archetypally French. High seriousness without cheap effects or emotional conventionality (Gounod's operas illustrate the problem) would not be restored until later in the century, with the works of Saint-Saëns (to some extent), Franck, Fauré and Debussy. In the middle decades – those of glory for Verdi in Milan, Wagner in Dresden, Brahms in Vienna and Liszt in Weimar – Paris tried to maintain its position as the musical capital of Europe, but the effort showed. Though Wagner and Verdi were drawn to the Opéra for individual productions (Wagner for *Tannhäuser*, Verdi for *Les vêpres siciliennes* and *Don Carlos*), with mixed results, the single overwhelmingly powerful centre of musical creativity that Paris once had been, no longer existed anywhere.

NOTES

[1] J. Mongrédien, *La musique en France des Lumières au Romantisme, 1789–1830* (Paris, 1986), 189.
[2] D. Whitwell, *Band Music of the French Revolution* (Tutzing, 1979), 16–17, 59–66.
[3] B. Brévan, *Les changements de la vie musicale parisienne de 1774 à 1799* (Paris, 1980), 130.
[4] M. Carlson, *The Theatre of the French Revolution* (Ithaca, NY, 1966), 114–15, 210–13, 220–23, 238–40.
[5] Carlson, *The Theatre*, 238; C. Pierre, *Les hymnes et chansons de la Révolution* (Paris, 1904), 17.
[6] Cited in C. Pierre, 'Notes sur les chansons de la période révolutionnaire', *Revue musicale*, iv (1904), 181.
[7] F. Vernillat and P. Barbier, *Histoire de France par les chansons* (Paris, 1956–61), iv, 78–84.
[8] Brévan, *Les changements*, 132; see also M. Vovelle, 'La Marseillaise', in *Les lieux de mémoire*, ed. P. Nora (Paris, 1984–6), i, 85–136.
[9] Vernillat and Barbier, *Histoire*, iv, 233–41.
[10] M. Ozouf, *Festivals and the French Revolution*, trans. A. Sheridan (Cambridge, Mass., and London, 1988), 282.
[11] Description in Carlson, *The Theatre*, 96–9 and plate IX; Voltaire had been denied church burial in 1778 because of his outspoken anti-clericalism.
[12] Ozouf, *Festivals*, 271–7.
[13] *Music in the Western World: a History in Documents*, ed. P. Weiss and R. Taruskin (New York, 1984), 319–20; cf Pierre, *Les hymnes*, 143–4.
[14] Official printed programme, in M.-L. Biver, *Fêtes révolutionnaires à Paris* (Paris, 1979), 192–8; confirming sources cited in D. L. Dowd, *Pageant-Master of the Republic* (Lincoln, Nebraska, 1948), 120–24.
[15] Ozouf, *Festivals*, 268–71.
[16] See, for example, C. Palisca, 'French Revolutionary Models for Beethoven's *Eroica* Funeral March', in *Music and Context: Essays for John M. Ward* (Cambridge, Mass., 1985), 198–209.
[17] F. Robert, *La musique française au dix-neuvième siècle* (Paris, 2/1970), 8–9, 17–19; and A. L. Ringer, 'J.-J. Barthélemy and Musical Utopia in Revolutionary France', *Journal of the History of Ideas*, xxii (1961), 355–68.
[18] Examples cited, from reports by John Quincy Adams and other travellers, in W. L. Chew, *Das Leben in Frankreich zwischen 1780 und 1815 im Zeugnis amerikanischer Reisender* (Tübingen, 1986), 403–8.
[19] R. P. Locke, 'The Music of the French Chanson, 1810–50', in *Music in Paris in the Eighteen-Thirties*, ed. P. A. Bloom (Stuyvesant, NY, 1987), 431–6.
[20] W. Benjamin, 'Paris – the Capital of the Nineteenth Century', trans. Q. Hoare; repr. in *Charles Baudelaire: a Lyric Poet in the Era of High Capitalism* (London, 1973).
[21] *La musique à Paris en 1830–1831*, ed. F. Lesure (Paris, 1983), 15–38.

[22] J. Gourret, *Ces hommes qui ont fait l'Opéra* (Paris, 1984), 119–20.

[23] Cited in S. Huebner, 'Opera Audiences in Paris, 1830–1870', *ML*, lxx (1989), 206–25.

[24] Ibid., and original text of letter (1 May 1831).

[25] R. P. Locke, *Music, Musicians, and the Saint-Simonians* (Chicago and London, 1986).

[26] Cited in J. Fulcher, *The Nation's Image: French Grand Opera as Politics and Politicized Art* (Cambridge, 1987), 66.

[27] Lesure, *La musique à Paris*, 41–112.

[28] K. Pendle, 'The Boulevard Theaters and Continuity in French Opera of the 19th Century', and N. Wild, 'La musique dans le mélodrame des théâtres parisiens', in *Music in Paris*, ed. Bloom, 509–35 and 589–610.

[29] Cited in M. Root-Bernstein, *Boulevard Theater and Revolution in Eighteenth-Century Paris* (Ann Arbor, 1984), 133.

[30] Brévan, *Les changements*, 110.

[31] J. Combarieu, *Histoire de la musique* (Paris, 2/1950), ii, 399–402; D. Charlton, *Grétry and the Growth of Opéra-comique* (Cambridge, 1986), 250–51.

[32] Brévan, *Les changements*, 117–22.

[33] Carlson, *The Theatre*, 238; M. E. C. Bartlet, 'Politics and the Fate of *Roger et Olivier*, a Newly Recovered Opera by Grétry', *JAMS*, xxxvii (1984), 128–31, 137–8.

[34] Castil-Blaze [François Henri Joseph Blaze], *De l'opéra en France* (Paris, 1820), i, 30.

[35] W. Dean, 'German Opera', *NOHM*, viii (1982), 467, 472.

[36] E. J. Dent, *The Rise of Romantic Opera* (Cambridge, 1976), 47–94; W. Dean, 'French Opera', *NOHM*, viii (1982), 50–57, 62, 44.

[37] Cited in Dean, 'French Opera', 70.

[38] Root-Bernstein, *Boulevard Theater*, 264, n.1; Carlson, *The Theatre*, 114, 131–4, 164, 171–2, 182–4.

[39] Mongrédien, *La musique*, 70–77, 53–9.

[40] Huebner, 'Opera Audiences', 215.

[41] N. Goodwin, 'Dance, §VI, 1: 19th century, Theatrical', *Grove 6*, 204.

[42] R. P. Locke, 'The Music of the French Chanson, 1810–1850', in *Music in Paris*, ed. Bloom, 431–56.

[43] P. Gossett, 'Music at the Théâtre-Italien', in *Music in Paris*, ed. Bloom, 327–64.

[44] Cited by G. Favre, in *NOHM*, viii (1982), 584.

[45] A. Caswell, 'Loïsa Puget and the French *romance*', in *Music in Paris*, ed. Bloom, 97–115.

[46] Cited in Mongrédien, *La musique*, 188.

[47] Henri Blanchard (1850), cited in F. Douglass, *Cavaillé-Coll and the Musicians* (Raleigh, N. Carolina, 1980), i, 80 (also pp.8, 34, 37, 72, 82, 101, 105, 109); cf N. Dufourcq, *La musique d'orgue française* (Paris, 2/1949), 118.

[48] B. S. Brook, 'The Symphonie Concertante: an Interim Report', *MQ*, xlvii (1961), 493–4.

[49] *Le concert de la rue Feydeau*, cited in Mongrédien, *La musique*, 206–7.

[50] Cambini (1811), in L. Schrade, *Beethoven in France: the Growth of an Idea* (New Haven, Conn., 1942/R1978), 3.

[51] B. Schwarz, *French Instrumental Music Between the Revolutions (1789–1830)* (New York, 1988), 52–4.

[52] Cited in ibid., 182.

[53] B. S. Brook, *La symphonie française dans la seconde moitié du xviiie siècle* (Paris, 1962), i, 467–82.

[54] A. L. Ringer, 'The *Chasse* as a Musical Topic of the 18th Century', *JAMS*, vi (1953), 158–9; see also Schwarz, *French Instrumental Music*, 32–3, 68, 79–80.

[55] Mongrédien, *La musique*, 256.

[56] J. M. Levy, 'Quatuor concertant', *Grove 6*.

[57] Mongrédien, *La musique*, 287; full letter in G. de Rothschild, *Luigi Boccherini: his Life and Work*, trans. A. Mayor (London, 1965), 131–3 (cf 65–72).

[58] *Catalogue of the Works of Boccherini*, ed. Y. Gérard, trans. A. Mayor (London, 1969), 259–60.

[59] F.-J. Fétis, *Biographie universelle des musiciens* (Paris, 2/1873/R1963), i, 10.

[60] J.-M. Fauquet, *Les sociétés de musique de chambre à Paris de la Restauration à 1870* (Paris, 1986), 66.

[61] Mongrédien, *La musique*, 294–306.

[62] A. Main, 'Liszt's *Lyon*: Music and the Social Conscience', *Nineteenth-Century Music*, iv (1980–81), 228–43.

[63] *Revue et gazette musicale* (30 Aug 1835), in Weiss and Taruskin, *Music in the Western World*, 367

[64] C. R. Suttoni, *Piano and Opera: a Study of the Piano Fantasies Written on Opera Themes in the Romantic Era* (diss., New York U., 1972), 299–312.

[65] J. Kallberg, 'Chopin in the Marketplace: Aspects of the International Music Publishing Industry', *Notes*, xxxix (1982–3), 535–69, 795–824.

[66] H. F. Chorley (1841), in A. Carse, *The Orchestra from Beethoven to Berlioz* (Cambridge, 1948), 80–81.

[67] A. Elwart, *Histoire de la Société des concerts du Conservatoire impérial de musique* (Paris, 2/1864), 69–84.

[68] J.-M. Nectoux, 'Trois orchestres parisiens en 1830', in *Music in Paris*, ed. Bloom, 474, 493–4.

[69] Cited in E. Bernard, 'Les abonnés à la Société des concerts du Conservatoire en 1837', in *Music in Paris*, ed. Bloom, 41–54.

[70] D. V. Hagan, *Félicien David, 1810–1876* (Syracuse, NY, 1984).

[71] *The Memoirs of Hector Berlioz*, ed. and trans. D. Cairns (New York, rev. 3/1975), chap.54, p.416.

[72] Ibid., postscript, 474.

BIBLIOGRAPHICAL NOTE

G. Wright's *France in Modern Times: From the Enlightenment to the Present* (New York and London, 4/1987) offers a level-headed account of the period's oft-polemicized political events and economic, social and intellectual developments; Wright is refreshingly aware of his own liberal bias and offers extensive historiographical essays (slightly longer in the third edition, 1981) that focus on alternative and enriching interpretations, whether Marxist or conservative, anecdotal, structuralist or econometric.

Studies in English devoted to the Revolution of 1789 include: L. Gershoy, *The French Revolution and Napoleon* (New York, rev. 2/1964); G. Lefebvre, *The French Revolution*, 2 vols., trans. E. M. Evanson, J. H. Stewart and J. Friguglietti (London, 1962–4); G. Lefebvre, *Napoleon*, 2 vols., trans. H. F. Stockhold and J. E. Anderson (New York, 1969); *New Perspectives on the French Revolution: Reading in Historical Sociology*, ed. J. Kaplow (New York, 1965); F. Furet and D. Richet, *French Revolution*, trans. S. Hardman (London, 1970); A. Soboul, *The French Revolution 1787–1799*, 2 vols., trans. A. Forrest and C. Jones (London, 1974); F. Furet, *Interpreting the French Revolution*, trans. A. Sheridan (Cambridge, 1981); *A Critical Dictionary of the French Revolution*, ed. F. Furet and M. Ozouf, trans. A. Goldhammer (Cambridge, Mass., 1989); and Simon Schama, *Citizens: a Chronicle of the French Revolution* (New York, 1989).

The festivals are diversely treated in J. Robiquet, *Daily Life in the French Revolution*, trans. J. Kirkup (London, 1964); L. Hunt, *Politics, Culture, and Class in the French Revolution* (Berkeley, 1984); D. L. Dowd, *Pageant Master of the Republic: Jacques-Louis David and the French Revolution* (Lincoln, Nebraska, 1948); E. Kennedy, *A Cultural History of the French Revolution* (New Haven, 1989); and M. Ozouf, *Festivals and the French Revolution*, trans. A. Sheridan (Cambridge, Mass., 1988). Texts and pictures documenting the festivals are gathered in Michael Vovelle's *La Révolution française: images et récit, 1789–1799*, 5 vols. (Paris, 1986); see also Pierre, *Les hymnes*, and Brécy, *La Révolution* (both listed under 'Music' below).

Concerning the whole 60-year period, E. J. Hobsbawm sets French developments, including cultural ones, into a worldwide context of political and industrial change in *The Age of Revolution: 1789–1848* (New York, 1962), as does (quite differently) C. Breunig, *The Age of Revolution and Reaction, 1789–1850* (New York, 2/1977). Other points of view are offered in A. Cobban, *History of Modern France*, 3 vols. (Baltimore, 1957–65); *A Century for Debate, 1789–1914: Problems in the Interpretation of European History*, ed. P. N. Stearns (New York and Toronto, 1969); G. Rudé, *Debate on Europe: 1815–1850* (New York, 1972); and the *New Cambridge Modern History* (Cambridge, 1957–79), viii–x.

The Early Romantic Period

Literature and the visual arts

The arts and branches of literature, as well as aesthetic, religious and social thought, are explored by a team of experts in *The French Romantics*, ed. D. G. Charlton, 2 vols. (London, 1984). F. W. J. Hemmings provides a delightful if somewhat anecdotal overview in *Culture and Society in France, 1789–1848* (Leicester, 1987). Still valuable on literature (also on visual art and music) are the insights in Arnold Hauser's *The Social History of Art*, iii–iv (New York, 1957–8).

The branch of literature most crucial for music in this period is explored in M. Carlson, *The Theatre of the French Revolution* (Ithaca, NY, 1966); idem, *The French Stage in the 19th Century* (New York, 1972); M. Root-Bernstein, *Boulevard Theater and Revolution in Eighteenth-Century Paris* (Ann Arbor, 1984); and W. D. Howarth, *Sublime and Grotesque: a Study of French Romantic Drama* (London, 1975). On other literary genres, see *French Literature and its Background*, ed. J. Cruickshank (London and New York, 1968–70), iii–iv; M. Z. Shroder, *Icarus: the Image of the Artist in French Romanticism* (Cambridge, Mass., 1961); G. Brereton, *An Introduction to the French Poets* (London, 2/1973); and F. C. Green's still valuable overview of *French Novelists from the Revolution to Proust* (London, 1931). Provocative and wide-ranging studies include J. Smith Allen, *Popular Romanticism in France: Authors, Readers, and Books in the 19th Century* (Syracuse, NY, 1981); and, on 'high' Romanticism, J. Barzun, *Classic, Romantic, and Modern* (Chicago, rev. 2/1961), and R. Wellek, *A History of Modern Criticism* (New Haven, Conn., 1955–68), ii–iii. L. Guichard's *La musique et les lettres au temps du Romantisme* (Paris, 1955/R1984) deals well with music journalism and with the musical writings of Stendhal, Honoré de Balzac, Gérard de Nerval and George Sand.

The visual arts are well but differently served by J.-J. Lévêque's *L'art et la Révolution française, 1789–1804* (Neuchâtel, 1987), W. F. Friedländer's *David to Delacroix*, trans. R. Goldwater (Cambridge, Mass., 1952), H. Honour's broadly conceived *Romanticism* (London, 1979) and, focussing on the mid-nineteenth century, T. J. Clark's imaginative studies *The Absolute Bourgeois: Artists and Politics in France, 1848–1851* (London, 2/1982) and *Image of the People: Gustave Courbet and the Second French Republic, 1848–1851* (London, 1972). Special insight into the place of music in French society can be gained from the drawings of Daumier and others: Y. Fromrich, *Musique et caricature en France au dix-neuvième siècle* (Paris, 1973); B. Farwell, *French Popular Lithographic Imagery, 1815–1870*, 12 vols. (Chicago and London, 1981–); and Cohen, *Gravures musicales* (cited under 'Music' below). Further bibliography on the visual arts (and on literature and French Romanticism in general) is given in the individual chapters of Charlton, *French Romantics*, and of *France: a Companion to French Studies*, ed. Charlton (London, 1979).

Music and musical life

A solid study of the years 1789–1830 – and particularly valuable on orchestral concerts and sacred music – is J. Mongrédien's *La musique française des lumières au romantisme* (Paris, 1986), though the musical works themselves are better treated in *NOHM*, viii (1982), especially chaps.2, 12 and 13, on opera, song and choral music, and in several of the studies (e.g. Favre, Gougelot and Noske; and Schwarz's *French Instrumental Music*) cited below. Still valuable are the chapters on French music in J. Combarieu, *Histoire de la musique* (Paris, 2/1950–55), ii–iii. Representative contemporary texts on music are gathered in *Music Aesthetics in the Eighteenth and Early Nineteenth Centuries*, ed. J. Day and P. le Huray (Cambridge, 1981). The music of the revolutionary festivals is painstakingly documented in C. Pierre's *Les hymnes et chansons de la Révolution: aperçu général et catalogue* (Paris, 1904) and Robert Brécy's *La Révolution en chantant* (Paris, 1988); an effective overview is J. Tiersot's *Les fêtes et les chants de la Révolution française* (Paris, 1908); and Pierre provides a substantial sampling of the music in his *Musique des fêtes et cérémonies de la Révolution française* (Paris, 1899).

Paris: Centre of Intellectual Ferment

Vivid details on musical life are to be found in the specialized studies of *Music in Paris in the 1830s*, ed. P. A. Bloom (Stuyvesant, NY, 1987), in W. Weber's *Music and the Middle Class: the Social Structure of Concert Life in London, Paris, and Vienna* (London, 1975) and in many of the works cited in the notes above. The piano cult, from manufacture to salon to virtuoso recital, is spread engagingly before the reader by Arthur Loesser in *Men, Women, and Pianos: a Social History* (New York, 1954); the pre-Romantic phase is treated more elaborately in G. Favre's *La musique française de piano avant 1830* (Paris, 1953/R1978). Richly rewarding are A. Carse's classic study *The Orchestra from Beethoven to Berlioz* (Cambridge, 1948), Boris Schwarz's belatedly published *French Instrumental Music Between the Revolutions: 1789–1830* (New York, 1988), J. Cooper's *The Rise of Instrumental Music and Concert Series in Paris, 1828–1871* (Ann Arbor, 1983), H. Gougelot's *La romance française sous la Révolution et l'Empire* (Melun, 1938–43), F. Noske's *French Song from Berlioz to Duparc* (New York, rev. 2/ 1970 by R. Benton and F. Noske, trans. Benton), J. Chazin-Bennahum's *Dance in the Shadow of the Guillotine* (Carbondale, Ill., 1988), I. Guest's *The Romantic Ballet in Paris* (London, 2/1970) and H. Searle's *Ballet Music* (New York, rev. 2/1973), as well as a number of works on opera: E. J. Dent's *The Rise of Romantic Opera*, ed. W. Dean (Cambridge, 1976), W. Crosten's *French Grand Opera: an Art and a Business* (New York, 1948), P. J. Smith's *The Tenth Muse: a Historical Study of the Opera Libretto* (New York, 1970), K. Pendle's *Eugène Scribe and French Grand Opera of the Nineteenth Century* (Ann Arbor, 1979), P. Barbier's *La vie quotidienne à l'Opéra au temps de Rossini et de Balzac: Paris, 1800–1850* (Paris, 1987), J. Fulcher's *The Nation's Image: French Grand Opera as Politics and Politicized Art* (Cambridge, 1987), N. Wild's profusely illustrated *Décors et costumes du xixe siècle*, i: *Opéra de Paris* (Paris, 1987), C. Join-Dieterle's equally striking *Les décors de scène de l'Opéra de Paris à l'époque romantique* (Paris, 1988), and the comments on Meyerbeer in A. Porter's *Music of Three Seasons: 1974–1977* (New York, 1978). Valuable for opera and much else are the pictures in Fromrich and Farwell (both cited above under 'Literature and the visual arts') and in *Les gravures musicales dans 'L'illustration', 1843–1899*, ed. H. Robert Cohen, 3 vols. (Quebec, 1982–3).

Approaching the era through its leading performers and composers can be revelatory of larger issues as well: H. Bushnell, *Maria Malibran: a Biography of the Singer* (University Park, Penn., and London, 1979); A. Fitzlyon, *The Price of Genius: a Life of Pauline Viardot* (London, 1964); B. Schwarz, *Great Masters of the Violin* (New York, 1983); G. de Courcy, *Paganini the Genoese*, 2 vols. (Norman, Oklahoma, 1957); J.-J. Eigeldinger, *Chopin: Pianist and Teacher*, trans. N. Shohet, K. Osostrowicz and R. Howat, ed. Howat (Cambridge, 3/1986); *S. Heller: Lettres d'un musicien romantique à Paris*, ed. J.-J. Eigeldinger (Paris, 1981); E. Perényi, *Liszt: the Artist as Romantic Hero* (Boston, Mass., 1974); A. Walker, *Franz Liszt*, i, *The Virtuoso Years, 1811–1847* (London and Ithaca, NY, rev. 2/1988); F. Liszt, *An Artist's Journey: 'Lettres d'un bachelier-ès-musique', 1835–1841*, trans. and annotated C. Suttoni (Chicago and London, 1989); B. Deane, *Cherubini* (London and New York, 1965); J. Mongrédien, *Jean-François Le Sueur: Contribution à l'étude d'un demi-siècle de musique française, 1780–1830*, 2 vols. (Berne, 1980); B. Friedland, *Louise Farrenc, 1804–1875: Composer, Performer, Scholar* (Ann Arbor, 1980); H. Weinstock, *Donizetti and the World of Opera in Italy, Paris and Vienna in the First Half of the Nineteenth Century* (New York, 1963); H. Macdonald, *Hector Berlioz* (London, 1981); J. Barzun, *Hector Berlioz and the Romantic Century*, 2 vols. (New York, rev. 3/1969); D. Cairns, *Berlioz, 1803–1832: the Making of an Artist* (London, 1989); D. Kern Holoman, *Berlioz* (Cambridge, Mass., 1989); and the indispensable *The Memoirs of Hector Berlioz*, ed. and trans. D. Cairns (New York, rev. 3/1975).

Chapter III

Vienna: Bastion of Conservatism

SIGRID WIESMANN

> For everyone, surely, who can enjoy the good things of life,
> especially for the artist, perhaps quite especially for the musical
> artist, Vienna is the richest, happiest, and most agreeable residence
> in Europe. Vienna has everything that marks a great capital in a
> quite unusually high degree. It has a great, wealthy, cultivated, art-
> loving, hospitable, well-mannered, elegant nobility; it has a wealthy,
> sociable, hospitable middle class and bourgeoisie, as little lacking in
> cultivated and well-informed gentlemen and gracious families; it has
> a well-to-do, good-natured, jovial populace. All classes love amuse-
> ment and good living, and things are so arranged that all classes
> may find well provided and may enjoy in all convenience and
> security every amusement that modern society knows and loves.[1]

Johann Friedrich Reichardt's enthusiastic characterization of Vienna's
brilliant musical life during the first decade of the nineteenth century
confirmed the impressions of many a visitor at a time when not only
Ludwig van Beethoven but musicians from all parts of Europe made
their home at least temporarily in the booming capital of the Austrian
Empire. The city's culture depended primarily on two classes that
formed the upper ranks of society in the wake of the reforms
introduced by Joseph II before the turn of the century: the old
aristocracy and the new officialdom that had arisen from the urban
bourgeoisie and petty nobility. The aristocracy was traditionally
cosmopolitan in background and outlook; it spoke and wrote French
or Italian and favoured music and architecture in the representative
Baroque manifestations which survived in Austria far longer than
elsewhere. The new bureaucracy, on the other hand, charged with the
centralization of the multi-national state, used German as its official
language and among the arts looked above all to German literature.
Virtually all important writers of the period, Heinrich Joseph von
Collin (for whose *Coriolan* Beethoven wrote a famous overture) no less
than Franz Grillparzer and Adalbert Stifter, were state officials. By
contrast, the *poeti caesarei* (court poets) were all Italians – Apostolo
Zeno and Pietro Metastasio as well as Giovanni Brambilla. In the
field of spoken drama they saw themselves primarily as classical

34. The family of the Viennese notary Dr Josef Eltz at Ischl: painting (1835) by Ferdinand Georg Waldmüller, an artist whose work is typical of the 'Biedermeier' style fashionable in early nineteenth-century Vienna

tragedians, but their principal activity as librettists tied them closely to music, the chief domain of the high aristocracy.

Bourgeois musical culture was by no means a new development, but only the nineteenth century had all the hallmarks of a specifically bourgeois era. What distinguished it from the preceding period in Austrian history was the decline of the traditional artisan who had made up much of the central layer of the bourgeoisie in the sixteenth and seventeenth centuries but was now relegated to the status of petty bourgeois. The nineteenth-century Austrian bourgeoisie was formed largely by a rapidly growing class of officials, products of the academic reforms of the later eighteenth century, who became the carriers of a bourgeois culture quite separate from that of the nobility, the clergy, the peasants, the labouring class and, indeed, the petty bourgeoisie. And it was mostly this relatively small minority that favoured what is usually referred to as art music.

Beethoven's patrons were nevertheless, with very few exceptions, members of the aristocracy. They were the ones who offered him financial support when he threatened to leave Vienna for the court of Napoleon's brother Jérome at Kassel. Indeed, Beethoven, the proud republican, derived most of his aesthetic as well as material encouragement not from the bourgeoisie but from representatives of the higher aristocracy. Unlike Schubert, a native of Vienna, Beethoven, who spent two-thirds of his life there, never found any meaningful relationship to the city's literary middle-class culture. True, he planned to write an opera with Grillparzer, who eventually eulogized him at his funeral; but it is difficult to imagine that the two communicated in any deeper sense. Beethoven, after all, was rooted in the tradition of Rousseau and 'storm and stress', and nothing was more alien to the spirit of Austria, as the literature which appealed so particularly to imperial officialdom demonstrates. Grillparzer's devotion to the state, in which he saw an earthly reflection of the divine order, amounted to an act of faith that furnished the stuff of which tragedy is made, precisely because that conception of the state also implied the willingness of the individual to surrender some of his or her innermost human substance. Such a viewpoint was, of course, incompatible with the philosophy of a Beethoven who placed individual values, the 'voice of the heart', above all else.

The Viennese, therefore, honoured Beethoven, whose international fame they respected, as something of a monument admired preferably from afar. Apart from the spectacular successes of 1814, his works were rather infrequently performed. Reichardt, wishing to call on Beethoven towards the end of 1808, found that 'people here take so little interest in him that no one was able to tell me his address, and it really cost me considerable trouble to locate him'.[2] When he did so, it was in the rear of the same aristocratic residence that contained the apartments of Countess Erdödy and Prince Lichnowsky: Beethoven was in fact no worse off than a musical celebrity like Antonio Salieri, Mozart's nemesis, who occupied 'a fine-looking house of his own'.[3]

By and large, the city's musical taste remained centred on the works of Haydn and, to a lesser degree, of Mozart, until Vienna too was seized by the Rossini fever that swept through Europe after 1813, when *Tancredi* and *L'italiana in Algeri* caused a sensation. In the meantime, Mozart's pupil Johann Nepomuk Hummel, born in nearby Pressburg (now Bratislava) in 1778, represented Viennese taste far better than Beethoven. First, he was closely connected with Haydn, whose position as Kapellmeister at Eszterháza he assumed in 1804; second, he had studied with Albrechtsberger as well as Salieri and could thus rely on his knowledge of the whole Viennese tradition. While Beethoven, who had some of the same teachers, prided himself as early as 1802 on his 'new manner', Hummel made a career of opera, church and chamber music, above all brilliant piano concertos which he performed with glittering displays of dexterity, elegance and cantabile touch that fascinated large audiences everywhere.

Mozart's pupil Franz Xaver Süssmayr (1766–1803), on the other hand, represents something of a psychological puzzle, if only because he never again reached the compositional heights to which, in the shadow of his master, he managed to ascend with his completion of Mozart's Requiem. Several of his operas were none the less successful; one, *Der Spiegel von Arkadian* (1794), had no fewer than 113 performances in the decade after its première. Peter von Winter (1754–1825) belongs more or less in the same company, even though he spent much of his life as Hofkapellmeister in Munich. His most successful opera, *Das unterbrochene Opferfest* (1796), began its triumphant march through central Europe in Vienna. And this work, long regarded as the best German opera between Mozart's *Die Zauberflöte* and Weber's *Der Freischütz*, was succeeded in turn by *Das Labyrinth* (1798), with which Emanuel Schikaneder hoped to have found a worthy sequel to *Zauberflöte*.

It is characteristic of Vienna's musical culture that Joseph Weigl (1766–1846), who came from Eisenstadt and in 1827 at the age of 60 inherited the position of court Kapellmeister from his teacher, Salieri, composed operas chiefly in Italian, apart from his international success *Die Schweizerfamilie* (1809) and its immediate predecessor *Das Waisenhaus*. Rapidly growing nationalism, a pervasive trend almost everywhere, was not yet an issue in Viennese music – at any rate, no

35. *Beethoven out walking in Vienna: drawing by Johann Peter Theodor Lyser, first published in 1833 in the Hamburg periodical 'Cäcilia'*

more than in Dresden. The prevailing linguistic mix was binding on all composers irrespective of their origin. Salieri, for example, composed a German Singspiel, *Der Rauchfangkehrer.*

The Salzburg-born Sigismund von Neukomm (1778–1858), true cosmopolitan that he was, left Vienna for St Petersburg and Paris before moving as far as Rio de Janeiro and returning via Lisbon to London and finally Paris. He wrote Russian songs, English anthems and Latin masses, French songs, German and Italian operas and an oratorio on a text by Klopstock, *Christi Grablegung.* This kind of non-discriminating attitude in aesthetic matters typified the musical life of Vienna as much as that of Paris, thanks primarily to an internationally connected, multilingual nobility. Seen in this light, Salieri (1750–1825) would seem to pass muster as a representative of Viennese Classicism, considering that he was not only Hofkapellmeister but also conductor of the Tonkünstler-Sozietät and longtime director of the conservatory of the Gesellschaft der Musikfreunde, both of which he served as one of the city's musical pillars, administratively no less than as a creative and re-creative musician.

The ultimate fate of Vienna as the leading musical city in Europe was to a large extent tied to the late eighteenth-century rise of instrumental music, which opened new modes of thought about the nature and function of music in general; in many ways this thinking was out of line with the city's aristocratic tradition. That Vienna managed nevertheless to maintain its pre-eminence for at least another two decades is confirmed not only by Reichardt's report (quoted above), written at a time when Beethoven's creative power had begun to leave its decisive imprint on friend and foe alike. Beethoven's fortunes and misfortunes were themselves part of the changes in Viennese musical life. In 1800, when he soundly defeated the popular pianist Daniel Steibelt in a much-publicized improvisation contest, this astonishing feat inevitably evoked memories of a similar event that had pitted Mozart against Clementi nearly two decades earlier. Since he first settled in Vienna in 1792, Beethoven had made an increasing mark on Viennese music primarily as a virtuoso performer; he was in growing demand, for private concerts and musical parties in the palaces of the aristocracy as well as in the often hardly less magnificent homes of the newly risen upper bourgeoisie. And he was expected, like all eighteenth-century performers, to write compositions for his own use and that of his pupils and patrons. He met these traditional expectations brilliantly with works centred on his principal instrument, the piano. From the outset, however, Beethoven shunned virtuosity for its own sake; yet he did not avoid technical difficulties where they were called for by a composition's underlying idea.

By 1800 Beethoven had turned his attention to the 'serious' genres that were to remain associated with his name ever after, if only because he endowed them with entirely new characteristics – the piano sonata, symphony and string quartet. Still, the most successful piece in his concert of 2 April 1800 was not his Symphony in C op.21, but the Septet op.20 dedicated to the Empress Maria Theresa. It was this sparkling work in the tradition of the eighteenth-century divertimento which, more than any other, established Beethoven as a composer to be watched. It was published within two years by Hoffmeister, who brought out almost simultaneously an arrangement for string quintet. Beethoven eventually transcribed it as a trio for clarinet, violin and piano for his musical physician and friend Johann Schmidt. Among its emulators for the benefit of Viennese audiences were Hummel, Spohr and, indeed, Franz Schubert.

Beethoven continued to make his sacrifices to Viennese taste for many years, though with declining interest and intensity. His ballet *Prometheus*, which contains the dance-tune that prompted the finale of the Eroica Symphony, and by derivation the whole of it, found far more admirers among the Viennese than the symphony that inspired so many Romantics in Germany and elsewhere. Beethoven's position at the threshold of Romanticism has been the subject of perennial debate. What is relevant in this context, however, is the fundamental conception of his artistic mission that placed him apart from his Viennese contemporaries, a phenomenon *sui generis* at odds with everything Viennese. To some extent even that truly Viennese musician Schubert, who as a member of the next generation might have been expected to accept the Beethovenian bequest wholeheartedly, did so only to a limited degree and in his characteristically modest fashion.

'Viennese Romanticism', in short, is something of a contradiction in terms, given the peculiarities of an Austrian or south German Catholic musical culture that developed along quite different lines from those followed by the Protestant north. Few Austrians cared about aesthetic matters in philosophical terms: fully immersed in music itself, they had little use for thinking about it. Austrian theory from Albrechtsberger to Sechter and Bruckner focussed on questions pertaining to musical craftsmanship. Philosophical issues, so dear to Berlin and Leipzig theorists from Dehn to Hauptmann and Riemann, held little interest for Austrians, and their writings by and large eschew musical aesthetics altogether. Musical Romanticism of the north German variety was inseparable from literary and philosophical concerns, and they permeated the aesthetic reflections of a Wackenroder even earlier than did any compositional practice. Such intertwining of music, literature and philosophy was characteristic of Weber and E. T. A. Hoffmann (not to mention Schumann and Wagner), but by the same token incompatible with Viennese musical

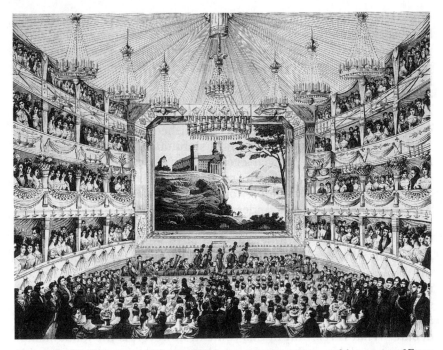

36. Interior of the Theater an der Wien in 1832, decorated for the anniversary of the accession of Franz II: engraving by A. Geiger after J. C. Schöller

culture which was, at bottom, non-literary.

Hardly by accident, programme music of the mid-century variety never found ready acceptance in Vienna, nor did the Austrian capital spawn any great song composers between Schubert and Hugo Wolf. By the time Wolf produced his astonishing corpus of lieder within the span of little more than a decade, even Vienna had yielded to the conquering hero Richard Wagner. Characteristically, Schubert called his lyrical piano pieces simply 'impromptu' or 'moment musical', just as the Bohemian Václav Tomášek (1774–1850) labelled his 'eclogues'. Schumann and Chopin used terms like 'ballade' and 'novellette' to stress the literary connection. Even Beethoven followed the Viennese tendency by referring to his short piano pieces as 'bagatelles'. Viewed in this light, the controversies between the adherents of absolute and programme music, so called, as represented by Eduard Hanslick and Franz Brendel respectively, were but relatively late manifestations of long-standing irreconcilable differences between the musical expectations and experiences of Protestant Germany and those of Catholic Austria.

Basically, Vienna remained a conservative operatic city well into the nineteenth century. Attempts to replace Italian with German opera met with little success. Occasionally the same work was given simultaneously in different theatres in Italian and German. The kind of passionate discussion of pertinent political issues that took place in Berlin about 1820 had no place in the Viennese context, at least not before 1848.

The centrality of opera in Viennese musical life inevitably affected the role of instrumental music, which in the north had found such important literary promoters in Tieck, E. T. A. Hoffmann and Rochlitz. Decades passed before orchestral concerts adequate to the demands of Beethoven symphonies became a regular part of the winter season. Nor was there an appropriate hall designed for such purposes until the Musikverein opened in 1870. Meanwhile, Ignaz Schuppanzigh instituted public quartet evenings as early as 1804, ten years before Baillot did the same in Paris. The immediate creative result was Beethoven's op.59 (1809), the 'Rasumovsky' Quartets, explicitly written with an eye on a professional rather than an amateur ensemble. The very idea of 'public chamber music' may seem paradoxical, but it points accurately to the ambivalent character of a genre that owed its existence largely to Beethoven, and especially to his op.59. It was the transplanting of the quartet from a private domestic sphere to the public concert which favoured the quasi-

37. 'Die Liedler': one of a series of drawings (1822) by Moritz von Schwind illustrating his friend Schubert's setting (1815) of words by Josef Kenner

symphonic style of Beethoven's later chamber works and, of course, others written under his influence. The public, on the other hand, and to a large extent the critics too, continued to insist on 'intimacy' as an inherent and desirable characteristic of all chamber music, undaunted by the fact that the ever-larger halls in which it was now performed militated against any such qualities.

If the symphony, as ideally represented by Beethoven's Eroica, turned the orchestral concert into an entirely new experience, and if, by the same token, his op.59 did much to move chamber music into the public realm, transcending its traditional constraints in the process of ensuring its future, the German lied as transformed by Schubert called no less for new venues, specifically the lieder recital, as we know it to this day. Thus, the three principal elements of modern concert life were, at least indirectly, outgrowths of Viennese conditions during the first quarter of the nineteenth century.

In the meantime, the institutional aspects of the city's musical life were anything but ideal. Musical events in the aristocratic palaces suffered often from overcrowding and poor acoustics. The unheated theatres were quite unsuited for winter concerts like Beethoven's long Akademie of 22 December 1808. Reichardt, who attended it, gave a vivid account of this problematic, seemingly endless affair which included the first performances of the C minor and F major symphonies (subsequently known as nos.5 and 6) as well as the G major Piano Concerto played by Beethoven himself. The concluding Choral Fantasy op.80 was not even finished when the composer sat down at the piano. Reichardt had acccepted

> the kind invitation of Prince von Lobkowitz to join him in his box . . . There we sat in the most bitter cold, from half past six until half past ten, and confirmed for ourselves the maxim that one may easily have too much of a good thing, still more of a powerful one . . . the singers and orchestra were made up of very heterogeneous elements, and it had not even been possible to arrange one full rehearsal of all the pieces on the program, every one of which was filled with the greatest difficulties. How much of the output of this fruitful genius and tireless worker was none the less performed during the four hours will astonish you.[4]

Small wonder that, by the time the programme reached the C minor Symphony, even someone as favourably inclined towards Beethoven as Reichardt found it 'very elaborate and too long'. Towards the close of that long evening everything threatened to fall apart when, shortly after the beginning of the Choral Fantasy, the musicians lost their places, and Beethoven, 'thinking no longer of his public or of his surrounding, shouted out that one should stop and begin over again'. 'You can imagine', added Reichardt, 'how I and all his other friends suffered at this. In that moment, indeed, I wished that I had had the courage to leave earlier after all'.[5]

A year later, in the wake of the financial collapse caused in large part by the French siege, the nobility, which had carried the principal burden of Beethoven's yearly income as well as the wages of their private orchestras, ceased to be a major cultural force. But, even though the bourgeoisie was as yet lacking in experience in such matters, the number of concerts increased steadily and before long competed with opera for the attentions of the new public. There were, of course, no guidelines as to programme content or, for that matter, venues. What later came to be known as symphonic or philharmonic concerts, centred largely on the works of Beethoven and other serious orchestral music, remained a relatively minor aspect of a musical culture governed by various forms of entertainment, including such as were meant to edify the educated middle classes. It was that ultimate cultural ideal, in fact, which prompted the founding of the Gesellschaft der Musikfreunde in 1812. But it took another 30 years for Otto Nicolai to start the first series of philharmonic concerts billed as such.

For decades, concert dates remained tied to special events: weddings, birthdays, anniversaries, dedication ceremonies etc. In 1825 Beethoven's friend Ignaz Ritter von Seyfried organized a concert to commemorate the anniversary of Mozart's death. For the opening of a new bridge, Johann Strauss the elder composed a waltz. Churches, theatres, restaurants, ballrooms and the assembly hall of the university offered more or less suitable venues. Revenues from concerts were, as a rule, divided unequally between the organizers and the musicians. In 1823 Beethoven's famous pupil Ignaz Moscheles received as much as a half of the receipts of his concert at the Kärntnertortheater, but its director, Domenico Barbaja, had made an exception, no doubt the result of Moscheles's negotiating skills as well as his celebrated reputation. The level of solo performance, both vocally and instrumentally, was by all indications high. Orchestras and choruses, on the other hand, consisted largely of amateurs and were notoriously under-rehearsed, which may explain, for example, the simple choral style of so many secular oratorios, their serious texts notwithstanding. The singers, though generally educated, were often deficient in musical skills, and bourgeois musical tastes were still in their formative stages. It was a long time before the adherents of serious music could be considered a group apart from those who merely sought musical entertainment. In the later nineteenth century a stunt like Carl Czerny's arrangement of Rossini's overture to *Semiramide* for sixteen pianos might not have been tolerated by serious audiences; in its time it was a huge success.

The importance of Beethoven for establishing concert life modelled after Parisian precedent can hardly be overestimated. The difficulties

38. Schubertiade, probably at the home of the Fröhlich sisters: drawing by Waldmüller from his 1827 sketchbook. Schubert and Josefine Fröhlich sit at the piano, with the bass Johann Michael Vogl behind; those listening are thought to be Franz Lachner (left), the violinist Ludwig Kraisil and the dramatist Franz Grillparzer

contemporary audiences encountered at a first hearing of his symphonies produced a need for repeat performances, and this led to the formation of permanent orchestral repertories. But that happened rather late. The heady days of the Vienna Congress, when concert followed concert and Beethoven had a great triumph with his exceedingly popular 'Battle Symphony' (*Wellingtons Sieg oder Die Schlacht bei Vittoria*), were followed by many years of decay under the oppressive regime of Count Metternich. Beethoven virtually retired from musical life, complaining bitterly about the Viennese and his many enemies among them. Rossini was the man of the hour, rivalled eventually only by Nicolò Paganini. Beethoven's later works were of little consequence for public musical events. In some ways his fame was greater in London where his cause was being promoted by his former pupil and faithful friend Ferdinand Ries among others. Certainly, his Ninth Symphony was written for performing forces far superior to those readily available in Vienna. Even to the east things looked better, especially in Bohemia. Beethoven, for one, thought of his *Missa solemnis* originally as a work to be given its première at the installation of his favourite pupil, the Archduke Rudolph, as Archbishop of Olmütz.

Schubert, by temperament anything but a public figure, was by no means as unknown as some of his biographers would lead one to believe. Rather, unlike Beethoven, Schubert appealed from the outset to like-minded individuals, circles of friends whose musical world was that of the home. The Schubertiads described in the memoirs of his friend Sonnleithner were intimate concerts, the opposite in content and atmosphere of virtually all operatic and public concert performances with their excesses of virtuosity. What was lacking in the seven years between Schubert's first publication (1821) and his untimely death was the kind of musical opportunity the nobility had offered earlier in the century when Beethoven flourished in palatial residences. Bourgeois salons of the sort that proved so important for Romantic Berlin hardly existed in imperial Vienna.

That is not to say, however, that the broader public ignored Schubert altogether. On 7 March 1821 the charity concert organized by the Gesellschaft der adeligen Damen at the Kärntertortheater included, among other novelties, Schubert's *Erlkönig* sung by his friend Vogl, a vocal quartet (*Das Dörfchen*) and the male chorus *Gesang der Geister über dem Wasser*. The prominent Viennese musician Adalbert Gyrowetz conducted and Fanny Elsler starred in the tableaux that formed part of the highly varied programme. Thereafter Schubert's songs were heard repeatedly at public concerts, though not as often as his vocal quartets.[6] Schubert's instrumental works were rarely played, but some were given at Schuppanzigh's subscription concerts in the 1820s: his Octet, a couple of quartets and the E♭ Piano Trio op. 100.

39. Title-page of the first edition of Schubert's 'Erlkönig' (1821), a setting of Goethe composed in the late autumn of 1815

Encouraged by his growing success, especially with the D minor Quartet ('Death and the Maiden'), Schubert gave a concert of his own on 26 March 1828, consisting entirely of chamber music and songs. Characteristically, it was ignored by the critics, one of whom, after pages of enthusiastic outpourings prompted by a Paganini concert, reported truthfully that numerous friends and patrons had applauded the composer generously. About the works performed, not a single word.[7]

It is likely that Schubert would have found a place in the musical life of Vienna before long, but his death in 1828 precluded any such possibility. The same holds to a lesser degree for a slightly older contemporary, Jan Hugo Voříšek (1791–1825) who, together with his teacher Václav Tomašek, championed the new genre of the lyrical piano piece – which, of course, was also one of Schubert's strengths. Such pieces are by definition little suited to public concerts, but rather satisfy the needs of amateurs and domestic musical gatherings. In a sense, the lyrical piano piece, which was to gain such crucial importance for early Romantic music, was a logical outgrowth of Viennese conditions, even though both its principal exponents, Tomašek and Voříšek, had been born and raised in Prague.

The expanding musical needs of the rising bourgeoisie were also met by a series of music festivals centred on the oratorios of Handel and Haydn. In neighbouring Germany, such festivals turned into celebrations of liberal hopes for political freedom and national independence. In Vienna these festive occasions, mounted in the Winterreitschule (the city's largest hall), were large-scale cultural manifestations in which the educated bourgeoisie that formed the nucleus of the state bureaucracy took special pride. Typically, works by French composers, including Méhul and Cherubini, were performed next to those of Handel, Haydn, Mozart, Beethoven and, indeed, Rossini. While these concerts contributed to the gradual formation of nineteenth-century canons of taste, ideology was of no import. What mattered was that such public events were designed to offset the prevailing fashion for vocal and instrumental virtuosity, with its often purely commercial spin-offs, including dishes, clothing and hairstyles named after Paganini, whose portrait also appeared on medals, jewellery boxes and walking-sticks. The Austrian five-guilder note was known as 'Paganinerll' and Paganini parodies of all sorts abounded. After what some regarded as a huge Paganini hoax came the Jenny Lind craze and the Henriette Sontag fever. Few of the virtuoso talents that evoked so much enthusiasm had roots in Vienna. But that did not prevent the city from becoming, just a few years after the deaths of Beethoven and Schubert, the centre of what Hanslick referred to as 'the musical bric-à-brac typical of a period of intellectual inactivity and the greatest political degeneration in Austria'.[8]

Even so, there were those who spared no effort to counteract the superficialities of a musical life whose most talented creative figures were Johann Strauss the elder and Joseph Lanner, Vienna's famous waltz kings. One such was Raphael Georg Kiesewetter (1773–1850) who organized concerts of early music in his home from 1816 to 1842. He had amassed a large collection of scores far in excess of what he could use in the pioneering scholarly publications with which he laid the foundations for the study of Renaissance music. Kiesewetter invariably stressed vocal traditions. But older instrumental music, too, found a champion in Simon Molitor, who also used his home for the purpose. Political ideology played a role in the activities of male singing organizations which, during the Metternich period, caused an occasional minor revolution in the concert hall, to paraphrase an expression coined by Kurt Tucholsky in connection with the largely abortive revolution of 1918.

Opera, the traditional focus of musical interest, continued for a long time to outweigh any serious concern with and about instrumental music. But even in opera there was little opportunity for native talent to assert itself at a time when Rossini reigned supreme. German opera in particular had few chances. Weber's *Euryanthe*, first performed in Vienna in 1823, met with only a lukewarm reception (admittedly, its

40. Performance of Handel's 'Belshazzar' in the Winterreitschule, 6 November 1834: lithograph

diffuse libretto was no help). One of the few that made the grade was Konradin Kreutzer's *Nachtlager von Granada* (1834), based on a play by Friedrich Kind, the librettist of Weber's *Der Freischütz*. It was one of the few successful German operas that bridged the gap between Weber and Wagner – a typical Singspiel with a Romantic flavour considered so peculiarly German that it was performed in German even in countries where opera was generally given in the local language. Kreutzer's experience abroad appeared to confirm that a specific national orientation, far from impeding success, could actually be of considerable benefit. (Kreutzer, though Kapellmeister of the Kärntnertortheater since 1822, was no more Viennese in origin than Otto Nicolai, who became Hofkapellmeister in 1841 and a year later founded the philharmonic concerts. Nor did Kreutzer and Nicolai remain in Vienna for any length of time.)

Musical standards declined before they had a chance to reach the levels associated with cities like London or Paris. When Frances Trollope, the prolific writer of Romantic travelogues, visited the Vienna opera in 1836, she found that 'they have not a single voice in any degree capable of sustaining an opera in such a style as one seems to have a right to expect in Vienna'.[9] Not one to give up easily, she went to hear a performance of *Don Giovanni* which, she concluded, would be her last attempt, 'unless they get some vocal recruits'. Nor did she have much favourable to say about instrumental music: 'Handel, Mozart, Haydn, and the like are banished from "ears polite", while Strauss and Lanner rule the hour. Nevertheless, there is not one to whom you can speak on the subject, but will utter a very elegant phrase in honour of their very immortal composers'.[10] The imperial chapel hardly fared better. After a disappointing High Mass at St Stephen's, she felt that 'the voices of the Jews of Vienna have made those of the Christians appear feeble by comparison'.[11] What had provoked this perhaps surprising judgment was a visit to the Vienna synagogue where Salomon Sulzer, a cantor of outstanding vocal qualities and a composer in his own right, had organized a boys' chorus that attracted interested outsiders from far and wide. Sulzer eventually was appointed professor of singing at the Vienna Conservatory, contributing greatly to the raising of vocal standards in the Austrian capital and, thanks to an increasing number of students from outside the city, elsewhere as well.

The years between the political upheavals of 1830 and 1848 produced a number of innovations. Relative old-timers like Hummel were expected to conclude their concerts with a free fantasy and their 'solo' appearances relied heavily on an orchestra, in an accompanying role as well as for the ubiquitous overtures that framed virtually every such public event; but in the 1830s solo sonatas began to be included in programmes. By 1836 Sigismond Thalberg dared to perform without an orchestra. That he did so was no doubt related to the tendency of leading pianists to think of their instrument as a two-handed orchestra, as it were. Orchestras were likely to be helpful under these circumstances, mostly as separate but equal instrumental foils or partners. And that is precisely how Schumann, Liszt and Brahms treated the orchestra in their concertos. For the time being, however, its role remained perfunctory, as was still the case with Chopin. Liszt, Thalberg and Chopin had enthralled Viennese audiences in the 1820s. But it was only during the 'virtuoso period' between the two revolutions that their enormous prestige permitted them to proceed musically in ways that might well have been unacceptable before.

The 1830s also witnessed the gradual replacement of that staple of virtually all concerts, the aria, by the lied, except in the most sophisticated orchestral programmes like those of the *concerts spirituels* and the Gesellschaft der Musikfreunde. This new convention offered lesser local talents welcome opportunities. Josef Dessauer, for example, proved a fine melodist in his songs even though as an opera composer he never quite made the grade. (Dessauer, like so many other active participants in Viennese musical life, hailed from Prague.) In Vienna the purveyors of light orchestral music carried the day, led by Strauss and Lanner, those two masters who never ceased to astonish grateful admirers with new musical evidence of the climate of frivolity – if not necessarily superficiality – typical of the atmosphere before 1848. In the words of Hanslick:

> How trivial was public musical life at the end of the thirties and in the early forties! Sumptuous and trivial alike, it vacillated between dull sentimentality and scintillant wit. Cut off from all great intellectual interests, the Vienna public abandoned itself to diversion and entertainment. Not only did the theaters flourish; they were the chief subject of conversation and occupied the leading columns of the daily newspapers. Musical life was dominated by Italian opera, virtuosity, and the waltz. Strauss and Lanner were idolized.[12]

The philharmonic concerts were given in the Grosser Redoutensaal, the large ballroom in which Strauss and Lanner alternated as conductors of their dance music; but the departure in 1847 of Otto Nicolai (to become director of the Berlin Opera) in effect put an end to a flourishing enterprise that had been initiated on 27 November 1842. Nicolai was not only a remarkable conductor and organizer, whose performances of Beethoven's Ninth Symphony had finally been worthy of this extraordinary work, but also the composer of that delightful, skilfully wrought Shakespeare opera, *Die lustigen Weiber von Windsor*, excerpts from which were first heard at his Viennese farewell

41. *'The Grand Galop of Johann Strauss': engraving by A. Geiger after J. C. Schöller from the supplement to 'Wiener Theaterzeitung, Wiener Szene' (1839). Together with the waltz, quadrille and polka, the galop (usually reserved for the finale) was one of the most popular ballroom dances of the nineteenth century*

concert on 1 April 1847. During Nicolai's tenure in Vienna, concert life generally had enjoyed an unprecedented boom. According to Hanslick, the 1842–3 season offered a total of 120 concerts, and in 1845–6 as many as 130. Fashionable virtuosos still dominated the scene, but their heyday had already passed. Nor was there now much interest in the numerous charitable concerts that had been a mainstay of concert life for decades.

Perhaps it was the impact of Nicolai's philharmonic concerts that shocked the more sophisticated members of the public, as well as critics, into realizing that the new music produced to the west and north of Vienna had passed them by. Those crucial developments were, of course, indebted to the Romantic spirit that animated so much German intellectual and artistic creativity. But even Mendelssohn, the most Classical of the German Romantics, remained virtually unknown in Vienna. His oratorios, so popular elsewhere, could not break into a tradition limited largely to Haydn's *The Seasons* and *The Creation*. As Hanslick observed, Mendelssohn's *St Paul* was known in the USA before it came to Vienna, where it received no more than a lukewarm reception. Unlike Prague, which rivalled Leipzig in the performance of new works, Vienna continued

101

to prefer 'the legs of Fanny Elsler'.[13] Clara Schumann made little impression on the Viennese with her appearances during the 1846–7 season.

Opera continued to tread well-established paths as well. The Kärntnertortheater, where the court opera was housed, presented opera in Italian until it fell victim to the revolution of 1848. Its offerings, whether on the stage, in the dining-room or at the gambling-table, reflected the tastes of the commercial genius Domenico Barbaja, the director whose other domain was La Scala, Milan. As a result, Donizetti was appointed imperial court composer (a title vacated in 1791 with Mozart's death) in return for which he composed some of his last works, *Linda di Chamonix* (1842) and *Maria di Rohan* (1843) and revised his *Don Sebastiano* to suit Viennese tastes.

In the realm of church music, still hampered by the financial consequences of the secularization of church property in 1804, the need for new institutional foundations led to the creation of church music organizations in a number of Viennese parishes. But as church music was now largely left to lay people, composers like Joseph Eybler (1765–1846) were forced to limit themselves to relatively simple styles. There was a growing interest in early church music, though, in keeping with the emerging historicism that had caught the imagination of many educated dilettantes. Even so, the Caecilian movement, which had numerous adherents in neighbouring Bavaria, lagged in

42. The third-act terzetto from Donizetti's opera 'Maria di Rohan', written for Vienna and first performed at the Kärntnertortheater (5 June 1843), with Eugenia Tadolini, Giorgio Ronconi and Guasco

Austria, where *a cappella* music as yet found little favour. The oratorio, on the other hand, tended to remain close to church music in both style and content, as Eybler's *Die vier letzten Dinge* shows. Patriotic themes, in the tradition of Handel, had been popular earlier in the century, when Maximilian Stadler wrote *Die Befreiung Jerusalems* (1809) on a text by Heinrich von Collin in honour of the Austrian resistance to Napoleon. Pre-March Vienna, by contrast, had little taste for works that intertwined religious and patriotic sentiments.

During the lifetime of Haydn and Mozart Vienna held considerable promise as a music-publishing centre. The firm of Artaria, who had received his imperial privilege as a music dealer, decided in 1778 to bring out publications of their own, no doubt stimulated by the mounting popularity of both Haydn and Mozart. Their privilege, the first of its kind, expired in 1791 and was not renewed until 1806, when Beethoven had long since established himself as Vienna's leading composer, a fact of which Artaria took full advantage, at least until Rossini became the rage. Meanwhile, Artaria did much to promote the little-known works of Schubert. Beethoven also had extensive dealings with Tobias Haslinger and Anton Diabelli; it was the latter who commissioned numerous composers to write variations on the theme on which Beethoven composed his monumental Diabelli Variations op.120, which, except for Bach's Goldberg Variations, have virtually no rival in a genre traditionally associated with the lighter side of musical creativity.

Not surprisingly, given the indolent state of Viennese musical affairs during the first half of the nineteenth century, other cities, Leipzig in particular, tended to do better in the field of publishing, an increasingly lucrative business serving a rapidly expanding musical public. The history of early nineteenth-century musical journalism is a case in point: while the Leipzig *Allgemeine musikalische Zeitung* was published regularly and punctually for seven decades from the time its first number was issued by Breitkopf & Härtel in 1798, the *Wiener Allgemeine musikalische Zeitung* (like Haslinger's *Allgemeiner musikalischer Anzeiger*) survived only for a few years and with considerable difficulty. Their mostly short-term editors, J. F. Castelli, Ignaz von Mosel, Ignaz von Seyfried and Franz August Kanne, were anything but professional musical journalists.

Even so, the era before March 1848 was by no means as dead a period in Viennese music as has often been maintained. Thanks to Joseph Lanner and Johann Strauss the elder, Vienna became the fountainhead of developments in entertainment music that left profound and lasting traces in musical life everywhere. The number of leading musicians who sought fame as well as financial rewards in the Austrian capital testifies to the lively interest of the Viennese in a form of art they considered their own. In their ways, the waltz kings, of course, were hardly less representative of true Viennese spirit than Schubert and many lesser talents before them. Ironically, however, interest in Schubert (many a valiant effort by his brother Ferdinand notwithstanding) remained minimal, whereas the waltz soon became not only big business but to all intents and purposes the popular identification mark of a city passionately dedicated to maintaining the status quo. Certain groups of the public nevertheless appreciated some of the more radical departures from musical convention. The visit of Hector Berlioz during the 1845–6 season created much excitement in spite of the sharply divided critical reaction. Berlioz presented much of his symphonic output in six well-attended concerts that included two complete performances of *Roméo et Juliette*. 'In Berlioz', Hanslick later wrote, 'the Viennese public got acquainted with an isolated peak of modern musical romanticism, whose existence it had not even suspected'.[14] Apparently, his somewhat unorthodox appearance was a factor in the relatively positive response to so much novel music. He was soon forgotten, at any rate, and did not return until twenty years later, when he conducted *La damnation de Faust* at a concert of the Gesellschaft der Musikfreunde.

The events of March 1848, momentous though they were for music in most European capitals, had little effect in Vienna. The opening of the Italian opera season, scheduled for 1 April 1848, had to be cancelled in the face of the surge of nationalist feeling that motivated the revolutionaries and that their actions in turn engendered. Paradoxically, the opening work was to have been Verdi's *Ernani*, which in Italy had appealed precisely to the pervasive desire for national freedom. No such considerations, however, could erase the fact that Italian opera in German-speaking Vienna was by definition unacceptable at a time of fervent reaction to everything foreign. Ballochino, the opera's director, was forced to resign and the singers disappeared. Three years later Italian opera was back, when a new company moved into the Kärntnertortheater.

During the turbulent months after the March upheaval young people, students in particular, were much in evidence, and musicians scrambled to satisfy their musical needs and interests. There was choral singing of old and new patriotic tunes and various theatres offered students not only free entrance but also specially organized events. Thus, the Theater an der Wien, now renamed Nationaltheater, on 24 April 1848 presented a programme that consisted almost entirely of choruses on various fighting texts glorifying national independence to raise funds for a new culturally orientated student association. Opera performances in German often included additional songs or, at the very least, new verses extolling freedom, much as had been the case under similar circumstances in Paris in the 1790s. The expected beneficial effects of the 1848 revolution on the art of music and musical life in general, however, proved an illusion. Theatres remained largely empty, periodicals ceased to appear and the widespread uncertainty regarding the nation's future was hardly conducive to artistic activity of the highest order. The Gesellschaft der Musikfreunde and its conservatory barely managed to survive.

As a municipal entity Vienna differed fundamentally from cities like Paris and London during the period under consideration. Schubert's friend Sonnleithner still had every reason to refer to the seat of imperial power as a large conglomeration of small towns. It took a thorough reorganization, both politically and architecturally, later in the century to arrive at a viable cultural environment ready to sustain the creative effect of a Brahms or Bruckner, who settled in Vienna shortly ahead of the building boom that shaped the city as it exists to this day. In the meantime, the same political regime and social ambience persisted virtually unchanged, except that the aristocratic salons had vanished, while their bourgeois counterparts never achieved the significance they had attained in Berlin, Vienna's rapidly emerging rival to the north. With the virtuoso onslaught of the third and fourth decades of the century, even highly skilled dilettants retreated from their once-active roles as performers to the passive anonymity of a public mesmerized by acrobatic musical feats. Characteristically, at a time when the Romantic movement generated an unprecedented spate of individual musical creativity almost everywhere else, Austria consoled herself with a Habsburg myth predicated on the supposed timelessness and universality of the imperial realm and hence also the perennial validity of past achievements in art, music and literature. The fact that, under these conditions, Vienna remained a well-nigh proverbial centre of attraction for musicians and music-lovers from all parts testifies to the robustness of an underlying vitality that has proved impervious to the horrors of war, revolution and political terror, not to mention economic disasters and endemic social problems; this vitality, time and again, has elicited the very best from genuine talent at all levels of musical enterprise.

This chapter has been expanded and revised by the Editor.

NOTES

[1] J. F. Reichardt, *Briefe geschrieben auf einer Reise nach Wien* (Amsterdam, 1810), as trans. in *Source Readings in Music History*, ed. O. Strunk (New York, 1950/R1965), 728.

[2] Ibid, 733.

[3] Ibid.

[4] Ibid, 737.

[5] Ibid, 738–9.

[6] E. Hanslick, *Geschichte des Concertwesens in Wien* (Vienna, 1869), 284.

[7] Ibid, 285.

[8] Ibid, 364.

[9] F. Trollope, *Vienna and the Austrians* (London, 1938), i, 367.
[10] Ibid, 372.
[11] Ibid, 379.
[12] As translated in *E. Hanslick: Vienna's Golden Years of Music,* ed. H. Pleasants (New York, 1950), 6.
[13] Hanslick, op cit, 369–70.
[14] Ibid, 358.

BIBLIOGRAPHICAL NOTE

General

Unlike Vienna shortly before and after the beginning of the twentieth century, the imperial seat of power that was home to both Beethoven and Schubert has received relatively little attention of late, at least in the English-speaking world, perhaps because cultural life under a conservative regime like that of Prince Metternich holds few attractions for a generation that takes 'progress' for granted. Even so, the city itself never lost its romantic fascination among English-speaking travellers and music-lovers. Yet, curiously, few comprehensive studies of the long-time capital of the Austrian Empire are currently available for further consultation. Possibly the best of these, dealing extensively with the period under discussion, is I. Barea's *Vienna* (New York, 1967), of which some 200 pages are devoted to the city's crucial Baroque legacy, the Biedermeier spirit that prevailed during the later years of Beethoven and Schubert and the revolutionary period that followed. Barea discusses political events, intellectual currents and demographic and architectural developments as well as the arts and entertainment, drawing on a host of primary and secondary sources.

Noteworthy among English eyewitness reports, from a general as well as specifically musical point of view, are *A Mozart Pilgrimage being the Travel Diaries of Vincent and Mary Novello in the Year 1829*, ed. R. Hughes (London, 1955), and above all F. Trollope's *Vienna and the Austrians* (London, 1838). Trollope, in her nearly 70 'letters' to imaginary friends, touched upon virtually every aspect of life among the various social classes in pre-March Vienna, inevitably stressing, however, 'polite society' and its pleasures.

The literary scene

Franz Grillparzer, the leading Viennese dramatist of the period, was the subject of a pioneering study by G. Pollak, *Franz Grillparzer and the Austrian Drama* (New York, 1907), and more recently of P. Drake's dissertation *Grillparzer and Biedermeier* (Waco, 1957). *The Musical Element in the Viennese Volksstueck and in the Dramas of Grillparzer* is explored by E. F. Saverio (Richmond, 1925). A comprehensive account of the man in the literary and general artistic context of his time is given in W. E. Yates, *Grillparzer: a Critical Introduction* (Cambridge, 1977). Grillparzer's important *Autobiographie*, introduced by A. Grünberg (Vienna, 1959), is available only in German, as are the *Erinnerungen* of that other major literary force and one-time director of the Burgtheater, Heinrich Laube (vols. viii and ix of his *Ausgewählte Werke*, Leipzig, 1906). Literary life, the theatre and censorship are expertly discussed in H. Rieder's *Wiener Vormärz* (Vienna, 1959).

Politics

Metternich, the all-powerful politician and *spiritus rector* of the Vienna Congress, is the focus of A. Cecil, *Metternich, 1773–1859: a Study of his Period and Personality* (London, 3/1947). A. Palmer, in *Metternich* (London, 1972), covers some of the same ground but favours issues above personality matters. G. de Bertier de Sauvigny, in *Metternich and his Times* (London, 1962), quotes extensively from pertinent correspondence. C. A. Macartney devotes about half of his extensive treatment of *The Habsburg Empire 1790–1918* (London, 1968) to the first 50 years of the nineteenth century.

Musical institutions

As for music and musical institutions in particular, current scholarship tends to neglect socio-economic and/or political studies in favour of largely descriptive discussions of stylistic characteristics and structural analyses, frequently in *ex post facto* terms which, on the whole, reveal little if anything of the creative motivation or context. Before the spectacular rise of musicology as an academic discipline, a single individual the famous (or, as the view may be, notorious) critic Eduard Hanslick managed to produce an extensively documented four-volume history of Viennese concert life that has lost none of its intrinsic validity and usefulness. Though never translated into English, it has become available again in a single-volume German reprint (*Geschichte des Concertwesens in Wien*, Hildesheim and New York, 1979). Hanslick organized his chapters according to musical genres and supported his cogent comments with an admirable array of facts, names and dates, as well as excerpts from the contemporary press. Concert and programme listings for the first decade of the century are accessible in the appendices to *Concert Life in Haydn's Vienna* by M. S. Morrow (Stuyvesant, NY, 1989). Meanwhile Hanslick's is again the authoritative voice with respect to opera, unquestionably Vienna's central musical genre, then as now. His autobiography, *Aus meinem Leben* (London, *R*1971), gives a particularly vivid personal account of the events of 1848. Some of the pertinent passages are printed in English in the introduction to H. Pleasants's *Vienna's Golden Years* (London, 1950), a volume of selections from the hundreds of extensive reviews Hanslick wrote from the late 1890s onwards.

M. Prawy's lavishly illustrated history of *The Vienna Opera* (New York, 1969) owes its basic reliability to the many primary sources consulted. However, the author was clearly less interested in early nineteenth-century developments than in the hundred years or so that followed the revolution of 1848. H. Kralik's identically titled study (Vienna, 1953), though far more even-handed, is also less detailed. *300 Jahre Wiener Operntheater: Werk und Werden*, by E. Pirchan, A. Witeschnik and O. Fritz (Vienna, 1953), goes beyond either of those publications, especially in regard to technical questions. Though duly covering composers, producers and performers, this particular book displays a rare awareness of the crucial physical conditions under which operatic performances took place. A good deal of space is assigned to valuable discussions of the structural characteristics of various houses, the design and inherent possibilities of their stages and equipment etc. K. Kobald's *Alt-Wiener Musikstätten* (Vienna, 1974), in turn, draws attention to that easily overlooked but characteristic concert venue, the Viennese inn, where many a Beethoven and Schubert work was first performed. Musical contributions of the legitimate stage were the subject of a Viennese exhibit in 1976, and its catalogue, *Musik im Burgtheater*, offers a chronological listing of incidental music performed. The most recent brief survey of institutions, venues and musical genres is found in chapter 14 of *Musikgeschichte Österreichs*, ed. R. Flotzinger and G. Gruber (Graz, Vienna and Cologne, 1979).

Musical life

The socio-political setting for music during the Metternich era, a time of steady decline in Eduard Hanslick's eyes, is the central issue in A. M. Hanson's *Musical Life in Biedermeier Vienna* (Cambridge, 1985), a revision of a dissertation. Hanson documents in eminently readable form various aspects of official policy, including censorship, as well as economic conditions, and in this light reviews virtually the entire spectrum of Viennese musical activity during the last decade of both

The Early Romantic Period

Beethoven's and Schubert's lives. Viennese social divisions and habits and their musical ramifications at mid-century are the subject of a portion of W. Weber's *Music and the Middle Class: the Social Structure of Concert Life in London, Paris and Vienna* (New York, 1975). While Weber treats such questions in rather dry academic, mostly statistical terms. M. Brion conveys a well-rounded, though hardly in-depth, impression of *Daily Life in the Vienna of Mozart and Schubert* (New York, 1962). Brion rightly stresses the oft-neglected fact that 'the fortunate city' catered to the showmanship of an Emanuel Schikaneder and the spirited dances of the waltz 'kings' Strauss (father) and Lanner far more readily than to the instrumental music of Beethoven, let alone Schubert. E. Gartenberg's slender but well-written *Vienna: its Musical Heritage* (Universty Park and London, 1968) deftly makes up in atmosphere what it lacks in originality.

Ultimately, of course, it is the music composed and/or performed in Vienna which counts. And virtually any worthwhile biography of the principal composers from Beethoven to Strauss will necessarily consider also the environment to which they responded. *Thayer's Life of Beethoven*, rev. and ed. E. Forbes (Princeton, 1970), is still the outstanding example, even though the original was written over a century ago. A typically biassed yet valuable study from a disciple's pen is *Beethoven as I Knew him* by A. F. Schindler, ed. D. W. MacArdle (New York, 1972). Of particular value are documentary collections like *The Letters of Beethoven*, collected, trans. and ed. E. Anderson, 3 vols. (London, 1961), *Beethoven Letters, Journals and Conversations*, trans. and ed. M. Hamburger (New York, 1960), or O. E. Deutsch's *Schubert: a Documentary Biography* (London, 1977). Much of the fundamental importance for any real understanding of the musical city that was Vienna between the revolutions remains, however, concealed in contemporary musical writings, such as musicians' auto-biographies, travel accounts and, above all, periodicals – foremost among them, even with regard to Vienna, the Leipzig *Allgemeine musikalische Zeitung*. Unfortunately, most of these invaluable sources have been reprinted only in their original languages, especially German. Among the notable exceptions are *Louis Spohr's Autobiography* (New York, 1969) and Ignaz Moscheles's *Fragments of an Autobiography* (Wolfeboro, 1979), which refer repeatedly to Viennese musical conditions during the period under consideration.

Chapter IV

Berlin: 'Music in the Air'

CHRISTOPH-HELLMUT MAHLING

'Music is part of the air you breathe; you absorb it through the very pores of your skin. One meets it everywhere, in concert hall, church, theatre, in the streets, in the public gardens',[1] wrote Hector Berlioz from Berlin, when he visited the city on his travels through Germany in 1842–3. He was depicting the extensive musical life of Berlin at this period and mentioning the principal places where music was played in public and for the public, accessible to everyone. Only during the first half of the nineteenth century, however, had the phenomenon described by Berlioz developed such lively diversity.

Musical life in Berlin had received fresh stimuli in the eighteenth century, particularly through the reorganization of the Hofkapelle under Frederick II. Major contributions were made by its leading members, including C. P. E. Bach, Franz and Georg Benda, Johann Gottlieb, Carl Heinrich Graun and Christoph Nichelmann. Like many other musicians, they supported musical activities in the city as well as serving the court. This was partly because at court the emphasis was on chamber music, and after 1742 on opera, while other kinds of music were hardly performed. As in other cities, the amateur musicians of Berlin used to meet privately or in public buildings to make music together, with the aid of professionals. For instance, the Musikübende Gesellschaft, founded in Berlin in 1749, met at the house of the organist Sack and in 1755 gave the first performance of Carl Heinrich Graun's Passion *Der Tod Jesu*. There was also the Musikalische Assemblée, directed by C. F. Schade, and musical gatherings at the house of the Hofkapellmeister, Johann Friedrich Agricola (which in 1770 became amateur concerts at the Corsica House, given by Ernst Friedrich Benda among others), and the *concerts spirituels* on the Parisian model, founded by Johann Friedrich Reichardt in 1783. In 1787 Johann Karl Friedrich Rellstab established the Konzerte für Kenner und Liebhaber, held first at the English House and then at its founder's home. These concert institutions were important in the semi-public musical life of the city.

The Hofkapelle was prominent only when it performed operas at Carnival, although at this period it also took part in many benefit concerts. Moreover, the Hofoper was largely committed to Italian opera. German-language operas and Singspiels were the province of the Nationaltheater, founded by Doebbelin in 1786 and subsidized by the king. As early as 1799 the lack of large-scale concerts was felt to be a deficiency, particularly puzzling in view of the large number of available musicians, some of them extremely proficient. In 1802 no fewer than 248 professional musicians were registered as living in Berlin.[2] The writer of a report from the city in the *Allgemeine musikalische Zeitung* of January 1799 remarks:

> Least of all can I accustom myself here to the fact that with the great number of excellent virtuosos in the royal orchestra – such as Ritter the great bassoonist, those two outstanding cellists, the Duports, and their worthy pupils Hausmann and Gross, the excellent violin-ists Haak, Möser and Seidler, a fine french horn player in Le Brun and two very good clarinettists in Bähr and Tausch – that with all this wealth of virtuosos, no proper concerts on a large scale are given either at court or in the city. To be sure, I have often attended single concert performances by foreigners or by natives of Berlin . . . but still, there is seldom anything really complete.[3]

Thus it seems to have been less a lack of facilities or goodwill that affected musical life than the conflict between trends in musical taste: more precisely, between tradition and progress, the old and the new. Although a new tendency began about 1800, it took almost another three decades for a definitive change to occur in the city's music. When that came, knowledge of the musical conditions in other big cities which served as models, especially Vienna, London and in particular Paris, was a large contributory factor.

The court was still at the centre of musical life until the end of the eighteenth century, despite all endeavours in the city itself, but crucial changes took place during the first half of the nineteenth century. The French Revolution of 1789 had a noticeable effect, as did the general political and social regroupings at the turn of the century. 1806, when Napoleon entered Berlin, was as much a watershed as 1848, the year of revolution. Musical activity was shifting towards the city itself, growing and expanding all the time. There were two important factors: the ever-increasing emancipation of the middle classes and the rapid rise in Berlin's population. Whereas the population was about 172,000 in 1800 (including some 33,300 soldiers), by 1850 it had risen to about 420,000 (including some 18,000 soldiers).[4] The high proportion of soldiers should not be overlooked. As the population grew, so did the demand for music, for entertainment as well as for thoughtful and aesthetic appreciation. And no class of society could or would do without its musical entertainment: neither the nobility and the prosperous patrician financiers, nor the upper and lower middle classes, nor the servant and working classes.[5] More thought was given to supplying this demand, and the venues of musical performances and the price of tickets influenced the structure of concert audiences, although the form and content of concert programmes on the whole displayed only slight differences.

INSTITUTIONS

The reconstruction of Prussia began in 1807. That year the two Berlin theatres, the royal Hofoper and the Nationaltheater, merged under the same management; August Wilhelm Iffland, previously director of the Nationaltheater, was appointed director-general. Performances were public and open to anyone on payment of the admission fee. In 1807, too, the orchestras of the two theatres were amalgamated into a single, large orchestral body; the musical direction was in the hands of Vincenzo Righini and Friedrich Himmel. From now on the royal Kapelle thus enlarged – along with the orchestra of the Royal City Theatre, opened in 1824 chiefly for the performance of Italian opera – was not only the principal theatre orchestra but also the main permanent orchestra to occupy an established place in the musical life of Berlin. This was important since it meant there were always many orchestral players available who could perform as soloists, in groups or as a small orchestral unit in other, supplementary concert events.

The primary function of the Kapelle was to act as the court and opera orchestra. It was not called upon to give concerts at court so often as to play for an increasing number of operatic and theatrical performances, which also meant that it was very seldom available to the promoters of other concerts. Further claims on its time and availability came in 1842 when it took over the symphony soirées held every other Wednesday during the winter season and hitherto run by Carl Möser as subscription concerts. Wilhelm Taubert was in charge of this series. There were also financial reasons that made it almost impossible for private concert promoters to recruit an orchestra. As the *Berliner musikalische Zeitung* put it in 1846: 'A *concert*? No. The Kapelle asks a fee of three thalers for every member. Add to that the hire of a hall, the costs of heating, lighting, attendants and writing out parts, and it comes to so large a sum that only a rich man and not a poor musician could afford it'.[6] It is not surprising that the same journal enthusiastically hailed the endeavours of Wilhelm Wieprecht to found a new orchestra, to be mainly at the disposal of native Berliners but also available to non-residents giving concerts in the city. These efforts led to the founding of the Euterpe Orchestral Society, which gave its first concert on 31 January 1849.

The quality of the concerts at which the royal Kapelle performed deteriorated noticeably over the decades. The programmes had attracted adverse criticism as early as 1846, and that criticism was extended to the orchestra itself in an article 'Musical Berlin Today' published in 1850:

> There is a lack of that musical authority which not only holds the orchestra carefully together but dominates, mentally unites and inspires it. And there are many material shortcomings, compared to former times. The strings are thin in tone, devoid of substance, fullness or powerful bowing, the basses dull. Of the wind instruments, the trombones and trumpets are mediocre in quality, the sound is not noble and clear . . . the tuning not precise enough . . . this is no longer the Kapelle of Spontini's day.[7]

The royal orchestra represented the conservative musical element to a greater extent than almost any other institution in Berlin. Only against that background can we see why progressive elements turned elsewhere, outside the traditional institutions. The success of private orchestras up to the time of the Bilsesche Kapelle, and indeed of Hans von Bülow with his Meiningen group in 1882, was a direct consequence of this state of affairs

*

After 1807 the royal opera also experienced a period of artistic buoyancy. It staged Spontini's *La vestale* (1811) and *Fernand Cortez* (1814), Méhul's *Joseph in Aegypten* (1811) and Boïeldieu's *Jean de Paris* (1813), as well as Weber's early operas *Silvana* (1812) and *Abu Hassan* (1813). Karl von Brühl, who took over the management of the theatre from Iffland in 1814, put on stage plays too, but he concentrated in particular on opera. With the appointment of Gasparo Spontini in 1820, the orchestra gained an outstanding conductor and teacher who led it to great heights. His successor Giacomo Meyerbeer, appointed in 1842, built on his work. Spontini also improved the social standing of orchestral musicians and ensured that they were guaranteed pensions in old age and for their surviving dependents.

The singers and chorus participated in this musical prosperity. Famous women singers like Wilhelmine Schröder-Devrient, Angelica Catalani, Anna Milder-Hauptmann, Leopoldine Tuczek, Jenny Lind, Pauline Marx and Pauline Viardot-García shone, along with such outstanding members of the permanent ensemble as Johanna Eunicke, Caroline Seidler and Josephine Schulze-Kilitschky, and leading men like the baritone Eduard Devrient, the bass Joseph Fischer and the tenors Eduard Mantius and Joseph Tichatschek. The bill included Gluck's *Alceste* (1817), Meyerbeer's *Emma von Roxburg* (1820) and Mozart's *Così fan tutte*, and above all operas by Rossini such as *Tancredi* (1818), *Otello* (1821), *Il barbiere di Siviglia* (1822), *Elisabetta, regina d'Inghilterra* (1824) and *La gazza ladra* (1824). Other

43. *Designs by Karl Friedrich Schinkel for two operas performed by the Berlin royal opera:*
(a) Hall of Stars of the Queen of Night in Act 1 of Mozart's 'Die Zauberflöte' (1816)

(b)Temple of Diana at Ephesus in Act 1 of Spontini's 'Olimpia' (1821)

operas performed were Spontini's *Olimpie* (1821), with a libretto revised by E. T. A. Hoffmann, Spohr's *Jessonda* (1825), conducted by the composer, and Weber's *Euryanthe* (1825) and *Oberon* (1828). Karl Friedrich Schinkel's scenery for Mozart's *Die Zauberflöte* and operas by Gluck and Spontini created a great sensation. Many operas had their first performances in Berlin, among them E. T. A. Hoffmann's *Undine* (1816), Spontini's *Agnes von Hohenstaufen* (1827), Heinrich Marschner's *Hans Heiling* (1833), Meyerbeer's *Das Hoffest von Ferrara* (1843) and *Ein Feldlager in Schlesien* (produced in 1844 for the reopening of the opera house after a fire), and Otto Nicolai's *Die lustigen Weiber von Windsor* (1849). However, the most important event for operatic history was the successful première of Weber's *Der Freischütz* on 18 June 1821, with the composer conducting; at the very least, it challenged the supremacy of Italian opera.

After August 1825 Italian operas, in particular the works of Rossini, were at the heart of the repertory of the recently opened Residenztheater. There Henriette Sontag had her triumphs, for instance in Rossini's *L'italiana in Algeri*, thanks to which this theatre, patronized and thus supported primarily by the middle classes, competed temporarily also in purely musical terms with the Hofoper, which concentrated on the staple repertory of the leading opera theatres at home and abroad: it offered works by Auber (*La muette de Portici*, performed

44. *The Berlin Schauspielhaus (right), built by K. F. Schinkel (1818–21), where the première of Weber's 'Der Freischütz' took place on 18 June 1821 (the German Cathedral is on the left): lithograph (c1840) by L. E. Lütke*

in 1829; *Fra Diavolo* in 1830), Bellini (*I puritani, La sonnambula*), Cherubini (*Ali Baba* in 1835), Donizetti, Halévy, Lortzing (*Zar und Zimmermann* in 1839), Marschner (*Der Templer und die Jüdin, Hans Heiling*), Méhul, Meyerbeer (*Robert le diable*), Rossini (*Guillaume Tell*, among others) and Spohr (*Faust, Die Kreuzfahrer*). Wagner's *Der fliegende Holländer* was given on 7 January 1844, but only after fierce arguments between the manager Karl Theodor von Küstner and Meyerbeer, the new Hofkapellmeister (he was appointed in 1841).

PRIVATE CONCERTS

> Two gentlemen previously mentioned, Herr Kantor Adlung and Herr Musikdirektor Bohrer, have tried to remedy the total lack of concert music, which is felt all the more keenly by music-lovers as our city becomes better able to provide it. They have announced twelve concerts, which they began to give in the middle of last month. That very lack, and the extremely reasonable price of entrance (attendance at a single concert costs the subscriber only eight groschen), may have helped to fill the hall even more than the choice and performance of the pieces.[8]

This report is from 1802; subsequently concerts were held in the theatre hall on 17 November 1803 and 'every following Tuesday' in the winter season. At the time they were 'the only public institution of this kind we have here, and though they do not fill the gap left by those concerts of sacred music which the royal Kapelle ceased to give some eight or nine years ago, yet they are of great significance, and could become even more important'.[9] The programmes show considerable variety and a liking for the three great Classical Viennese composers, particularly Beethoven. The programme for the ninth subscription concert, on 7 March 1805, was as follows:

PART 1

New Symphony in D major, revived and now played with even greater precision	*Beethoven*
Scena (Madame Eunicke)	*Cannabich*
Double Clarinet Concerto, soloists Herr Bliesener and Herr Reinhardt	*Tausch*
Scena (Herr Fischer)	*Righini*

PART 2

Introduction to the opera *Medea*	*Cherubini*
Violin Concerto, soloist Herr Mauser	*Kreutzer*
Rondo (Madame Eunicke)	*Righini*
Overture to *Figaro*	*Mozart*

The political and military events of 1805–6 led to the cancellation of the concerts 'for lack of subscribers'. However, in November 1807 there is mention of a subscription concert given 'in a hall in the Hôtel de Paris', probably the first of the Bliesener brothers' concerts, which later became very popular. In May 1808 the horn player and chamber musician Georg Abraham Schneider began his Sunday concerts 'in imitation of the popular Viennese Sunday concerts in the Augarten',[10] and they continued on a larger scale the next winter. But Schneider's enterprise did not survive for long: the concerts ceased in 1811. Obviously the reorganization of the royal orchestra, which meant that its members could not play elsewhere so often, and the ban on using the theatre hall for 'outside' performances had worked against them.[11] The royal Kapelle was now required to give concerts of its own in the theatre hall in the winter of 1811–12. But the Bliesener brothers' subscription concerts in the Hôtel de Paris continued.

On 4 March 1812 'Concertmeister Carl Möser', who had much to do with the development of regular concerts in Berlin, gave one of his own. It was such a success that he was able to give another on 17 March 'by request'; on 5 April he played a violin concerto by Kreutzer at the 'concert of the royal orchestra . . . on behalf of the pension fund for widows of its members . . . to great applause'.[12] He organized his first quartet soirées in the winter season of 1813–14, but did not neglect his large-scale concerts and after 1819 there was a new hall for them, built by Schinkel at the Hofjäger 'on the left side of the Thiergarten'. The quality of the Bliesener brothers' concerts also improved, obviously under the influence of Möser's.

The directorate general was responsible for organizing five concerts in the theatre in the winter season of 1821–2, conducted by the musical directors Seidel and Schneider. Among other works, Mozart's symphonies in G minor, E♭ major and C major and several of Haydn's symphonies were performed 'in full'.[13] But the erratic attitude of the directorate-general towards concerts, the trend towards the intensification of concert life and the increasing esteem in which Beethoven's works were held worked to the advantage of Möser's progressive attitude. His concerts were regarded as models, especially as they often featured first Berlin performances. In these favourable circumstances it could only be a matter of time before Möser, whose achievements had been recognized by the king with the title of 'Musikdirector und wirklichen ersten Concertmeisters',[14] felt it appropriate to supplement his quartet soirées with regular symphony soirées, or transform them into such concerts.

Möser – full of ideas and, not least important, a good businessman too – knew how to use every opportunity for a concert. Such occasions were provided, for instance, by anniversaries of the births and deaths of the great masters, which were regularly celebrated, at first primarily as social occasions, later as concerts. From about 1827 or 1828 Möser's quartet soirées, symphony soirées and memorial concerts became permanent institutions, making up a considerable part of the musical life of Berlin until 1842. As early as 7 July 1826 he had given an open-air concert in

> a garden square surrounded by trees, and reinforced the orchestra with amateurs. Musicians of the Royal City Theatre were also invited, but apparently were prevented from appearing . . . Had so great a number of players been brought together in a concert hall, the effect must have been imposing indeed . . . The choice of pieces left almost nothing to be desired for an open-air concert. Beethoven's Pastoral and 'Battle' Symphonies, the overtures to Weber's *Oberon*, Spontini's *Olimpie* and Spohr's *Faust*, songs for men's voices by Zelter and Flemming – so much good and great music has perhaps never been brought together before in a Berlin concert.[15]

Möser's soirées were regarded as particularly valuable because 'the great symphonies of the three heroes of German music alternate with more recent compositions in the symphonic genre, and also with *classical* quartets'.[16] The performances were of a high standard, and here Möser's prominent position as Konzertmeister of the royal Kapelle and teacher in the orchestral school set up by Spontini gave him an advantage: it allowed him to recruit the ablest musicians. The orchestral school, or training school for the royal Kapelle, was itself soon expanded into a complete second orchestra when 'the best oboists of the local regiments were encouraged to take part in its ensemble rehearsals'. The *Berliner musikalische Zeitung* added, not without a hint of criticism:

> Möser's services to this second orchestra do indeed deserve recognition. However, he is now accused of having used it for private purposes. Even if, not unexpectedly, artistic purposes were thereby served, since it was *this orchestra* which did most to pave the way for the symphonies of the German masters in Berlin and win understanding for them, yet the school was not set up to serve private purposes.[17]

The success of Möser's ventures and the ever-increasing demand for similar musical entertainments gave rise to imitations. Thus, the Ganz brothers first presented what they called 'morning diversions' in the winter season of 1831–2. These were so well received that as early as January 1832 the brothers were able to announce a 'second cycle of six Morning Entertainments'. One reason for their popularity was the number and diversity of the pieces performed; another is revealed in a comparison of 'Möser's Evening Entertainments' with 'the Ganzes' morning diversions':

In both, tribute was paid to a greater or lesser degree to the pure sense of art, and if the quartets, quintets and symphonies Herr Musikdirector Möser chose tended to be from the classics, in the sphere of more elevated instrumental music, then the brothers Ganz had the merit of giving public performances of a number of the most recent compositions, thereby in particular offering younger, rising talents an opportunity to test their powers.[18]

In the winter of 1833–4 'the performances of quartets given every other Saturday by Herr Hubert Ries, Herr Maurer, Herr Böhmer and Herr Just, all of them members of the royal Kapelle'[19] are mentioned for the first time. And early in 1834 the *Allgemeine musikalische Zeitung* reported that Beethoven's String Quartet op.131 had been heard 'with particular interest' at one of Möser's soirées, 'performed with great precision and purity by four young players, Herr Zimmermann, Herr Ronneburger, Herr Richter and Herr J. Griebel'. These were the two quartet ensembles which from now on regularly gave chamber music soirées side by side with Möser's evenings.

String quartet ensembles encountered strong competition in the trio soirées founded in 1844 by 'Herr Steifensandt and the Stahlknecht brothers', playing the piano, violin and cello. They were given once a fortnight and were a great success, not least because of the use of the piano, which was becoming an increasingly fashionable instrument. Zimmermann eventually added the piano to his Quartet Association and took to describing his concerts as 'Soirées for Chamber Music'.

CHORAL CONCERTS

Among the 'concerts for art's sake', as Ludwig Rellstab described them, were some offering large-scale choral works, particularly oratorios. In the first decades of the nineteenth century four institutions could offer such pieces: the royal opera chorus, a choir recruited 'from the public singing schools' of the Berlin secondary schools, the choir of 'Cantor Adelung's private school'[20] and, most important, the choir of the Singakademie (choral society) founded by Carl Friedrich Christian Fasch in 1791.

The work most regularly performed at Passiontide in Berlin – usually several times – was Carl Heinrich Graun's *Der Tod Jesu*. One performance was usually given on Good Friday. Johann Sebastian Bach's *St Matthew Passion*, after its revival by Mendelssohn and the Singakademie on 12 March 1829, also became a staple item in Holy Week. Haydn's oratorios *The Creation* and *The Seasons* were particularly popular in Berlin, *The Creation* being a clear favourite. Other works heard were Mozart's Requiem, many of Handel's oratorios, including *Alexander's Feast*, *Messiah*, *Judas Maccabaeus*, *Jephtha*, *Israel in Egypt*, *Solomon*, *Joshua* and *Belshazzar*, as well as oratorios and choral works

45. The Berlin Singakademie: engraving (c1830) by Finden after von Klose

by Mendelssohn, Zelter and Friedrich Schneider. Oratorios by Rungenhagen (*St Cecilia*) and Schumann (*Das Paradies und die Peri*) were also performed, as were Righini's *Te Deum*, Cherubini's Requiem and Prince Radziwill's music for Goethe's *Faust*.

1827 was a crucial year for the Singakademie: it acquired its own premises with a concert hall superior to almost all other halls in Berlin, not least because of its excellent acoustics; the Philharmonic Society founded by Eduard Ritz in 1826[21] took over the 'orchestral accompaniment, as a favour' in its performance of large choral works, making it largely independent of the royal Kapelle so its expenses were much reduced; and the social cachet of its performances was increased because from 1827 members of the royal family frequently took part. The availability of an independent hall and orchestra may well have been one of the factors causing the Singakademie's annual four subscription concerts to contribute, from the winter of 1829–30, to the permanent series of the Berlin season.[22]

In 1837 Julius Schneider took over from the organist Hansmann (who had succeeded Kantor Adlung) as director of the Singverein. He too arranged a series of subscription concerts, beginning in the winter of 1839–40. The Singakademie and Singverein were thus the leading choral societies of Berlin. At the services for festival days in the Catholic church of St Hedwig 'Masses by Haydn, Mozart, Vogler, Danzi, etc.' were performed 'by a number of good voices and an orchestra suitable for the limited space', as mentioned in the report of the death of the singer Georg Gern and the memorial service for him, at which Mozart's Requiem was performed by members of the theatre and the royal Kapelle.[23]

Finally, mention must be made of the royal court and cathedral choir. After its reorganization in the spring of 1843 it gradually came more into the public eye and eventually, particularly in the latter half of the nineteenth century, it was regarded as the equal of the large, older choirs. The *Allgemeine musikalische Zeitung* of 4 January 1844 reports:

> Since Christmas, a new order of service has been introduced at the court and cathedral church. On the first day of the festival divine service began with a psalm *a cappella* composed by Herr General-musikdirektor Mendelssohn-Bartholdy, and sung by the reorganized cathedral choir. They also sang the chorus from Handel's *Messiah*, 'Unto us a child is born' etc, very movingly and with full orchestral accompaniment. (A part of the royal Kapelle was especially engaged and paid for this extra service.)[24]

The quality of the choir rose so rapidly that 30 of its members were in London giving concerts as early as 1850.

Other choral societies gradually formed, though it was some time before they took part in public concerts. In 1809 Zelter founded a Liedertafel (male chorus). It was to meet once a month, with a membership of 20–25, 'to derive amusement and pleasure from the singing of cheerful songs while enjoying a frugal meal . . . offering poetry and music a place where their works might be enjoyed as fully as possible'.[25] Most of its members came from the upper reaches of the civil service and from professions in the sciences and arts. Only members of the Singakademie who could write verse or compose music were accepted; most important, they had to be good singers, since they had to sight-read. The members' expenses were not inconsiderable: besides paying for a two-course meal they paid an entrance fee and a quarterly membership fee. As a rule only someone proposed by an existing member could join. None the less, membership was much sought after. The songs consisted principally of patriotic and cheerful choral pieces with a musical structure presenting no great difficulties, such as Zelter's *Und sitz' ich in der Schänke, bei einem Glase Wein, so denk' ich dein in Ehren, lieb Weib so hold und rein.*

Other societies were founded on the model of Zelter's Liedertafel. 1819 saw the formation of a second Liedertafel (its members including Bernhard Klein, E. T. A. Hoffmann and Theodor Körner), partly in reaction to the exclusiveness of Zelter's, and in 1829 Julius Schneider's Liederverein was founded (it merged with the 'provincial Liedertafel' in 1844). In 1842 Wieprecht and Flodoard Geyer founded an 'academy for men's voices' of which Franz Liszt was appointed honorary director in 1843. That year saw the founding – or rather reorganization – of the Berlin Cathedral choir, and in 1849 the Stern'sche Gesangverein gave its first public concert. After 1850 there was a great increase in the activities of male choruses, not least as a result of political and social developments. The *Taschenbuch für deutsche Sänger* (1864) mentioned no fewer than 89 choral societies, for mixed voices as well as male voices.[26] They all gave concerts, whether publicly or simply in the restaurant they frequented. Sometimes they provided support for each other's concerts, and at major performances large choirs often joined forces.

OTHER CONCERTS

Concerts given by musicians living in Berlin – including the royal Kapelle – were divided into those intended to serve 'art alone' (and of course the artist too) and those given as charity or benefit concerts primarily for non-musical reasons. The performer had to act as concert agent in charge of organization, from announcing the forthcoming concert to booking a suitable hall and selling tickets. In this, as with finding other musicians or even an orchestra, a musician was often dependent on the help of musical colleagues. Mutual help and support for such concerts was important, and musicians took it for granted.

After 1810 fewer occasional concerts were given by musicians resident in Berlin. One reason was that the number of regularly scheduled concerts and soirées increased. Their organization was in the hands of a few musicians who, not least because of their prominent positions in the royal Kapelle, could arrange them relatively easily and without too much risk – in particular of a financial nature. So musicians were more anxious to be heard performing at such events than to give a concert of their own (it was different, of course, once a musician had achieved a certain degree of fame). Another reason was the increase in concerts by foreign virtuosos. The standards and skill of these visiting musicians heightened public demands and expectations to such a degree that only the very best Berlin musicians could venture to stand comparison.

Benefit or charity concerts made up the larger part of the 'additional' events. Since their principal aim was to assemble as large an audience as possible, the programme had to be attractive, offering something for everyone. Consequently, in contrast to those concerts given strictly for art's sake, 'mixed programmes' were the order of the day, and they were given for a multiplicity of purposes. On 8 October 1800, for example, the 'Directorate of Fasch's Singakademie' put on 'a solemn and very well executed performance of Mozart's Requiem . . . to benefit the Citizens' Aid Institute'; the takings came to 'over

121

1500 talers'.[27] Birthdays of members of the royal family were often the occasion for a concert in aid of some appropriate charitable foundation. Particularly in the war and postwar years of 1813–17, concerts were given to assist citizens in need and soldiers and disabled veterans. At one, arranged by the Kapellmeister, Weber, on 8 May 1816, at which Beethoven's 'Battle Symphony' and his oratorio *Christus am Oelberge* were performed, over 1096 thalers were taken 'for an institute to be built for blinded defenders of the fatherland'. When Spontini was made musical director of the Berlin Opera in 1820, he received, among other things, the promise of an annual concert for his own benefit. Later, the takings went into the Spontini Foundation he had set up to support members of the opera orchestra and chorus. This is perhaps the only example of a benefit concert that nearly became an institution.

After 1830 benefits decreased in proportion to other concerts but they were never given up entirely. For instance, Count von Brühl organized a performance of Haydn's *Creation* in the garrison church 'for the benefit of the victims of the flood at Tilsit . . . which was heard by some 6000 people with the liveliest enthusiasm'.[28] In 1847 and 1848 a midday Sunday concert was given, 'in aid of the Berlin Institute for the Provision of Nourishment, and to provide the humble poor with free fuel', in the concert hall of the royal opera house 'in the

46. Interior of the concert hall in the Berlin Schauspielhaus: engraving by Thiele after Schinkel

presence of the royal family'.[29] When Lortzing died in Berlin in January 1851 many concerts were given 'to assist his bereaved family'.

At the same time, the expansion of musical activity resulted in concerts becoming more differentiated according to the performers, the audiences for which they were intended, the content of their programmes and their venues.[30] Thus more and more military bands, salon orchestras and choral societies, particularly male-voice choirs, gave charity concerts, since they appealed to almost all social classes. However, these and comparable concerts that did not serve art alone often received harsh criticism. For instance, the journal *Signale für die musikalische Welt* reported in 1850 that:

> the concerts held for charity, festive occasions and patriotic purposes, which are given for reasons of servility and personal interest, cut the ground from under the feet of true artistry . . . it is not usual for musical taste to reign supreme in them, as may be seen clearly enough from the poor state of public musical performances in Berlin, although the city has such a wealth of intelligent circles that good taste, now as ever, is very well represented indeed; yet the people of these circles prefer not to attend public musical performances, whose high prices are in disproportionate relation to their value, and will abandon such reticence only on certain special occasions when more enjoyment seems likely or the prevailing fashion in society demands it.[31]

After the 1848 revolution 'district concerts' financed by the lending banks were held in the various districts (over a hundred of them) into which the city had been divided in the summer of 1848 for political purposes. In 1850 the *Neue Berliner Musik-zeitung* commented:

> the institution of the lending banks mediates between music and politics. Music here, as so often, performs the noble function of moving people to charity and alleviating human suffering. Recognition should be paid to the fact that the most outstanding musical talents of Berlin, with altruistic readiness, have volunteered their services for these concerts, arranged in almost all districts of the city for the support of poor citizens of those areas.[32]

As charity concerts of this kind were given throughout the city, the venue frequently had to be a small room in an inn. That was not felt to be an obstacle, however, since these concerts were intended to appeal to members of those social classes which felt more at ease in familiar surroundings than in a concert hall. Moreover, a ball was often held after the musical performance, providing what was obviously a necessary incentive to attendance at the concerts themselves (this often meant that audiences, anxious to get the music over with, were inattentive and created something of a disturbance so that the dancing might begin).

*

Musicians from outside the city contributed a great deal to the varied musical life of Berlin. Except during the war years, Berlin was a profitable place for travelling artists, and their visits increased steadily, particularly after the first three decades of the nineteenth century. In part as a result, there was scarcely a day in the winter months when no concert was held. The organization and planning of concerts thus became more complicated. Whereas it had been possible at the beginning of the century to organize an ad hoc musical performance within a few days, such a concert was inconceivable around the middle of the century without long preparation and advance announcements. It was simpler for outside musicians to appear in an existing series, and they often performed at Möser's soirées. They were thus largely relieved of cares about the audience and the organization of the concert. The latter also applied to guest appearances by famous virtuosos which were usually arranged in advance by Berlin musicians or institutions, a state of affairs advantageous to both sides. The visit of the 47-year-old singer Catalani in 1827 is a good example; she prepared for her public appearance by singing at private soirées and the division of takings was typical, [33] as was her participation in several concerts where she sang arias not in the original key but transposed to a lower register.

Prices for concerts by visiting musicians seem to have been very high. On her first visit to Berlin in 1816, Catalani had asked 'three thalers for a seat in the hall, and four for one in a box'. Even at a charity concert on 27 July 1816, offering an 'opportunity for the less prosperous to hear this superb singer', the price of a ticket was 'only one thaler 12 groschen'. Despite these high prices, 'well above the common run', the singer gave eight concerts in June and July 1816, two 'for the benefit of charitable institutions'.[34]

A few of the concerts given by outside musicians may be mentioned here. On 13 March 1805 Louis Spohr and 'Demoiselle Alberghi from Dresden' performed together in the hall of the royal Nationaltheater. Weber and Heinrich Bärmann (first clarinettist in the Munich Kapelle) had great success with a concert they gave in Berlin on 15 March 1812 and had to give a second by popular request. Nicolò Paganini was also received with enthusiasm in March 1829, when he gave four concerts. From 1832 Clara Wieck (later to marry

47. Recital by Joseph Joachim and Clara Schumann: pastel (20 December 1854) by Adolph Menzel

Schumann) visited Berlin regularly. At first solo piano compositions made up most of her programmes but later she increasingly played the piano part in chamber music, supported by members of various Berlin chamber music societies. In 1832 the Müller brothers' string quartet from Brunswick excited much admiration.[35] In May 1838 Charles de Bériot and Pauline García gave two enthusiastically received concerts, and in the 1844–5 season Jenny Lind, the 'Swedish nightingale', was immensely successful in Berlin.

   Since there were now more and more musicians from outside staying in the city at the same time – whether preparing to give concerts or already in action – they would sometimes also perform in those of their colleagues. From the end of December 1841 until February 1842, Liszt not only gave eleven concerts of his own but took part in a great many others, for instance in those given by the Italian tenor Pantaleoni, 'thereby ensuring him a packed hall in the Hôtel de Russie', and in a benefit concert of the Society for the Support of Destitute Teachers.[36] Early in 1843 Liszt appeared in two of a series of four concerts given by the pianist Döhler, in which they played a sonata for piano duet by Moscheles and the well-known *Hexameron*, variations on themes from Bellini operas, by six composers. The piano virtuosos Dreyschock and Clara Wieck and the violin virtuoso Ernst, on the other hand, were in Berlin virtually at the same time during the winter of 1839–40, but never gave concerts together, though Pauline Viardot-García sang at a concert given by Clara Schumann on 1 March 1847.

48. Piano recital by Liszt: frontispiece to 'Berlin as it is and . . . drinks' (1842) by Adam Brennglas

OTHER MUSICAL VENTURES

At the theatre, music was not merely incidental in the narrow sense; there would be some kind of opening music (a sinfonia or overture) and it was usual to entertain the audience with music in the entr'actes (the intervals between acts). There were few things musicians liked less than having to play at the theatre – the pay was low, the audiences inattentive, the repertory constantly changing. Their performances were correspondingly lacklustre, as was public response. Accordingly, musicians living in Berlin or visiting the city were offered the chance of introducing themselves to the public in the entr'actes; in certain circumstances, and if they appealed to the audience enough, they might then give a concert of their own. This arrangement was advantageous to all concerned, especially as concerts between the acts of plays were soon being regularly announced in the press – and more or less comprehensively reviewed there as well. Whole symphonies might be performed in this way: 'The achievement of the Royal City Theatre orchestra deserves mention: it recently played Beethoven's "Pastoral" Symphony and his Eroica with great precision as entr'actes. The fact that these fine but difficult pieces of music had such a lively appeal to a rather mixed audience bears witness to the progress of intellectual culture'.[37]

There were other musical activities. For instance, in the autumn of 1816 a kind of *collegium musicum* was founded at the university, which on 23 March 1817 gave its first public concert, a 'musical entertainment', offering 'a symphony in D major by Mozart, a violin concerto by Kreuzer', Beethoven's Choral Fantasia and variations for piano as well as 'songs by Th. Körner (*Reiterlied, Schwertlied, Lützows Wilde Jagd*) set for four voices by C. M. von Weber, and a finale by Mozart'.[38] Earlier, in 1811, a 'society of thе students of this city' had given a concert 'in the hall of the Werkmeisterschen Museums'.[39]

Music must have flourished in the schools too. A report in the *Allgemeine musikalische Zeitung* of December 1819 tells us: 'No less happy has been the progress of the pupils' music society at the Berlin-Cologne Gymnasium. In their last concert, on the 4th, the young people performed Cherubini's *Lodoïska* and Beethoven's *Prometheus* overtures, and a symphony by A. Romberg, a violin concerto by A. Rode and a piano concerto by Dussek; they were much applauded and showed their talents and precision in a very pleasing way'.[40] In February 1837 the Cologne Real-Gymnasium gave a performance of Handel's *Samson*, conducted by the musical director Lecerf.

The *Neue Berliner musikalische Zeitung*, which began publication in 1844, arranged a series of free concerts for its subscribers in the same year, introducing 'younger talents in particular'.[41] The Society of Musicians arranged annual soirées and in 1849 celebrated the fifteenth anniversary of its foundation in its own concert hall. Music and literature came together in another very popular type of entertainment, the 'musical and declamatory soirées', as they were called, usually organized by actors and actresses.[42]

Music was often used to enrich and adorn functions of other kinds. On 6 January 1852, for instance, 'the exhibition of the six transparency pictures was closed to the accompaniment of singing by the royal Cathedral choir'; and the same year 'The exhibition of tableaux vivants, embellished by the accompaniment of vocal and instrumental music, [was] becoming more and more accepted in the higher reaches of our society'.[43] The royal orchestra under Meyerbeer and the cathedral choir and soloists had to take part in such 'exhibitions'. Special occasions, particularly festive royal events, were usually celebrated with suitable musical offerings. The festivities on the accession to the throne of King Friedrich Wilhelm IV, celebrated in October 1840, were on a particularly grand scale: as well as the music during divine service in the cathedral on 15 October (the day of the homage ceremonies) there was a performance of Naumann's *Vater Unser* in the garrison church and the Singakademie performed Handel's *Te Deum*.

The semi-public court concerts in the royal palace in Berlin or at Sanssouci were divided into those held with some regularity, the programmes of which had to be approved by the king, and those arranged for certain artists on the king's order. For a musician to perform in one of these concerts was not simply a special honour but a source of additional income. It is not possible to establish the criteria whereby this privilege was extended, but the degree of fame the artists enjoyed obviously played a considerable part. On 9 January 1847, for instance, one such court concert was held at the palace with a number of international musicians taking part: 'Mme Viardot-García sang an aria by Handel from the opera *Alcina*, some Spanish songs, and a duet from Rossini's *Semiramide* with Fräulein Tuczek. The Moralt brothers from Munich played the violin and cello. Mme Fechner from Warsaw appeared as pianist and Fräulein Jenny Thalheim from Vienna as harpist'.[44] Jenny Lind received particular marks of distinction. In 1847 she had:

> the honour of singing in a specially arranged court concert at Sanssouci. Besides their Majesties the King and Queen, the royal princes, the Archbishop of Ollmütz and the Prince of Weimar, heir to the throne, were present. Fräulein Jenny Lind was very well accompanied by Herr Meyerbeer, the General-Musikdirector, at the piano, and supported by the performance of two compositions for piano by the court pianist Dr Kullak.[45]

MUSICAL AND LITERARY SALONS

Concerts in private salons existed side by side with public concerts. They frequently served not just as musical entertainment but to introduce an artist to a small circle of influential and knowledgeable music-lovers in preparation for a public appearance. When great virtuosos performed at such private soirées it was usually out of friendship for the host. However, certain new works were given their first performances to a small audience on such occasions. Charitable purposes might also be the occasion of a private soirée, as might the anniversary of the birth or death of Haydn, Mozart or Beethoven.

Among the leading literary and musical salons of Berlin were those held by Karl and Rahel Varnhagen, the bookseller Hans Parthey, later his daughter Lili and son-in-law Bernhard Klein, and later still their daughter Elisabeth (who was married to the Egyptologist Richard Lepsius). Other salons were those of Abraham Mendelssohn, father of Felix, and Herz Beer, Meyerbeer's father. At quite an early date 'singing teas' were given in the Nicolai house by Parthey's parents-in-law. Salons were a mixture of political discussion club, coffee-house, musical and literary society and sometimes the setting for a convivial dance as well. Intellectuals, historians, philosophers, scientists, poets, writers, professional musicians and music-lovers, nobles, officers and well-to-do businessmen met there as well as representatives of the great Jewish families, in whose houses these gatherings were often held. All these made up the audience, and at least some also performed. The leading singers and instrumental soloists of the time were guests at salons: they included Sontag,

49. *'Die Theegesellschaft' ('singing tea'): painting (1850) by J.P. Hasenclever*

Paganini, Milder-Hauptmann, Lind, Joachim, Liszt, Clara and Robert Schumann and Moscheles. At the 'singing teas', as Zelter told Goethe, there were 'perhaps more than 50 such family circles which take pleasure in singing'; people with less musical training could join in. Gustav Parthey painted the picture of a musical salon at the Brüderstrasse house, with his future son-in-law Bernhard Klein (later Musikdirektor of Berlin University) acting as conductor. Oratorios by Handel (including *Judas Maccabaeus*, *Semele* and *Messiah*) were performed there, as were Mozart operas.

Members of the rising musical generation often presented their own work at salons, whether as singers, instrumentalists or composers. Such was the case in the Mendelssohns' house, for instance; young Felix could have his compositions performed by extremely gifted people, and at the same time he could submit himself to expert judgment, since guests at the house included Karl Friedrich Zelter, one of Felix's teachers, Adolph Bernhard Marx, Ferdinand Hiller, Eduard Rietz, Eduard Devrient, Moscheles, Weber, Spohr, Meyerbeer, Chopin and Liszt. Unfortunately we have few accounts of these musical occasions, but a letter written by Felix's mother on 27 February 1821 to her cousin Henriette von Pereia-Arnstein in Vienna may give at least some idea of them. She mentions Mendelssohn's first dramatic efforts:

> Dr Casper, who was with him in Paris last summer, was working on the libretto of an operetta while in that city, and Felix began setting it to music at the end of September. His father made it a condition

that no one was to hear anything about it until it was finished, and indeed, except for Fanny, no one saw so much as a note until rehearsals began. On his father's birthday, 11 December, the family sang it privately, to the piano . . . He expressed a lively wish to his librettist to hear it some time with full instrumental accompaniment, and no doubt you will have guessed that we fulfilled that wish. We chose 3 February, his birthday, when he reached his twelfth year, and the preparations, rehearsals, etc, entertained us not a little. A delightful theatre was erected in the big drawing room, all complete; the middle of the space was taken up by the orchestra, chosen from the best members of the royal Kapelle, with Felix seated at the piano among them. The back of the room was raised, and crammed with spectators. In the Singspiel, Fanny played the part of the chamber-maid, Stümer took a tenor part, and Dr Casper, . . . and a good friend of ours the bass parts.[46]

Mendelssohn's early operettas, such as *Die beiden Pädagogen* (1821), *Die wandernden Komödianten* (1822) and *Der Onkel aus Boston* (1822–3), may well have been performed in the same or a similar way. The last of his musico-dramatic works, *Die Heimkehr aus der Fremde* op.89, composed in 1829 for his parents' silver wedding anniversary on his return from England, was also performed in the parental home with the help of family members and friends. Eduard Devrient directed the performance. Other compositions by Mendelssohn, such as his early symphonies, chamber music and piano works, usually received their first performances there too.

In December 1826 there was a performance of Weber's *Oberon* in the house of the publisher Schlesinger: 'In front of a numerous company, Mme Schulz, Herr Stümer, etc, played most of the parts, accompanied on the fortepiano by Herr Dorn and Herr Felix Mendelssohn'.[47] When Henry Litolff first visited Berlin, in the summer of 1845, he was introduced at a private soirée.[48] It was followed by a series of public concerts at which the virtuoso was enthusiastically acclaimed. It is worth remembering, too, that the violinist Joseph Joachim was first heard at Fanny Hensel-Mendelssohn's musical Sundays in 1843.

The number of musical salons in Berlin was clearly increasing, thus giving rise to differences in both musical quality and in the social composition of the 'audience'; to an ever greater extent, salons seem to have constituted a counterweight to the extensive public musical life of the city, which could hardly any longer provide people with a comfortable sense of being among kindred spirits. They were also places where contemporary music received encouragement.

OTHER ASPECTS OF THE 'MUSIC BUSINESS'

At Carnival, concert life in the city came to a halt. Instead there were great numbers of masked balls and other dances of all kinds. And they all required music. We do not know exactly who the musicians were on such occasions or what music they performed but we can get a general idea; for instance, we are told that in 1832 'the Carnival is still in full swing. The masked balls in the Colosseum, like the subscription court balls in the concert hall of the Royal Theatre, are much attended, and in addition there are a great many private musical soirées and balls'.[49] And February 1841 is said to have been 'as rich in music and dancing as in snow and ice'. Apparently there was a ' "superfluity" of balls and masquerades, but fewer concerts than soirées were held'.[50]

The 600–700 people who came annually to 'take the cure' at the Struve-Soltmann Mineral Water Spa, opened on 2 July 1823, also had musical entertainment. The spa orchestra, the composition of which remains unknown, played in a pavilion in the garden in summer and in the hall of the establishment in winter. This orchestra was engaged on a permanent basis. Music also seems to have played a special part 'in Herr Werner's excellent coffee-house in Unter den Linden', a kind of 'artists' café':

50. *Dancing at the Berger's dance hall, Berlin: engraving (c1795)*

> The Thursday soirées of Herr Musikdirektor Beutler, held in Herr Werner's café, are very popular in a select and lively circle, on account of the variety of entertainment offered by instrumental music, singing, supper and sociable dancing, and it has particular charms in the presence of interesting lady performers such as Mme Devrient and the very proficient harpist Fräulein von Holst from London.[51]

Entertainments in restaurants were also the occasion for introducing new and (generally) mechanical musical instruments, such as a 'phisharmonica' and a 'flageolet' introduced in 1830 'at the Tivoli'.[52]

Concerts featuring foreign folksongs and folk music were always received in Berlin with acclaim and much admiration for the performers, as can be seen for instance in the success of Mme Viardot-García with her Spanish songs. Other successful performers included the 'five Rainers from the Tyrol' with their folksongs,[53] and 'the 40 Pyrenean singers' who made 'a great impression in the illuminated garrison church' with their singing in 1841 and made another guest appearance in 1851.[54]

MILITARY BANDS AND PRIVATE ORCHESTRAS

The character of musical activity on a popular level, however, was determined by the military bands and in particular by the so-called 'private orchestras' or 'salon orchestras', which became increasingly common from 1840. They gave their concerts in halls, but also in large restaurants and similar establishments and outside during the summer. There was scarcely an open-air restaurant in the suburbs that had no music.

The first report of a concert by a military band with a military male-voice choir dates from 1821.[55] One reason why it was mentioned may have been that it took place on 1 December in the Jagor Hall, a proper concert hall; another could have been that the programme was much the same as those of the familiar 'traditional' concerts which offered mixed programmes, in this case nine items, including overtures by Spontini and Méhul, excerpts from operas by Gluck, Boieldieu and Weber. Also, it was a charity concert attended by the king. The reviewers praised not only the fine execution of the works but the way they had been arranged for wind instruments, apparently by Weller, director of the military band of the 2nd Regiment of Guards, which gave the concert. The choir was conducted by its chorus master Leidel. From then on frequent mention was made of both in the musical press. The band must indeed have been very good, for in 1823, at a large vocal and instrumental concert in the hall of the Royal Theatre, its musical director G. A. Schneider ventured to perform a work of his own, a 'Jubilee Overture for two choirs, performed by the royal Kapelle and the choir of the 2nd Regiment of Guards'.[56] Concerts by military bands included solo concert pieces. Weller and Neidhart[57] were the best-known directors of military music at this time.

An 'entertainment' at the Tivoli, organized by the singer Blume in 1830, was reported in the *Allgemeine musikalische Zeitung*:

> Wind music alternated with four-part songs and choruses (of male voices) . . . Most suitable for the time and place was the battle music played by the military band out of doors . . . Such an entertainment is to be held once a month during the summer at the Tivoli, which is now the favourite pleasure garden of the people of Berlin. Every Sunday, music for wind band and fireworks are included in the admission price of ten groschen. The usual kind of military concerts also take place in other pleasure gardens near the city. Weller's band is notable, like Neidhart's, for its precision and the excellent arrangements of well-chosen operatic pieces, overtures and symphonies, even symphonies by Beethoven.[58]

This is the first mention of the performances by wind bands of Beethoven's symphonies and his 'Battle Symphony', which became an established part of the musical life of Berlin. (Beethoven's symphonies were not the only ones to be arranged in this way; symphonies by Haydn and Mozart were performed too.)

These open-air concerts offered a wider public the chance of hearing and becoming acquainted with music usually played only in the concert hall before a well-defined audience. But that audience too enjoyed open-air concerts, regarding them as a kind of continuation of the winter season. They were thus considered almost on a par with other concerts in the musical life of the city. It is scarcely surprising that with the popularity of military music and the high level of accomplishment of all the bands stationed in Berlin, outdoor concerts were sometimes on a very large scale.

The organization of such concerts was facilitated when in 1838 Wilhelm Friedrich Wieprecht, who had been a violinist in the court theatre since 1824, was appointed director of all the guards' military ensembles. Taking over from Schneider, he had all these bands at his disposal. He worked to improve the programmes of military concerts, and earned much praise for his reorganization of Prussian military music. His concerts must have been on a very high musical level, for in 1845 even the journal *Signale* wrote of one:

> The number of performers was about 130 military bandsmen. The programme began with Richard Wagner's overture to *Rienzi*. (Other works played were Meyerbeer's overture to *Das Feldlager* and Mendelssohn's overture *Meeresstille und glückliche Fahrt*.) The major

work of the evening was the Eroica Symphony – heroic in performance as well. Several marches and a torch dance by Meyerbeer were
very effective.[59]

After the 1840s, military music experienced stiff competition from
the increasing number of 'private orchestras' or 'salon orchestras'.
Concerts of wind music alone were no longer in demand. The military
bands had to adapt: their members learnt to play string as well as
wind instruments so they could also offer the repertory of the salon
orchestras. In 1849 Wieprecht was able to found an orchestral
ensemble called 'Euterpe', mainly made up of former military bands-
men. Together with the Hofkapelle this ensemble was available for
concerts and was soon giving its own subscription concerts. Most
important, it could also provide a replacement for any kind of military
band in large concerts.

Johann Strauss the elder and his orchestra (enlarged to 28 musicians
in 1833) paid a successful visit to Berlin in December 1834; at first he
had no perceptible effect on concert activities – at least, no orchestra
'à la Strauss' was formed. But from 1840 onwards a great number of
such private orchestras sprang up. They were the 'modern' orchestras,
their repertories ranging from dance music to the Classical symphony.
They usually gave weekly concerts, performing not only music by
Haydn, Mozart, Beethoven, Weber and Mendelssohn but also works
by contemporary composers such as Richard Würst and August
Conradi. The orchestra was generally reinforced on these occasions
and the programmes were much like those of the established concerts.
Sometimes a symphony formed merely the second part of a programme
divided into three large sections. The quality of these orchestras seems
to have been outstanding, the difference between them and the
concerts of the royal Kapelle thus consisting mainly in their admission
price: the music played by the Kapelle for an exclusive audience for a
thaler could reach a wider public for two and a half or five groschen.[60]
When Josef Gungl arrived with his orchestra in 1843 he immediately
endeared himself to the people of Berlin by his relatively low ticket
prices.

The number of concerts given by these salon orchestras increased,
not just in the summer but in winter too. There was even a
subscription for the concerts held at the Kroll establishment. The
venues and the quality of the orchestra affected the constitution of the
audience. In this respect, Gungl was the clear favourite of elegant
society. However, he was also the favourite of the musical 'progressive'
party in Berlin, since he and his orchestra performed works not played
at the royal Kapelle concerts, not least because of the influence of the
prevailing school of musical criticism led by Ludwig Rellstab. Gungl's
orchestra must have been extremely good: 'He has fine talents in his

orchestra, and he can get them because he pays them just as well as the members of the royal Kapelle are paid. Schubert's Symphony in C major, and Gade's Symphony in C minor, have been repeated several times'.[61]

Intense as competition was between the private orchestras and between conductors like Gungl, Laade, Liebig, Canthal, Hünerfürst, Manns, Strauss, Meyer and Engel, they all showed great solidarity when a colleague was in need. Not only was a joint concert given in aid of the Lortzing family, but when there was a fire at Kroll's in which the orchestra and its conductor Manns lost their instruments and printed music, another joint concert was organized on their behalf.

The private orchestras had now become considerably more important than the royal Kapelle in Berlin concert life because of their numbers and their custom of giving a weekly concert with a serious programme. Their quality and skill can hardly be overestimated. It should be remembered that later, under Julius Stern, Liebig's Kapelle became the Berlin Symphony Kapelle, and that Bilse's Kapelle, active in Berlin from 1867 onwards, gave rise to the Berlin Philharmonic Orchestra in 1882. Nor can it be too strongly emphasized that these private orchestras had to adapt to public taste more than the royal Kapelle did: they lived, after all, by their audiences. They had a special educational importance too. Not only did they allow citizens of the humbler social classes, including students, to hear the works of great composers, they also, most significantly, gave the rising musical generation a chance to gain experience by performing in works that used a reinforced orchestra. It was such orchestras that really made Berlin a city of music.

*

The varied picture Berlioz painted of musical life in the city in 1842–3 is borne out by the article on Berlin in Meyer's *Konversations-Lexikon* (1862):

> Much was also done for intellectual entertainment, as promoted by plays, concerts, and similar pleasures ... Concerts of great importance were those given by the royal cathedral choir and the symphony concerts of the royal Kapelle, as well as the performances of the Singakademie. The majority of major artists, both of Berlin and from outside, gave concerts in the city; in summer there was no lack of military concerts, and the concerts given by the Liebig Kapelle deserve special mention here, their fine execution and low prices of admission having a most beneficial effect upon the formation of taste in the city. Very attractive to the public of Berlin as a whole, with their concerts and dances, are the Elysium and the grandiose

> Kroll establishment, where people of high and low degree assemble, some as performers, others as spectators ... Two very tasteful pleasure gardens in Berlin are known as 'flower gardens', the Teichmann in the Thiergarten Strasse, and the Möwe in Potsdamerstrasse. The Kroll and Faust establishments are the finest of the winter gardens, and the Kroll gardens by the Brandenburg Gate outdo anything else of the present kind in Germany in size and elegance; other 'flower gardens' are those of the Empress of Russia and of the Hennig brothers.

And yet lively as the musical life of Berlin looked on the outside, it eventually stagnated. The same works were performed almost the whole time and the activities of the private orchestras made little difference. The Berlin public, led by the music critics who set the tone, was basically conservative. Consequently, progressive musicians could get a hearing only very slowly and with great difficulty: they objected to the rigidly stereotyped programmes of the musical institutions and to the attitude of music criticism which led public taste down a one-way street. As early as 1831, Gottfried Wilhelm Fink, editor of the *Allgemeine musikalische Zeitung*, wrote:

> In the sphere of concert and chamber music we also suffer from great imbalance, arising from the routine of custom and convenience, and lack of acquaintance with the meritorious works of recent times ... We get nothing but frequent repetitions of the quartets of Haydn, Mozart and Beethoven, although of course they are fine works at any time, of the last-named composer's magnificent symphonies, and of the same cycle of operas by Auber, Rossini, with a few Singspiels by Mozart or from France.[62]

In 1848 there were 53 performances of symphonies by Beethoven, from among nos.1–8, almost as many as there were performances of symphonies by Haydn (36) and Mozart (20) put together. Only three new symphonies were played. From 1 January to 31 March 1849 (still in the 1848–9 season) there were 24 performances of Beethoven's symphonies, including a complete performance of the Ninth, fourteen of symphonies by Haydn, three of symphonies by Mozart and two of symphonies by other composers.

The question therefore was no longer one of whether music was being played but of what was performed. New music, even then, was unpopular with the public. So at first, despite all efforts, things mostly remained the same. Only in 1846 and thereafter was the problem addressed again, and intensively; proposals were even made for founding another orchestra principally to perform modern works. In 1846 Hieronymus Friedrich Truhn wrote with cutting sarcasm on the deficiencies of Berlin concerts and in 1848 he even drew up a 'thermometer chart of symphony soirées'.[63]

If efforts were being made about 1850 to bring more liveliness and modernity to the concerts of the major institutions and their programmes, and if a more objective and open-minded attitude could now be discerned in concert criticism, then after 1848 another aspect came to the fore: an endeavour to acquaint the middle and lower classes of society with works by great composers to a wider extent than previously. As G. Engel put it in 1850:

> It is now over ten years since open-air concerts, at which dances, light overtures and so forth were customarily performed, began to rise rather above their usual level. During the summer, excellent orchestras began performing symphonies as well as the customary kind of light music, first in the so-called 'flower gardens', giving concerts once a week. Soon the Liebig Kapelle followed suit: Friday was the usual day set aside for classical music; younger composers being in the lead. Less successful was a similar venture made at the Kroll establishment: concerts of this kind were not so popular as to make the big hall there suitable for them, and soon they ceased again, but they have been revived by Wieprecht, who for some time has been giving large concerts at Kroll's on Sundays. Their programmes are very varied, including four-part works for male voices and symphonies as well as overtures, dances etc. The prime objective was to make classical music accessible to the usual Sunday audience, and its great popularity is proof of the heights to which musical taste has risen in all circles of Berlin.[64]

NOTES

[1] Ninth letter, to M. Demarest, in *The Memoirs of Hector Berlioz*, ed. and trans. D. Cairns (New York, rev. 3/1975).

[2] See A. Meyer-Hanno, *Georg Abraham Schneider (1770–1839) und seine Stellung im Musikleben Berlins* (Berlin, 1965), 53.

[3] *AMZ* (1799), cols.271–2.

[4] The following figures can be drawn from H. J. Meyer, *Neues Konversations-Lexikon*, iii (Leipzig, 2/1862), 243, and ii (Leipzig, 4/1888), 756; and from B. Hofmeister, *Bundesrepublik Deutschland und Berlin*, i (Berlin and Darmstadt, 1975), 13, 50: *c*1800 – 172,000 (including *c*33,300 soldiers); 1804 – 182,157; 1815 – 193,000 (according to the municipal statutes); 1820 – 201,900 (including 16,071 soldiers); 1840 – 309,950; 1848 – 419,000; 1849 – 410,726; 1855 – 420,000. The *Vossische Zeitung* of 31 Jan 1848 speaks of 'some 450,000 inhabitants'.

[5] See also C.-H. Mahling, 'Music and Places for the Performance of Music as a Reflection of Urban Social Stratification in the 19th and Early 20th Century', in *IMSCR*, xii *Berkeley 1977*, 307–11.

[6] F. Geyer, 'Ein Beitrag zur Geschichte der Gegenwart', *Berliner musikalische Zeitung*, iii (1846).

[7] *Signale für die musikalische Welt*, viii (Leipzig, 1850), 242–3.

[8] *AMZ* (1802), col.222.

[9] *AMZ* (1804), cols.248–9; a 'resumé' of the concerts is added as a survey. See also ibid, cols.481–2. In the 1804–5 season the concerts were given in groups of eight and four; see *AMZ* (1805), col.255.

[10] *AMZ* (1807–8), col.558.

[11] As the orchestra consisted of professionals as well as amateurs, its existence was immediately endangered if it was made difficult for professional musicians to perform. In addition the theatre hall was exclusively reserved for performances by the royal Kapelle; see

The Early Romantic Period

AMZ (1811), cols.605–8.

[12] *AMZ* (1812), cols.274 and 319.

[13] *AMZ* (1821), cols.29, 249–59 and 348; see also *Zeitung für Theater und Musik*, i (Berlin, 1821), 31.3.

[14] *AMZ* (1825), cols.669–70.

[15] *Berliner Allgemeine musikalische Zeitung*, iii (1826), 242 and 246f; see also *AMZ* (1826), col.611.

[16] *AMZ* (1832), col.75.

[17] F. Geyer, 'Ein Beitrag zur Geschichte der Gegenwart, 2', *Berliner musikalische Zeitung*, iii (1846).

[18] *AMZ* (1832), cols.331–2.

[19] *AMZ* (1833), cols. 820–21.

[20] *AMZ* (1802), col.397.

[21] This Philharmonic Society is not to be confused with the Philharmonic Association founded later by Leopold Ganz; see *AMZ* (1836), col.793.

[22] See *Signale für die musikalische Welt*, i (1843), 371, and ii (1844), 2 and 67.

[23] *AMZ* (1830), col.251.

[24] *AMZ* (1844), col.79.

[25] H. Kuhlo, *Geschichte der Zelterschen Liedertafel von 1809 bis 1909* (Berlin, 1909), 22.

[26] *Taschenbuch für deutsche Sänger*, i, ed. E. Kral (Vienna, 1864), 16.

[27] *AMZ* (1800), col.87.

[28] *AMZ* (1837), col.472; a later report (ibid, col.553), mentions an attendance of 'over 4000 persons'.

[29] *Neue Berliner Musik-zeitung*, i (1847), 33, and ii (1848), 44.

[30] See Mahling, 'Music and Places'.

[31] *Signale für die musikalische Welt*, viii (1850), 242–3.

[32] *Neue Berliner Musik-zeitung*, iv (1850), 130.

[33] Sharing the profits often led to complications, as when the famous singer Gertrud Elisabeth Mara gave several concerts with the royal Kapelle during her guest performances in Berlin in February 1803; see *AMZ* (1803), cols.406–7, 408–9 and 452–3.

[34] *AMZ* (1816), cols. 500 and 604.

[35] *Iris im Gebiete der Tonkunst*, iii (1832), 100.

[36] *AMZ* (1842), cols.236 and 291.

[37] *AMZ* (1834), cols.111–12 and 157.

[38] *AMZ* (1817), col.279.

[39] *AMZ* (1811), col.229.

[40] *AMZ* (1820), col.51.

[41] *AMZ* (1844), col.242.

[42] One such soirée was held on 11 December 1843 in the hall of the Hôtel de Russie, with 'about a dozen artists and virtuosi': *Signale für die musikalische Welt*, ii (1844), 2; see also *Berliner Musikzeitung Echo*, iii (1853), 29.

[43] *Berliner Musikzeitung Echo*, ii (1852), 14 and 38.

[44] *Neue Berliner Musik-zeitung*, i (1847), 34.

[45] Ibid., 350.

[46] Quoted from R. Elvers, 'Hausmusik bei Mendelssohns 1821', in *Das Liebhaberorchester* (Berlin, 1961), 9.

[47] *AMZ* (1827), col.60. 'A few days later Herr Schlesinger put on a version of . . . Weber's *Oberon* in his fine room, giving us a foretaste of what a future performance of the opera will provide'.

[48] *AMZ* (1845), col.745; see also R. Hagemann, *Henry Litolff*, privately published (Herne, 1978), especially p.10.

[49] *AMZ* (1832), col.219.

[50] *AMZ* (1841), col.245.

[51] *AMZ* (1831), col.15.

[52] *AMZ* (1830), col.408.

[53] *Berliner Allgemeine musikalische Zeitung*, iii (1826), 413.

[54] *Iris im Gebiete der Tonkunst*, xii (1841), 68; see also *Echo*, i (1851), 29.

[55] *Zeitung für Theater und Musik*, i (Berlin, 1821), 194; *AMZ* (1822), col.39.

[56] *Zeitung für Theater, Musik und bildende Künste*, iii (1823), 199.

[57] The spelling of his name differs: it may be Neidhard, Neidhart or Neithardt.

[58] *AMZ* (1830), cols.491–2. Mention is made in June 1830 (*AMZ*, col.409) of the fact that 'now . . . the garden concerts out of doors' are beginning again. A popular feature was the combination of music and fireworks; see, for example, the *Vossische Zeitung* (11 May 1831).

[59] *Signale für die musikalische Welt*, iii (1845), 229–30; see also *Echo*, ii (1852), 239.

[60] See C.-H. Mahling, 'Zur Frage der "Bürgerlichkeit" der bürgerlichen Musikkultur im 19. Jahrhundert', *Musica*, i (1977), 13ff; 'Zur Beethoven-Rezeption in Berlin in den Jahren 1830 bis 1850', *Beethoven Congress: Berlin 1977*, 351.

[61] *Signale für die musikalische Welt*, v (1847), 349.

[62] *AMZ* (1831), cols.379–80.

[63] *AMZ* (1848), cols.146–7.

[64] G. Engel, 'Bildender Einfluss der Bezirks-Concerte', *Neue Berliner Musik-zeitung*, iv (1850), 129ff. The 'Sunday audience' mentioned here contained all classes of society, particularly the artisan and working class.

BIBLIOGRAPHICAL NOTE

The extensive body of literature on the musical history of Berlin includes many publications not strictly speaking academic. Some of the more popular studies, however, offer remarkably lively pictures of musical life. The following list contains only major works devoted to musical life in Berlin in general and the city during the first half of the nineteenth century in particular. Basic surveys are given in the articles on Berlin in *MGG* and (more briefly) in *Grove 6*.

For a general discussion emphasizing the operatic and concert repertories of the Berlin Hofkapelle and royal opera see A. Weissmann, *Berlin als Musikstadt: Geschichte der Oper und des Konzerts von 1740 bis 1911* (Berlin and Leipzig, 1911). Further publications on the history of the royal theatre and opera in Berlin are A. E. Brachvogel, *Geschichte des Kgl. Theaters zu Berlin*, 2 vols. (Berlin, 1877–8); J. Kapp, *Geschichte der Staatsoper Berlin* (Berlin, 1942); H. Fetting, *Die Geschichte der Deutschen Staatsoper* (Berlin, 1955); and W. Otto, *Geschichte der deutschen Staatsoper Berlin: von der Gründung der Kapelle bis zur Gegenwart* (Berlin, 3/1969).

Specialist essays and new material on the music in Berlin in the first half of the nineteenth century may be found in *Studien zur Musikgeschichte Berlins im frühen 19. Jahrhundert*, ed. C. Dahlhaus, Studien zur Musikgeschichte des 19. Jahrhunderts, lvi (Regensburg, 1980). The beginnings of public musical activity among the middle classes are the subject of A. Meyer-Hanno's *Georg Abraham Schneider (1770–1839) und seine Stellung im Musikleben Berlins* (Berlin, 1965). The growing importance of choral singing is traced in G. Schünemann's *Die Singakademie zu Berlin 1791–1941* (Regensburg, 1941) and H. Kuhlo's *Geschichte der Zelterschen Liedertafel von 1809 bis 1909* (Berlin, 1909). There is an account of the development of male-voice choirs in *Taschenbuch für deutsche Sänger*, ed. E. Kral (Vienna, 1864). The literary and musical salons that played such a special role in the musical life of Berlin are at the centre of R. Elvers, 'Hausmusik bei Mendelssohns 1821', in *Das Liebhaberorchester* (Berlin, 1961); K. Höcker, *Hauskonzerte in Berlin* (Berlin, 1970); and I. Drewitz, *Berliner Salons: Gesellschaft und Literatur zwischen Aufklärung und Industriezeitalter* (Berlin, 3/1984).

Eyewitness accounts of music and musical life in Berlin are part of *The Memoirs of Hector Berlioz*, ed. and trans. D. Cairns (New York, rev. 3/1975), and E. T. A. Hoffmann's 'Briefe über die Tonkunst in Berlin', in *Schriften zur Musik* (Munich, 1963). The best and most topical information, however, comes from contemporary newspapers and music journals, such as the paper that appeared six times a week (every day but Monday) from 1810, the *Königlich privilegierte Berlinische Zeitung von Staats- und gelehrten Sachen*; also known as *Vossische Zeitung*, it contained theatre programmes, concert announcements and reviews by Ludwig Rellstab and others. Another general paper was the *Haude- und Spenersche Zeitung*, published in Berlin from 1808.

The Early Romantic Period

Music journals published in Berlin include: *Zeitung für Theater und Musik* (1821–; after its third year of publication it was known as the *Zeitung für Theater, Musik und bildende Künste*); *Berliner Allgemeine musikalische Zeitung* (1824–); *Berliner Musikalische Zeitung* (1844–); *Neue Berliner Musik-zeitung* (1847–); and *Berliner Musikzeitung Echo* (1851–). Musical activities in Berlin were also covered by the following journals circulating throughout Germany and Austria: *Allgemeine musikalische Zeitung [AMZ]* (Leipzig, 1799–); *Iris im Gebiete der Tonkunst* (Berlin, 1830–); and *Signale für die musikalische Welt* (Leipzig, 1843–).

Chapter V

Dresden and Leipzig:
Two Bourgeois Centres

SIEGHART DÖHRING

The musical history of Dresden and Leipzig in the early nineteenth century illustrates, with particular clarity, aesthetic and ideological tendencies in the development of a national and middle-class musical culture. In these two cities, as throughout Germany at the time, the classes of society that set the cultural tone were much concerned with the idea of national music, in particular a national opera to be at least equal, and if possible superior, to Italian and French models. In the field of instrumental music, German composers had produced major works in the very recent past; but though a national continuation of this tradition was seen as desirable, it was not yet assured.

There was a considerable gulf between the idea and the reality of a national art, particularly in the sphere of opera, with all the prestige it carried: about 1800 there were only the rudiments of German opera as an independent genre. The fact that the national drama so desired in the eighteenth century did now exist was both an incentive and a source of misconception. The plays of Lessing, Schiller and Goethe were felt to be specifically German literature, even though their historical stature was actually founded on their universal aesthetic qualities and their claims to worldwide validity. The way in which the champions of a German national opera closed their eyes to these tendencies, countering the aesthetic cosmopolitanism of the great European capitals with a national 'Aesthetik der Provinz',[1] can be interpreted only as the expression of a deep-rooted sense of inferiority concealed by aggressive polemics. The only freedom of discussion for the politically powerless middle classes was in the realm of art: they could express their political convictions through their views of the arts. Although the successful resistance to Napoleon's campaign of conquest in 1813 gave strong encouragement to the national movement throughout Germany, the restoration of the old order meant that German backwardness was felt all the more acutely by those keener intelligences who could not but recognize defeated France as a culturally superior, more liberal and thus more progressive nation.

The outcome of the war had particularly unfortunate consequences for the kingdom of Saxony and its two major cities, Dresden and Leipzig. In addition to military sacrifices, peace brought material and political burdens. Since King Friedrich Augustus I had supported Napoleon and was thus on the losing side, conquered Saxony was put under a Russian and then a Prussian governor-general. In 1815 the Congress of Vienna restored the kingdom to its former ruler, but only as a rump state reduced to less than half its size because of the territories ceded to Prussia. These events plunged the politically and culturally committed middle classes into a crisis of identity. This was particularly so in traditionally conservative Dresden, and to a lesser extent in the more modern city of Leipzig. Because of the lack of financial means for putting liberal ideas into practice, the people saw themselves thrust back into an authoritarian order from which, in spite of all disillusionments, they were nevertheless unable to detach themselves. This conflict between aspirations and the ability to realize them encouraged resentment against everything foreign – and consequently led to intellectual isolation. Typical of the climate of provincial mediocrity, for instance, was the Dresden Liederkreis, a society of local writers and artists which influenced the city's cultural life for a long period and tried to counteract the impact of its most important native poet, Ludwig Tieck. This lack of cosmopolitan outlook, to which various contemporary observers bear witness, must be borne in mind if we are to understand the national party's vehement attacks on Italian opera and its uncritical championing of the German genre.

DRESDEN

Musical development proceeded in the two cities with emphasis on different areas, an outcome of their different social structures. Opera, the most ostentatious of musical genres, was dominant in the capital city of Dresden. There had been an Italian court opera since 1667, when it was the third such institution to be founded in the German-speaking states. It reached its zenith under Hasse in the mid-eighteenth century but was dissolved in 1763 as a consequence of Saxony's defeat in the Seven Years' War. For several decades, private opera companies subsidized by the court took its place. At the same time, in the second half of the eighteenth century, the German Singspiel became established as a popular genre, particularly with the performances by Joseph Seconda's company in the Theater auf dem Linckeschen Bade outside the city.

In 1813 the Russian governor-general merged the Italian opera, the German theatre and the Hofkapelle into a 'state institution'. After the king's return, this state institution was dissolved and a new Italian Hofoper was set up on 1 January 1817. A few weeks later a German

51. The Königliches Hoftheater, Dresden, built by Gottfried Semper (1837–41): anonymous lithograph

Opera was associated with it. The Italian Opera existed as an independent body until 1832. After decades of makeshift performing arrangements, the magnificent Hoftheater built by Gottfried Semper in 1841 symbolized the concentration of musical life in Dresden, now as previously, on opera. Concerts given by the 'musical academies' of the Hofkapelle were always of secondary importance, and so was chamber music; regular public performances of chamber music by quartets consisting of members of the court orchestra began about 1811, though they did not become a formal institution until the Tonkünstlerverein was founded in 1856. The societies known as the Dreyssigsche Singakademie (founded in 1807) and the Liedertafel (founded in 1830) were on the pattern of their famous Berlin models.

The setting-up of an independent German Opera as part of the Hofkapelle in 1817, under the direction of Carl Maria von Weber, was an innovation not only for Dresden but for the entire German-speaking area. Apart from those municipal operas formed about 1700 in completely different historical and artistic circumstances, its only precursor was the National Singspiel in Vienna, founded by Joseph II in 1778, which lasted for ten years. The decision to set up a German Opera in Dresden should not be regarded as an expression of artistic bias in favour of German music, since the continued existence of a specifically Italian Opera was assured at the same time, in conditions that clearly show that court sympathy was on its side. A major factor in the decision was the personal support of von Vitzthum, the

143

theatre manager: his belief that popular German operas would be more profitable carried weight with the court, which was in a state of financial weakness.

The historical significance of the undertaking should not lead us to overestimate its immediate effect. By international standards, the Dresden Opera was not in the first rank and its German section was provincial. Weber soon found that his artistic ambitions were severely hampered by an orchestra of only average ability, a weak chorus and poor soloists and most of all by a largely uneducated public with unsophisticated tastes. With a few exceptions, such as the brief engagement of the young Wilhelmine Schröder-Devrient, the soloists were actors with some singing ability. By dint of exhausting work, Weber succeeded in raising standards, but he was never able to make the German company as important as its Italian counterpart. On the whole German opera remained a popular entertainment and Weber had to accept the painful fact that his contemptuous comment on the Prague public could equally be applied to the audience at his German Opera in Dresden: 'Kasperl is just the thing for them'.[2]

In any case, the repertory of a genuine German opera company was only just coming into being. In particular, apart from a few more or less experimental exceptions, there were no large-scale vernacular operas. The repertory mainly consisted of Singspiels, Liederspiels and musical burlesques. Moreover, the term 'German operas' in the superficial sense was taken to include all works performed in the German language, including those merely translated. Thus the repertory included not only Mozart's *Die Entführung aus dem Serail* (performed in 1818) and *Die Zauberflöte* (1818), but also *Don Giovanni* (1821), as well as Weigl's *Das Waisenhaus* (1817) and *Die Schweizerfamilie* (1818), Himmel's *Fanchon* (1817) and Kauer's *Das Donauweibchen* (1821), Méhul's *Joseph* (1817) and *Hélène* (1817), Cherubini's *Lodoïska* (1817) and *Les deux journées* (1819), Boïeldieu's *Jean de Paris* (1817), Isouard's *Cendrillon* (1819) and other mainly French operas. Contemporary German operas of good quality were rare: they included Spohr's *Jessonda* (1824), Weber's *Der Freischütz*, which he produced in Dresden in the year of its Berlin première (1821), and *Euryanthe*, whose success in Dresden in 1824 compensated for its lukewarm reception at its Viennese première the previous year.[3]

The artistic aspirations of Weber as *praeceptor Germaniae* in the field of opera were completely at odds with this situation. He saw his championship of German opera not least as an educational task, and he used the local press as well as the stage as his forum. He introduced his new productions with the publication of 'Musico-Dramatic Notes' intended 'to facilitate the assessment of those operas appearing for the first time at the Royal Theatre of Dresden

52. Carl Maria von Weber: portrait by Ferdinand Schimon (1797–1857)

by providing information on their artistic history'. Of particular significance was the article of 1820 in which he introduced to the Dresden public *Emma di Resburgo*, the successful Italian opera by his old friend Meyerbeer. After dismissing the work's alleged 'Rossini fever' as a passing aberration on the part of Meyerbeer's 'genius', he ended by expressing his hope that the composer would soon 'return to his German fatherland and join those few who truly respect art, helping to construct a national German opera . . . and thus at last establishing us in that position among artistic nations whose foundations in German opera were so firmly laid by Mozart'.[4] This article provoked vigorous controversy in the press – and Weber again joined in. A section of the public, and some critics, were very much on his side. Thus one critic hailed the success of Weber's *Euryanthe* in Dresden as not just an artistic but a national event: 'Truly, it is not one man's triumph of which we speak, but a triumph of German music itself, shared with its consecrated priest! Hail to German art, showing us yet again, with this masterpiece, that it may enter the lists with all other European nations!'[5]

Legitimate as Weber's endeavours on behalf of a national German opera may seem in principle, the strongly ideological character of his argument is unmistakable. A polarizing opposition of Italian to

German opera, as propounded by Weber in journalism following 'patriotic' lines, contradicts the facts. This is particularly true of Dresden, where German opera, still under-developed, presented no serious competition to the long tradition of Italian opera – a fact that could be ignored only by taking a coloured view. At the beginning of the nineteenth century Italian opera was no longer solely Italian, nor was German opera yet independently German. Since the mid-eighteenth century, Italian and French opera had moved towards each other in a process of mutual exchange, producing hybrid genres which also included elements of Classical Viennese instrumental music. Stylistic borrowing from Italian and French opera had always been a condition of the existence of German opera, which was really still Singspiel. To insist about 1820 on a specifically national path in opera was to run counter to its actual development, which was tending towards a universal style of music drama and a synthesis of genres. In Dresden this tendency was represented by the two last Italian Hofkapellmeisters, Ferdinando Paer and Francesco Morlacchi, and finally – contradicting his artistic theories – by Weber himself in his last operas.

Paer, a native of Parma, was a celebrity in Europe in 1802 when he was appointed to the Dresden court (initially in a guest capacity). His opera *Camilla*, written for Vienna in 1799, had provided a good example of the new mixed genre uniting elements of the *opera buffa* and *opéra comique* with the modernized type of *opera seria*. Paer's sound command of technique and richness of instrumental colour were the result of a thorough study of Mozart's works. He developed this style further in his Dresden operas, *I fuorusciti di Firenze* (1802), *Sargino* (1803) and in particular *Leonora ossia L'amore coniugale* (1804). Although Paer's *Leonora* is overshadowed by Beethoven's later setting of the same subject (*Fidelio*, 1805–14), it is a fine work on a high musical level and needed to fear no comparisons in its time. With these works and his later operas Paer dominated the stages of Europe for decades.

Morlacchi, on the other hand, appointed Hofkapellmeister at Dresden in 1810 and later the main target of the national party that formed round Weber, was of lesser artistic stature, and his influence was largely restricted to Dresden. *Tebaldo e Isolina*, the only opera of his to retain a place in the repertory for some time, owed its success largely to the castrato Velluti, for whom the role of Tebaldo was written. He sang it on many European stages after its first performance in Venice in 1822. *Tebaldo e Isolina* corresponds in its musical form to the genre of the new Rossinian *opera seria*, but it seems stylistically regressive and particularly indebted to the older type of *opera seria* in its elegant, academically pale melodic line. However, Morlacchi's stage works[6] cannot be said to correspond to that malicious distortion of the Italian opera represented as the allegorical figure of an aging prima donna in Weber's fragmentary novel *Tonkünsters Leben*.[7]

Paer and Morlacchi were outshone by the genius of Rossini, to whom the future development of Italian opera belonged – a development made international by Rossini himself when he followed the example of the French 'reform operas' of Gluck and Spontini in his later Neapolitan works. However, the hallmark of Italian opera of that period, whether by Morlacchi or Rossini, which in spite of all differences of musical quality stamped it as the most modern genre of musical theatre until the advent of grand opera, was the musical dramaturgy developed from theatrical practice; for the first time, opera seemed to have been conceived 'scenically' as a total aesthetic and dramatic entity. And this new musical dramaturgy, developed largely by librettists (the most experienced and versatile of which, Gaetano Rossi, was the author of *Tebaldo e Isolina*), inevitably forced composers to think in dramatic terms.

The absence of any specific formal approach was the principal cause of the failure of virtually all early attempts to establish German opera as an independent genre on a level with Italian and French opera. Weber no doubt thought in dramatic terms, as both composer and man of the theatre. But even if the conversation reported by Lobe, in which Weber set out the dramaturgical system of *Der Freischütz*, must be regarded as a piece of literary fiction, the fact remains that Weber tried hard to arrive at musical and dramatic unity, compositionally as well as theatrically.[8] His dramatically inspired tonal colouring, no less than his careful attention to the dramatic aspects of production, bears witness to that. These elements, however, are ephemeral and do not permeate or determine the entire structure of text and music, which retain many characteristics of Singspiel and *opéra comique*. And the same can be said of *Euryanthe*, in spite of the elimination of spoken dialogue. The 'Romantic' character of Weberian opera remains as unresolved as the national element. The Romantic colour and aura which his works certainly possess to a high degree do not amount to 'Romantic opera' as a new genre. Indeed, there was no dramatic Romantic opera, in the sense of a unified, fantastic creation involving music, libretto and staging, until Meyerbeer's *Robert le diable* (1831) and Wagner's *Der fliegende Holländer* (1843). But the fact that Weber's German Romantic opera was as yet more of an ideal than a reality – a premonition of future developments – in no way diminishes his historical importance as composer and theatre director, or the significance of the German Opera of Dresden.

The fruits of Weber's dedicated labour were harvested by his successor, Carl Gottlieb Reissiger, though Reissiger's own contribution to the rapidly rising artistic reputation of the Dresden Opera should not be underestimated. Reissiger's committed work as Kapellmeister was of more importance to the musical life of the city than were his compositions, which besides choral and chamber works included several operas, among them *Die Felsenmühle* (1831), a very popular work in its time. During the Reissiger period, too, an event of great consequence in the cultural life of Germany occurred: the closing of the independent Italian department of the Dresden Opera in 1832. The symbolic significance of this administrative act – a concession by the court to the nationalistic forces that had emerged strengthened by the events of 1830 – was considerable, but it had few immediate practical consequences: all it really meant was that the administration of the two departments, long interlinked, was now merged under German management. Italian and French operas were still performed in Dresden; their share in the repertory actually increased, with the successful works of Rossini, Bellini, Auber and Meyerbeer (though these operas were sometimes sung in German). Morlacchi remained in his post and foreign singers continued to appear. However, German singers were gaining in status, among them the sopranos Agnes Schebest, Wilhelmine Schröder-Devrient and Pauline Marx, the tenor Joseph Tichatschek and the baritone Anton Mitterwurzer. The orchestra gained a high reputation with notable virtuosos leading their respective sections: the violinists Anton Rolla and Carl Lipinski as leaders, the cellist Johann Friedrich Dotzauer and the flautist Anton Bernhard Fürstenau, among others.

Thus the Dresden Opera was flourishing from both the artistic and administrative viewpoints when, in the person of Richard Wagner, a figure came on to the scene whose work and influence were to determine the company's direction for the rest of the century. The successful première of Wagner's *Rienzi* (1842) was a brilliant prologue to his activity as Kapellmeister, a post he took up a few months later. Though the first performances of *Der fliegende Holländer* (1843) and *Tannhäuser* (1845) were only in the nature of a *succès d'estime*, they consolidated his reputation as a controversial but original opera reformer. He left his mark on the repertory with new productions and revised versions of the operas of Gluck (*Armide* in 1843, *Alceste* in 1846, *Iphigénie en Aulide* in 1847) and a revival of Spontini's *La vestale* in 1844, conducted by the composer. As composer and Kapellmeister, Wagner made it clear that he intended to pursue further Weber's ideas of a national German opera, and the solemn transfer of Weber's body from London to Dresden in 1844 was seen as symbolic of that attitude. His performance of Beethoven's Ninth Symphony in 1846, in the former opera house in the Zwinger Palace, also had overtones of artistic politics.

Wagner saw himself as a 'German artist' in the tradition of Weber and Beethoven, but in fact he depended on Italian and French models, in particular on Meyerbeer's grand opera as the most highly developed form of musical drama of its time.[9] However, the three

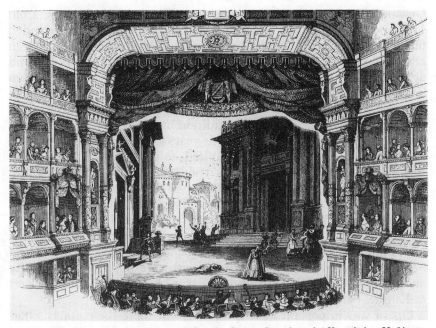

53. Wagner's 'Rienzi' (closing scene of Act 4), first performed at the Königliches Hoftheater, Dresden, on 20 October 1842: engraving from the Leipzig 'Illustrierte Zeitung' (12 August 1843)

operas he produced and composed in Dresden, together with *Lohengrin* which though composed in Dresden had its première in Weimar, indisputably raised German opera as a genre to the rank of its Italian and French counterparts. With an instinct for drama that was unusual in German opera and that carried the novice opera composer over technical hurdles he had not always fully mastered, Wagner fused the different ideas offered by contemporary opera – declamatory melody, the dramatic use of tone-colour, reminiscence motifs, scenic integration into a personal entity. His influence laid the foundations of the Dresden Opera's subsequent international reputation. For a brief period his operas disappeared from the Dresden stage when, as a result of his involvement in the revolutionary events of 1849, he temporarily became *persona non grata*, but even in the 1850s they were back in the repertory, which they dominated for the final decades of the nineteenth century. As the first centre of Wagnerian opera, therefore, the Dresden Opera was in the vanguard of operatic progress.

LEIPZIG

In Leipzig, a great centre of commerce with its trade fairs, known as 'little Paris' in the eighteenth century, musical life had always been much more varied, with marked emphasis on concerts. The

The Early Romantic Period

Gewandhaus concerts in particular dominated the city's music from 1781 and throughout the nineteenth century. Their influence extended further, as pioneers of regular civic concerts. Although there had been an established opera company in Leipzig between 1693 and 1720 and again from 1817, and a number of opera performances had been given in the interim, the musical theatre was never as important there as in Dresden. On the other hand, the reputation of Leipzig's church music was legendary; its centuries-old tradition had been brought to a peak by Johann Sebastian Bach during his years as Kantor of St Thomas's, and in the nineteenth century it united, to great mutual effect, with the tradition of the Gewandhaus concerts. During the nineteenth century, too, Leipzig saw the foundation of many choral societies, the oldest and most influential being the Singakademie (1802) and the Liedertafel (1815). The cultural breadth of musical life was enhanced by the fact that several of the leading musical journals of Germany (including the *Allgemeine musikalische Zeitung*, the *Neue Zeitschrift für Musik* and *Signale für die musikalische Welt*) were published in the city and the music-publishing firms of Breitkopf & Härtel and Hoffmeister & Kühnel (subsequently Peters) were based there.

Opera was important in Leipzig, too, but there the emphasis had always lain elsewhere. In the eighteenth century the German Singspiel rather than Italian opera was dominant; the impresario Heinrich Gottfried Koch was its organizational founder and Johann Adam Hiller its first important composer. By 1781 ten of Hiller's Singspiels had been produced in Koch's Komödienhaus, newly opened in 1766 and sometimes called the 'cradle of the German Singspiel'; they included works which later became extremely popular, for example *Lottchen am Hofe* (1767), *Die Liebe auf dem Lande* (1768) and *Die Jagd* (1770). When Koch left Leipzig in 1773 his successors, among whom were Abel Seyler and Pasquale Bondini, continued the Singspiel tradition in the context of a mixture of drama, opera and ballet. In 1788 Guardasoni's company gave guest performances of Mozart's *Le nozze di Figaro* and *Don Giovanni* in the recent original Prague productions.

Operatic activity entered a new phase with the founding of a permanent Stadttheater. In spite of a slight predominance of Italian and French music, the theatre prided itself on its productions of the most important new works, such as Weber's *Der Freischütz*, which was performed there only a few days after its Berlin première, Spohr's *Jessonda* and Marschner's *Der Vampyr*, given its première in Leipzig in 1828.[10] Although of lesser artistic reputation than the Dresden Hoftheater, the Leipzig Stadttheater had great social and cultural importance for the rising liberal middle classes, since Leipzig was one of their strongholds in Germany. The operas of Albert Lortzing were an artistic reflection of the thinking and taste of this middle-class public in the period preceding the revolution of March 1848. Lortzing was employed at the Stadttheater from 1833 to 1845 as a singer and actor and, more important, as composer and librettist of his own stage works. Setting out from the Singspiel tradition, and influenced by Mozart and the instrumental colour of Romantic opera, he created his own genre of German comic opera, particularly with *Die beiden Schützen* (1837), *Zar und Zimmermann* (1837) and *Der Wildschütz* (1842), all of which had their premières in Leipzig. His operas, all with spoken dialogue, created a sophisticated form of entertainment containing a good deal of social criticism but free of narrow nationalism.[11]

However, concerts were more important than opera in Leipzig in the first half of the nineteenth century. The roots of the Leipzig concert tradition went back to the eighteenth century, to the founding of the Grosses Concert in 1743; this private society was modelled on concert organizations in other European cities, such as the Parisian Concert Spirituel which had been in existence since 1725. The Grosses Concert engaged musicians from concert to concert. Admittance was by subscription; women accompanying a subscriber were admitted free, as were visitors to Leipzig for the great trade fairs. The concerts, in private houses and large rooms in public hostelries, were under the artistic direction of Johann Friedrich Doles, a pupil of Bach, and later of Johann Adam Hiller. After the latter had fallen out with the administrators of the Grosses Concert in 1771, he founded the Musikausübende Gesellschaft in 1775, which consisted of professional and amateur musicians and gave 30 concerts a year.

As the Grosses Concert ceased its activities in 1778, Hiller's society took on the role of legitimate successor. The construction of its own concert hall, the Gewandhaus, opened in 1781 by Hiller's ensemble, marked the beginning of a new era: a tradition was founded that has lasted (with interruptions) until the present day and which served as a model for nineteenth-century concerts far beyond the boundaries of Germany. Hiller was succeeded as Kapellmeister by Johann Gottfried Schicht in 1785, Johann Philipp Christian Schultz in 1810 and Christian August Pohlenz in 1827. They rehearsed the vocal works but the direction of instrumental music was the province of the orchestral leaders; among these, August Matthäi, who took up his position in 1803, made a notable contribution to chamber music in Leipzig by founding the Gewandhaus Quartet. Several early performances of Beethoven's symphonies, the First in 1801, the Third in 1807 and the Fifth in 1809, testify to the rapid rise of orchestral standards. There were also performances of Haydn's *The Creation* in 1800 and *The Seasons* in 1801, in which the choir of St Thomas's took part.

The prestige of the Gewandhaus concerts reached a highpoint in 1835 with the appointment of Felix Mendelssohn as director of both

54. Felix Mendelssohn: portrait (1829) by James Warren Childe

vocal and instrumental music; the famous violinist Ferdinand David was leader. Until his death in 1847, Mendelssohn was at the centre of Leipzig musical life, taking full advantage of the artistic and organizational possibilities inherent in his position. Not only did he compose major works that continued the Classical tradition in the spirit of Romantic historicism, conducting them in fine performances (including the G minor Piano Concerto in 1835, the oratorio *St Paul* and the D minor Piano Concerto in 1837, the Scottish Symphony in 1842 and the Violin Concerto in 1845), but he was also an admired teacher who enriched and extended the Leipzig tradition of 'historical concerts' with works by Bach, Handel, Haydn, Mozart and Beethoven. His performances of the Ninth Symphony were legendary; his performance of Bach's *St Matthew Passion* in St Thomas's in 1841 was epoch-making. Mendelssohn effectively promoted the work of contemporary composers, notably Schumann, giving the premières of his First and Fourth Symphonies in 1841, his Second Symphony in 1846 and the oratorio *Das Paradies und die Peri* in 1843; he was responsible for the posthumous first performance of Schubert's C major Symphony, the

Ninth, in 1839. Mendelssohn's programme planning for the Gewandhaus concerts was a model for the nineteenth-century orchestral
repertory in its mixture of music of past and present. Finally,
Mendelssohn founded the Leipzig Conservatory (1843) and engaged
musicians of international stature as teachers, among them the great
pianist and composer Ignaz Moscheles.

Leipzig had a long tradition of publishing and journalism, which
contributed a great deal to the city's cultural liberalism. The history
of book printing in Leipzig goes back to the first half of the sixteenth
century and the trade fairs and the university contributed to its rapid
growth. In the eighteenth century the city also became a centre of
German music printing, previously concentrated chiefly in south
Germany (in Augsburg, Mainz and Nuremberg). The publishing
house founded in 1719 by Bernhard Christoph Breitkopf was in the
forefront of this development. Initially it mainly published scientific
literature, but with Georg Christian Schemelli's *Musikalisches Gesang-
Buch* (1736) and the third and fourth editions of *Die Singende Muse an
der Pleisse* (1741 and 1747) by Sperontes (Johann Sigismund Scholze),
Breitkopf brought out two of the most important musical collections of
the period. The firm changed to music publishing under Bernhard's
son, Johann Gottlob Immanuel Breitkopf, who entered his father's
printing works in 1745 and the publishing house in 1762. His new
method of music printing revolutionized the trade, and as publisher of
Carl Philipp Emanuel Bach, Hiller and Haydn, among others,

55. Interior of the old Leipzig Gewandhaus: engraving (c1840)

Breitkopf quickly became one of the leading firms in Europe. A year after his death, in 1795, his son Christoph Gottlob Breitkopf sold the business to Gottfried Christoph Härtel, and since then it has borne the name Breitkopf & Härtel. From 1798, thanks to Härtel, the firm began publishing complete editions of Mozart, Haydn, Clementi, Dussek and other composers, as well as editions of Bach's motets (1802–3), chorale preludes (1803–5) and the *Well-Tempered Keyboard* (1819); they were not like modern scholarly editions, but their historical significance in bourgeois musical life during the nineteenth century can hardly be overestimated.

Franz Anton Hoffmeister and Ambrosius Kühnel set up another music-publishing house in 1800, the Bureau de Musique, which was taken over by Carl Friedrich Peters in 1814 and later became world-famous under his name. A large factor in its success was that it was the first to use the innovatory flatbed process for printing music. Among the house's publications were the first complete edition of Bach's works for keyboard and organ, an edition of Mozart's quartets

56. *Programme of a concert at the Leipzig Gewandhaus, 12 April 1846, with Jenny Lind and Mendelssohn*

57. *Rehearsal of the Leipzig Gewandhaus orchestra under Julius Rietz (Mendelssohn's successor) in 1850: lithograph after a drawing by the cellist Carl Reimers*

and quintets and Forkel's pioneering biography of Bach. To appreciate its achievements, one has to think of the financial risk involved in publishing editions of earlier music at a time when the idea of a 'classical repertory' was still unknown.

At the beginning of the nineteenth century, Leipzig was also a centre of newspaper and magazine publishing in the German-speaking area: 'the best daily papers came from Leipzig, the best political journals, the best popular magazines and the best professional journals'.[12] In 1844 the *Leipziger Lesegesellschaft*, unique in its time, had at its disposal over two hundred scientific and literary periodicals, almost a hundred political journals and various local news-sheets and pamphlets. Many journals, though produced in Leipzig, were intended for distribution further afield, since the city had only some 50,000 inhabitants, and the cosmopolitan trend in Leipzig journalism at the time can be explained at least in part by its concern for readers beyond the immediate region. The general political papers, which consisted chiefly of the conservative *Leipziger Zeitung*, owned by the state of Saxony, and the liberal *Leipziger Allgemeine Zeitung* (*Deutsche Allgemeine Zeitung*), published by the firm of Brockhaus, were less concerned with music reporting than the more literary journals; the latter were led by the *Zeitung für die elegante Welt*, which became a prominent platform for progressive artistic aspirations before 1848, particularly under the editorship of Heinrich Laube in 1833–4 and 1842–4.

In the first half of the nineteenth century a number of important music journals were published in Leipzig. The *Allgemeine musikalische*

The Early Romantic Period

Zeitung, founded by Härtel in 1798, was the first German music journal to continue publication for any length of time. Under the editorship of Johann Friedrich Rochlitz (until 1819), and with such distinguished contributors as Ernst Theodor Amadeus Hoffmann, it became a stimulating and high-quality forum for professional and general aesthetic musical discussion and criticism. Rochlitz's journalistic enthusiasm played a considerable part in the dissemination of Beethoven's works in Germany. Although in principle it had never relinquished its original position, about 1830 the *Allgemeine musikalische Zeitung* found itself at the conservative end of the spectrum of music journalism. Schumann's *Neue Zeitschrift für Musik*, which first appeared in 1834, may thus be regarded as a counterblast from a younger generation of composers and critics who viewed themselves as revolutionary. It was part of the journal's aim to offer the creative artist a platform, 'to give him, too, an organ wherein to express himself in the written word, as well as by his own influence'.[13] Though Schumann, who edited the journal until 1844, was anxious to follow an independent artistic line, he neither could nor would avoid biassed judgments. In his missionary fervour, he did not want to promote the progress of music in general: he wanted to point the way. This latent ideological line was to become clearer under the editorship of Schumann's successor, Franz Brendel, who exclusively promoted the 'new German school'. Whereas the *Allgemeine musikalische Zeitung* and the *Neue Zeitschrift für Musik* were intended for the professional, musically educated reader, *Signale für die musikalische Welt*, which first appeared in 1843, was addressed to the amateur music-lover.

NOTES

[1] The phrase is from C. Dahlhaus, 'Motive der Meyerbeer-Kritik', in *Jahrbuch des Staatlichen Instituts für Musikforschung Preussischer Kulturbesitz 1978* (Berlin, 1979), 35.

[2] Letter from Weber to Gänsbacher, 1 Dec 1814 (L. Nohl, *Musikerbriefe*, Leipzig, 1867, 243); see also W. Becker, *Die deutsche Oper in Dresden unter der Leitung von Carl Maria von Weber, 1817–1826*, Theater und Drama, xxii (Berlin, 1962). Kasperl was a character in Viennese popular comedy and a traditional half-wit figure in puppet theatre.

[3] Becker, op cit, 72–95.

[4] *Abend-Zeitung* (1820), i, nos.17–18 (C. M. von Weber, *Ausgewählte Schriften*, ed. W. Altmann, Deutsche Musikbucherei, xvii, Regensburg, 1928, 259–63; also Weber, *Kunstansichten*, *Ausgewählte Schriften*, Taschenbücher zur Musikwissenschaft, xxiii, Wilhelmshaven, 1978, 211–15).

[5] *Literarischer Merkur* (1824), no.43, 8 April, quoted from Becker, *Die deutsche Oper*, 67.

[6] See J. Budden, 'German and Italian Elements in Morlacchi's *Tebaldo e Isolina*', in *Francesco Morlacchi e la musica del suo tempo (1784–1841): Perugia 1984*, 19–27.

[7] *Tonkünstlers Leben* (1809–20; unfinished), in Weber, *Ausgewählte Schriften*, 338ff.

[8] J. C. Lobe, 'Gespräche mit Carl Maria von Weber', in *Fliegende Blätter für Musik*, i (Leipzig, 1855), 27–34, 110–22; also in Lobe, *Consonanzen und Dissonanzen* (Leipzig, 1869). L. Finscher has shown that this conversation is in fact a back-projection on Lobe's part of the dramaturgy of

Meyerbeer and Wagner; see 'Weber's *Freischütz*: Conceptions and Misconceptions', *PRMA*, cx (1983–4), 79–90, especially 88ff.
   [9] For the origins of Wagnerian music drama, see R. T. Laudon, *Sources of the Wagnerian Synthesis: a Study of the Franco-German Tradition in the 19th Century Opera*, Musikwissenschaftliche Schriften, ii (Munich and Salzburg, 1979).
   [10] O. Fambach, *Das Repertorium des Stadttheaters zu Leipzig 1817–1828*, Mitteilungen zur Theatergeschichte der Goethezeit, ii (Bonn, 1980).
   [11] R. Rosengard, *Popularity and Art in Lortzing's Operas: the Effects of Social Change on a National Operatic Genre* (diss., Columbia U., 1973), especially Part 3, 'German Popular Opera: the Stylistic and Social Definition of Lortzing's Genre', 612–47.
   [12] H. Kirchmeyer, *Das zeitgenössische Wagner-Bild*, i: *Wagner in Dresden*, Studien zur Musikgeschichte des 19. Jahrhunderts, vii (Regensburg, 1972).
   [13] R. Schumann, in *NZM*, i (1834), 1.

BIBLIOGRAPHICAL NOTE

General music history

A concentrated summary of social, institutional and intellectual history is offered in the first part ('Social and Stylistic Forces affecting German Opera in the First Half of the 19th Century') of R. Rosengard's *Popularity and Art in Lortzing's Operas: the Effects of Social Change on a National Operatic Genre* (diss., Columbia U., 1973). A general summary of development in Dresden is given by G. Jäckel, 'Aspekte der Dresdner Kulturgeschichte', in *Die italienische Oper in Dresden von Johann Adolf Hasse bis Francesco Morlacchi*, ed. G. Stephan and H. John, in Schriftenreihe der Hochschüle für Musik Carl Maria von Weber, xi (Dresden, 1987), 417–27; and in W. Becker, *Die deutsche Oper in Dresden unter der Leitung von Carl Maria von Weber 1817–1826* (Berlin, 1962). For Leipzig see F. Schmidt, *Das Musikleben der bürgerlichen Gesellschaft im Vormärz (1815–48)* (Langensalza, 1912). These texts provide references to specialist literature about the political history of Saxony.

Opera, concerts, printing and publishing

The standard work on the history of opera in Dresden is R. Prölls, *Geschichte des Hoftheaters zu Dresden: von seinen Anfängen bis zum Jahre 1862* (Dresden, 1878). Particular aspects are covered by O. Landmann in 'Die italienische Oper in Dresden nach Johann Adolf Hasse: Entwicklungszüge 1765–1832', in *Die italienische Oper in Dresden von Johann Adolf Hasse bis Francesco Morlacchi*; and by Becker in *Die deutsche Oper in Dresden*. Essays on specific topics, a chronology and fine illustrations are in *Oper in Dresden: Festschrift zur Wiederöffnung der Semperoper*, ed. H. Seeger and M. Rank (East Berlin, 1985). A list of performances and catalogue are in O. Fambach, *Das Repertorium des Königlichen Theaters und der italienischen Oper zu Dresden 1814–1832*, Mitteilungen zur Theatergeschichte der Goethezeit, viii (Bonn, 1985). A brief history of opera in Leipzig during this period is in F. Schulze, *Hundert Jahre Leipziger Stadttheater: ein geschichtlicher Rückblick* (Leipzig, 1917). A list of performances and catalogue are again covered by Fambach, *Das Repertorium des Stadttheaters zu Leipzig 1817–1928*, Mitteilungen zur Theatergeschichte der Goethezeit, iii (Bonn, 1980).
   The Leipzig Gewandhaus concerts were of crucial importance to the establishment of a civic tradition of theatre-going in the nineteenth century and their history has been recorded many times. The standard work is A. Dörffel's *Geschichte der Gewandhausconcerte zu Leipzig* (Leipzig, 1884, 2/1972). There are general descriptions, continuing up to quite recent times, in E. Creuzberg's *Die Gewandhaus-Konzerte zu*

The Early Romantic Period

Leipzig, 1781–1931 (Leipzig, 1931) and (though extremely brief) in F. Henneberg's *Das Leipziger Gewandhausorchester* (Leipzig, 1962, rev. 2/1972; Eng. trans., 1962). See also literature on Mendelssohn. For other concert activity and church music in both cities see the articles on Dresden and Leipzig in *Grove 6* and *MGG*.

An informative introduction to contemporary music printing, especially in Saxony, is in the first chapter of H. Kirchmeyer's *Das zeitgenössische Wagner-Bild*, i: *Wagner in Dresden* (Regensburg, 1972). See also literature on Schumann, the *Neue Zeitschrift für Musik* and, for the history of the most important publishing houses, the specialist literature in *Grove 6* and *MGG*.

Composers

Literature on individual composers can offer insight into musical life in the cities in which they worked. There is no monograph on Paer. Specialist studies of Paer's work in Dresden are in R. Engländer, 'Ferdinando Paer als sächsische Hofkapellmeister', *Neues Archiv für sächsische Geschichte und Altertumskunde*, i (1929), 204–24, and A. Kobuch, 'Ferdinando Paer in Dresden', in *Die italienische Oper in Dresden von Johann Adolf Hasse bis Francesco Morlacchi*. A survey not confined to Morlacchi's life and work but also covering historical, cultural and institutional milieu is available in G. Ricci des Ferres-Cancani's *Francesco Morlacchi (1784–1841): un maestro italiano alla corte di Sassonia* (Florence, 1956). Individual aspects are covered in *Francesco Morlacchi e la musica des suo tempo (1784–1841): Perugia 1984*. Weber's writings on music are available in various selected editions, the only complete collection being in C. M. von Weber, *Sämtliche Schriften*, ed. G. Kaiser (Berlin and Leipzig, 1908). The best general study is offered by J. Warrack, *Carl Maria von Weber* (London and New York, 1968, 2/1976). A survey with emphasis on biography and on the content and success of Marschner's operas is offered in A. D. Palmer's *Heinrich August Marschner, 1795–1861: his Life and Stage Works* (Ann Arbor, 1980).

Although Spohr did not work in Dresden or Leipzig, his works formed an important part of the opera and concert repertories there in the first half of the nineteenth century. His *Lebenserinnerungen* are important not just as biography but also as documentation of contemporary music history, first printed in full according to the autographic records in an edition by F. Göthel (2 vols.; Tutzing, 1968). Parts of the bibliography and the work-list, as well as a historical survey (with extensive illustrations) are available in *Louis Spohr: Festschrift und Ausstellungskatalog zum 200. Geburtstag*, ed. H. Becker and R. Krempien. Also useful are D. M. Mayer's *The Forgotten Master: the Life and Times of Louis Spohr* (London, 1959/R1981) and C. Brown's *Louis Spohr: a Critical Biography* (Cambridge, 1984) – the former predominantly biographical, the latter also analysing his works. The best recent biography of Lortzing, both for social history and for analysis of works, is R. Rosengard's *Popularity and Art in Lortzing's Operas* (diss., Columbia U., 1973). Another view is offered by H. Schirmag, *Albert Lortzing: ein Lebens- und Zeitbild* (East Berlin, 1982).

It is not possible to single out a selection of writings on Wagner specific to Leipzig and Dresden from the vast range of literature available. A good foundation is still provided by E. Newman, *The Life of Richard Wagner*, 4 vols. (London, 1933–47/R1976). An original work on Wagner's years in Dresden, containing considerable information, is H. Kirchmeyer's *Das zeitgenössische Wagner-Bild*, i: *Wagner in Dresden*.

A book of fundamental value which summarizes earlier research is E. Werner's *Mendelssohn: a New Image of the Composer and his Age* (New York, 1963; rev. in Ger. as *Mendelssohn: Leben und Werk in neuer Sicht*, Zurich, 1980). For aspects of Mendelssohn's biography and his work see *Felix Mendelssohn-Bartholdy*, ed. G. Shumacher (Darmstadt, 1982), and W. Konold, *Felix Mendelssohn-Bartholdy und seine Zeit* (Laaber, 1984). Schumann's critiques and music essays, mostly written for the *Neue Zeitschrift für*

Musik, were first published in four volumes under the title *Gesammelte Schriften über Musik und Musiker* (Leipzig, 1854). The most complete edition, with enlarged addenda and more extensive annotation, is the fifth, ed. M. Kreisig (Leipzig, 1914). On Schumann's music publishing activities see H. Pleasants, *The Musical World of Robert Schumann* (New York and London, 1965), and L. Plantinga, *Schumann as Critic* (New Haven, 1967/R1977).

Chapter VI

Italy: the Centrality of Opera

JOHN ROSSELLI

When the young Napoleon Bonaparte led a French army into Italy in 1796 it marked the end of an unusual half-century of peace for a much-invaded country. It also launched a series of revolutions, imposed by the French with the help of a minority of intellectuals rather than generated from within. Wars and repeated changes of government ensued until, nearly twenty years later, the victorious allies fastened on Italy an Austrian hegemony; this in turn lasted, with occasional troubles, until Austria and the other Italian states were severely shaken by the revolutions and nationalistic movements of 1848–9. Independence and unification were to follow within little more than a decade.

On entering an Italian town, a French general of the Napoleonic period would, as one of his first acts, commandeer for himself and his officers a number of free boxes at the opera house. Not that French generals were particularly music-loving: they wanted boxes because opera, by the late eighteenth century, was Italy's best-known product. It was also the centre of social life for the educated classes, even in troubled times, unless fighting was actually going on in the streets. By appearing in the state box – formerly the preserve of the local ruler or governor – the general would show who was in charge. The presence of a ruler (or his representative) was crucial to Italian musical life. The ruler's personal taste or inclinations, however, were by now subordinated to the practice of a musical network which had its own organization and which dealt wholly in opera.

Musical life in 1796 still centred largely on courts, certainly in the capitals of the ten petty monarchical states; leading aristocratic families exerted a somewhat more diffuse influence in the republican capitals Venice, Genoa and Lucca, soon to lose their status. A court still represented a concentration of wealth in the midst of a poverty-stricken country; and its display was often meant not merely to stress a ruler's status but also his political will to the educated classes under the eye of his authority. Ferrara, a city of the utmost importance in the development of music in the Renaissance period, dwindled into insignificance after its absorption into the Papal States and the loss of its court; much the same happened to Turin when it was temporarily absorbed into Napoleonic France, and it would happen to ex-capitals such as Parma and even Venice after Italian unification. In contrast, Lucca, not at other times a leading musical centre, had a period of glory in 1820–47 when the Bourbon dukes to whom it had been allotted ran Italy's only gambling casino: this both paid for a lavish opera season and attracted tourists.

Courts were still economically and politically important to musicians, but they had lost much of their power of creative patronage. At the turn of the seventeenth and eighteenth centuries the heir to the throne of Tuscany could still dominate the state's musical life and influence the development of opera by, for instance, commissioning a string of works from Alessandro Scarlatti and then dropping him in favour of another composer. In the same period great churches and abbeys demanded a steady supply of new oratorios, motets and other sacred works, as did such notable institutions as the Venice orphanages where girls were trained to sing and play instruments to a famously high standard.

Vocal music – already dominant, though not absolutely – could still be regarded as divided into three roughly equal types: theatre, church and chamber, whose corresponding genres were opera, sacred music and secular cantata, each with its distinct vocal style.[1] In a musical world so organized, the composer was aptly called *maestro di cappella*; many did direct church choirs or teach in charitable institutions besides writing operas and cantatas. But during the eighteenth century the centre of musical life gradually shifted to the opera house. During the Napoleonic period, that was where cantatas were performed (to mark some festive occasion) and even oratorios (lightly disguised as 'sacred dramas', in effect operas on a biblical theme, reserved for Lent). Composers continued writing for the church, but few leading musicians now held the sort of post that called for a steady output of sacred works: to be a *maestro di cappella* represented security or a fall-back position for those not markedly successful in the theatre. Opera was king, and could keep good musicians fully employed.

Long-term social changes explain this shift, as well as changes in taste and feeling. Religious sentiment among the educated classes (though scarcely among the population at large) became increasingly lukewarm; the monastic orders dwindled and some were suppressed by the pope or by 'enlightened' rulers well before the French Revolution.[2] The Venice orphanages and the Naples conservatories that similarly brought up boys (not all of them orphans) as musicians entered a period of crisis around 1760 from which they failed to recover; the reasons are not clear but may have had to do with inflation.[3] Italy, poor as it was, had some share in the general expansion of the European economy from about 1730.

In these conditions a network of opera houses giving professional performances, which had begun to take shape in the last years of the seventeenth century, could expand steadily throughout the eighteenth. One Italian town after another built a new theatre or replaced an existing wooden (perhaps temporary) one with a permanent, often lavish and elegant structure. The writer who asserted in 1785 that 'every small town, every village has a theatre'[4] was exaggerating, but Italy probably had more theatres, more widely scattered, than other countries of similar size. The first official census of theatres in united Italy, carried out in 1871 after a period of further building, listed 940 theatres in 699 towns; some of the towns had only a few thousand inhabitants, and some of the theatres held as few as 50.[5]

About 1800 the network was densest in the area of north and central Italy roughly defined by lines drawn between Milan, Trieste and Rome. Much of the south lay outside it and came in only gradually in the course of the nineteenth century. However, it also extended outside the Italian peninsula. Because parts of Italy were, or had been, ruled by Habsburgs (Spanish or Austrian), Vienna and Madrid, Prague and Barcelona in effect formed part of it; so did outposts of Italian cultural influence such as Malta and Corfu. Italian opera had also been taken up by princely courts in the many German states and as far afield as St Petersburg and Lisbon, as well as by groups of aristocrats and business and professional people in London; there it was a luxury export, as it was to be in the nineteenth century in many parts of the world, especially (from about 1825) the Americas.

With opera thus developed, an Italian ruler could no longer have a marked share in the creation of new works. King Charles Felix of Sardinia (1821–31) liked to choose subjects and vet librettos and he sometimes demanded fewer arias and more concerted pieces; but although he treated the royal theatre at Turin as his drawing-room – he would sit in his box munching breadsticks during the performance – it was the normal operatic fare of the day that was given there. Other rulers took a detailed interest not so much in what was performed as in how it was performed and by whom; they looked out for anything that might disturb public order. Charles III, King of Naples until 1759, had built the Teatro San Carlo (then the largest theatre in Europe), even though he was uninterested in music, as a means of building up the monarchy's prestige and keeping his nobles under his eye. Preoccupations of this kind deepened after the revolutionary period: in 1825 the chief minister of the Austrian territories in northern Italy was anxious to keep La Scala open because it attracted 'to a place open to observation during the hours of darkness a large part of the educated population'.[6]

Courts, though important, were no longer indispensable as the focus of musical life. Even in Turin and Naples, headquarters of a centralizing monarchy, non-royal theatres multiplied after the Napoleonic period. Outside the capital cities the old tradition of Italian town life – steeped in municipal pride and drawing the allegiance of groups who in England would have spent most of their time on their country estates – ensured keen support, often strengthened by rivalry between one town and the next. Reggio Emilia felt the need to keep up with the state capital, Modena, and therefore made a point of putting on new (or at any rate very recent) and elaborately produced operas during its summer fair season,[7] an example followed by Padua and Bergamo among others. Smaller towns in practice formed regional networks, taking their operas from a neighbouring larger town. Successful new operas circulated rapidly, as a rule within a few years; even the biggest hits among the late eighteenth-century comic operas were virtually finished after ten or fifteen years, though revivals might still occasionally be given in small towns. Constant creation of new operas was the mark of a leading city. All the capital cities insisted on novelty and some, like Turin, struggled to do so even after the revolutionary period when conditions began to change.

About 1789 the leading cities were Naples, Milan, Venice, Rome and Bologna. Naples was still enjoying, but no longer fully earning, its fame as the capital of Italian music. Its celebrated music schools were in decline, but the San Carlo orchestra was still rated the best in the country. In the quarter-century or so after the Napoleonic wars it managed a further burst of creativity, largely thanks to the presence first of Rossini (bolstered by an exceptionally high subsidy) and then of Donizetti. But by 1840 it could be described with some plausibility as 'away from the centre of operatic affairs'.[8]

Milan had some way to go before becoming, in the course of the nineteenth century, the centre of musical Italy; meanwhile its new theatre, La Scala (opened in 1778 to replace one that had burnt down), was admired, and the office that supervised it carried an undefined authority as the arbiter of contractual disputes elsewhere. Venice, with its tourist trade and its half-dozen opera houses, was probably the most fertile source of new works, especially comic operas. Rome, also a tourist centre, kept a fairly important place in spite of a papal court that was at times indifferent or hostile.

A special case was Bologna. Though not a capital, it had established itself as the headquarters of the singing profession and an important city for musicians of all kinds, partly for the same geographical reason that was later to make it the hub of the railway network: it was the crossroads of north and central Italy. It had also become a centre of musical learning, known to the rest of Europe chiefly through the celebrated scholar Padre Martini (1706–84) and the Philharmonic Academy, to which Mozart was admitted at fourteen. It had been the first city in Italy to put on one of Gluck's reform operas (*Alceste*, 1778), just as it was later to be the first to put on Wagner (*Lohengrin*, 1871), though by that time it had lost its pre-eminence to Milan.

Whether in a large city or a small town the opera season was the centre of social life – for the nobility, their servants and such middle-class people as an impoverished country could show: lawyers, doctors, army officers, a few bankers and merchants and, under the *ancien régime*, a good many priests and monks. Only the grandest theatres specialized exclusively in opera; the very grandest, the San Carlo in Naples and La Fenice in Venice (opened in 1792), staged nothing but *opera seria*, the stately opera on historical or mythological themes that had been regarded through most of the eighteenth century as the proper fare for kings and princes, accompanied as a rule by equally grand ballet. Most other theatres put on a variety of performances, not only opera (serious or comic) but plays, occasional 'academies' (concerts) by visiting instrumentalists, equestrian or acrobatic displays, even performing monkeys.

The theatre calendar was carefully arranged. Opera, as everyone knew, was the most exalted genre and, within opera, *opera seria* its supreme form; a particular season, usually Carnival (running from 26 December to Shrove Tuesday), was the fashionable one. Lesser genres were put on in other seasons or, if the city had more than one theatre, in less fashionable houses. These distinctions were marked in the most practical way: in fashionable seasons or theatres it cost more to get in and the audience was correspondingly more aristocratic. Nor was any of this left to the free play of the market: it was laid down in detail by government regulation. A season commonly offered two operas, as a rule new to the town and often newly commissioned. Each might be performed twenty times unless it was a total flop; in that case a third, 'fall-back' opera might have to be put on in a hurry to take its place. A large part of the audience came to every performance.

Italians of the upper classes, as foreign visitors often remarked, did not entertain much in their cavernous *palazzi*: these were virtually impossible to heat in winter, and even nobles with great estates were often short of money. It was easier to meet at the theatre, generally on four or five nights a week during the season. Not only could one talk to friends in their boxes, queuing up if need be to sit beside one's hostess; the boxes had dressing-rooms attached to them where servants prepared food and drink, and the theatres had large handsome foyers the main purpose of which was to accommodate the playing of games – games of chance such as faro and roulette through much of the eighteenth and early nineteenth centuries, more innocuous ones like backgammon after gambling had been suppressed. If the opera and ballet were satisfactory, an Italian could thus spend a large part of his or her waking life in a high state of sociability and enjoyment: 'for

58. Interior of a box at La Scala, Milan: engraving (1844) after A. Focosi

eight sous', the French novelist Stendhal wrote from Milan in 1814, 'a good Milanese has a fine time from a quarter past seven until half past midnight, nose in the air, taking in marvellous things' (he himself felt sated after a couple of hours and went into someone's box to talk).[9]

In these conditions it is not surprising that Italian audiences were regarded by foreign visitors as the noisiest in Europe – this at a time when no audience anywhere kept totally silent. People might be relatively quiet during the ballet, the German composer Otto Nicolai reported, 'but during the opera they all chatter like canary birds that cry all the more sharply the louder the music is played'.[10] There is some exaggeration here: even at the twentieth performance, people attended to an aria or a duet they admired. What is more, if we are to believe the great British baritone Charles Santley (who trained in Italy in the 1850s), some of the noise was constructive: 'Without interrupting the performance, they express their approbation with a murmur of satisfaction'.[11] When they listened they did so phrase by phrase, and they might whistle (the Italian equivalent of hissing) at a note sung flat the moment after they had cheered a well-shaped trill.

The Italian audience was not unlike the crowd at a modern sporting event: riot was fairly common. It wanted displays of executive skill, not just from singers but from composers and scene designers; within a narrow range of experience it was highly knowledgeable and eager for new enjoyments, but it was conservative and would tolerate only piecemeal changes, whether in the form of the music or the libretto or in styles of singing or playing. This attitude came to seem unworthy to foreign musicians in the Romantic period, who by then were looking for exalted sentiment and a total artistic impression. Hence the strictures of Berlioz, who wrote that Italians wanted to swallow an opera like a plate of macaroni, and Nicolai, according to whom Italian audiences wished only to 'listen to sounds, watch scenery and movement, pass the time and have fun'.[12] Hence too the unmistakable way such audiences (with the prospect of twenty performances before them) made their feelings known when they were not having fun.

Even with so conservative an audience, Italian music changed, but it did so gradually over a long period. Nearly three-quarters of a century passed from about 1750, when the old *opera seria* form that had carried all before it began to lose impetus, to around 1820 when Rossini established a new model for Italian opera; even then Rossini summed up the old ways as much as he pioneered the new. The change paralleled that in the visual arts from Rococo or late Baroque, with their cult of the delicately pleasurable or majestic, to the neo-classical hankering after the 'sublime', theoretically founded on antique grandeur and simplicity but often in practice taking outsize, eccentric or deliberately alarming form. In Italian music the chief vehicle for the new simplicity was comic opera: though comic opera itself virtually disappeared in the process, its forms and procedures largely shaped the very different Italian opera of Rossini's successors.

The *opera seria* of the mid-eighteenth century was the art form ideally suited to the absolutist courts. Generally based on the chaste and subtle librettos of Pietro Metastasio (1698–1782), which dozens of composers set over and over again, it concerned itself solely with the great, above all with monarchs shown, in the end, as magnanimous. It dealt in emotional self-contradictions, settled in reconciliation rather than in passion. It ignored collectivity and had no chorus; its individuals were separate, abstract and, though 'historical', scarcely bound to time or place. Metastasio gave drama (embodied in recitative) great importance, but it was the solo aria, with its generalized sentiment and elaborately embellished da capo, on which composers and audiences concentrated. To this form expensive virtuoso singers were central; chief among them were the castratos, for the astonishing sounds only they could produce seemed apt for such artificial and exalted works.

Opera seria was bound to run into trouble once the Rousseauian cult of the natural, the austere and the particular came to be widely shared, not to mention the deepening interest in history as development and the increasing criticism of absolute monarchy and aristocracy. Castratos, though accepted in the early eighteenth century (in spite of jokes and prohibitions), came to seem increasingly absurd and the operation that made them was seen as repugnant. That seems to be why fewer notable castratos came forward as opera singers in the closing decades of the century; the last (and for years the only) one, G. B. Velluti, retired in 1830, though in the church, an even more conservative institution, castratos were employed until the end of the nineteenth century.

Some of the republicans who took office in the wake of Bonaparte's army wished to suppress opera in favour of morally elevating spoken tragedies; they denounced *opera seria* as extravagant, expensive and as making for 'softness' and 'licence', criticism that was to be echoed in the 1848 revolution, when some democrats wished to close down La Scala. But although this austere strain did not last – the Napoleonic regime soon accommodated itself to existing élites and habits – composers and librettists had for some time, well before the French Revolution, felt the need to move *opera seria* away from its old rigid form. Metastasio's words were cut and adapted, choruses came back, concerted pieces crept in. These changes can be detected in Mozart's *Idomeneo* and *La clemenza di Tito*, the only serious late eighteenth-century operas most people are now likely to hear.

Idomeneo and *La clemenza* are somewhat anomalous (being intended for a non-Italian audience and shaped by Mozart's singular genius). More representative is Domenico Cimarosa's *Gli Orazi e i Curiazi* (1796), whose culminating night scene with the oracle builds up fragments of aria, arioso, recitative and chorus, together with some effective woodwind figuration and pointing, to cause a shudder we may think of as 'Gothick'; elsewhere the work is florid and melodious, with some straining after the neo-classical grandeur suggested by its then fashionable subject (the patriotism of republican Rome). Similar experimentation went on elsewhere, as in Manfroce's *Ecuba* (1812), a work as yet barely rescued from oblivion and showing the influence of French neo-classical opera, and in Johann Simon Mayr's

59. *Commemorative fan (c1819) with a portrait of Rossini and music and characters from his operas*

Medea in Corinto (1813). Though in effect an Italian composer, Mayr was steeped in Haydn and Mozart; his *Medea* shows an odd mixture of 'sublime' declamation (in which the great soprano Giuditta Pasta later awed London and Paris audiences) and highly elaborate orchestration that sounds not so much symphonic as arbitrary.[13] Cimarosa and Mayr were here wearing their togas, with a touch of style from beyond the Alps. But they were in the first place practitioners of comic opera, as, from 1810, was the young Rossini in his earliest stage works.

The late eighteenth century was the golden age of Italian comic opera, not perhaps in terms of intrinsic quality (the librettos at least of some early eighteenth-century comic operas were bolder in their satirical and realistic attack than almost anything produced after about 1750) but as a genre of which the public could not get enough. The great hits of the period were nearly all comic operas, most of them now forgotten; they included not Mozart's masterpieces (which for a long time made little headway in Italy) but such simpler works as Guglielmi's *La pastorella nobile* and Sarti's *Le gelosie villane* – titles embodying the rustic subjects then fashionable – as well as several by Giovanni Paisiello (1740–1816) and Domenico Cimarosa (1749–1801), the leading Italian composers of the day. Of all these, only Cimarosa's *Il matrimonio segreto* (1792) is still performed.

These, however, represent the tip of a large iceberg. Even a sampling of the librettos and music of comic operas of the period shows how repetitive they were. Because of the censorship exercised by all the Italian states, their subjects were replete with innocuous clichés: the cantankerous old man fooled by his wily maid, the vanity of rival opera singers, the comic foreigner and so on. Only in the very last years before the French Revolution do we find librettos dealing in political satire (Casti's *Il re Teodoro in Venezia*, 1784; music by Paisiello) or criticism of the nobility (Bertati's *La villanella rapita*, 1783; music by Bianchi, with later additions by Paisiello and Mozart).

The music too can sound to us remarkably similar from one work or number to the next. It may well be that habituation to stronger musical meat (as Stendhal was already complaining in the 1820s) makes us deaf to nuances and variations that were appreciated by contemporaries. The *galant* style of eighteenth-century music often sets this problem, and it was the Italian version of the *galant* style, with its emphasis on rhythm, graceful, short melodic line and easy harmony, that found its aptest expression in comic opera. Even to modern ears, however, there is a difference between the formulaic writing and banal orchestration of Bianchi and the inventive woodwind scoring and elegant vocal line of Paisiello and Cimarosa. Their misfortune is to have written for a pre-revolutionary aristocratic world in which the merely delightful (but not particularly dynamic) sufficed.

The strategist who built on the work of his predecessors and contemporaries to renew the model of Italian opera was the young Gioachino Rossini (1792–1868). 'Strategy' is the right term for his cautious yet far-sighted originality, now at length beginning to be acknowledged; it goes with the military element in his music, the piccolo and drum pointing of his perkiest tunes and the famous crescendo that overwhelms opposition. But although Rossini was an experimenter he was, paradoxically, by temperament a conservative; much of his work codifies past practice while giving it an extra touch of dynamism – fizz, speed, even vulgarity (not out of place in Napoleonic Italy with its *parvenu* kings and newly rich army contractors). His culminating Italian serious opera *Semiramide* (1823) is a kind of sum of a century's vocal accomplishment. At a more earthy level, such a device as lining up the characters and having them imitate animals, bells etc to express bewilderment – it made the Venice audience at *L'italiana in Algeri* (1813) 'struggle and gasp for breath, and wipe the tears from their eyes' – went back at least to the 1730s.[14] Audiences had never tired of it. But Rossini gave it a new rhythmic devilment.

The traditions he could draw on were those of the uneasily evolving serious opera, but above all those of comic opera and its bourgeois offshoot *opera semiseria*. The important part of this legacy was the set of musico-dramatic formal devices that had evolved in the late eighteenth century. Comic opera had always tended to bring the characters together at the end of an act for a scene of mutual expostulation and confusion; from about mid-century these finales exploited the device of having all the characters sing at once, each voicing a different emotion. This was something only opera could do, though it had taken composers a long time to realize the possibilities of an arrangement on the face of it so unrealistic. Once the finale was established, its potential became clear: for multiplying the discharge of comic or emotional effect, for carrying the action forward by bouncing the dramatic ball from one character to the next, for alternating bursts of energy with passages of contemplation in which the world seems to stand still, or simply for making a loud noise. By the 1780s finales had become extremely long, often built up as a chain of linked numbers none of them as elaborate as an aria. The supreme example is the finale to Act 2 of Mozart's *Le nozze di Figaro*, though what set the seal on the form for Italian audiences were such 'ensembles of confusion' (from astonishment to mayhem) as the Act 1 finale of *Il matrimonio segreto* or that, already mentioned, in *L'italiana in Algeri*.

Because rapid action was essential to the success of comic opera, singers' vocal lines could be less elaborate and demanding than was the norm in serious opera; verve and acting ability were not ignored in *opera seria*, but in comic works they counted for a good deal more than the ability to trill or decorate. Over a long period, from about 1790 to 1830, audiences gradually came to prefer less vocalization and more declamatory dramatic singing in serious opera too. Rossini's share in this was again paradoxical, for in his Italian works he loaded solo arias and duets with coloratura, much of it of a rapid, showy kind which in the past had often been left to singers' improvisatory powers. Yet some of the ensemble scenes that were most to influence Italian music, such as the tomb scenes in *Semiramide* or the 'scene of darkness' and the Jews' prayer by the Red Sea in *Mosè in Egitto*, achieve striking effects not through decoration but through a noble simplicity of line combined with bold harmony. In his French works of the late 1820s Rossini moved away from the more luxuriant forms of vocalization.

In this matter, the work of his Italian successors, though sometimes referred to as *bel canto* opera, represents the tail end of a declining tradition. A part like Norma in Bellini's opera of 1831, though exceedingly taxing, has less vocalization and more dramatic singing than almost any part in a serious opera of 1731; in Verdi's earlier works coloratura is confined to women and even then used only for specific dramatic purposes, to bring out a character's mixture of tenderness and vengeful ambition (Abigaille's 'Anch'io dischiuso' and

60. Alessandro Sanquirico's design for the scene in Nino's tomb in Act 2 of Rossini's opera seria 'Semiramide' as performed at La Scala, Milan, in 1824, the year after its première at La Fenice, Venice

'Salgo già' in *Nabucco*, 1842) or her febrile, willed gaiety (Violetta's 'Sempre libera' in *La traviata*, 1853).

Comic opera, finally, could absorb new fashions that blurred the distinction between 'high' and 'low' genres. In particular it absorbed the eighteenth-century bourgeois or 'tearful' comedy, though in the Italian opera world, with its hierarchical outlook, this was for a time given the special label *opera semiseria*. It was the kind of work that took a serious view of ordinary people and their feelings and brought them through various ordeals to a happy ending while pointing a moral. Domestic virtue threatened and rewarded was often the theme – parental affection, wifely fidelity, honesty and innocence won earnest praise. Sentiments of this kind (easily overflowing into sentimentality) were characteristic of the rising middle class in the economically advanced countries, Britain and France; it is not surprising that an early example in Italian opera, Piccinni's *La buona figliuola* (1760), should have been based on Richardson's novel *Pamela, or Virtue Rewarded*, or that some later examples were influenced by the French 'rescue opera' set in an exotic or historical locale.

In Italy, smiling through tears, the effect aimed at in this kind of work, was sometimes attained by a vocal line of apparently simple pathos, moving slowly stepwise within a narrow range but in fact calling for great control of vocal colour and expression. An example is Paisiello's *Nina* (1789), in which one of the first of many such lovelorn heroines loses and recovers her reason. Bellini was to draw conscious inspiration from *Nina* in the making of *La sonnambula* (1831), a work which, with its millrace and perilously sleepwalking bride, shows how sentiments fit for an early Victorian sampler could be made to yield real sweetness and truth.

Rossini meanwhile had written several works in this vein; the most striking is *La gazza ladra* (1817), with a realistic contemporary setting. His Cinderella, too (*La Cenerentola*, 1817), had moments of *Nina*-like pathos. His chief contribution, however, was to set his seal on the process – carried forward both by him and by his immediate predecessors and contemporaries – that united all Italian operatic genres into a single form; it was prevailingly, indeed deepeningly, serious in content, but far less aristocratic in tone and more dynamic in thrust than the old *opera seria* and, in its structure and vocal writing, drew a good deal on comic and sentimental opera.

Rossini's decisive part in this process was for long obscured: until a few years ago he was remembered chiefly as a master of comic opera. That is odd, for *Il barbiere di Siviglia* (1816) and *La Cenerentola* were among the last of their kind, whereas some of his serious operas, neglected over the past century or more, were admired and influential in their own day. Comic opera did not flourish in the post-Napoleonic climate of earnestness and reaction. Laughter was now subversive. By

1823 an experienced man of the theatre could write that comic opera was 'almost proscribed by modern taste'.[15] Rossini, however, had made his name almost overnight with two works put on within four months in 1813, *Tancredi* and *L'italiana in Algeri*, the former serious, the latter comic, but each containing a good deal of music that could have found a place in the other. Here and elsewhere he was apt to attend to the musical pattern without worrying too much about the detailed sense of the words he was setting; his contribution to the new model of Italian opera was above all formal. It ensured that when his successors full-heartedly took on the themes offered by the European Romantic movement, their work was sustained by a kind of classical order.

The main characteristic of early *opera seria* had been a clear differentiation between recitative (which carried forward the dramatic action) and aria (a display of feeling, with time suspended). The aria itself, when as so often it was a da capo aria, had as its ruling principle repetition, with embellishments, of its long first section; after a second section making a brief diversion into another key, rhythm or mood, the listener's pleasure lay in identifying both the familiar elements of the first section and the unexpected, improvised ornamentation introduced by the singer. The changes codified by Rossini made for more forward movement. 'Dry' (*secco*) recitative, with keyboard accompaniment only, began to disappear, giving way first to orchestrally accompanied recitative and then to tighter structures, either forms of arioso or bits of sung dialogue inserted into aria forms, but in any case no longer embodying an attempt at sung speech. The basic form of the aria (as of the duet or other concerted piece and of the chorus) was now of two main sections, the first as a rule slower, the second faster; each of these might be divided further into sub-sections, but the overall forward thrust instilled by a meditative start leading to a more energetic finish was essential. The fast section (cabaletta) typically marked a change in the dramatic situation: a character comes to a sudden resolve, a chorus hears a piece of unexpected news.

In time, librettists and composers were to grow expert at stretching this slow–fast framework to cover an entire scene. There would now be an extended middle section in which the crucial change was conveyed not just by a few bars from an excited messenger but by a whole musical movement. Perhaps the most famous scene in Italian opera, the Miserere in Verdi's *Il trovatore*, is technically such a middle section; it should (but often in performance does not) lead up to a cabaletta, whose function is, as usual, to propel the action forward in a mood of urgency and bring down the curtain to enthusiastic applause.

An early example of a whole scene built from a sequence of numbers, and involving a number of characters and a chorus essentially on the model of the old comic-opera finale, is the impressive opening 'scene of darkness' in Rossini's *Mosè in Egitto* (1818); equally innovatory was to be the string of duets that make up the highly dramatic and moving confrontation between Violetta and Germont in Verdi's *La traviata*. In each of these the aria convention is seemingly ignored, and yet the basic movement from contemplation to action still informs the musical structure. In finales Rossini bequeathed to serious opera the comic-opera pattern of a collective pause (often known as *largo* though not always marked as such) before the headlong final section or *stretta*. The pause in comic opera was conventionally one of bewilderment; in serious opera it made possible a moment of grandiose expansiveness or sorrowful contemplation in which the audience would be caught up before the *stretta* in high excitement propelled the emotional action to a close.

Rossini's model took little notice of what was to become the dominant school in Europe and America: German symphonic music. This at one time led critics and historians to write off Rossini and his successors as opportunists or crude sensationalists or ignoramuses. Yet Rossini (like Verdi after him) was much better versed both in old music and in contemporary foreign music than he liked to reveal. He was in fact a student of Haydn's and Mozart's music, and during his Italian career he was subjected to tedious repetitive criticism to the effect that he was importing heavy German orchestration. Though he and others, like Mayr, took something from Germany and France, the Italian tradition on which he built remained largely independent; the lines along which it grew had nothing to do with symphonic development.[16]

Like some other neo-classical artists, Rossini held to an ideal of detached formal beauty, little concerned with the inner lives of human beings. This, in his Italian serious operas, is reflected in many numbers (solo arias especially) whose sinuous vocal line may be elegant, brilliant, heroic, on occasion bombastic, but seldom moving. Then, too, the military element – the crescendos and quick march rhythms – has a way of cropping up at what now seem incongruous moments. In his own day Rossini carried all before him and Italian composers of his and the next generation had no choice but to imitate him.[17] In the 1820s in particular a spate of operas by composers now forgotten (and some by the young Donizetti) closely followed his model.

When Rossini left for Paris in 1823 it might have seemed that Italian music had successfully made the gradual transition from the *ancien régime* model, rather as the old sovereigns, restored to power in 1814–15 after the fall of Napoleon, had by and large incorporated the social and administrative changes wrought by the Napoleonic empire. Italian opera was about to enter a period of creative activity beyond precedent. A little later, in the mid-1830s, musicians began to look for expressive means bolder than those of the Rossinian model; this slightly anticipated a period of political turmoil that ran deeper than the limited, often backward-looking revolts of the immediate postwar period.

In the system of opera production in which Rossini and his successors worked, the organization of seasons, the regulation of theatres and audience behaviour and the censoring of texts were treated as affairs of state, minutely controlled by government and the upper classes, some of whose members were in fact the government. At the same time the careers of musicians, composers and singers in particular, took them on individual paths round an operatic circuit that spanned a number of states and local centres of power. Government regulation of a fussy, at times despotic, kind co-existed with a musical free market. The men who struggled to bridge the two were the impresarios, intermediaries who acted both as clients of the great and as semi-independent businessmen. Governments and groups of leading nobles, bankers and professional men regarded it as their business to see that operas were produced at the right times and with appropriate lavishness; they also insisted on approving the choice of composer, the text of the libretto and the singers, not to mention the colour and materials of the costumes. They did not, on the whole, regard it as their business to train musicians, except insofar as traditional ties of family and patronage produced a supply of artists more or less spontaneously.

Italy was a country where family connections did most to determine careers. Instrumentalists were often the children of musicians and learnt from their parents; if the father played in one of the monarchical or municipal orchestras with (in effect) lifelong membership, he would try to pass his instrument and his job on to his son. Composers and singers were of less predictable talent, but they too often grew up in families of professional musicians or served a kind of apprenticeship with one person, as Donizetti did with Mayr. The old music schools of Venice and Naples, as we have seen, were in serious decline. Those of Venice disappeared, and in any case they had always set themselves against allowing their girls to become professionals. The Naples schools were eventually merged into one: it trained Bellini, but did not otherwise match the extraordinary galaxy of composing and singing talent that had come out of the Naples schools in the eighteenth century. The Milan school, founded by the Napoleonic government on the model of the new Paris Conservatoire, is famous for having rejected the young Verdi (as it happens, on not unreasonable grounds). It was the first of a series of schools, founded at intervals through the nineteenth century, that were to institutionalize musical training, though many aspiring singers continued to go to individual

175

teachers, themselves often retired or only moderately successful performers. How music education worked is not clearly known, but up to 1848 it was almost certainly far more dependent on family background and individual, practical apprenticeship than on set curricula. Once a young composer was trained (and had perhaps thrown off a few instrumental works as prentice pieces), his goal was to have an opera put on in a professional season. This, if he had talent, was not difficult; trouble came later.

Around the turn of the eighteenth and nineteenth centuries, and in leading theatres even later, the whole purpose of an opera season was to stage new works. At La Scala, the peak decade of creativity, measured in the number of new operas produced, was 1831–40, with 38; in the same period the San Carlo was still expected to put on each year five operas that had not previously been heard in Naples, three of them expressly composed for the city. Elsewhere the old productive rhythm slackened somewhat after 1815 – in Venice, where much of the earlier output had been comic opera, and in some capitals like Turin and Parma that could no longer afford a steady diet of new creations. Nevertheless, until the 1840s the expectation was that each opera should be a new experience. Revivals were about as welcome as repeat programmes are on television today: they were liked if they had been highly popular in the first place, and provided there were not too many of them. Indeed the length of time and the conditions in which operas were created had a good deal more in common with those of television than with present-day opera production.

Operas had always been written fast; even Monteverdi's court opera *Arianna* (1608) had to be written to a deadline. Around 1800 it was not unusual for the libretto and music of an *opera seria* each to be written in a fortnight. As instrumentation became more complex the composer needed a little longer, from three to six weeks; a slow worker like Bellini took at least seven weeks (and even then needed a year to work up preliminary sketches, whereas Donizetti and Pacini in most years composed two, three or even four operas). What made the productive rhythm of early nineteenth-century operas so unrelenting, particularly from the 1820s, was the multiplication of theatres and seasons. The operatic year now filled out: Lent was annexed as an open season for opera on secular subjects; theatres that had given only one season of opera a year now gave several; new theatres opened. Artists and managements had to keep going almost all the year round.

A composer might contract in June (when he had just seen his latest work on the stage) to write an opera for the forthcoming Carnival season, compose an intervening opera for the autumn season, receive Act 1 of the libretto for the Carnival opera (if it was on time) in early November, compose the last act in the second half of December as rehearsals went on, and accompany the first performance from the keyboard on 26 December – all this in three different towns, widely separated, with much correspondence and horse-drawn travel in between, not to mention delays and mishaps such as could easily intervene to make the schedule still tighter. Impresarios, singers, scenery and costumes were bound by much the same timetable, complicated by the passport and customs regulations of the Italian states: individuals or costumes travelling the 125 or so miles from Florence to Parma, for instance, normally crossed three frontiers. No wonder a swarm of agents, often living from hand to mouth, grew up to speed the traffic of contracts and shipments.[18]

By the early nineteenth century a successful composer need no longer attach himself to a sovereign, a cathedral or a teaching institution; those were positions to fall back on if his career should falter. He was a free agent, though bound to a busy commercial merry-go-round. The moment he stepped into a theatre, however, or had anything to do with the men who controlled it, he could not help being aware of his place in a hierarchical society.

The layout of the theatre auditorium itself was a means of displaying the hierarchy's upper sections. From the seventeenth century, Italian theatres were built on the horseshoe or rectangular plan, with tiers of boxes surrounding a stalls space. (The word 'stalls' is used here to denote the ground floor of the auditorium.) The larger theatres generally had four to six tiers; the second (like the 'piano nobile' in town houses) was always the official and aristocratic one, with the prestige of the other tiers diminishing the further away they were from the second. These tiers took up most of the seating space; even the last was often divided into boxes, and the most aristocratic theatres, such as La Fenice in Venice, resisted well into the nineteenth century any attempt to convert it into an open gallery. The stalls were only partly filled with benches (along with a number of closed seats that could be unlocked on payment of an extra charge); the rest was standing room.

Before the French arrived in 1796, a leading opera house displayed the nobility's predominance in the most obvious way. Not only did nobles occupy the best tiers of boxes, wearing brightly coloured clothes and, in some theatres, enjoying special privileges (candles in the boxes, torches at the exit). But their servants also occupied larger parts of the rest: upper servants in the stalls, footmen in the topmost tier, or peering through grilles let into the back walls of their masters' boxes, preparing food and drink in the dressing-rooms attached to them, lounging about the corridors and relieving themselves on the spot: all this while enjoying free entry or special low prices of admission.

Differential pricing was another means of displaying hierarchy. Nobles paid more for entry than did local citizens; so did the

61. La Fenice, Venice (lithographs by Barozzi after G. Pividor): (a) the fire that engulfed the theatre on 13 December 1836

(b) the interior soon after it was rebuilt in 1837 (this lithograph was dedicated to the contralto Karoline Unger)

'foreigners' (people from out of town or from other Italian states as well as tourists) who could be found in the stalls; men paid more than women. Army officers, on the other hand, might pay less than citizens and might also have the first three rows of stalls benches reserved for them. Professional men, officials, tradesmen, students and ecclesiastics found room in the stalls or, if they were well off, in the boxes; artisans, shopkeepers and soldiers were in the top tier, especially if it was an open gallery. Labourers and peasants – the vast majority of the Italian population – were nowhere.

This hierarchical order, maintained throughout the opera season, would be relaxed for the masked balls (held in the theatre, with the stalls covered over) that marked both the end of Carnival and the highspot of the social year. Masked balls enabled titled ladies to dance with tradesmen; even then the regulations demanded that everyone should be 'decently dressed', another way of keeping out the majority. Masks were potentially subversive. Governments distrusted them and in the post-revolutionary period often forbade them. By the 1860s masked balls were on the decline.

This hierarchical array was one aspect of musical life in which the period of revolutionary and Napoleonic rule made a difference. Milan, the Napoleonic capital, gave the lead and held it. Differential pricing was abolished; though it came back in other towns after the wars, it gradually disappeared as regulations were amended throughout the succeeding half-century. The overwhelming servant presence abated, as much through gradual changes in manners as through regulation. Noblemen now wore the dark frock-coats introduced by English gentlemen and could no longer be readily distinguished from other 'well-bred men and women' who kept no carriage.

Whenever a musician signed a contract or engaged in the day-to-day business of an opera season, he or she had to reckon with the hierarchy in another aspect: its control of theatres and of what went on in them. There were tiers of control just as there were tiers of boxes. There were owners, box-holders, official regulators and, serving all of them, impresarios. In practice these categories might overlap. The owner of a theatre might be the ruler, or a municipality, or the noble family that had built it for prestige and profit (that was how public opera houses had arisen in the first place) or, increasingly in the late eighteenth century, an association of nobles and professional men. Box-holders might own their boxes and help to finance the season. Official regulators had to approve prices, contracts and every detail of production and performance. These groups often quarrelled over one of the many mishaps that can arise in so complex a business as opera production. Yet they had certain motives in common. One was a real desire to see as lavish an opera season as possible: princes and cardinals took great trouble to recruit the best singers and even

62. Masked ball at La Scala, Milan, from a calendar of 1859

bassoonists. Another was fear of excess expenditure; periods of inflation and slump, as in the 1810s, made for bankruptcies and maimed or interrupted seasons. A third, powerful motive was fear of public disturbance; in the despotic states of the old disunited Italy even a trifle (like a take-off in a comic opera of a local eccentric) might seem to threaten the peace.

Cost, then as now, was crucial. Serious opera in particular was almost certain to sustain a loss. It seemed unthinkable without expensive virtuoso singers and, in leading theatres, elaborate new scenery and new costumes; there, a clause in the management contract stipulated that soloists' costumes must be made exclusively of silk and velvet. Costs rose from the late 1820s, almost certainly because singers' fees – which seem always to have accounted for roughly half of the total production costs[19] – were driven up by the spread of Italian opera into ordinary theatres all over Europe and the consequent rise in demand. This meant regular and increasing government subsidy. The box-holders could no longer meet the shortfall; in the earnestly moral atmosphere of the nineteenth century the gambling monopoly formerly awarded to the impresario, which had financed lavish opera and ballet seasons, was suppressed everywhere except in Lucca and rulers were unwilling to alienate the educated classes by raising prices by more than by the most gingerly steps.

The resulting official subsidy (paid for by consumption taxes that fell most heavily on the poor) built up deep resentment: when elected governments came into being, just after the period under consideration, they lost little time in cutting back subsidy and plunging opera houses into crisis. Meanwhile, even in a privately owned theatre like La Fenice in Venice, subsidy enabled government or municipal officials to impose on the proprietors the expensive creation of Rossini's *Semiramide*, or the engagement of the equally expensive Giuditta Pasta at a time when she was past her best. On the other hand, falling or mean levels of subsidy probably hastened the decline of Naples and Rome as musical centres: in Rome, as Berlioz found (where the papal government provided only a minimal subsidy), barbers doubled as musicians; sets and even costumes might be made of paper.[20]

Government regulatory powers affected musicians in all sorts of ways; in this matter there was little to choose between republican and reactionary governments. The regulations generally banned whistling and encores and forbade applause in the presence of the ruler, unless he chose to applaud first, which he sometimes did not. All this went against the grain (deliberately so, it seems); police and soldiers were accordingly posted all over the theatre. It was common for members of the public to be arrested for obstreperous whistling, impresarios for putting on a production that went badly wrong, stagehands for allowing mishaps, even eminent singers for refusing to sing. As a rule those arrested were released after a few days, especially if they expressed contrition or otherwise gave way; the point was to demonstrate the paternal authority of government. The game was well understood and individuals with bargaining power, in particular famous composers or singers, could to some extent hold their own.

Censorship was only one among many such regulatory powers. It did not become an important issue until the years just before and after the 1848 revolutions. Classical ideas still ruled the libretto: the cult of dignity, together with the need for brevity, kept out anything too specific. Librettists used a poetic vocabulary that ruled out the 'low' and the workaday. Donizetti's *Lucrezia Borgia* (1833), thought unseemly because it put a pope's daughter on the stage, with a little ingenuity could be and was transferred to several other locales. But when the censors (as a rule literary men) got to work on Verdi's *Rigoletto* (1851) they did not confine themselves to keeping out politics and religion and guarding against immorality; they objected to 'low' words such as 'buffoon' and 'sack', and in some Italian cities these words had to come out.[21] This was an extreme case; Hugo's original play had got into trouble even in France, and in choosing it Verdi was consciously breaking new ground.

The impresario, engaged as he was in mediating between artists and exacting superiors, might or might not make a difference to musical creativity. Most nineteenth-century impresarios came from the musical and theatrical professions or were tradesmen connected in some way with theatres and their owners. Most were bazaar traders in outlook; most concerned themselves at best with quality and punctuality of execution – singers were 'goods' and opera was a 'product'. One or two, however, stood out. Domenico Barbaja, a semi-literate café waiter from Milan who became a gambling promoter, army contractor and builder on a large scale, ran the Naples royal theatres for most of the period 1809–41; the crowning feature of his lavish seasons at the San Carlo was a series of ambitious new operas by Rossini, with the great singer Isabella Colbran (Barbaja's mistress, later Rossini's wife) in the leading parts. Barbaja – a *mafioso* and a blusterer, but also a large-spirited man with an unusual taste for Haydn and Mozart – thus made a difference in Rossini's career. Alessandro Lanari, a busy impresario who was a thorough and exacting professional, had special talents as a producer; Verdi accordingly entrusted him with the first performances of *Macbeth* (1847), a work that called for special care.

By the late 1820s the system of opera production was expanding. Thanks to subsidy, its economics were better than they had been (or were to be after 1848). War and revolution no longer took up people's

energies. Politics was banned, newspapers were thin and uninform-
ative, reading novels had not yet become a habit. Opera was one of
the few safe subjects: musical journals proliferated, and they were
attentively read. Looking back in 1869, a writer maintained that 'no-
one who has not lived in Italy before 1848 can realize what the theatre
meant in those days . . . The success of a new opera was a capital
event that stirred to its depths the town lucky enough to have
witnessed it, and word of it ran all over Italy'.[22] Allowing for
exaggeration ('the town' probably meant the upper and middle
classes, their dependants and the people who worked for and around
the theatre), there was in this a core of truth.

It was at this point that Italian musicians responded to some
of the deeper impulses of the European Romantic movement. The
best of their work has maintained itself in public favour ever since,
even when critical opinion has been against it; it has now risen in
critical esteem as well. At the lowpoint in its critical fortunes George
Bernard Shaw wrote of 'that ultra-classical product of romanticism,
the grandiose Italian opera in which the executive art consists in a
splendid display of personal heroics, and the drama arises out of the
simplest and most universal stimulants to them'.[23] That is well put.
Rossini's legacy ensured the economy and restraint of classical forms.
Yet Italian opera of the 1830s and 40s was also Romantic.

*63. Design by Alessandro Sanquirico for a scene from Vincenzo Schira's ballet 'Maria Stuarda'
(with choreography by Galzerani) performed at La Scala, Milan, on 10 February 1826; ballets of
this period contained mimed action*

The Early Romantic Period

'Romantic' is a notoriously multi-faceted term. So far as it denotes an interest in the wild, the remote, the exotic, Italian opera can be said to have put on its outward trappings but discarded much of its inward intent. Italian *opera seria* had long allowed some exotic subjects – Turkish, Persian, Chinese, even Red Indian – but this made no difference to the treatment of either words or music; even sets and costumes were fanciful, though a greater interest in historical or geographical accuracy can be seen as a consideration during the last third of the eighteenth century.

When the first wave of English Romantic literature reached Italy, through French translations and adaptations, librettists were as quick to fillet Scott and Byron as their predecessors had been to fillet Voltaire's Turkish or Red Indian tragedies. But they and the composers with whom they worked showed little more interest in conveying the spirit of remote times or places. The scene designer might do wonders with Loch Katrine or the Wolf's Crag, the costume designer might people them with (perhaps inaccurate) tartan, but Rossini's *La donna del lago* (1819) and Donizetti's *Lucia di Lammermoor* (1835) could be taking place anywhere, at any time, for all that the music and even the text convey. At most, some evocative writing for horns suggests a wooded spot amid echoing hills: that is as far as Italians were prepared to take the Romanticism of Otherwhere.

They were just as resistant to the Romantic fascination with the uncanny, the supernatural, the outpourings of the unconscious. Rossini and his librettists simply left the fairy element out of the Cinderella story: what remained was hard realistic farce with touches of sentiment. In Verdi's *Macbeth* the witches (in their better choruses) are shrilly malevolent and the scene of the apparitions is impressive with its hollow offstage music cunningly orchestrated. But the composer made no attempt to open a window on frightening reaches of the unknown as Weber did in the Wolf's Glen scene of *Der Freischütz*; what concerned Verdi was human emotion in this world.

Nor were Italians given – except, as we shall see, in a special, limited sense – to the Romantic concentration on the individual's inner experience, apprehended as an invisible world more valid than the outer one with its lying shows. This northern Romantic theme culminated in Wagner's *Tristan und Isolde*, a work long resisted by Italian audiences. Vocal music is ill-suited to the expression of unconscious yearnings, since it requires visible, audible human beings to communicate in a more than usually outgoing way; Wagner himself had to entrust much of that expression to the orchestra. Italians' long-standing obsession with the voice ensured that any composer who, like Rossini, showed interest in orchestration more varied than routine string accompaniment with woodwind pointing ran into repeated charges of 'Germanism'. Instrumental writing might become

64. Title-page of the first edition (four-hand piano score) of Verdi's 'Macbeth' published by Ricordi (1847)

blatant, as in parts of Verdi's early works when the orchestra doubles the voice; it could never become predominant. Even madness, the individual's ultimate retreat into an inner world, was kept within the scheme of human interaction: 'Qui la voce', the mad scene for Bellini's heroine in *I puritani*, distils a keen, pure pathos (the voice wandering through fragments of a melodic pattern never exactly repeated), but the singer's utterances are carefully framed and distanced by the sorrowing comments of the other characters.

Nor, finally, did Italian opera go far towards involving the audience in a total world of illusion, an aspect of Romantic theatre which Wagner, again, was to carry to its culminating point at Bayreuth by darkening the theatre and sinking the orchestra out of sight. Italy's tradition of selfconscious theatre, going back to the *commedia dell'arte*, was reflected in Gozzi's eighteenth-century fables in which clown figures comment on the action, and again in Felice Romani's libretto for Rossini's *Il turco in Italia* (1814); here one of the characters is supposed to be writing the opera as it unfolds. Such was the disregard of illusion that – as a visiting German soprano was surprised to find at the Turin royal theatre in 1788 – singers who had just finished a scene would sit in the directors' box at the side of the stage, in costume and in full view of the audience.[24] Such practices, we may assume, vanished soon afterwards, but nothing could stop singers from breaking off to acknowledge applause. Enthusiasm at great feats of singing and acting was the sought-after effect, not illusion.

What then was Romantic about Italian opera? The acceptance of elemental passion as a fit subject for musical art to express. The historical or local trappings of works by Scott, Byron, Hugo were most of them pared away; the characters' headlong or concentrated emotions were if anything made more direct. The means by which Italian opera moved away from Rossinian detachment were varied. Vincenzo Bellini (1801–35) developed a partly new treatment of the vocal line; just after his death the now forgotten Saverio Mercadante (1795–1870), reflecting what seems to have been a fairly widely shared need for change, tried for greater brevity, energy and harmonic richness in a group of reform operas; about 1825–30 Italian audiences belatedly joined northern Europeans in accepting unhappy endings; in the 1830s vocal casting and vocal writing changed radically so as to bring Italian opera into a new, more straightforwardly erotic balance; religious music too found a more ardent impulse; Gaetano Donizetti (1797–1848) and especially Giuseppe Verdi (1813–1901) in their works of the 1830s and 40s developed the Rossinian model with a new concision and rhythmic energy. Elemental passion was not always erotic. It could be familial or patriotic, as in some of Bellini's and many of Verdi's operas. It could be outraged pride or vaulting ambition, as in *Norma* or *Macbeth*. But its expression could no longer be confined to the decorous, however grand.

Bellini was recognized at the time as a special talent. There is more forward propulsion in his work than has been allowed, though his fast music is not always up to the stirring war chorus in *Norma*. His special gift, however, was for a long, sinuous, unforced yet unexpected melodic line, unique in its concentration and plangency (if there is a parallel it is with Chopin's piano music; the two were near contemporaries and seem to have worked out their musical personalities independently). His orchestration, often a matter of the simplest chords or plucked figures, became much richer in *I puritani*. If Italian music attained the Romantic dwelling on inner experience, it was in such things as Norma's heart-searchings over her children (on which Verdi was to build for Rigoletto's tremendous disclosure of his inner life, 'Pari siamo!'). In the idyll of *La sonnambula* Bellini treats the villagers' domestic feelings with grave attentiveness.[25] But the inner life so acutely voiced remains that of the single human being; there is no merging, no sense (as in Weber or Wagner) of infinities beyond.

The feeling that the Rossini tradition needed to be renewed seems to have been widely shared in the later 1830s. Mercadante's statement of his intentions stands out:

> I have . . . varied the forms, banished trivial cabalettas and crescendos; concision, less repetition, more novelty in the cadences; due regard paid to the dramatic side; the orchestration rich but without swamping the voices; long solos in the concertati avoided, as they oblige the other parts to stand idle to the detriment of the action; not much big drum and very little stage band.

But very similar demands were put forward at the same time in private letters to the composer Nicola Vaccaj from a civil servant who was an amateur singer.[26] Giovanni Pacini (1796–1867), who like Mercadante had started as an imitator of Rossini, felt the need to retire temporarily and work out a new style. Mercadante's 'originality' in structure and scoring may sound laborious, and Pacini's, when he came back, grotesque; they are evidence of an unease that was to be resolved by Verdi.

By this time tragic, even lurid subject matter was generally accepted. The old *opera seria* ended happily, whatever the violence done to history or to dramatic logic. The reason usually given was that audiences, especially when made up of great people, should not be upset by having to witness dreadful events. This attitude died hard: when an opera by Vaccai about Joan of Arc was given at Naples in 1827 for the queen's name day, the work was adapted to allow Joan to escape.[27] By then, however, it was becoming normal for an opera to end with the death of one or more of the characters. This trend was to culminate in Verdi's *Il trovatore* (1853). The four main characters brandish at each other throughout their incandescent love and hate; in the closing minutes one poisons herself, one is beheaded and two go mad.

This change of temper also found expression in the element central to opera, the voice. Eighteenth-century vocal casting, especially in *opera seria*, favoured high voices – castratos and women. Tenors were old men and tyrants. Basses were oracles or captains or were left out. In comic opera men's voices were used more. But the vocal palette was prevailingly light, as the palette of early eighteenth-century painting and interior decoration was light. Opera also continued an earlier practice of turning upside down the normal distribution of vocal range between the sexes. It was not unusual for a castrato soprano to sing alongside a female contralto; if the female singer was singing a man's part (or better still the part of a man disguised as a woman, or a woman disguised as a man) we may assume the resulting sexual ambiguity gave pleasure. Again, it was in tune with a common lack of differentiation in eighteenth-century painting between the features of (beardless) men and those of women.

There were always some exceptions, such as the tenor Anton Raaff,

65. *Giovanni Battista Rubini as Gualtiero (a role he created) and his wife Adele Comelli as Imogene in Bellini's opera 'Il pirata' (1827)*

the first Idomeneus. The decline of the castrato gave more scope to normal men's voices, particularly tenors. Well into the 1820s, however, they remained by and large lyric tenors capable of ornate singing, who in their upper range used their head voice or falsetto register and did not attempt full resonance from the chest. G. B. Rubini, who created the very high male leads in Bellini's *Il pirata*, *La sonnambula* and *I puritani*, could go up to high F and G: a sound (still produced by a few tenors) that is thrilling but rather sexless.

At this time opera also gave prominence to the prima donna, who after Rossini's day tended to be a soprano. The habit of giving a male part to a high voice died hard: the castrato was for a time replaced by a female contralto singing breeches parts (known as *musico*, the old polite term for a castrato), hence the splendid love duets for soprano and contralto in Rossini's *Semiramide* and in Bellini's Romeo and Juliet opera, *I Capuleti e i Montecchi* (1830). The last well-known composer to write *musico* parts was Donizetti; Verdi always resisted them.[28] While these changes were taking place composers also started to write leading parts for basses capable of rapid florid singing, as against the patter-singing basses of comic opera; some of the finest, such as Filippo Galli and Luigi Lablache, could manage both.

A strongly Romantic aspect of nineteenth-century Italian music was thus the heterosexualization of the vocal casting. This was complete once the *musico* vanished and (at almost exactly the same time) the *tenore di forza* or powerful dramatic tenor came in. Legend has it that the French tenor Gilbert-Louis Duprez, who sang in Italy in the 1830s, was the first to sing a 'chest high C' – to devastating effect. But other tenors were probably experimenting with a higher extension of the chest voice before Duprez made his mark.[29] The new kind of tenor part is exemplified by Edgardo in Donizetti's *Lucia di Lammermoor*, written for Duprez. It is compact of ardour, defiance, headlong erotic impulse; though it benefits from elegant singing, nothing in it is merely decorative. By *Il trovatore* the tenor voice has been established as the musical equivalent of a perpetually flashing blade; the business of opera was now the union-in-confrontation of the natural voices of man and woman close to their thrilling upper extremes. A Martian attending a performance, it has been said, would at least learn that on earth there are two sexes.

Whether by listening to music in an Italian church the Martian would have found out that there is a God, is a question to which conflicting replies were given at the time; it is still a controversial issue. A religious revival was an important part of the Romantic movement all over Europe. A common accusation by northern European visitors was that in Italy, seemingly untouched by this deepened religious feeling, church music was debased and operatic – either written on operatic lines or lifted from actual operas. The truth is hard to determine: most Italian church music of this time is unknown, because with opera as the reigning form the more successful a composer was the less likely he was to write for the church, and vice versa. There is no doubt that church organists often played operatic selections; to that extent Italy, a conservative country, made no more distinction than Bach or Vivaldi had between secular and religious styles.

There had long been an imprecise notion that the 'Palestrina' (that is, the contrapuntal) style of the late sixteenth century was the appropriate one for new church music. In the eighteenth century the great scholar Padre Martini was already critical of composers who wrote church music in the new *galant* style as if they were working for the theatre. He could have been talking about the young Cimarosa, who wrote solo motets with orchestra in a style not readily distinguishable from that of an operatic aria.[30] In the first half of the nineteenth century the great example was Rossini's *Stabat mater* (partly written 1833, completed 1841). Yet the aria most often denounced, 'Cujus animam', in its form is not like any aria in a Rossini opera. It is dramatic rather than operatic. At this relatively late stage in Rossini's career the work as a whole is ardent, highly coloured. If it were a painting we might mention pre-Raphaelitism being not far off: it does not spoil the comparison that there is a good deal of 'Victorianized' contrapuntal writing.

While Rossini was breaking his silence to honour the Virgin, Donizetti and the young Verdi were paring down the structures of Rossinian opera to achieve a more rapid discharge of energy. At its crudest this meant announcing the opening melody of an aria in the orchestra and then breaking it off uncompleted. Rossini had found it necessary, even in the *stretta* to the Act 1 finale of *L'italiana in Algeri*, to repeat the musical pattern for the sake of symmetry; Donizetti, in his later operas, and Verdi pressed on to a quick curtain. In Verdi's work concision ruled to the point of making the action seem absurdly rushed in some cases; his ultra-rapid choruses of conspirators and the like lent themselves to parody in his own day by Gilbert and Sullivan. Present-day audiences care less or not at all; they probably realize that these operas are built on non-naturalistic musical and dramatic structures with a cogency of their own. Yet another device by which Verdi in particular achieved unremitting forward movement was the displacement of the point of greatest musical interest from the start to the latter part of an aria. This parallels his habit of fastening on the third line of a four-line stanza for the climax of a sub-section in the larger structure. In plotting an opera as a whole Verdi insisted on each act being shorter than the previous one.[31]

Modern appreciation of Donizetti and early Verdi has not been free from concentration on some of their weakest features, ultimately derived from the military element in Rossini: quick march rhythms and martial scoring in cabalettas (even at the most serious moments), doubling of the vocal line by the brass, over-use of band music on and off stage. The pleasure these give, we may suspect, is that of deliciously absurd 'camp' objects. Yet there is much more to Donizetti and (needless to say) to Verdi.

Donizetti was an old-fashioned composer, not in his style but in his readiness to turn out some 65 operas in 27 years, to dismantle or tinker with them at the behest of singers and managements, to be the honest craftsman – all good eighteenth-century attitudes. Yet he really was a craftsman; most of his mature operas hold some pleasant surprise within a certain sameness of cut and idiom that was already remarked upon in his day. One such is the grotesquely sinister little encounter between two minor characters in *Lucrezia Borgia*; another is his ability to knit together a complex series of numbers through a recurrent theme, one whose seeming triviality works as tragic irony (a fine example is the marriage contract scene in *Lucia di Lammermoor*). He was adept at writing gratefully for a well-trained voice and his comic music is fresh and amusing, not only in the familiar *L'elisir d'amore* and *Don Pasquale* but in a number of shorter works.

'Amusing' is not a word for the young Verdi, though some modern writers have argued in favour of *Un giorno di regno* (1840), his only comic opera until *Falstaff* over half a century later. With Verdi's operas of the 1840s, the full energy and daring of the literary Romantic movement informed Italian music; unlike many musicians, he was a reader, and he knew his Shakespeare and Schiller (in translation) as well as the contemporary Victor Hugo and Manzoni and some extravagant Spanish dramatists. He virtually dictated his own librettos and was the first Italian composer both to conceive the notion of having his works performed as he had written them and (thanks to the coming of effective copyright) to enforce it. In spite of his disclaimers he was the composer-artist; a composer-craftsman he had to be in Italian conditions, and the strain told, though by the late 1840s he was unquestionably the country's leading musician and his fame had spread abroad.

Fierceness and noisiness were matters for complaint among some who heard these early works; they were also the works' passport to success in a fierce and noisy decade. Today we may enjoy the onrush and the sense of raw power, but we are likely to be more impressed by the soaring nobility and grandeur of some of the music (as in the trio of baptism in *I Lombardi alla prima crociata*, 1843, or the scene by the tomb of Charlemagne in *Ernani*, 1844) and by the extraordinary penetration of Verdi the music-dramatist. The sleepwalking scene in *Macbeth* is not Shakespeare 'set to music', though the words follow the original closely. Verdi has re-created the scene in music whose melody and harmony seem simple yet uncannily right – desolation made music; the command of rhythm is important too, the keeping-up of a gentle, fate-like pulse. Earlier, Lady Macbeth's toast in the banqueting scene, which used to be deplored as trivial, is again just right in the flashy brilliance that masks her unease. The speed of the movement, its short-breathed phrasing (an inheritance from comic opera), are essential to the effect.

We have also learnt to discriminate among these early operas: *Macbeth*, *Ernani* and *Nabucco* stand out, but there are fine things in all of them. In Italy they are collectively known as the 'risorgimentale' operas. People commonly assume that because the Risorgimento sums up the complex of nationalist and allied movements that led to Italy's independence and unity in 1860–70, these operas must express straightforward nationalist sentiments; the notion is often extended to other operas of the period. The story is told of how audiences called out 'Viva VERDI!', the composer's name standing for 'Vittorio Emanuele re d'Italia'. The matter is in fact a good deal more complex; it needs to be disentangled from nationalist myths perpetuated after independence. Timing is crucial. A great deal changed during the 1840s and the period of revolution and repression in 1848–9 made for further profound changes in feeling.

Italian music was bound up with courts, governments and local aristocracies. Not surprisingly, most artists did their best to keep on good terms with their patrons. Few seem to have been active nationalists before 1848; most seem to have been taken up with music and theatre and concerned with politics only as a potential interference with their work. Rossini was an ironic conservative, Pacini an outright reactionary, Bellini and Donizetti were non-political (and Donizetti solicited, obtained and kept a court appointment in Vienna, the capital of the empire that was supposedly oppressing his country). Even Verdi in 1842–3 dedicated the scores of *Nabucco* and *I Lombardi* to two Austrian archduchesses, one of them his own sovereign. Yet times changed. Verdi would probably not have dedicated his works to members of the Austrian imperial family in the troubled years that just preceded the 1848 revolutions, and most certainly not in the years that followed them. Even the resonance of individual operas changed. *Norma*, with its Gaulish rebels, could be given peaceably in the presence of the visiting Austrian emperor in 1838, yet it seemed a nationalist rallying cry just before the revolution ten years later.[32]

The Romantic interest in collectivity, already evident in Rossini's *Mosè in Egitto*, could point in the direction of nationalism. But this sense of the people as something greater than the sum of individuals was politically ambiguous. It could be a conservative theme, as in Burke and Sir Walter Scott. In music it was most conspicuous in Verdi's early works. *Nabucco* followed on from *Mosè* in its biblical theme of exile, its use of the chorus and its solemn prayer. The famous chorus of the Jews by the waters of Babylon, 'Va pensiero sull'ali dorate', is sung in unison, in itself a political gesture: the singers are at one in the most obvious way. It speaks of a lost fatherland to be redeemed; the swinging slow 3/4 tune soars with a heart-catching leap and a shift into harmony (even though at the non-inflammatory words 'golden harp'; there is a more forthright cabaletta to come). Yet the chorus was passed by the censors; the opera was a great success, repeated almost at once all over Italy, and there is no sign that it bothered any of the old governments.

66. Barricade on the Porta Tosa, Milan, 22 March 1848: painting by Giulio Borra

Probably the chorus (like the similar one in *I Lombardi*) expressed a broad sense of human fellowship and a feeling for Italy's lost glories, shared by many in the audience. Its nationalism was what the Germans call 'folkish', directed at celebrating the oneness of its people and culture but without as yet drawing any specific political consequences. It could therefore be accepted by people some of whom were beginning to think of an independent but federal Italy, with the existing states left intact. In a wider sense, any call such as Verdi's upon deep collective emotions was bound to subvert the existing order. Later, in *La battaglia di Legnano* (1849), Verdi was to write a stirring scene for the Italians victorious against the armies of the Holy Roman Empire, the predecessor of Austria. But that was put on in republican Rome during the revolution. When the republic fell a few months later Verdi was ready to shift the action to the sixteenth-century Netherlands and show it under another title.

The 1848 revolutions severely jolted the opera world which had shown such busy creativity over the previous quarter-century. War followed revolution. Theatres stood virtually empty. A serious economic crisis had preceded the revolution and was now deepened by it. The upper classes were hard hit. Seasons were cancelled; others were put on only because the returning governments primed the pump with extra subsidies (that was how *Rigoletto* reached the stage in Venice in 1851).[33] Singers, though under protest, had to accept less than their usual fees. The opera business did not recover fully until 1853–4.

67. *Costume designs for the first production of Verdi's 'Rigoletto' at La Fenice, Venice, 11 March 1851*

By that time changes that had been under way since the mid-1840s were making themselves felt. The old, relentless rhythm of production had begun to flag soon after 1840. In 1844 the San Carlo formally cut down the number of new works it required, and although La Scala made no such declared change it did not put on as many new operas as in previous years. Routine performances of operas that had been heard before and that were more than a few years old became acceptable. The expression 'repertory opera' seems to date from the mid-1840s. Singers were expected to have a repertory they could sing at short notice. In many theatres this probably meant performances of deteriorating quality: a day's rehearsal or none, with the prompter kept busy.

At the same time a new kind of opera house was beginning to appear: large, built by non-noble entrepreneurs, unsubsidized and appealing to a more popular audience than the old royal or aristocratic theatres – though 'popular' still meant artisans, shopkeepers, commercial travellers and clerical workers rather than labourers or peasants. Their managers could seldom afford to commission new works; the new theatres and repertory opera therefore grew up together. A successful opera such as *Norma* or *Rigoletto* would now be given throughout the country, year in year out, with no sign of the public tiring of it.

A successful Italian composer was no longer forced to go on turning out new works at a Donizettian rate. That rate was merely normal for most composers up to the mid-nineteenth century because they depended on an original commission for nearly all their income: in practice they could not stop performances of pirated scores. After 1840, when the first effective copyright treaty between Italian states was signed, they were increasingly able to live off repertory performances. Verdi was the first to take advantage of the new situation. He altered the terms of his contracts and, after the three great 'popular' operas (*Rigoletto, Il trovatore, La traviata*, 1851–3), spaced out his works at ever longer intervals.[34] This made possible the creation of more studied, more complex but also more problematic works such as *Simon Boccanegra* (first version, 1857) and *La forza del destino* (1862).

Verdi's three 'popular' operas in any case summed up Italian opera of the previous quarter-century. They are among the handful of works any opera house in the world must put on at frequent intervals, tough creations that can withstand rough and ready performance, but rewarding care and skill with unsuspected beauties. Of the three, *Il trovatore* was the most traditional and the one that came closest to summing up past practice, though at a new level of continuous excitement. The other two, in different ways, were more experimental. *Rigoletto* combined the grotesque, the appalling and the tragically heroic in a Shakespearean way new to audiences brought up on classical distinctions between the genres; some have detected in the sufferings of its grim, misguided father the shade of the *Lear* Verdi meant, but failed, to write. The work turns its back on the aria-and-cabaletta convention – there is just one, plainly a concession to the tenor; much of the rest is a string of duets, and the sinister last act is built out of fragments of sung dialogue and brief concerted pieces, held together by tiny recurrent themes.

La traviata was innovatory, too, in its knitting together of the confrontation between the heroine and the young man's father by means of a string of duets, and in such a master-stroke as the tenor's offstage voice at the end of Act 1 suddenly repeating his earlier declaration of love interwoven with the soprano's febrile repudiation onstage: two voices and two movements in an opposition that presages union. The subject matter and its treatment were new in that Verdi brought the intimate pathos of the old *opera semiseria* to bear on a modern story hinging on bourgeois respectability and money, with an unhappy ending; there is no hint of the 'sublime' in Violetta's self-sacrifice, but, on the contrary, a humanity brought out by the delicacy of her vocal line and of much of the scoring. Woman as victim was a subject with a great operatic future, but in *La traviata* it is kept this side of masochism or sentimentality by the restraint of classical forms lithely handled.

For all the worldwide success of these three works, Italian opera now entered an awkward period of change. Over much of Europe the 1848 revolutions had shaken the old order beyond recall. In the Italian states they eroded the old court-based hierarchies and dynastic loyalties. But they also damaged people's confidence in dreams of liberation and other ideal solutions to life's problems. A selfconsciously tough realism now seemed to many people to be in order, whether in politics or in the arts.

The elemental passion on which Italian opera had fed was no longer enough. Opera would have to take notice of the intellectual concerns of nineteenth-century civilization. It would have to give audible and visible expression to the great abstract ideas – history, society, liberty. Only now, in the 1850s, did Italy seriously begin to absorb the Paris grand operas that did just that, in particular those of Meyerbeer and Halévy. Parisian grand opera had exerted some influence in Italy, in part through Rossini's French works which virtually created the form (*Guillaume Tell* circulated in Italy in spite of its anti-Austrian stance, with its libertarian sentiments and sometimes its title disguised, but it was not greatly liked), in part too through the Paris experiences of Verdi and Donizetti. But the great success of *Les Huguenots*, *Le prophète* and *La juive* made the 'ultra-classical' structures of Italian opera seem ultra-simple. Something richer, more self-consciously learned and artistic would be needed.

Verdi apart, however, Italian composers for many years were unable to renew their musical idiom in an effective way; Verdi's own development was highly individual and carried no school with him. When a successful group of composers arose once more with the *verismo* school of the 1890s it started from new premises.[35] Even someone like Shaw who loved Italian Romantic opera thought the march of progress had left it irretrievably behind. Only with the questioning of progress in our own century has the best of it been acknowledged as a mighty survivor.

NOTES

[1] A well-known but backward-looking treatise on singing, P. F. Tosi, *Opinioni de' cantori antichi e moderni* (Bologna, 1723/R1968), distinguishes the three styles and objects to modern singers' contaminating one with another.

[2] See O. Chadwick, *The Popes and European Revolution* (Oxford, 1981), which gives particular attention to Italy.

[3] M. F. Robinson, 'The Governors' Minutes of the Conservatorio Santa Maria di Loreto, Naples', *RMARC*, x (1972), 1–97, gives detailed local reasons for the decline of the Naples schools. Inflation, documented in R. Romano, *Prezzi, salari e servizi a Napoli nel secolo XVIII* (Milan, 1965), may be an over-arching explanation: it was damaging to institutions dependent on more or less fixed income such as rents.

[4] S. Arteaga, *Le rivoluzioni del teatro musicale italiano* (Venice, 1785), iii, 321–2.

[5] E. Rosmini, *La legislazione e la giurisprudenza dei teatri* (Milan, 1872), ii, 581ff.

[6] Count Strassoldo to Viceroy of Lombardy-Venetia, 1 Aug 1825, in J. Rosselli, *The Opera Industry in Italy from Cimarosa to Verdi: the Role of the Impresario* (Cambridge, 1984), 82.

[7] See *Teatro a Reggio Emilia*, ed. S. Romagnoli and E. Garbero (Florence, 1980).

[8] Saverio Mercadante to Francesco Florimo, 7 April 1840, in S. Palermo, *Saverio Mercadante* (Fasano, 1985), 208–9. There was in this statement some special pleading – Mercadante, an established but financially not very successful composer, was dickering for a higher salary as prospective director of the Naples Conservatory – but he would scarcely have put it forward if it had been quite implausible.

[9] Stendhal, *Correspondance*, ed. H. Martineau and V. Del Litto (Paris, 1962), i, 791–2.

[10] O. Nicolai, *Briefe an seinen Vater*, ed. W. Altmann (Regensburg, 1924), 185.

[11] C. Santley, *Student and Singer* (London, 1892), 83–4.

[12] H. Berlioz, *Voyage musical en Allemagne et en Italie* (Paris, 1844), 218–20; Nicolai, *Briefe*, 58–60.

[13] See, for the little-known Calabrian composer Nicola Manfroce (1791–1813), and for a different estimate of Mayr's work, P. Isotta, 'I diamanti della corona', in his edition of the librettos of Rossini's *Mosè in Egitto/Moïse et Pharaon/Mosè* (Turin, 1974), especially pp.206–14. There is a recording of *Medea in Corinto* (Vanguard VCS 10087/9).

[14] Stendhal, *Life of Rossini*, ed. and trans. R. N. Coe (London, 1956), 75–6; M. F. Robinson, *Naples and Neapolitan Opera* (Oxford, 1972), 208.

[15] G. Valle, *Cenni teorici-pratici sulle aziende teatrali* (Milan, 1823), 8–10.

[16] At Florence, a selfconsciously cultivated city, there was some interest, particularly from the 1820s, in German symphonic music and especially in Beethoven: see M. De Angelis, *La musica del Granduca* (Florence, 1978).

[17] See, for a more wholehearted appreciation of Rossini's serious operas, the article by P. Gossett in *Grove 6*, and R. Osborne, *Rossini* (London, 1986), as well as Isotta's essay (see n.13).

[18] For a detailed account of opera production in Italy in this period, see Rosselli, *The Opera Industry*.

[19] L. Bianconi and T. Walker, 'Production, Consumption and Political Function of Seventeenth-Century Opera', *EMH*, iv (1984), 224, 230; Rosselli, *The Opera Industry*, 50–65.

[20] Berlioz, *Voyage musical*, 164, and *Mémoires* (Paris, 1870), chap.39. See also G. Radiciotti, *Gioacchino Rossini* (Tivoli, 1927–9), i, 177.

[21] M. Lavagetto, *Un caso di censura: il 'Rigoletto'* (Milan, 1979), 107–28.

[22] M. Lessona, *Volere è potere* (Florence, 1869), 298.

[23] G. B. Shaw, *Music in London 1890–94* (London, 1932), ii, 178.

[24] 'Eine Selbstbiographie von Gertrud Elisabeth Mara' (ed. O. von Riesemann), *AMZ*, 3rd ser., x (1875), 59.

[25] For a perceptive estimate of *La sonnambula*, see F. Degrada, 'Prolegomeni a una lettura della *Sonnambula*', in *Il melodramma italiano dell'ottocento: studi e ricerche per Massimo Mila* (Turin, 1977), and in Degrada, *Il palazzo incantato* (Fiesole, 1979).

[26] Mercadante to Florimo, 1 Jan 1838, quoted in J. Budden, *The Operas of Verdi* (London, 1973–81), ii, 6. The complete letter is in Palermo, *Mercadante*, 178–9; the letters of G. Viezzoli to Nicola Vaccaj, 1836–8, are in Archivo Vaccaj, Biblioteca Comunale, Tolentino (see especially letter of 22 March 1838). The best guides to the development of Italian musical forms in this period are the introductory chapters in Budden, op cit, and F. Lippmann, 'Vincenzo Bellini und die italienische Opera seria seiner Zeit', *AnMc*, no.6 (1969); rev. It. trans. in M. R. Adamo and F. Lippmann, *Vincenzo Bellini* (Turin, 1981).

[27] G. Vaccaj, *Vita di Nicola Vaccaj* (Bologna, 1882), 107–10.

[28] A later breeches part such as the (soprano) page Oscar in Verdi's *Un ballo in maschera* (1859) belongs to a different tradition of women singing the parts of children or adolescents.

[29] Giovanni David seems to have been doing so shortly before he created the very high-lying (and heroic) part of Rodrigo in Rossini's *Otello* (1816): E. Celani, 'Musica e musicisti in Roma 1750–1850: 3', *RMI*, xxii (1915), 28–9. Domenico Donzelli, for whom Bellini wrote the demanding part of Pollione in *Norma* (1831), was another tenor who combined flexibility with power.

[30] His *Quoniam* and *Gloria patri* have been recorded in a delightful performance by Arleen Augér, part of a Schwetzingen Festival recital (Deutsche Harmonia Mundi 1C 065–99807). Padre Martini's criticism (of Pergolesi's church music) in C. Burney, *A General History of Music*, ed. F. Mercer (London, 1935/*R*1957), ii, 924.

[31] See Budden, *The Operas of Verdi*, i, 32–3, 141, and ii, 39–41; L. Dallapiccola, 'Parole e musica nel melodramma', *Quaderni della RaM* (1965), no.2, p.117; rev. in *Appunti* (1970); Eng. trans., *PNM*, v/1 (1966), 121.

[32] For a more detailed discussion, see Rosselli, *The Opera Industry*, 165–9. 'Viva VERDI!' in the sense mentioned was heard at the fourth performance at La Scala of *Simon Boccanegra*, about the end of January 1859; the first performance took place on 24 January, just over a fortnight after King Victor Emmanuel of Sardinia had made a speech (9 January) that was generally taken as heralding a war of independence. The war started on 29 April: C. Gatti, *Il Teatro alla Scala nella storia e nell'arte (1778–1963)* (Milan, 1964), i, 130–31. This seems to be the first recorded instance, and almost the last, since the war rapidly brought Italian unity.

[33] J. Rosselli, 'I costi dell'operazione', in *Musicacittà*, ed. L. Berio (Rome and Bari, 1984) [programme of 47th Maggio Musicale, Florence].

[34] J. Rosselli, 'Verdi e la storia della retribuzione del compositore italiano', *Studi verdiani*, ii (1983), 15, 21–3.

[35] Budden, *The Operas of Verdi*, ii, chap.1.

BIBLIOGRAPHICAL NOTE

General background

The most incisive and up-to-date general account in English of this period in Italian history is S. Woolf's *A History of Italy 1700–1860* (London, 1979). It is a political, social and economic history and ignores the arts; the names Rossini and Verdi do not appear. One reason is that the book originally appeared as part of vol.iii of *Storia d'Italia*, ed. R. Romano and C. Vivanti, 6 vols. in 9 pts. (Turin, 1973–6), alongside an essay on cultural life by N. Badaloni, which, in line with the usual priorities of Italian intellectuals, does not mention Rossini or Verdi either. An older, once highly influential view still worth considering is that of Benedetto Croce in his *History of the*

Kingdom of Naples, trans. F. Frenaye, ed. H. S. Hughes (Chicago, 1970; originally published Bari, 1925). It may be contrasted with A. Gramsci's *Il Risorgimento* (Turin, 1949; part trans. in Gramsci, *Selections from the Prison Notebooks*, ed. and trans. Q. Hoare and G. Nowell-Smith, section 'Notes on Italian History').

The literary and intellectual background is well dealt with by A. Colquhoun, *Manzoni and his Times* (London, 1954). On the visual arts Hugh Honour's *Neo-Classicism* (London, 1968) does much to illuminate a movement difficult to come to terms with today. Significantly, the same author's *Romanticism* (London, 1979), though well aware of Italian developments, gives them little space. The liveliest single work on Italy during and just after the Napoleonic period is by the great contemporary novelist Stendhal, *Rome, Naples et Florence* (Paris, enlarged 2/1826; several modern editions). His *Life of Rossini*, ed. and trans. R. N. Coe (London, 1956; originally published Paris, 1824), is not a reliable biography but another highly entertaining, opinionated essay by a man who knew Italy and its musical world at close quarters.

The musical world

A good starting-point is G. Pestelli's *The Age of Mozart and Beethoven*, trans. E. Cross (Cambridge, 1984; originally published Turin, 1979). Mozart himself was a keen observer of the Italian musical world just before our period: see *The Letters of Mozart and his Family*, ed. and trans. E. Anderson (London, rev. 3/1985). So was Charles Burney in *Music, Men, and Manners in France and Italy, 1770*, ed. H. E. Poole (London, 1969). The two most distinguished studies of the changing aesthetics and practice of Italian opera in this period are F. Lippmann, 'Vincenzo Bellini und die italienische Opera seria seiner Zeit', *AnMc*, no.6 (1969), also available in Italian in M. R. Adamo and F. Lippmann, *Vincenzo Bellini* (Turin, 1981), and the chapter 'Verdi and the World of the Primo Ottocento', in vol.i of J. Budden's *The Operas of Verdi*, 3 vols. (London, 1973–81). There is a further essay by Budden in *A Verdi Companion*, ed. W. Weaver and M. Chusid (London, 1979), where B. Cagli sketches the business of opera in nineteenth-century Italy, a subject dealt with more fully by J. Rosselli, *The Opera Industry in Italy from Cimarosa to Verdi: the Role of the Impresario* (Cambridge, 1984).

The visual side of opera is magnificently illustrated and learnedly expounded by Mercedes Viale Ferrero in vol.iii of *Storia del Teatro Regio di Torino*, ed. A. Basso, 5 vols. (Turin, 1976–88). The six-volume *Storia dell'opera italiana*, ed. L. Bianconi and G. Pestelli (Turin, 1984–), of which four volumes have already appeared, will eventually include essays by P. Weiss and others on opera in the eighteenth and nineteenth centuries; it is designed to set opera in its social context and to discuss it according to its creative and productive aspects, where the earlier *Storia dell'opera*, ed. G. Barblan and A. Basso, 6 vols. (Turin, 1977), is organized more according to schools and individual composers. The last volume of the Barblan-Basso history includes extensive discussion by F. Cella of the development of the libretto, a subject dealt with in English by J. Black, *The Italian Romantic Libretto: a Study of Salvadore Cammarano* (Edinburgh, 1984): this, as the sub-title makes clear, concentrates mainly on the librettist of *Lucia di Lammermoor* and *Il trovatore*.

Individual composers

The best modern studies of Rossini in book form are those by L. Rognoni (Turin, rev. 3/1977) and, in English, by R. Osborne (London, 1986). Osborne represents the recent tendency to set a high value on Rossini's serious operas, most eloquently spoken for by P. Isotta in his essay 'Il diamanti della corona', part of his edition of the librettos of *Mosè in Egitto/Moïse et Pharaon/Mosè* (Turin, 1974). A modern edition of

The Early Romantic Period

Rossini's correspondence is being prepared at the Centro Rossiniano di Studi at Pesaro, as is one of Verdi's at the equivalent institute at Parma.

For Bellini and Donizetti the best sources are in many ways their published letters: Bellini, *Epistolario*, ed. L. Cambi (Milan, 1943), and Donizetti, *Vita, musiche, epistolario*, ed. G. Zavadini (Bergamo, 1948). The finest study of Verdi is that (already mentioned) by Budden, who has also published a one-volume account of the composer's life and works in the Master Musicians series (London, 1985; best read in the corrected paperback edition, 1986). A work that offers remarkable, at times controversial, insights is G. Baldini's *Abitare la Battaglia*, ed. F. D'Amico (Milan, 1970; trans. R. Parker as *The Story of Giuseppe Verdi*, Cambridge, 1980). In spite of the English title it is mainly a critical essay on the operas down to *Un ballo in maschera* (1859). The essays on all these composers in *Grove 6* (by P. Gossett, Lippmann, W. Ashbrook, Budden and A. Porter) are all of high quality and have been reprinted in a separate volume, *Masters of Italian Opera* (London, 1983).

Chapter VII

London: the Professionalization of Music

JOEL SACHS

To appreciate the nature of music and musical life in London in the early nineteenth century, one needs first to look at the city itself. From Joseph Haydn's time to Felix Mendelssohn's, London was in a state of immense flux. Already enormous at the turn of the century, it had more than a million inhabitants, twice as many as Paris, four times as many as Vienna. At the 1851 census London's population had passed two and a half million. In that same time, the developed land of the metropolitan area grew from a rectangle roughly bounded by the present Park Lane, Marylebone Road, the eastern edge of the City and an east–west line just across the Thames, to a sprawl reaching out to Kensington, Hampstead, areas north and east of the City and many new southern suburbs. London's role in Britain was also changing: in the 1790s it was a small city visited only out of necessity by the aristocracy and landed gentry who controlled Britain; by the middle of the century it was the financial and commercial capital of an immeasurably rich world empire. The inseparability of art from life is, of course, hardly unique; but in a city fairly bursting with money, the progress of that relationship is especially fascinating.

The disparity of wealth between those who could enjoy the arts and those who could not was particularly brutal in London because of the vastness of the poor population and its proximity to the rich. For the destitute majority, music was an informal pleasure, experienced on the streets and in taverns, sung roughly but with passion, witnessed only at the cheapest venues of entertainment. This music for and from the masses will remain only poorly understood, however, because of the paucity of surviving descriptions and compositions. The rich, of course, had the leisure to enjoy music and left plentiful evidence to that effect. Unlike the Viennese, however, Londoners were ambivalent about music. Sometimes treasured, sometimes taken for granted, music implied everything from tawdry mediocrity, vigorously marketed, to the highest quality, appealing only to a limited audience. And the struggle to establish music's place can be traced through several phases, from the years of formation, to intense professionalization, stability and prosperity, and finally to a musical world with the characteristics of today's.

THE TURN OF THE CENTURY

Surviving documents[1] reinforce the impression that public concerts were infrequent before the last decade of the eighteenth century. Since the 1730s – possibly even earlier – the Lord Chamberlain had been charged with regulating stage entertainment and protecting the monopolies of the patent theatres (Drury Lane and Covent Garden). In the early 1790s, however, his office also asserted its power to licence concerts, a power exercised infrequently in the past. The ledgers in which licences were recorded show a rapid increase in compliances about 1794, suggesting that public concerts were assuming greater significance. This points to the beginning of a period of flourishing music-making about 1790. But, since entertainment was unsubsidized, the typical concert price of half a guinea was beyond the reach of most people, who were lucky to have an income of £50 a year. Even the 'middle class', whose income has been reckoned as starting at about £150, could hardly afford to go to formal musical events.

Money was by no means the only criterion for concert and opera attendance. To ensure a socially uniform audience, some concerts were accessible only to people of impeccable reputation and the transfer of tickets to individuals other than the buyer's immediate family was prohibited. A music-lover contemplating buying a series subscription, therefore, had to bear in mind that illness or indisposition might cost him dearly. Non-transferability, though burdensome for administrators, survived into the 1840s. And some music was presented exclusively at events so private that we know almost nothing about them. Financial and social factors required that all concerts and Italian opera performances be restricted to the short spring social season. During the season the wealthy converged on the capital from their country estates for the parliamentary session, and the glitter of London at this time attracted continental visitors. It was this temporary concentration of power and money which rendered London's expensive concerts viable.

Contemporary writers[2] describe music-lovers as divided into factions: 'ancient', 'modern' or 'classical'. 'Ancient' signified Baroque music – Handel, Geminiani, Corelli and other Italians, but not J. S. Bach, who remained more or less unknown. The small 'ancient' group felt overwhelmed by the devotees of modern music – the virtuoso instrumental music (primarily concertos) and opera arias, as well as the salon music with which the wealthy educated their daughters. Programmes and attendance were governed by the many virtuosos, mostly from abroad, who, attracted by English wealth, had come to London for decades; with their skills and talents, they had seized the imagination of audiences. Musical immigration temporarily increased in the early 1790s with the arrival of refugees from France, including such luminaries as Giovanni Battisti Viotti, Jan Ladislav Dussek and Mme Gautherot, a French violinist. Devotees of 'ancient music' were contemptuous of the modernists, who scarcely knew contemporary composers like Haydn and Mozart. The works of the latter, and symphonies, overtures and chamber music generally, were increasingly referred to as 'classical' music. This use of the term differs from ours: 'classical' composers, to whose numbers Beethoven, Hummel, Weber and others would be added, belonged to the musical avant garde of their time.

The foreign presence in London was most concentrated in the Italian opera company at the King's Theatre (at the bottom of the Haymarket). This focus of culture was perennially on the brink of destruction. Its exclusive audience contrasted vividly with the rougher crowd at the patent theatres, Drury Lane and Covent Garden, where seats were filled with a broad spectrum of humanity ranging from the educated to prostitutes and thieves. Italian opera attracted its audience with star singers engaged at fantastic cost. Singers earned as much as £5000 a year – not including concert, party and country festival earnings – and had almost total control

68. *Riot over the raised ticket prices, following the opening of the second Covent Garden Theatre on 18 September 1809: etching by George Cruikshank*

over the company. The orchestra, however, was badly paid because players were in abundant supply. Nevertheless, the best performances were reputedly as good as any in Europe, a fact that may have eluded many in the audience, who cared far more about the opportunity to talk even during the performances. What counted most was to be seen. Those with a real interest in art usually favoured the ballet, performed during intervals or after the opera.[3]

In spite of its legal monopoly on Italian opera, the King's Theatre was not supported by government or crown subsidies. Under normal circumstances an opera house with such an outrageous budget would not have survived, the less so as it was encumbered by numerous bankruptcies, lawsuits, desperate managers and an embarrassed crown, which owned the land under the theatre (at one time, the stage and the auditorium were owned by different creditors). The opera house remained open only because its construction, like that of many European theatres, had been financed by the sale of 'property boxes': one purchased a long lease on a box and could use the seats personally or sell them at a handsome profit. If the opera house closed, the box owners, many of them powerful, stood to lose heavily. The guardians of society therefore had to ensure it remained open: staging an inoffensive repertory effectively displayed the expensive cast; but cynicism about the opera house pervaded the musical world. While the King's Theatre enjoyed the monopoly of Italian opera, it was not permitted to perform anything else. The management, therefore, brought new operas from Italy and engaged resident composers and librettists to

69. The King's Theatre: (a) interior, showing the lyre-shaped auditorium designed by Novosielski: engraving (1809) by Pugin after Rowlandson

(b) two studies of the band in 1806 by John Nixon; the players include Anthony Ashe (flute) and the brothers Petrides (horns), top, and Dahmen (cello), bottom right

create new works. These house teams produced little, even though they included Antonio Sacchini, resident composer in the 1770s, and Lorenzo da Ponte, librettist there from 1792. Some 85% of the repertory was imported and little of it retained its original form since singers demanded new arias and cuts were made to leave time for the desired ballets. Moreover, only a handful of operas, by Bianchi, Cimarosa, Martín y Soler, Paisiello, Sacchini and Sarti, survived beyond a single season.

London had 'English opera' at Covent Garden, Drury Lane and other smaller theatres. This consisted chiefly of adaptations of continental operas, cut, rearranged and provided with additional songs and instrumental music, to the point that the original was almost unrecognizable, by composers who included Charles Dibdin and Stephen Storace. This repertory was of slight dramatic importance, but it drew audiences and allowed such singers as Elizabeth Billington, John Braham and Nancy Storace to earn salaries not far below those of their Italian counterparts (who, however, sang far fewer performances each season). English opera was presented all the year round, rather than just in the season, and to a much less exclusive audience.

Whereas opera had a tradition as public entertainment, concerts

70. Oratorio at Covent Garden (the first theatre): watercolour (1790s) by Benedictus van Assen

were only now breaking away from the private domain.[4] Virtually every public concert was called a 'benefit concert', that is, one presented for the financial benefit of its organizers (most of whom were musicians). Among the few concerts not undertaken as individual speculation were occasional festival programmes, the twelve-concert series of the Concert of Ancient Music, the Lenten oratorios (low-priced semi-sacred performances at Covent Garden or Drury Lane) and the few true fund-raising events in aid of professional entertainers' charities or in response to a disaster or the hardship of a respected individual. The preferred venues were all in the largely residential West End: the Hanover Square Rooms, the Argyll Rooms (near Oxford Circus), the King's Theatre concert room and the assembly rooms of Willis or Almack, near St James's Palace. A few events still took place at taverns in the business districts (such as the Crown and Anchor in the Strand). The aim of a benefit was, of course, to fill the hall with the best class of person.

Some organizers presented entire series of benefits by subscription. The viability of such undertakings had been demonstrated by J. C. Bach and C. F. Abel between 1765 and 1782; their series was succeeded by Wilhelm Cramer's Professional Concerts (1783–93), which in turn faced the formidable competition of J. P. Salomon. Salomon had invited Haydn to London as composer-in-residence in 1791, and in doing so accomplished the near-miracle of elevating modernist tastes from the trivial. The Professional Society fought back in 1792 by engaging Haydn's former pupil, Ignace Pleyel, but its declining popularity coincided with the end of the boom in serious instrumental concerts. The declaration of war by France, on 1 February 1793, restricted the flow of foreign artists and caused the demise of Cramer's society. Haydn returned in 1794, his chief legacy being the twelve 'London' symphonies, his last. Salomon continued with a reduced series in 1796, but for the better part of two decades neither he nor anyone else had much luck with concerts featuring contemporary instrumental music. Deprived of continental talent, Salomon discovered that English musicians did not draw crowds. By contrast, vocal concerts, even those featuring English singers, flourished.

Early nineteenth-century programmes usually mixed instrumental and vocal solos with ensemble pieces. Benefits in particular appealed to the well-to-do, with popular entertainments offering few artistic challenges. An all-instrumental concert was therefore unthinkable. The orchestras could be large or very rudimentary, but rehearsal time for the overtures, concertos and accompaniments was minimal and the results were often poor. Salomon's and Cramer's concerts had been notable exceptions in this respect, too. The concerts' extreme length – sometimes three or four hours – has been cited as evidence of London's hunger for music, but audiences arrived late, left early and did not worry about disturbing the hardier listeners.

Most benefits catered to the modernists who, unlike the devotees of ancient music, demanded constant variety and titillation. Both could be found in the arias and concertos featuring virtuosos, and the 'ancients' had reason to complain that the old, honoured concerto style had degenerated into mere soloistic display. Concertos, of course, were generally executed by the composer and were rarely published except in transcription. The more renowned soloists of the 1790s included the pianists Muzio Clementi, Johann Baptist Cramer, the prodigies John Field, Johann Nepomuk Hummel and Daniel Steibelt, as well as the violinists George Bridgetower and Felix Janiewicz. But countless others, including leading orchestral string and wind players, had their own following. The handful who played 'masterpieces' were women or children. From among the latter, a few, including Mozart (a London resident during his childhood), Clementi and Hummel, rose to adult fame. The chief difference between the aria and concerto cults is the fact that almost no singers were composers; instead they made arias their own through ornamentation, a practice that could be musically disastrous. Serious musicians' contempt for concertos and arias lasted until the discovery, as it were, of the mature Mozart led to the elevation of the genres.

A concert involving many musicians was a major undertaking that necessitated high ticket prices to pay for renting the hall, the musicians' fees, advertising, refreshments and guards. While the prospect of making a profit was alluring – Haydn reported receipts of

£350 (nearly double what he had been guaranteed) from his 1791 benefit[5] – many promoters lost money and relied on the good will of professional colleagues. Losses could be tolerated, however, because a successful benefit promised long-term reward through exposure to wealthy potential pupils and well-connected people who could provide entrée into the lucrative orbit of private concerts and parties. A benefit was therefore thought essential for any visiting virtuoso. With such high stakes, programmes and publicity took extreme forms. One advertisement shortly after the turn of the century announced a performance by a child harpist who was to undertake the unprecedented feat of performing a duet for two harps by himself. Garish or deceptive publicity grew. In the 1820s, posters were even glued to carcasses in the butchers' shops. Also, an advertised famous singer might appear only briefly, if at all.

While the wealthiest people flocked to concerts of modern music, the ancient style appears to have been the refuge of the elderly, especially older aristocrats who clung to established values in an epoch of threatening change. They mostly went to events organized by the Concert of Ancient Music; founded in 1776 and granted royal patronage in 1785, it aimed to perform the great works of earlier composers, and compositions less than twenty years old were excluded. The subscription list was limited to the highest levels of society and each committee member in turn arranged an evening's programme. The society's orchestra numbered some 50 players, as did its (all-male) chorus, at first drawn from the chorus of Westminster Abbey and the Chapel Royal. Concerts consisted mainly of Handel's works but the repertory included music by Italian Baroque composers and numerous English glee composers. Under its noble directors, and apparently with little contradiction by its conductor William Greatorex (who held the post from 1793 to 1830), the same works appeared season after season. However, programmes also offered Renaissance and early Baroque music, then almost unknown, thus helping to sow the seeds for the mid-nineteenth-century Renaissance revival.

The demand for Ancient Concert subscriptions is perhaps the clearest example of the beneficial effects of royal patronage. Although the king made no direct monetary contributions, his patronage helped fill an auditorium. Many members of the royal family were musical, and when George III became permanently insane in 1810, even those with little respect for the free-spending Prince of Wales had to admit that his musical tastes would bring cultural benefits. The level of music-making at court did in fact rise drastically both in quantity and in quality. While most of the court's musical activity took place outside London, especially at Brighton, St James's Palace was the setting for many a concert, and appointment to its band brought

71. Ticket for a Harmonic Society amateur concert at the Great Room, Cateaton Street, 6 September 1810

income and a pension. Some court positions, however, were given as sinecures to non-musicians, who engaged deputies.[6] Meanwhile the public gardens, especially Vauxhall and Ranelagh, offered concerts, operas, pastiches, concerto performances and fireworks to audiences drawn from a wide sector of the populace, though hardly from the poor.

Sacred music was at a low ebb. An innovatory spirit did not characterize the leading churches like St Paul's Cathedral, whose boys spent most of their time singing in fashionable concerts; and in most Anglican churches congregational singing had all but disappeared. It was largely left to the Methodists to demonstrate the power of music in worship. Roman Catholic Masses were forbidden until 1835, except at the chapels of foreign embassies. A few organists of such chapels became leaders of London music, for example Vincent Novello, who introduced the masses of Haydn and Mozart at the Portuguese Chapel. And there were other voices from the church crying out for higher musical standards: Samuel Wesley (nephew of John Wesley) chose this inappropriate time to attempt a complete edition of J. S. Bach's music; and John Wall Callcott, organist of St Paul's, Covent Garden, worked to promote higher standards.[7] Luckily, these voices did not go entirely unheard.

RISING PROFESSIONALISM, c1810–1823

After stagnating through most of the first decade of the century, concert life rapidly improved. Certain energetic musicians initiated many of the new ventures, but the rapid increase also mirrors the growth of London itself. By 1810, with five years of war still ahead, the pace of development had quickened noticeably. The Prince Regent's huge projects, which culminated in Regent's Park and Regent Street, heralded an age of expansion that accelerated with the end of the war. London now enjoyed prosperity, all manner of speculative enterprises and some industrialization. The flourishing, affluent middle class avidly sought culture and became more assertive: the arts began to change.

London's musicians, cut off from sophisticated instrumental music for twenty years, seized the moment. There was no official encouragement of concerts, but musicians knew that the government was unlikely to interfere with their ideas. (Opera managers, however, had to contend with constant meddling.) On 24 January 1813, at the home of William Dance (a prominent violinist, conductor and contractor), an influential group of musicians met to consider the state of the profession; they included Dance, the pianist, composer and publisher Johann Baptist Cramer and his brother the violinist François (sons of the director of the 1790s Professional Concerts), the singer Philip Anthony Corri and, according to some accounts, the pianist Charles Neate. Out of their meeting grew the Philharmonic Society.[8]

A philharmonic society had existed as early as 1730 at the Crown and Anchor Tavern, but it was an amateur organization. In 1802, John Wall Callcott had formulated a plan for a philharmonic society but his would have offered only lectures to its members. The 1813 Philharmonic Society, however, was to organize a series of orchestral performances through which London musicians could become acquainted with modern music. At first their performances were intended only to edify the members themselves and their associates and families. They came to include an audience, but would-be subscribers needed recommendations by a musician-member, since the founders wanted to exclude people with no real interest in serious music. The fashionable – the bane (and the financial rock) of concert life – would have no claim to tickets. Even so, in view of ticket prices, four guineas for eight concerts with a discount for professionals, subscribers had to be prosperous.

Daring restrictions were imposed on the repertory; no solos, whether vocal or instrumental, would be given (concertos with

multiple soloists and vocal ensembles were permitted). The Philharmonic Society was proposing to form the first large, permanent
symphony orchestra, and the solo repertory did not make good use
of resources (the concertos of Mozart and Beethoven were still
virtually unknown). The rules had a social motivation too: virtuoso
stars were the idols of the fashionable, and the Philharmonic wished
its listeners to concentrate on compositions. Sceptics predicted that
these regulations would lead to the society's early demise, but
resources and taste had been underestimated. The Philharmonic's
refusal to pander to the rich became an asset, and tickets were
soon in great demand. Within a few years, the concerts were packed
with nearly 800 people, more than 600 of whom were external subscribers. The society accumulated a substantial surplus, which it
soon put to good use. The cooperative structure of the Philharmonic
ensured that the orchestra could be drawn largely from members and
associates who were not paid (apart from a few extras, primarily
wind players). Thus the musicians were perceived as dedicated
professionals. Within a few years the orchestra grew to have nearly
50 string players – almost twice as many as Salomon's 1790s
orchestras – double flutes, oboes, clarinets and bassoons, four horns,
two trumpets, three trombones, timpani and extra wind or percussion
as required.

The Philharmonic's real accomplishment, however, was demon-
strating that high standards of programming could attract a large
public. The society was quite unlike the others active at the time: the
Ancient Concert, still vigorously dedicated to the past, and the Vocal
Concerts (1791–1822) of Harrison, Bartleman and Knyvett. Only at
the Philharmonic could the greatness of new music be appreciated.
Early accomplishments included first London performances of several
of Beethoven's overtures and the Fifth Symphony, and other new
symphonies and overtures presented during the season of Cherubini's
residency (modelled on the old Haydn concerts), as well as works by
Ferdinand Ries, Friedrich Kalkbrenner, Camille Pleyel, Hummel and
countless others.

In 1815, during the third season, a group of musicians aware that
the society was accumulating a surplus saw no reason to perform
without pay. They formed a rival orchestra, using the old name
Professional Concerts, thus threatening the future of both. After one
season, the Philharmonic emerged the winner, though at a cost: its
orchestra now had to be remunerated. It is probably not merely co-
incidental that during the struggle for its survival the Philharmonic's
guidelines were amended to permit opera arias and, not long afterwards, solo concertos. Discoveries of works by Mozart helped to
justify the change, but the orchestra – Europe's first full professional
symphony orchestra – had now become dependent on box-office

receipts. At the same time the organization had become more complex and the cooperative structure more unwieldy. Nevertheless, a city that offered little high-quality music for nearly twenty years had suddenly spawned an institution without rival in Europe: a professional orchestra of almost unprecedented size and, by 1820, a properly run concert organization, independent of government subsidy or bureaucratic interference, which enhanced musicians' social and intellectual status. Women musicians were admitted as a special class of professional subscribers.

Those hectic and exciting years also witnessed problems that were to become endemic to London's musical life. Many refugees from Napoleon had been founding members and associates of the Philharmonic, contributing ideas, compositions and performing skills. Their accomplishments provoked antagonism as English musicians were passed over during balloting for Philharmonic membership. At the end of the war, in 1815, most of these refugees returned to the Continent, provoking criticism of their lack of lasting loyalty to Britain. Soon other Europeans, enjoying the new freedom to travel, arrived and competed against the English for precious performing opportunities. Where music should have united, it divided. The exodus had dramatically drawn attention to the perils of relying on foreigners.

The Philharmonic Society presented eight concerts each season, between mid-February and June, and these came to follow the same pattern: a symphony, an aria, a chamber work, a vocal ensemble and an overture in the first half, and after the intermission an overture, a vocal ensemble, a concerto, an aria and a symphony. But even these devoted audiences did not have the limitless stamina needed for such long programmes, and many people left before the end. (The final work was known to be played more out of obligation than commitment.) Also, even the best string quartet seemed puny when heard after a Beethoven symphony or a virtuoso aria, but it was still considered preferable to hear works in this context rather than not at all.

While the Philharmonic represented an enormous leap forward in quality, the level of these early performances was uneven. Members' skills were varied, and the ambivalence about conductorial authority that plagued English music in general had potent effects in the complex Philharmonic repertory. The English conductor sat at a keyboard instrument, giving cues to singers and possibly setting the tempos, much in the way he would have done in Baroque music. Real control was in the hands of the principal violinist, the leader. The Philharmonic leader was handsomely paid, whereas the conductors were unpaid: they were gentlemen. Musically this could be disastrous. The conductor and the leader could not be seen well by all the players and, worse, no-one had a real command of the music at a time when a thorough grasp of rapidly changing styles was essential. And the early conductors were not nonentities: they included Clementi and Cramer (the only conductors during the first two seasons), Cherubini, George Smart, Henry Bishop, Ferdinand Ries. The English resistance to giving control to the conductor helps explain why Beethoven's Third, Fifth, Sixth and Seventh Symphonies made poor initial impressions.[9]

The Philharmonic Society's success was not the only sign of a new musical epoch. At the King's Theatre, the Italian Opera had staggered through each season, struggling to keep its doors open in the face of an increasingly apathetic public and a host of creditors. But in 1817, with the selection of William Ayrton as musical director, things began to change. Ayrton, who had already made his mark at the Philharmonic Society, proceeded to stage the first British production of *Don Giovanni*; he filled the house for 23 nights, giving the company a new lease of life and transforming London opera (previous Mozart productions had not survived their initial season). The Covent Garden Theatre, limited to entertainments in English, reacted immediately with a bowdlerized *Don Giovanni* in a double-bill with *Hamlet*. (Sensing a fortune to be made from abbreviated masterpieces, Covent Garden whipped up adaptations by Bishop of *Il barbiere di Siviglia* and *Le nozze di Figaro* in 1818–19.)

Until 1818 music journals were few and short-lived; those that survived temporarily were either concerned with arcane topics of theory and aesthetics or, at the opposite extreme, with crassly marketed salon music. Coverage of music in the daily papers was unremarkable at best, focussing on the audience more than the event itself. The turning-point was the founding of the *Quarterly Musical Magazine and Review* in 1818. Although it was published in Norwich, the home of its founder and editor Richard Mackenzie Bacon (proprietor of the *Norwich Mercury*, a notable provincial organ of liberalism), the new monthly became the leading musical voice in London. Bacon strove for high standards and breadth of coverage and his columns remain an invaluable source of information about the musical world.

Much remained to be accomplished in professional musical education. Charles Burney had attempted to create a conservatory as an adjunct to the Foundling Hospital in 1774, but with no success. Nearly half a century later there was still no institution for musical education. One simply took lessons from a musician, occasionally in a formal apprenticeship. The war had precluded studying on the Continent, but Charles Neate went to Germany almost as soon as Napoleon had been pushed out. He spent some months in 1815 in close contact with Beethoven and later helped London keep abreast of new developments. Those who aimed to play in the opera or theatre orchestras found that entrée was most easily gained through one's teacher, for whom one might deputize (a practice that pervaded the orchestral world). Those who aspired to the solo world needed a master who could establish contacts among the elegant. The lack of opportunity for formal education was a sore point among musicians, who were sensitive to the disdain with which other professionals regarded them. The Philharmonic Society presented a collective force capable of creating an academy; even so, an energetic attempt (1814) failed for lack of crucial support from the Prince of Wales.[10]

Amateur musicians had a wide choice of instructors: thousands of piano and singing teachers were said to survive in London by instructing the young ladies of good households, who also might study the harp or flute. A proper woman did not play the violin, the holding of which revealed her profile immodestly; playing the cello was unthinkable. Respectable gentlemen, including noblemen, studied the piano or string instruments, while most wind and percussion were left to the lower classes. The economic life of musicians was nevertheless fraught with insecurity. The Royal Society of Musicians (and the New Musical Fund, for non-Londoners) provided pension and disability aid, but membership was limited and many musicians could not afford the premiums.[11] Life was especially hard for wind players, who had few pupils and frequently passed their old age in poverty. This affected orchestral standards: elderly musicians who had no financial resources kept performing long after they had passed their prime in order to avoid the poor house.

CONSOLIDATION: THE 1820s AND 1830s

The triumphs of the decade after 1810 heralded a golden age that secured London's position as a target for musical fortune-seekers. The Philharmonic's status, and the resulting scarcity of subscriptions, was continually cited as responsible for the rapid increase in the appreciation of classical music. Indeed, the highest mark of approval was now an engagement at the Philharmonic. Having the finest soloists and paying musicians a professional wage added greatly to the expense of its concerts. Still, by 1821 an accumulated surplus of some £2300 ensured stability and permitted the Philharmonic to undertake some interesting projects. In 1820, for instance, Louis Spohr, one of the most respected violinists in Europe, was engaged as leader and, effectively, composer-in-residence, producing new symphonies and chamber works. He was succeeded by the extremely effective Hanoverian composer-violinist Christoph Gottfried Kiesewetter, whose excessive wages, however (250 guineas in 1821, the same as Spohr's), provoked a backlash that eventually resulted in the return of leadership to local violinists.

New names, now familiar, graced the roster of soloists: Liszt (a teenager), Mendelssohn (not much older), Hummel, Moscheles, Mme Szymanowska and the Belgian violinist De Beriot among the instrumentalists; Lucia Elizabeth Vestris, Margarethe Stockhausen, Giuditta Pasta, John Braham, Henry Phillips and Domenico Donzelli among the singers. Resident soloists, though less in demand than the foreigners, also built fine careers: Lucy Anderson (later music teacher to Queen Victoria), Cipriani Potter, Charles Neate and various wind and string players. Potter in 1820 played the first Mozart concerto at the Philharmonic and later introduced Beethoven's C minor and G major concertos; Anderson played Beethoven's 'Emperor' Concerto and Mendelssohn the G major piano concerto.

The Philharmonic's resources allowed it to commission or purchase symphonic works for British premières. In the 1820s Beethoven's Ninth Symphony and *Die Weihe des Hauses* overture were first performed as well as works by Spohr, Weber and a host of others. Not until 1832, however, were efforts made to obtain new instrumental or vocal music from local composers. Unfortunately when some of the composers failed to complete their commissions, the cause

UNDER THE IMMEDIATE PATRONAGE OF

His Majesty.

PHILHARMONIC SOCIETY.

THIRD CONCERT, MONDAY, MARCH 21, 1825.

ACT I.

Sinfonia Letter T.	Haydn.
Terzetto, "Tutte le mie speranze," Madame CARADORI, Miss GOODALL, and Mr. VAUGHAN (Davide Penitente)	Mozart.
Quartetto, two Violins, Viola, and Violoncello, Messrs. SPAGNOLETTI, OURY, MORALT, and LINDLEY	Mozart.
Song, Mr. VAUGHAN, "Why does the God of Israel sleep," (Samson)	Handel.
Quintetto, Flute, Oboë, Clarinet, Horn, and Bassoon, Messrs. NICHOLSON, VOGT, WILLMAN, PLATT, and MACKINTOSH	Reicha.
Recit. ed Aria, Madame CARADORI, "Per pietà," (Cosi fan tutte)	Mozart.
Overture, Les deux Journées	Cherubini.

ACT II.

New Grand Characteristic Sinfonia, MS. with Vocal Finale, the principal parts of which to be sung by Madame CARADORI, Miss GOODALL, Mr. VAUGHAN, and Mr. PHILLIPS (composed expressly for this Society) - *Beethoven.*

Leader, Mr. F. CRAMER.—Conductor, Sir G. SMART.

To commence at Eight o'clock precisely.

The subscribers are most earnestly entreated to observe, that the Tickets are not transferable, and that any violation of this rule will incur a total forfeiture of the subscription.

It is requested that the Coachmen may be directed to set down *and take up* with their horses' heads towards Piccadilly.

The door in Little Argyll-street will be open after the Concert, for the egress of the Company.

The next Concert will be on MONDAY, APRIL 11.

TERZETTO.—*Mozart.*	RECITATIVE accompanied—
Tutte, le mie speranze	Mr. VAUGHAN.
Ho tutte riposto in te !	(Samson.)—*Handel.*
Salvami oh Dio	
Dal nemico feroce	Justly these evils have befall'n thy son :
Che m'insegue, e m' incalza	Sole author I, sole cause. My griefs for
Oh Dio salvami.	this

72. *Programme of the Philharmonic Society concert, 21 March 1825, at which Beethoven's Ninth Symphony received its London première (in 1817 the society had invited Beethoven to compose two symphonies; the Ninth, first performed in Vienna in 1824, was the eventual outcome of the commission)*

215

of native composition received a serious blow. The London première of Beethoven's Ninth Symphony conducted by George Smart in 1825 was a disaster. Beethoven, journalists wrote, had gone mad. A proposal to revive it in 1827 was voted down; but when finally, in 1837, it received another performance, under Ignaz Moscheles, the critics realized that Smart had done it a great disservice. The damage, moreover, had been greater than mere individual failure. Twelve years of disdain for the symphony, combined with performances – some very poor – of other new works that manifested demonstrably inferior imagination, had implanted in the public a growing distrust of modern music.[12]

Predictably, xenophobes and traditionalists cited the Ninth as evidence of the folly of consorting with foreigners. Professional hostility to foreigners was in fact growing. The most celebrated case was that of Moscheles. He had been hailed as a keyboard giant during his first concert tour to London in 1821, and, after several equally successful annual tours, established his home there, returning permanently to Germany only in 1846. A man of integrity, whose salon was a gathering-place for intellectuals, Moscheles quickly became one of the city's most innovatory musicians, devoted to improving the art and the profession. But his undisputed talent became a secondary consideration when Philharmonic membership was proposed, for Moscheles was Jewish; his widely publicized rejection inflicted lasting wounds on the society and contributed mightily to its later loss of public support.

The Concerts of Ancient Music also flourished in the 1820s. Unlike the Philharmonic, however, it seemed committed exclusively to the same arias and concerti grossi which reappeared season after season. Even Mozart's and Haydn's music, though well within the chronological limits, was ignored by a stale administration. The advent of Lord Burghersh (later the Earl of Westmorland) as a director in 1832, was too little too late, for energetic new organizations were usurping its function. The Sacred Harmonic Society (founded in 1832) performed oratorios and by moving to the 3000-seat Exeter Hall in 1836 broke the Ancient Concert's monopoly on the repertory. With the massive Handel commemoration at Westminster Abbey in 1834, the Sacred Harmonic Society showed that a large audience could be drawn to early music.

These years also witnessed the fruition of efforts to found a music school. After the Philharmonic Society's plan collapsed in 1814, the matter remained dormant until 1818, when the *Quarterly Musical Magazine* began campaigning for better musical education. The Philharmonic recommenced lobbying, and in 1822 its plan came within hours of royal endorsement. At the last moment, a group of aristocrats led by Lord Burghersh submitted a rival plan that the king quickly approved. Because many musicians resented having lost control of their profession's only school, the Royal Academy of Music opened in 1823 in a contentious atmosphere. Unfortunately, the musicians had good reason to fear aristocratic meddling: the student body had been reduced to 21 children aged ten to fifteen, the curriculum had been diluted to include Anglican education, and a foreigner, the French emigré harpist Nicolas Bochsa, was named secretary. This was a bitterly contested appointment. At first sight it appears that a campaign of slander was used by francophobic Englishmen to block the appointment of a brilliant man. Behind the apparent innuendo, however, were hard facts. Bochsa was not a political refugee, as he claimed, but a convicted felon who had fled Paris to avoid being branded and sent to the galleys for forgery, fraud and theft. In London he had become a bigamist; his gift of harps to the new Academy consisted of stolen property. But Bochsa was the darling of the aristocrats and his advancement quickened the desire of professionals to achieve independence from the upper class.[13]

The early years of the Royal Academy of Music, under its principal William Crotch, were beset with problems. Chronically underfunded, in 1827 it nearly closed. But Lord Burghersh, though an overbearing guardian, tirelessly raised money to keep it alive, and the Academy gradually began to play the role originally foreseen for it, feeding accomplished players into major London institutions, providing leaders for British composition and improving music education. It also furnished needed employment for teachers and added to the status of the musical profession.

By the mid-1820s many aspects of performance and education had been addressed and music in London finally had roots that even Britain's financial vicissitudes could not shake. But the narrow social base of audiences and the dearth of British composers of international stature still caused difficulties. Of course, there were many composers in Britain devoted to a unique genre, the 'glee'. A partsong in an inoffensive, archaic, quasi-Renaissance style, the glee was favoured for private singing parties (at which limitless wine lubricated the singing), performed at concerts such as the Ancient Concert or at certain benefits. But like English anthems and organ music, glees symbolized British composers' attachment to the past. English opera, dominated by Henry Bishop and performed at Covent Garden, Drury Lane and the Lyceum-English Opera House, was directed towards an unsophisticated audience. It blended a late Classical light style – homophonic, with minimal interference from the orchestra – with brazen borrowings from continental operas. Another productive area of British composition was salon music: songs and simple instrumental pieces, especially for piano, flute or violin, abounded in the 1820s. Only a few composers wrote modern, serious instrumental music, and many of them were familiar names, mostly foreign: J. B. Cramer, Clementi, Dussek. Cipriani Potter was probably the best of the younger generation; like most of his continental colleagues he composed symphonies in a style derived from Haydn, Mozart and early Beethoven.

By the 1830s, British composers were determined to assert themselves. In 1834 a group founded the Society of British Musicians, dedicated to 'the advancement of native talent in composition and performance'. It produced an annual series of reading sessions and concerts of new British music and eventually had some 350 members or subscribers.[14] Its library provided a ready source of music for interested performers, and regular reviews of the society's concerts in journals kept the names of British composers before the public. Internal rivalries, favouritism and apathy finally doomed the society in 1865, but not before this generation had paved the way for the rebirth of British composition.

All these battles depended on the support of the journals, which were steadily growing in number and influence. Inspired perhaps by the *Quarterly Musical Magazine*, William Ayrton founded the *Harmonicon* (1823–33), a monthly journal of musical news with a supplement containing new compositions. Ayrton, unlike Bacon, stressed current events, so the *Harmonicon*'s concert reviews, correspondence, articles on concerts and opera, news of the profession, biographies of composers and publication reviews enable one to form a much clearer picture of London musical life. After *Harmonicon*'s demise, Ayrton attempted a cheaper version called the *Musical Library*, but he faced plentiful competition from even cheaper music journals, some of which pandered to strident nationalism. Only one of the new enterprises lasted, however: the *Musical World* (1836–91), which became a major organ for professionals and amateurs under its indefatigable editor James W. Davison, a colourful and dreaded critic. (The *Musical Times*, founded in 1844, is still published but did not become widely influential until the second half of the nineteenth century.)

Musical journalism also spread into non-specialist publications. Of these, the *Athenaeum*, the magazine of the literary and scientific society (founded 1828), became the most important when, in 1839, it appointed Henry Chorley to review musical events. Chorley and Davison wrote in a lively style that could degenerate into scandal-mongering, but, like the period's countless memoirs, their writings are invaluable. These sources also reach into some hitherto obscure corners of music, especially the private salons. That low standards prevailed in exclusive circles is revealed in many accounts. A private concert given by 'a great military character' (probably the Duke of Wellington) was described as follows in the *Quarterly Musical Magazine* (1821):

Mr. L. was engaged and was about to play, when the Noble D— addressing himself to his foreign conductor, said, 'must this man play? it is very late.' 'O yes, my Lord D., he will delight everybody,' said the Signor, who dreaded the disappointment and wrath of the violinist. 'It is very late,' again yawned his Grace, and walking up to the musician's stand, he placed himself, as if in rapt attention, at the side. The symphony [i.e. the introductory ritornello of the concerto] began, and just as the violinist was preparing to display himself in the solo, the D. closed the book, as if the whole being concluded, to spare the artist the trouble, making an inclination of the head in approbation, saying at the same time, with an amicable reesibeelity [*sic*] of countenance, 'charmingly executed indeed, Sir.' The astounded musician was effectually silenced.[15]

But these demeaning experiences were profitable, and at fees of up to 25 guineas private parties could not be ignored. Favoured performers continued to make the rounds of the mansions, playing at as many as three parties a night.

In the 1830s the popularity of benefits was reaching its peak. An influx of foreign performers produced an unbroken series of novelties and attendance adequate to justify as many as 70 benefits a season. The Lord Chamberlain's office assumed the function of an ad hoc clearing house to minimize the damage caused when benefits competed for an audience on the same day. Promoters were forced to select dates earlier in the winter or later in the spring, outside the old social season, or to give 'morning' (2.00 p.m.) concerts. However, standards were still uneven and audiences frequently inattentive. The relative failure of Weber's 1826 benefit had shown that renown was no guarantee of a crowd. The threat of catastrophe was worst for English benefit givers.

No benefits equalled those of Paganini in 1831 and 1832. Charging double the usual prices and giving, in the 3300-seat opera house, an unprecedented number of concerts – 27 in 1831 – Paganini proved that the right attraction could draw an almost limitless audience and make the performer a rich man. His associates cleverly manipulated rumours about his greed and the groundless tale that he had murdered his wife, to whet the public's appetite for infamy (this insatiable appetite for sensationalism can also be seen in the gruesome crime reports in the daily papers). Yet even *The Times*, which had opposed Paganini's pre-arrival publicity, admitted that his violin playing surpassed magnificence. Paganini transformed concert life in London, as everywhere, by raising the expectations of audiences.[16] The damage he wrought on the older style of concert giving can be seen in the fate of Europe's master of pianistic refinement, Hummel: his 1830 trip to London had been a resounding triumph, but when he

73. *Paganini's début at the King's Theatre, June 1831: drawing by Daniel Maclise*

returned in 1831, he could not survive the competition of Paganini and played to half-empty houses.

The Italian Opera, continuing its extravagant practices, also enjoyed good times, producing a succession of operas by Rossini, Bellini, Donizetti, Auber and Meyerbeer (always in Italian), performed by the finest singers of Europe. But, *Harmonicon* observed, whereas Berliners were well enough informed to be able to clash over the relative merits of Rossini and Weber, Londoners still could not experience opera in German or French. A lone opera produced in German in 1805 had not set a precedent, and during most of the 1820s the monopoly of Italian opera held firm, protected by the Lord Chamberlain's unwillingness to license any other foreign music drama. The pressure for flexibility increased through the 1820s, however. Although no performance in German of Weber's *Der Freischütz* was permitted, Londoners in 1824–5 could choose from no fewer than six English-language productions of this already famous opera – all of them travesties. At Drury Lane, Bishop truncated Weber's score and added a hodgepodge of songs; at Covent Garden, the opera was cut and paired with a farce. One London production had no music at all. Covent Garden, knowing a good commodity, sent Sir George Smart to Germany to commission Weber to write and conduct an opera in English. He acquiesced; his 1826 sojourn in London for the première of *Oberon* ended with his death from tuberculosis in Smart's guest quarters.

The first break in the Lord Chamberlain's resistance came in 1829, when he granted Nina Sonntag a licence for two performances of *Die Zauberflöte*. Its success neutralized the threadbare argument that the public did not want German opera. In 1832, 1833 and 1834, German companies at the King's Theatre and Drury Lane led by Karl Guhr of Frankfurt, Hummel and Hippolyte-André-Baptiste Chelard of Munich presented extensive seasons in German and French, including *Fidelio, Der Freischütz* and *Robert le diable*. These companies were a revelation. Apart from their excellent repertory, which centred on a concept of opera quite new to Londoners, they could boast of high standards of choral singing, staging and conducting, cited as models for years to come. Yet after 1833 German opera again fell temporarily silent. Lengthy appeals to bring a company under the Berlin Kapellmeister Gasparo Spontini, in 1838, came to nothing.

The most far-reaching events in the opera world, however, followed the appointment of Pierre Laporte as manager of the King's Theatre in 1828. The French-born Laporte, a former actor, was one of the shrewdest of the managerial victims of operatic quicksand. In the early 1820s he had made a name in London by cleverly manipulating the law to stage unlicensed plays in French. Laporte had a pressing agenda: to bring the opera house under the management's control and break the singers' stranglehold. One of his first acts was to employ Nicolas Bochsa as music director; even the influential Ayrton, who knew the facts about Bochsa, could not prevent it. Bochsa immediately barred the orchestral players from accepting any outside employment that he did not approve – and he only approved that which he conducted. Had his plan succeeded, Bochsa would have dominated conducting and could have destroyed the Philharmonic orchestra by depriving it of its nucleus. Fortunately, many courageous players, in a remarkable act for Britain in 1829, resigned en masse. Ultimately Bochsa – who had been expelled from the secretaryship of the Royal Academy of Music – was fired. Already a bigamist, he absconded to Australia with Henry Bishop's wife.

Bochsa's greed had discredited Laporte's admirable goal of reorganizing the opera house, but only temporarily. Laporte's next move eventually changed the face of London music. His priority, understandably, was to avoid his predecessors' fate of bankruptcy (the astute Laporte had sponsored Paganini's benefits). To maximize his income, he had to increase rentals of the decrepit small concert hall in the opera building (the King's Theatre concert room); his

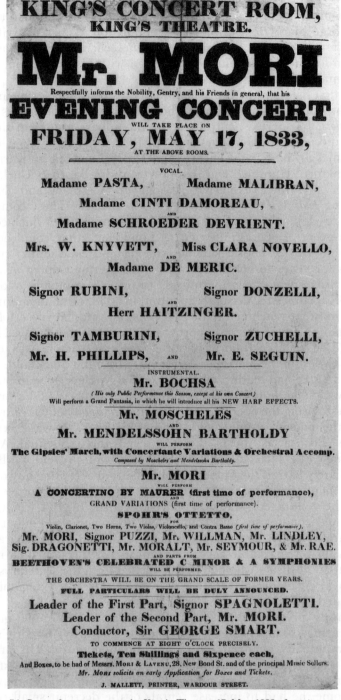

74. *Poster for a concert at the King's Theatre, 17 May 1833, featuring an unusually illustrious line-up of singers and instrumentalists*

plan, announced in 1829, was simple: the Italian opera singers could appear only in concerts held in the concert room. Since benefit givers had become dependent on opera stars, the effect would have been disastrous. Bookings of the concert room increased, but Laporte's business procedures were erratic until he engaged Benjamin Lumley, a young solicitor, as his assistant. In 1836 Lumley and Laporte applied the ban on singers ruthlessly, but it had an unexpected effect: after several poor seasons, promoters of benefits and the directors of the Philharmonic discovered the merits of French, German and even a few English singers. Interest shifted perceptibly towards non-Italian music. An even greater and more lasting result, however, was just round the corner.

TRANSITIONS: THE LATE 1830s AND EARLY 1840s

Even amid this prosperity, musical life was showing symptoms of instability. William IV's colourless reign dampened the previously festive air of the season. He detested music, and his reign might have been silent had he not married Adelaide of Saxe-Meiningen, who had a taste for music, gave concerts at court and developed her private band. But angry musicians saw that she had little interest in British composition.

Nevertheless, benefits still abounded, while the Philharmonic and especially the Ancient Concert were experiencing declining attendance. Many commentators noticed that musical culture had become dependent on the fashionable, and now that fashions were changing, music was in trouble. At the Philharmonic, the institution of transferability of tickets and the selling of limited quantities of single tickets attracted larger audiences, but soon the decline in attendance resumed. The Ancient Concert was in a worse state. Musicians were slow to recognize a major change in London life: concerts had been linked to the fashionable season and the burgeoning of music had intensified competition. Lower ticket prices would have extended the reach of fine music but, apart from the feared mixing of classes, no hall was large enough to permit offering 2000 tickets at 5s. instead of 700 at 10s.6d. Furthermore, the managers of the Drury Lane and Covent Garden theatres were forced to rely on low-grade entertainment to fill the seats. Such a fate was unacceptable to the purveyors of symphonies. Thus the central dilemma remained: how to draw a new audience without alienating the old one.

This controversy impinged on programmes. By the 1830s the repertory of both major institutions had fallen into a pattern: at the Ancient Concert, Handel still reigned supreme; at the Philharmonic, some 85–90% of the symphonies were by Haydn, Mozart and Beethoven (eight symphonies by Beethoven, about six by Mozart and perhaps fifteen by Haydn were repeatedly performed). Vocal music

223

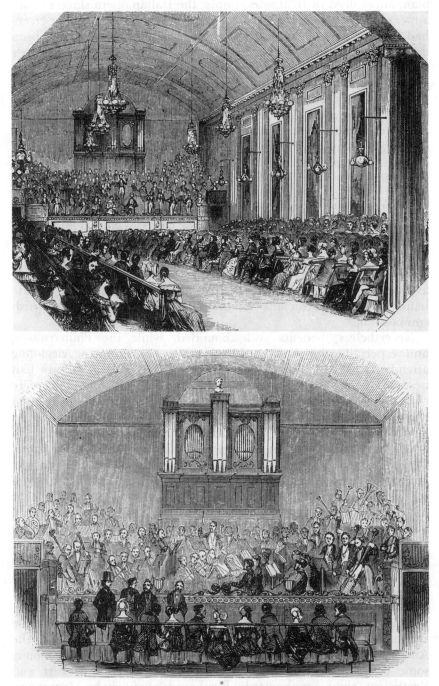

75. Two views of the Hanover Square Rooms, London, from the 'Illustrated London News' (24 June 1843); the close-up of the stage is said to show the orchestra of the Philharmonic Society

was also dominated by Mozart. New continental music had little to offer and might alienate audiences. The 1820s, apart from Beethoven, did not abound in first-rate symphonic compositions. Schubert's symphonies were still unknown; Berlioz's name was but a shadow. Even Schumann stated that symphonic production in the 1830s had been dismal.[17] However, when Mendelssohn's symphonies were performed, they were instantly incorporated into the repertory. Mendelssohn had everything London wanted in a musician: magnificent performing skills, winning new music and gentlemanly charm. By the mid-1830s he had become the city's new Handel and his reputation continued to increase with a string of triumphant premières, including concertos that even the sceptical could accept. His renown virtually proved the conservatives' point about the inferiority of new music: Mendelssohn's quality was so obvious that it needed no defenders. Nevertheless, distrust of modernity was increasing. The critics carped that the repertory was stagnant but slashed at almost all new compositions. Only new concertos, with their emphasis on the performing composer, were still sought avidly – each year some 85% of concertos performed was new – but they were tied to fashions in virtuosity and did not win the critics' respect.

Londoners were becoming aware that performing standards were not all they should have been. Baton conducting had been introduced by the German opera companies in the early 1830s and quickly taken up by Michael Costa at the Opera. When it penetrated the symphonic world, the liabilities of the traditional English system became glaring. (Spohr, in his memoirs, recalled introducing baton conducting in 1820, but his memory may have deceived him: there is no evidence for his claim.)[18] The more frequently Moscheles and Mendelssohn conducted, the more painful were the deficiencies of Smart, Bishop and the like. Moscheles and Mendelssohn also demonstrated that disciplined rehearsing produced good results. But the gentlemanly tradition died hard and inferior conductors still ruined fine music.

The old institutions were also being challenged by new types of concert. The growth of chamber music is a powerful example. In the winter of 1835–6, professional string players launched two series of chamber music concerts, whose success highlighted the defects of the Philharmonic programmes, in which chamber music was played between symphonic pieces. Furthermore, the chamber concerts were presented between the New Year and the opening of the social season, or even in the autumn, and in unusual locations. (The new concerts dared not dispense with singers, however.) The response showed that an audience was to be found among the business and professional classes, who had been neglected in favour of the seasonal visitors from country estates. This reduced the necessity for chamber music at the Philharmonic, and it was soon dropped. Other experiments were undertaken by individuals. Topical programming distinguished Moscheles's historical concerts of keyboard music in the late 1830s, at which the harpsichord reappeared after long obscurity and 'ancient' was at last united with 'modern'.[19] Liszt's 1840 'recitals' (the controversial title was his manager's idea) were not the same as modern solo concerts – Liszt also did not risk eliminating singers – but the idea of focussing an evening on a single instrument was novel.

The most momentous innovation, however, was 'cheap concerts'. Their model was the century-old Lenten oratorios at Covent Garden and Drury Lane, which had originated as sacred entertainments on Wednesdays and Fridays during Lent, when secular vocal entertainment was prohibited. By the turn of the century their sacred content was minimal. The oratorios, for which entry cost only a few shillings, exposed a new class to good music. Widely disdained by the finer folk, the oratorios' popularity was a portent of the future.[20]

More cheap concerts appeared occasionally during the late 1820s and 1830s. One series, the Societá Armonica, resembled the Philharmonic concerts, though without so impressive an orchestra. Most important, however, was the founding of Promenade Concerts in 1838, modelled on concerts given by Philippe Musard in Paris. At first the promenades were off-season, low-brow events serving popular music – quadrilles, waltzes, opera pot-pourris etc – with food and drink to an audience seated at tables. To the horror of the better London, people of rank began to frequent the promenades, which were quickly imitated. But it was a French emigré, Louis Jullien, who transformed the promenades and the audience for fine music with his Concerts d'Hiver, begun in 1841 at the Lyceum-English Opera House. Dressed in jewelled finery, receiving his silver baton from a liveried footman while he presented his handsome profile to the ladies, Jullien fused fine musicianship with a rare talent for promotion (his outdoor concerts included a pot-pourri based on the concluding scene of Meyerbeer's *Huguenots*, complete with rifle fire and fireworks). Even Jullien's most vociferous opponents had to grant that his players were excellent (he was resented for importing foreigners who reportedly undercut local wages). Soon he began including among the quadrilles a movement of a symphony or a concerto, and where the older institutions had failed he succeeded perhaps more than anyone else in attracting a new and more broadly based audience, though the ticket price still eluded the very poor.[21]

Jullien was only the most visible example of a change in the musical world. The Sacred Harmonic Society was also filling its hall through low-priced tickets. Hullah's and Mainzer's singing movement, based at Exeter Hall, was estimated to be giving instruction in

76. *Promenade Concert at Covent Garden: lithograph from Jullien's 'Annual' (1847)*

reading music to some 50,000 working-class children by the end of 1841. The Mechanics' Institutes were offering self-education in music. Daily newspapers, again expanding in number, were about to offer music criticism. In short, music was becoming a major factor in Victorian social reform.

British composers were increasingly determined to fight for recognition. Like all young composers in the post-Beethoven age, they had to struggle for attention. But they also lacked a tradition of accomplishment, especially in instrumental music, and needed to prove, as it were, their very existence. The British predilection for foreigners compounded their difficult position. Their success can be seen in the increasing numbers of active, serious composers in London in the 1830s, among them John Barnett, James Calkin, Thomas S. Cooke, James William Davison (the critic), John Henry Griesbach, Charles Edward Horsley, Frederick Bowen Jewson, Charles Lucas, George Alexander Macfarren, Thomas Mudie, Charles Neate, William Lovell Phillips, Cipriani Potter, Charles K. Salomon and Henry Westrop.

Of the younger English composers, William Sterndale Bennett (1816–75) came closest to international success; although he was not a chauvinist, he was adopted by the nationalists as their greatest hope for musical distinction, especially since he was one of the first products of the Royal Academy of Music. By the age of twenty Bennett was renowned as a pianist, organist and conductor, and during a visit to Germany in 1836 was warmly received by the Leipzig circle of Mendelssohn and Schumann (who were just a few years older than Bennett). Schumann wrote in the *Neue Zeitschrift für Musik* that a talent such as Bennett's gave one confidence in the future of the art.[22] Regular visits to the Continent ensued, bringing Bennett exposure that secured his reputation in Britain, where foreign esteem was crucial to success. In his mature years Bennett was one of the most influential voices in Britain, serving as principal of the Royal Academy of Music, professor of music at Cambridge University and conductor of the Philharmonic Society. But all these activities and the pressures of an inadequate income gradually eroded his energy for composition.

Apart from their artistic merit, Bennett's works clearly attracted Schumann and Mendelssohn because they displayed an idealism and a resistance to commercialism that was all too rare. But the Germans' admiration did not rest on an abstract idealism which Bennett represented. His best music – early orchestral works and piano music especially – possesses striking qualities of lyricism and depth. It is probably in his piano music that Bennett comes closest to current thinking. Nevertheless, though difficult, it eschews the crowd-rousing qualities of such contemporaries as Liszt and Sigismond Thalberg.

Technical difficulty in the absence of fashionable brilliance may help explain the rapid demise of Bennett's reputation, for he made demands that most amateurs could not fulfil and that professionals found insufficiently impressive.

Unlike British composers, musical industrialists were succeeding spectacularly and internationally. London by now had become a world centre for music publishing, thanks to a combination of free enterprise, aggressive marketing and cost-cutting production methods. Firms were led by entrepreneurial musicians including Cramer, Clementi, William Hawes and Samuel Chappell, as well as by book publishers who turned to music (among them Thomas Boosey). Some, like Robert Cocks,[23] had ingenious schemes such as issuing complete but unauthorized collections of the music of leading composers. Perhaps the most imaginative of the London publishers was Vincent Novello, whose early success came from his perceptive support of the choral singing movement.

Musical instruments began to play a major role in industry. The piano, benefiting from the fashion for musical training in middle-class families, was one of Britain's leading exports. Broadwood earned a place in history for its perfection of iron technology that led to the modern piano, and other London piano companies became lasting names – Chappell, Clementi, Cramer are but a few. Manufacture of pianos, harps and wind instruments flourished, while Londoners' ingenuity even led to rival designs for quickly retunable timpani, perfection of which was required for the contemporary advanced symphonic literature.

TOWARDS THE MODERN AGE: THE 1840s
By the 1840s accumulated strains were beginning to take their toll. The amount of activity each year was staggering and the struggle for survival thus more ferocious. The situation for the Ancient Concert and the Philharmonic had become desperate. Attendance at the Ancient Concert had declined irrevocably, and in 1848 it closed its doors. In 1841 and 1842 the Philharmonic Society seemed destined for the same fate. Attempts to add to the repertory failed: Berlioz's *Benvenuto Cellini* overture, for example, was hissed in 1841. Yet after several years of the most bitter criticism, journalists suddenly retreated, having realized (and admitted publicly) that they were destroying one of London's most valuable assets.[24] Meanwhile, the Philharmonic had cut wages, reduced its string section and terminated special projects. The worst victim of the economies was the contemporary composer: commissions for new works ceased. Other attempts at reform focussed on the conductor. Moscheles's and Mendelssohn's accomplishments underlined the need for a regular conductor with talent, power and charisma. But Mendelssohn was

now in Leipzig and Moscheles was preparing to join him in the new conservatory there. In 1846 Michael Costa of the Italian Opera at Her Majesty's Theatre (previously the King's Theatre), was appointed permanent conductor and granted what the press had recommended for years – more or less dictatorial power. Although many writers feared that Costa could conduct nothing more poly-phonic than an opera duet, he rose to the challenge and assured the survival of the Philharmonic. Both the level of performances and the variety of repertory, to which Costa added important choral-orchestral works, leapt forward. Nevertheless, the attitude to new music remained conservative.

Costa's arrival at the Philharmonic precipitated a spectacular upheaval in the opera world. Opera in London, as everywhere, had been a tug-of-war between singers and management. Pierre Laporte, with Benjamin Lumley, was the first to attempt seriously to bring the London company under management control, as we have seen. The climax came in 1840, when the cabal of singers had refused to perform unless all of them were re-engaged. Laporte and Lumley, to put them to the test, did not re-engage the baritone Antonio Tamburini. The result was not quite what they expected: the finer class of opera-lovers screamed for Tamburini and attempted to tear the theatre apart in the 'Tamburini riot'.[25] (The newspapers were amused to find that the leaders of Britain, who often preached about the morality of the lower classes, behaved at least as badly as the objects of their contempt.) Not long afterwards, Laporte died; Lumley took the reins, and relations between management and singers plummeted. The last straw for the singers was Lumley's refusal to allow Costa to accept the Philharmonic's first invitation to make him conductor (1845). The next year Costa resigned from the opera to join the Philharmonic, amid plotting for a new opera company.

The pressure for change had been in the air for years. When Alfred Bunn became manager of Covent Garden Theatre in 1833 he began to stage increasingly ambitious opera productions. Auber's *Gustavus III* had been an immense success and had launched the career of the Scottish soprano Jane Shirreff. In 1841–2, Adelaide Kemble made her auspicious début at Covent Garden in *Norma*. The new music director, the German-born Julius Benedict, brought greater polish to the performances. A guest season by the Brussels Theatre Royal Company, with the first London production of *Guillaume Tell*, again raised the spectre of competition for the Italian opera.

Coincidentally, during these years the grip of the Lord Chamber-lain's office had also been broken by parliament. Everything suggested that the time for a new opera company had come. The Royal Italian Opera at Covent Garden Theatre, formed by the unrepentant but magnificent singers from Lumley's company, and directed by Costa,[26] opened in 1847. Lumley, at Her Majesty's Theatre, counter-attacked by engaging Jenny Lind; and Jullien, having engaged Berlioz as music director for the 1847–8 season at Drury Lane, attempted to form an English Opera there. The multiplicity of operatic riches kept Londoners happy until Lind retired in 1849, after which Lumley's company began its slow decline. Lumley finally gave up in 1858; the theatre burnt down in 1867. More than a century later, the Royal Opera at Covent Garden still dominates London cultural life.

In the concert world, the Lord Chamberlain's control had deteriorated. By the late 1830s the licensing system was not functioning well and even its legality was questionable. A scandal involving the chief clerk led concert organizers to ignore the licensing requirement and in 1843 parliament ended it.[27] Even before licensing disappeared, however, concerts had been spreading throughout the expanding territory of London, as new halls outside Westminster opened in defiance of the Crown. (An auditorium on the south side of Oxford Street, in the City of Westminster, had to obey the licence requirement, whereas one on the north side, which lay outside Westminster, might not.) Unusual events abounded. Because of the civil reforms of the 1830s that eased the strictures on Roman Catholicism, important Catholic sacred works migrated from the embassy chapels to the concert halls, opening the doors to fresh repertory. The old benefit concert simultaneously declined and was soon scarcely to be found. The age of musical specialization had reached London, bringing with it greater variety.

Standards of performance also improved vigorously with Costa leading the Royal Italian Opera, the Philharmonic and the Sacred Harmonic Society. A new maturity and seriousness had become established. At court, Victoria and Albert were setting a tone for the better classes, turning the old band into a real orchestra, receiving such composers as Mendelssohn and Spohr at court, encouraging German instrumental music rather than Italian opera, and even giving support to British composers.

In short, the optimism of the Victorian age also marks this period's musical life. Only new music still bred scepticism. London's response to Liszt, Berlioz, Chopin and Schumann was fraught with mistrust of the continental avant garde. Romanticism and such innovations as chromatic harmony and programme music were regarded as symptoms of degeneracy. As a result, the Romantic movement passed London by. Strangely, London's anti-Romanticism was not rooted in the music itself, for almost no music by these composers was heard in the capital. Berlioz's music had been hissed, but Schumann's was not even played; his writings were considered ample warning of his dangerousness. Mendelssohn had sent Schubert's C major

Symphony to the Philharmonic in 1840, but it failed at a trial night and was not publicly performed for two decades. Liszt's writings were incomprehensible and he was 'not a gentleman'. As before, this retreat from the present did not apply to operas or concertos, but even the modern concerto was threatened by the formation of a repertory of masterpieces.

London was now at the crossroads. A geo-political monstrosity, it was devising new solutions to new problems. The musical world too was about to find new solutions to its problems. Perhaps the most significant factor was the successful challenge to London's cultural uniqueness by the new industrial cities of the north. These new cities, and the railways that connected them, would convert London's musical monopoly into a national culture.

NOTES

[1] Licence ledgers and other records of the Lord Chamberlain, in the Public Record Office, London.

[2] See, for example, the pages of *Harmonicon* (London, 1823–33) and the *Quarterly Musical Magazine and Review* (Norwich, 1818–c1929).

[3] Many memoirs of this period and newspaper accounts provide information about the economics of the opera world. One of the more fascinating is J. Ebers, *Seven Years of the King's Theatre* (London, 1828); see also D. Nalbach, *The King's Theatre, 1704–1867* (London, 1972).

[4] A comprehensive study of concerts in this period by J. Sachs is in preparation.

[5] J. P. Larsen, 'Haydn, Joseph', *Grove 6*.

[6] Information about music at court has been gleaned from contemporary newspapers, memoirs and miscellaneous references in the manuscript collection at the British Library, London.

[7] Wesley's and Callcott's papers dealing with these matters are in the British Library, manuscript division; Callcott's 1802 proposal is in Add.27669 f.47'–48.

[8] For the Philharmonic Society, see M. B. Foster, *History of the Philharmonic Society of London, 1813–1912* (London, 1912); a more comprehensive study of this organization for 1813–62 is being prepared by J. Sachs.

[9] Some information on conductors may be found in Foster, *History of the Philharmonic Society*; contemporary newspapers and periodicals, as well as memoirs, contain much that is instructive, which will appear in Sachs's forthcoming study of the Philharmonic Society.

[10] What little can be gleaned about this period is found in contemporary periodicals. Documents concerning the Philharmonic Society's attempt to form an academy are in the society's collection at the British Library and in the papers of Sir George Smart, British Library Add.41771; the struggle was also discussed in many articles apparently by R. MacKenzie Bacon in his *Quarterly Musical Magazine and Review*, especially 1819–24, and by Ayrton in *Harmonicon*, principally 1823–7.

[11] Documents about the Royal Society of Musicians are at its headquarters in London. Most information about the New Musical Fund is in the papers of Sir George Smart in the British Library.

[12] The most significant reviews of the performances of Beethoven's Ninth Symphony are in *Harmonicon* (1825) and the *Musical World* (1837).

[13] Bochsa's deeds and misdeeds were discussed by William Ayrton in *Harmonicon* on many occasions, 1823–9; a letter from Ayrton to the Lord Chamberlain (in the Public Record Office) traces Bochsa's misdeeds in detail.

[14] The history of the Society of British Musicians is best traced through the pages of the *Musical World* (1838–91) and *Athenaeum* (1828–1921).

[15] *Quarterly Musical Magazine and Review*, iv (1820–21), 433.

[16] For more information about Paganini's 1831 season, see *Harmonicon* and daily papers, especially *The Times* and the *Morning Post*, for the 1831 season. Additional discussion is in J. Sachs, *Kapellmeister Hummel in England and France* (Detroit, 1977).

[17] R. Schumann, *Gesammelte Schriften über Musik und Musiker*, ed. M. Kreisig (Leipzig, 1914), i, 424–30.

[18] Spohr's claim was reinforced by a mis-statement of George Hogarth in *The Philharmonic Society of London from its Foundation, 1813, to its Fiftieth Year, 1862* (London, 1862), 26–7, and repeated by Foster, *History of the Philharmonic Society*, and in most other sources about London music at that time. A. Jacobs, 'Spohr and the Baton', *ML*, xxxi (1950), 307–17, discusses the claim Spohr had put forward in his autobiography (Eng. trans., London, 1865/*R*1969) and showed that his memory must have deceived him.

[19] See J. Roche, 'Moscheles, Ignaz', *Grove 6*; also reviews in the *Musical World* (1837–).

[20] See J. Sachs, 'The End of the Oratorios', in *Music and Civilization: Essays in Honor of Paul Henry Lang* (New York, 1984), 186–92.

[21] See A. Carse, *The Life of Jullien* (Cambridge, 1951).

[22] R. Schumann, *Gesammelte Schriften*, i, 289.

[23] On Cocks, see J. Sachs, 'Authentic English and French Editions of J. N. Hummel', *JAMS*, xxv (1972), 203.

[24] See *Musical World* (14 Jan 1841), 18–19.

[25] On the Tamburini riot (30 April 1841) see Nalbach, *The King's Theatre*, pp.102ff.

[26] On Costa, see especially the *Musical World* and *Athenaeum* for 1845–6.

[27] The end of licensing requirements is discussed in Sachs, 'The End of the Oratorios', and in a forthcoming article on the licensing of German opera in London.

BIBLIOGRAPHICAL NOTE

The reader wishing an introduction to metropolitan London and its culture may turn especially to F. Sheppard's *London 1808–1870: the Infernal Wen* (London, 1971) and the later chapters of G. Rudé's *Hanoverian London, 1714–1808* (London, 1971).

Until recently, most historians of British musical life have dismissed the early nineteenth century as arid, offering as a reason the fact that no 'great' British composer emerged; this view has been rectified in the essays edited by N. Temperley for *The Athlone History of Music in Britain*, v: *The Romantic Age, 1800–1914* (London, 1981). Newspapers and periodicals offer glimpses of musical life; a useful collection of *Musical Times* articles is in P. Scholes's compendium *The Mirror of Music, 1844–1944* (London, 1947). There is a profusion of memoirs by composers, performers, amateurs, foreign visitors etc, often written to an exceptionally high literary standard. Two music critics left especially broad views of the period: J. W. Davison in *From Mendelssohn to Wagner, Being the Memoirs of J. W. Davison Forty Years Music Critic of 'The Times'*, compiled by H. Davison (London, 1912), and Davison's rival, H. Chorley (critic of *Athenaeum*), in *Thirty Years' Musical Recollections* (London, 1862). A sub-category of memoirist comprises the managers who were ruined by opera house economics: J. Ebers, *Seven Years of the King's Theatre* (London, 1828); A. Bunn (Drury Lane Theatre), *The Stage* (London, 1840); and B. Lumley (Her Majesty's Theatre), *Reminiscences of the Opera* (London, 1864). The early period is also the subject of the Earl of Mount Edgecumbe's *Musical Reminiscences, containing an Account of the Italian Opera in England from 1773* (London, 3/1828).

Many performers bared their lives in print. A central figure is Sir George Smart, the leading conductor in London from the 1810s to 1830. The life of Smart, a hoarder of documents and paraphernalia, is revealed in a volume of excerpts edited by B. Cox and C. L. E. Cox, *Leaves from the Journals of Sir George Smart* (London, 1907). For a view of London in the 1820s, turn to *Louis Spohr's Autobiography* (Eng. trans., London, 1865/*R*1969). For the period *c*1823–1848, an invaluable source is Charlotte Moscheles's memoir of her husband, *Life of Moscheles, with Selections from his Diaries and Correspond-*

ence, 2 vols. (London, 1873; adapted from the original German by A. D. Coleridge). John Ella, an important professional violinist and founder of the Musical Union, the mid-nineteenth-century élite chamber music society, described his career in *Musical Sketches, Abroad, and at Home* (London, 1869).

Several amateurs add to the picture of musical London: W. Gardiner, *Music and Friends; or, Pleasant Recollections of a Dilettante* (London, 1838 and 1853); Prince Hermann von Pückler-Muskau, *A Regency Visitor: the English Tour of Prince Pückler-Muskau, described in his Letters*, trans. S. Austin (London, 1832); and F. von Raumer, *England in 1835, being a Series of Letters Written to Friends in Germany during a Residence in London and Excursions into the Provinces*, trans. S. Austin, 3 vols. (London, 1836).

Among correspondence, especially important is H. C. Robbins Landon's *The Collected Correspondence and London Notebooks of Joseph Haydn* (London, 1959). Two books that are interesting but not so well known are R. Gotch's charming compilation, *Mendelssohn and his Friends in Kensington: Letters from Fanny and Sophy Horsley written 1833–36* (London, 1934), and *Letters of Felix Mendelssohn to Ignaz and Charlotte Moscheles*, trans. and ed. F. Moscheles (London, 1888).

Biographies of Beethoven, Spohr, Weber, Mendelssohn, Berlioz etc all make excellent reading. A few that deal extensively with London are L. Plantinga, *Clementi: his Life and Music* (London, 1977); A. W. Ganz, *Berlioz in London* (London, 1950); J. Warrack, *Carl Maria von Weber* (London, 1976); J. Sachs, *Kapellmeister Hummel in England and France* (Detroit, 1977); J. R. Sterndale Bennett, *The Life of William Sterndale Bennett, by his Son* (Cambridge, 1907); A. Carse's fascinating biography of one of the century's greatest showmen, *The Life of Jullien* (Cambridge, 1951); M. Cowden Clarke, *The Life and Labours of Vincent Novello* (London, 1864); J. Mewburn Levien, *Beethoven and the Royal Philharmonic Society* (London, 1927); and W. A. Ellis's monumental *Life of Richard Wagner*, v (London, 1906), which treats in almost frightening detail Wagner's 1855 sojourn. Two authors have written studies of the methods by which foreign composers published their works in England: A. Tyson, *The Authentic English Editions of Beethoven* (London, 1963); and J. Sachs, 'Authentic English and French Editions of J. N. Hummel', *JAMS*, xxv (1972), 203. Two specialized biographical dictionaries are also important: J. D. Brown and S. S. Stratton, *British Musical Biography* (Birmingham, 1897), and the dictionary of the dramatic and musical stage, *A Biographical Dictionary of Actors, Actresses, Musicians, Dancers, Managers, and other Stage Personnel in London, 1660–1800*, ed. P. Highfill and others (Carbondale, Ill., 1973–).

A general view of London's orchestras is found in A. Carse's *The Orchestra in the Eighteenth Century* (Cambridge, 1950) and *The Orchestra from Beethoven to Berlioz* (Cambridge, 1948). The Philharmonic Orchestra is the subject of two modern books: R. Elkin's *Royal Philharmonic* (London, 1947) and M. B. Foster's *History of the Philharmonic Society of London, 1813–1912* (London, 1912); both give invaluable listings of concert programmes from 1813. The Concert of Ancient Music is described in an important article, J. Matthew, 'The Antient Concerts, 1776–1848', *PMA*, xxxiii (1906–7), 55. The opera world has been treated by W. C. Smith, compiler of *The Italian Opera and Contemporary Ballet in London, 1789–1820* (London, 1953–4); H. S. Wyndham, *The Annals of Covent Garden Theatre from 1732 to 1897*, 2 vols. (London, 1906); F. Petty, *Italian Opera in London, 1760–1800* (Ann Arbor, 1980); D. Nalbach, *The King's Theatre* (London, 1972); H. D. Rosenthal, *Two Centuries of Opera at Covent Garden* (London, 1958); and G. Hogarth, *Memoirs of the Opera* (London, 1851).

A broad range of information about instrumental music may be found in N. Temperley's *Instrumental Music in England, 1800–1850* (diss., U. of Cambridge, 1959); for the virtuoso world, see T. B. Milligan, *The Concerto and London's Musical Culture in the late Eighteenth Century* (Ann Arbor, 1983). Concert halls are the subject of R. Elkin's *The Old Concert Rooms of London* (London, 1955). Among the fine treatments of social history are C. Ehrlich's studies of the socio-economic history of music, *The Piano: a History* (London, 1976) and *The Music Profession in Britain since the Eighteenth Century: a Social History* (Oxford, 1985); M. J. Gane's *Social Change in English Music and Music-Making, 1880–1970* (diss., U. of London, 1972); W. Weber's provocative study of audiences, *Music and the Middle Class: the Social Structure of Concert Life in London, Paris and Vienna* (New York, 1975); and E. D. Mackerness's *A Social History of English Music* (London, 1964).

Chapter VIII

Moscow and St Petersburg

GERALD R. SEAMAN

THE REIGN OF CATHERINE THE GREAT

> Yesterday I went again to a Russian opera, whose music is composed of ancient native airs . . . The words are by Her Majesty. The setting is splendid. The scene takes place in Russia in ancient times. All the costumes are absolutely magnificent; they are made of Turkish fabrics of the period and cut on the lines of the times. It features a legation of Kalmouks, singing and dancing in the Tartar manner . . . I have never seen a spectacle more varied nor more lavish; there were more than five hundred people on stage, but even though the little Grand Dukes and the four little Grand Duchesses were there with their governors and governesses, there were hardly 50 of us spectators, so exclusive is the Empress in granting admission to her Hermitage.[1]

> Their minds receive very little cultivation, for they can neither read nor write: all their learning consists in a few proverbs, which they transmit from father to son. The labourer sings behind his plough, the coachman on his box, and the carpenter on the roof of the hut where he is at work; their songs are generally upon love and their music is very monotonous . . . One village has sometimes more than one church, and churches are in general very numerous in Russia, because it is a work of great merit to found one. The ringing of bells is here almost continuous, as it is thought to be part of religious service.[2]

These two accounts, the first from 1791 by Count Valentin Esterházy, the French ambassador to the Russian court, and the second from a Scottish journal of 1789, give a vivid picture of Russian musical life in the late eighteenth century. On one side was the great mass of the people – peasants, largely illiterate, but drawing sustenance from the church and preserving jealously their rich heritage of folk music – and on the other the cultivated world of the nobility, whose love of Western culture manifested itself in the emulation of Western fashions, opera, chamber music and books. Peasant and nobility were mutually dependent and there were occasions when the two worlds met. It was not unknown for wealthy aristocrats to marry one of their

77. *The Hermitage (Catherine the Great's Winter Palace), St Petersburg, designed by Bartolomeo Francesco Rastrelli (begun 1754; early nineteenth-century engraving by Sabat and Schifler) with (below) its theatre designed by Quarenghi (1783–5)*

serfs, as did Count Sheremetev, while a number of children sired by
the nobility were given a good education, sometimes being sent to
study abroad, as in the case of Mikhail Matinsky (1750–*c*1820), a
gifted scholar and librettist.

Many types of music-making existed in Russia during the early
eighteenth century but it was not until Catherine the Great's reign
that Russian professional music truly came into being. These 34
years, from 1762, saw immense changes in all spheres, not least in
cultural life. A firm adherent of the ideals of Enlightenment (at least
in her early years), Catherine carried on an extensive correspondence
with leading European intellectuals, including Diderot, Voltaire and
Grimm, while her court, centred on the Hermitage and occasionally
resident at the palaces of Peterhof, Gatchina, Oranienbaum, Tsarskoe
Selo and Pavlovsk, became a meeting-place for celebrated foreign
composers and virtuosos. Manfredini, Galuppi, Sarti, Traetta,
Cimarosa and Paisiello were some of the distinguished visitors,
and Paisiello's *Il barbiere di Siviglia*, one of the most popular and
successful *opere buffe* of the eighteenth century, had its première at the
St Petersburg court in 1782. Catherine's court dominated musical life,
but its influence spread gradually throughout society.

*

Catherine was at first patriotic, and it is significant that 1772 saw
what appears to have been the first real Russian opera, *Anyuta*,
performed at Tsarskoe Selo. Its libretto was by M. Popov, but
the name of the composer is unknown and the music is lost. In the
hundred or so operas written in Russia in the last part of the
eighteenth century, of which roughly a third survives, folk elements
played a prominent part.

The first Russian opera to enjoy prolonged success was *Mel'nik-
koldun, obmanschchik i svat* ('The Miller-Magician, Cheat and Matchmaker'). The librettist, Alexander Ablesimov, a talented playwright,
stipulated the use of well-known folktunes, sung to his words. First
performed in Moscow on 20 January 1779, it is simple in subject and
almost certainly owed something to Rousseau's famous *opéra comique*,
Le devin du village, which was possibly given in Russian at the Theatre
of the Moscow Orphanage in 1778.[3] (The Moscow Orphanage had
opened in 1763, followed by that of St Petersburg in 1772, and music
formed an important part of the children's education.) The music,
arranged by Mikhail Sokolovsky, a violinist at the Moscow Petrovsky
Theatre, was later revised by and misattributed to Evstigney Fomin.

Catherine wrote a number of librettos, of which mention should be
made of *Fevey* and *Nachal'noye upravleniye Olega* ('The Early Reign of
Oleg'). They were staged extremely elaborately, the latter supervised

by Catherine herself, and we are fortunate that first-hand accounts of their performance survive in the letters of Count Valentin Esterházy. Two numbers in *Fevey* (1786), with music by Vasiliy Pashkevich (*c*1742–1797), are of particular interest, the song of Ledmer and the chorus of Kalmyks. Ledmer's song is a curious anticipation of the type of 'changing-background' technique which Glinka and his successors were to use with great effect in the following century, for the same tune is repeated incessantly against varied harmonization and orchestration. The Kalmyk chorus is an attempt at composition in an exotic vein, another facet to be developed in the nineteenth century.

One of the most gifted composers of the period was the Ukrainian Dmitry Bortnyansky (1751–1825) who, though better known for his sacred music, also wrote operas. Like several Russian composers (including Matinsky, Fomin, Berezovsky and Degtyaryov), Bortnyansky was sent to Italy to complete his musical training, having taken lessons from the distinguished Italian composer Baldassare Galuppi in St Petersburg. In Venice, Bortnyansky wrote three operas and was commissioned on his return to compose a further two: *Le faucon* (1786) and *Le fils-rival* (1787). *Le faucon*, to a French libretto by Lafermière based on a subject from Boccaccio's *Decameron*, was the first given at the court of Prince Paul, Catherine's son. The music is italianate and skilfully written, recalling in its smooth flowing lines the elegant sculptures of Canova and the classical structures of Cameron and Rastrelli.[4]

Mikhail Matinsky, the illegitimate son of Count Yaguzhinsky, was born in 1750 in Pokrovsk, near Moscow; he studied at Moscow University and was sent to Italy at his father's expense. From 1779 to 1802 he taught at the Smolny Institute for Daughters of the Nobility. He seems to have died in the mid-1820s. Matinsky was the librettist of the opera *Sanktpeterburgskiy gostïny dvor* ('The St Petersburg Bazaar'), which has survived only in its second version of 1792 under the title *Kak pozhivyosh', tak i proslïvyosh'* ('As you Live, So shall you be Judged'); whether he also composed the music is disputed: it may have been Pashkevich, but the surviving music is so much better than any of Pashkevich's that that is unlikely.[5]

Another gifted Russian composer was Evstigney Ipatovich Fomin (1761–1800) who also completed his musical training in Italy, studying under Padre Martini and being elected a member of the Bologna Accademia Filarmonica in 1785. Of Fomin's operas, particularly vivid is his *Yamshchiki na podstave* ('The Post-Drivers at the Post-Station') of 1787, to a libretto by N. A. L'vov.[6] (L'vov had collaborated with Jan Bohumir Práč in compiling one of the earliest collections of Russian folktunes (1790)). Most effective are the lively overture, which uses two folksongs, and the opening chorus, also based on folk material. Fomin's finest work is the two-act melodrama

78. Horn band in the uniform of the time of Alexander I: engraving by J. C. Nabholz

Orfey i Evredika ('Orpheus and Euridice'), written in 1791–2 and based on a libretto by Knyazhnin. Apart from unusual orchestral devices, it is also original in that Fomin introduces an offstage Russian horn band to strengthen the chorus of bass voices (symbolizing the gods).[7]

The Russian horn band was a remarkable phenomenon of the second half of the eighteenth century. It consisted of a band of serf musicians, each playing only a single note; their hunting horns varied in length from about three inches to over eight feet, giving a range of some four and a half octaves with chromatic intervals. One of the most famous horn bands was that developed by Jan Antonín Mareš, a Bohemian by birth, for Prince Narïshkin. According to one source, between 1753 and 1796 there were no fewer than nine such bands in St Petersburg as well as others in Moscow and the provinces. The music was written in a special type of notation and was sometimes of astonishing complexity.[8] Fomin's use of a Russian horn band in a dramatic work is a good indication of its popularity. The horn band survived until the mid-1830s.[9]

Lavish spectacle was typical not only of the court opera but also of sacred music, for just as Russian sculpture and architecture were strongly influenced by Italian culture, so Russian sacred music was influenced by such composers as Galuppi, for several years director of the imperial chapel, and Giuseppe Sarti, the distinguished director of the Italian Opera in St Petersburg (and teacher of the talented serf composer Stepan Anikiyevich Degtyaryov, 1766–1813). Bortnyansky is remembered particularly for his multi-voice sacred concertos, full of smooth part-writing and masterly contrapuntal technique. Sarti wrote sacred and secular oratorios, often conceived on a lavish scale and demanding huge forces. His *Te Deum*, for instance, written to mark the victory of Potyomkin at Ochakov in 1789, used not only a large orchestra, with soloists and chorus, but also bells and cannons.

Court cultural life left its mark in many spheres. Wealthy nobles, such as Count Sheremetev and Count Vorontsov, had their own theatres and serf orchestras, and in the magnificence of their performances they sought to rival those of the court, whose musical activities they imitated. Sheremetev had an opera troupe of serf artists and a large orchestra which often took part in Moscow concerts and whose repertory included overtures and symphonies by Haydn. Gradually the local nobility took an interest in opera, and opera companies of varying strength and ability were set up in country estates. Towards the end of the century opera performances in private houses became the fashion. Conditions for serf musicians, however, were often far from good, and contemporary newspapers include advertisements for musicians for sale along with domestic animals. Degtyaryov, composer of the patriotic secular oratorio *Minin i Pozharsky, ili Osvobozhdeniye Moskvï* ('Minin and Pozharsky, or the Liberation of Moscow', 1811), and the singer Praskov'ya Kovalyova (Zhemchugova), who later became Sheremetev's wife, were both Sheremetev's serfs.

As in other parts of Europe and the New World, there was an ever-increasing demand in Russia for uncomplicated new music to meet the needs of the musical amateur. Of great popularity were the works of the Polish composer Józef Kozłowski (1757–1831), whose polonaises were heard throughout fashionable society and enjoyed great popularity; they are found both in orchestral form and arranged for keyboard. Numerous accounts give details of the prevalence in cultured circles of the harp and guitar, not only as accompaniment to the sentimental songs and 'romances' of the period but sometimes in chamber ensembles. Such songs were written by Kozłowski, Grigory Teplov (1711–79) and Fyodor Dubyansky (1760–96). The guitar was especially popular during the 1790s and in the early nineteenth century, being promoted by such Italian composers as Sarti and Canobbio and by French émigrés from the French Revolution, who settled in Russian towns and estates as teachers of music and singing.

Just as the eighteenth century saw an increasing number of periodical publications in western Europe, so too in Russia did the first music journals start to appear. Such were the *Giornale musicale del Teatro Italiano di St Pietroburgo* (1795), edited and produced by

Bernhard Theodor Breitkopf, son of the Leipzig music publisher, and the *Magazin muzkal'nykh uveseleniy* ('Journal of Musical Amusements'), also of 1795, issued by Selivanovsky, a Moscow publisher and bookseller. Outstanding, though, are the two so-called *Karmannye knigi* ('Pocket-books for Lovers of Music'), produced in 1795 and 1796 by Johann Daniel Gerstenberg, an enterprising German who went to St Petersburg about 1790. Their content is diverse, containing calendars, portraits, descriptions of composers and musical forms, musical games, anecdotes and other materials, similar to those in comparable publications in western Europe. Where the Russian pocket-books differ, however, is in their printed musical content; the 1795 volume, for instance, contains six 'Russian Songs' by Dubyansky and 'Two Russian Songs with Variations' by Palschau. With their sentimental texts and plaintive melodies, such songs were extremely popular: they crop up constantly in anonymous vocal collections of the period.[10]

Associated with the increase in amateur music-making was the growth in the number of instrument makers and the appearance of music instruction books (translations of foreign works). Ivan Yevsta-fyevich Khandoshkin (1747–1804) was a musician at the Russian court and the finest violinist in Russia in the eighteenth century. He wrote sonatas for unaccompanied violin and combinations of strings and his sets of variations on Russian folktunes are evidence of his own remarkable virtuosity.[11]

Though foreign operas were usually given initially in the royal palace, they were often staged later at the Moscow and St Petersburg public theatres and in English translation. The English impresario Michael Maddox played a crucial role.[12] His public theatre was not the first in Moscow – being preceded by that of Locatelli, 1759–61, among others – but Maddox's activities, both as a producer of west European works and especially as an enthusiastic supporter of the first operas by Russian composers, were sufficient to give him an esteemed place in Russian culture of the period.

Maddox was born in England in 1742. A Jew, he arrived in St Petersburg impecunious and became a tight-rope walker; in 1772 he appears to have gone to Moscow where he gave 'mechanical and physical displays'.[13] Maddox attracted the attention of Prince Urusov, a passionate devotee of the stage, who had been granted by Catherine the Great the privilege of 'master of all stage performances in Moscow' but who had little practical experience; in 1776 an agreement was drawn up between them.

At first, performances were given at Count Vorontsov's house on the Znamenka, its theatre renovated and equipped with innovatory stage machinery, whose effects captivated the imagination of the Muscovite audiences. Performers were drawn from Colonel N. S. Titov's troupe and from dancers and actors trained at the Moscow

Orphanage. Among several notable productions at the Znamenka (or Russian) Theatre was the first performance of *The Miller-Magician, Cheat and Matchmaker* (see p. 238).

Permission was obtained for the construction of a more substantial theatre but before it was built, in 1780, the Znamenka Theatre burnt down. Prince Urusov withdrew but Maddox persisted. Further finance was raised, fresh plans drawn up and, in only five months, the new building was opened in Great Petrov Street, near Kuznetsky Most. As the *Moskovskie vedomosti* announced:

> For the satisfaction of the esteemed public to whom an announce-ment about today's opening of the newly erected Petrovsky Theatre has already been made, we consider it necessary to offer the information that this enormous building, constructed for the pleasure and entertainment of the people, which is 8 *sazhens* in height, 32 in length and 20 wide, containing 110 boxes, not counting the galleries . . . has been brought to a perfect conclusion and, in the opinion of the best architects and with the approval of the connois-seurs of the theatre . . . surpasses all the outstanding European theatres.[14]

According to a more recent description by Yury Khripunov:

> Its auditorium had a pit (with 20 benches and a few rows of stalls in front for distinguished guests), four tiers of boxes with 26 boxes in each tier and a gallery [*paradise* or *raëk*] for the general public . . . In all, not counting the galleries, the hall contained 800 people . . . The boxes in the so-called Italian style (representing, as it were, separate rooms, open to the side of the hall), according to the custom of the time, were let out for a year and were placed at the complete disposal of the owner, who could upholster them, paper them, furnish them and light them according to his taste.[15]

Khripunov also said that the stage was quite deep, being 11 *sazhens* from the proscenium to the 'horizon', and that the hall was illumi-nated with wax and tallow candles. It was possible to raise the floor of the theatre to make a ballroom suitable for fancy-dress balls.[16]

Well situated, close to the Kremlin (on the side of the present Bol'shoy Theatre) and equipped with excellent stage machinery, the theatre offered diverse entertainments. It was welcomed by Prince Dolgoruky, who extended Maddox's privilege for a further ten years. Maddox, who became a Russian citizen, did his utmost to secure the best performers, constantly advertising for new players and offering soloists 200–600 roubles per year 'according to capabilities'.[17] On opening the Petrovsky Theatre (also known as the 'Maddox' or 'Kamenny' Theatre), he offered a subscription to 75 performances during the season. Subsequently this number was increased to 100.[18]

Some idea of the style of performances at the Petrovsky Theatre is gained from an announcement of *Arlequin sorcier par sympathie*, a ballet-pantomime given on 8 May 1781, which appeared on the evening preceding in the *Moskovskie vedomosti*:

> This pantomime will be enriched by magnificent and entertaining transformation scenes, the like of which no-one has exhibited before. In the three acts Arlequin will change his costume eight times, and in such a singular manner that no-one will be able to remark it. All this will be accompanied by music, singing, play of firebrands [*jeux de brûlots*] and English dances. The music of this work is the composition of Mr Andrea Galletti.[19]

From 1780 to 1782 Maddox had leading actors and actresses among his performers and from 1782 to 1796 the choreographer Francesco Morelli played a prominent part in his productions. In 1784 the ballet school of the Moscow Orphanage was purchased by Maddox, who used it as a valuable theatrical training-ground.[20] As with many contemporary English and German theatres, the players were expected not only to act in the dramas and comedies but also to sing in the comic operas.[21] From its inception to 1805 some 425 Russian and foreign pieces were given at the Petrovsky Theatre, of which about a third were operas and the rest comedies, tragedies, dramas and ballets.[22] The operas by foreign composers included Cherubini's *Les deux journées*, Cimarosa's *Il matrimonio segreto*, Grétry's *Les deux avares*, Méhul's *L'irato*, Paisiello's *Il barbiere di Siviglia* and Salieri's *La scuola de' gelosi*.[23] Mozart's *Die Zauberflöte* was given in Moscow in 1794, only three years after its première in Vienna.

Maddox's entrepreneurial activities were by no means confined to the stage, and concerts were frequently given by foreign virtuosos, such as the double-bass player Joseph Zaneboni. As early as 1780, influenced by the immense popularity of the public gardens of Vauxhall and Ranelagh in London, Maddox had erected in a space adjoining the theatre a number of halls and pavilions, accommodating several thousand people. These, too, served as a venue for masquerades, comedies and comic operas, at which refreshments were provided and the entertainments were often concluded by fireworks,[24] all of which appealed to the Moscow populace – especially those seeking amorous adventures. On the boards of Maddox's Vauxhall Theatre (as it was called) were performed many foreign comic operas, including Monsigny's *Le cadi dupé* and Philidor's *Le bucheron, ou Les trois souhaits*, both in 1785.

In spite of the success of his theatrical productions, in 1789 Maddox's enterprise ended in bankruptcy and the theatre was taken over by the board of trustees, to whom he had mortgaged his property to the sum of 100,000 roubles. But his managerial skill was recognized and he was permitted to continue as director, receiving an annual salary of 5000 roubles and a free lodging.[25] Maddox's privilege was renewed for a further ten years and his company continued to attract outstanding Russian performers, among them the singer Elizaveta Sandunova.

In 1805 the Petrovsky Theatre was destroyed by fire and Maddox's entrepreneurial career was brought to a close. His theatrical troupe continued to perform in a private house until the following year, when, along with other performers, they were taken under the aegis of the state, following the institution in 1806 of a Moscow branch of the Imperial Theatres.[26] He was granted a pension of 3000 roubles by the state in recognition of his services. Little is known of him until his death in the province of Tula in 1822.

CIVIC MUSICAL LIFE, 1800–1850

Catherine II died in 1796, and the reign of Paul (1796–1801) was marked by a period of reaction. Far-reaching reforms, intended to curb the moral laxity of the Russian (and especially the St Petersburg) populations were implemented; the number of private orchestras was reduced and all dramatic and operatic productions were subjected to a double censorship both before and during production. The publication and import of foreign materials was restricted and it became increasingly difficult to travel abroad.

After Paul's assassination, however, and the accession of Alexander I (1801–25) there was an upsurge in creative activity and the years 1801–12 saw a marked increase in the publication of books. Eighteenth-century writers (unlike composers) had been mostly of noble birth (with the notable exception of the gifted scholar and poet Lomonosov), but early nineteenth-century writers were less often from the aristocracy, the civil service or the army. The same increase in intellectual activity was seen in Russian music, which in the early nineteenth century started to develop at a faster rate and to acquire a more distinctive national colouring.

The French Revolution and the Napoleonic wars, as well as the influence of Western Romanticism, left their mark on Russian life. Young Russians who had visited western Europe returned to their native land with a fresh outlook and a desire for reform. An element of sentimentalism began to appear in Russian literature and music, together with the influence of Romanticism. The writer Zhukovsky was particularly fascinated by German Romantic poetry. The novels of Scott, the poetry of Byron and the Greek and Roman classics were extensively read. Leading writers included Karamzin (1766–1826), Krylov (1769–1844), Zhukovsky (1783–1852), Zagoskin (1789–1852) and Griboedov (1795–1829) but they paled in quality before the brilliance of Alexander Pushkin (1797–1837), the creator and formulator of the modern Russian language. In music, Pushkin's counterpart was Mikhail Ivanovich Glinka (1804–57).

The Napoleonic wars had a lasting effect on Russian intellectuals; the growing awareness of Russia's cultural and economic backwardness, the fate of the Russian peasantry and increasing resentment at political oppression resulted in the formation of societies and aristocratic circles. These events were to culminate in the Decembrist uprising of 1825, a revolutionary outbreak crushed by Tsar Nicholas I (1825–55) only a few months after he came to power. Nicholas I's whole milieu, the atmosphere of reaction and repression, the role of the bureaucracy, the rise of the mercantile classes, as well as the general desire for reform, are all reflected in the works of Pushkin, Gogol (1809–52) and Lermontov (1814–41). Towards the middle of the century the element of realism became more apparent, as demonstrated by the paintings of Fedotov (1815–52), the music of Dargomïzhsky (1813–69) and the writings of the Russian critic Belinsky (1811–48), who was constantly striving after 'truth of expression'.

Alexander's reign saw considerable developments in drama, with the production of works in many different genres, including classical and Romantic tragedies, patriotic dramas based on national themes, sentimental dramas, comedies, melodramas and vaudeville. Overtures, orchestral entr'actes, choruses, vocal numbers, melodramas and ballets were often included in dramatic performances. Russian music, however, was still heavily dependent on foreign models. But concert life was developing, and the performance in 1811 of Degtyaryov's patriotic oratorio *Minin and Pozharsky, or The Liberation of Moscow* was a big event.

Before 1836, when the rebuilt Bol'shoy ('Grand') Theatre was opened in St Petersburg for opera productions, there had been no opera houses as such. Roles in operas and dramas were taken by the same cast; acting, singing and ballet were studied simultaneously at the theatre schools (the one in St Petersburg was established in 1783). Theatres were found not only in major towns but also on the large estates of the nobility, such as those of the Yusupovs in Arkhangel'-skoe (near Moscow), the Kamenskys in Orël or the Shakhovskoys in Nizhny Novgorod. Some of the serf theatres (Kamensky's and Shakhovskoy's, for example) were open to the public for a modest fee. The repertory of these theatres consisted of plays, together with French, Italian and Russian operas, including works by Grétry, Monsigny, Salieri, Paisiello and Martini. Sheremetev's serf theatres at Kuskovo and Ostankino were particularly magnificent: the best talent, both foreign and native, was employed on the technical side and the repertory was enormous, comprising some 116 pieces, including 73 operas (37 French, 23 Italian and thirteen Russian); there was also an excellent ballet company.

79. *Mikhail Ivanovich Glinka with his sister, Lyudmila Shestakova, in 1852*

The most popular dramatic form in the early nineteenth century was the vaudeville, an indispensable element in most Russian entertainments, whether ballet, opera or drama. Certain writers, including Shakhovskoy, Khmel'nitsky and Pisarev, specialized in vaudeville composition, often adapting French models to the Russian taste. The original satirical element was lost in Russian, but it was replaced by other features. The subject matter was diverse, the favourite themes at this time being patriotism, fantasy, parody and lower-class life. A special place in vaudeville was occupied by the solo couplet song which, in most cases, had an unchanging verbal refrain. Usually the music was strongly rhythmic, sometimes in a dance form such as the polonaise. If the situation called for it, a sentimental song or *romance* might be used. The vaudeville would usually be introduced by an overture, including elements of the solo songs heard later in the work, and would often be concluded by an ensemble, each soloist singing a couplet to a general refrain. The subjects of vaudevilles were sometimes taken from folk life and composers gave an authentic flavour to their work by using folk themes. Thus, Catterino Cavos (1776–1840), in his music to Shakhovskoy's patriotic opera-vaudeville *Kazak-stikhotvorets* ('The Cossack Poet', 1812), used Ukrainian melodies (one of which has survived as the popular song 'Yes, my darling Daughter!').

In the early nineteenth century, French and German Romantic operas began to appear on the Russian stage, among them works by Cherubini and Spontini and, from 1824, Weber's *Der Freischütz*. In the early 1830s the operas of Meyerbeer were given: *Robert le diable* had its first Russian performance in St Petersburg in 1834. A number of outstanding Russian opera singers were active at the time, including the bass Osip Afanasevich Petrov (1807–78) and the contralto Anna Yakovlevna Vorobyova (1816–1901), who later became Petrov's wife. Petrov was Ukrainian; having sung for several years with a provincial troupe he was 'discovered' in Kursk by the *régisseur* of the St Petersburg Theatres. He made his début in autumn 1830 at St Petersburg in *Die Zauberflöte*. His later roles included Bertram in Meyerbeer's *Robert le diable* in 1834, Ivan Susanin in *A Life for the Tsar* and Farlaf in *Ruslan and Lyudmila*. Vorobyova-Petrova was also gifted and is remembered as the creator of Vanya in *A Life for the Tsar* and Ratmir in *Ruslan and Lyudmila*.

In the first decade of the nineteenth century the Russian court was dominated by French opera, largely as a result of the work of Adrien-François-Boieldieu, conductor of the Imperial Opera in St Petersburg (1804–10). In the early 1830s a German opera company attracted attention by giving performances of French and Italian operas. Whereas Italian opera had dominated the musical scene in eighteenth-century Russia, its position in the early nineteenth century was far less secure. Italian productions were occasionally given in St Petersburg and attempts were made to form a private Italian opera theatre in Moscow in the 1820s (a permanent opera theatre existed in St Petersburg, 1829–31), but Italian opera was eclipsed and from the beginning of the 1830s disappeared from St Petersburg for more than ten years. However, in spring 1843 the famous Italian tenor Giovanni Battista Rubini (1795–1854) paid a short visit and took part in concerts and operas, which were extremely successful. In the autumn he again travelled to St Petersburg – but this time with an opera troupe that included such distinguished singers as Pauline Viardot-García and Antonio Tamburini. From then on Italian opera returned with new force, the Italian 'nightingales' often being bombarded with flowers grown specially by noble admirers in their own orangeries. The many notable visitors included Pasta, Salvi, Mario, Frezzolini, Tamberlik and Ronconi, all of whose performances are described in the contemporary Russian press. In the 1849–50 season 79 performances of 17 Italian operas were given in St Petersburg alone, a figure that was to increase in the seasons to follow.[26]

During the first half of the nineteenth century, Russian opera occupied a secondary place and even had Russian composers been given greater encouragement they would have been unable to offer serious competition to their foreign counterparts. Such operas as Blyma's *Starinnye svyatki* ('The Old Yuletide'), given in Moscow in 1800, the various versions of Stepan Ivanovich Davïdov's *Rusalka* (1803–7), the many operas of Alexey Nikolayev Titov (1769–1827), Cavos (1776–1840), Alexey Verstovsky (1799–1862) and Alexander

Dargomïzhsky, though sometimes enjoying local success, could not equal the craftsmanship and musical sophistication of contemporary European opera. Verstovsky's *Askol'dova mogila* ('Askold's Grave'), first given in Moscow in 1835 a year before Glinka's *Zhizn'za tsarya* ('A Life for the Tsar'), was immensely popular, being performed in the provinces until late in the century and owing much to Weber's *Der Freischütz*. But it was only with Glinka that a strong creative personality appeared. His influence, as may be seen from the Russian press, was modest until the mid-1830s.

Such was the official attitude towards native talent that from autumn 1846 St Petersburg was without Russian opera for three years, the troupe having been sent to Moscow, and it was only in spring 1849 that it returned on tour. Though it remained in St Petersburg from 1850, it was deprived of a permanent stage. Nevertheless, Russian operas continued to be performed. A regular opera company was established in Odessa for most of the nineteenth century, performing both Russian and west European works. If Russian composers could be said to excel at all, it was in the realms of the miniature – the comedy-vaudeville, the play with music, the vaudeville, the theme and variations and the song, examples of which were written by Daniil Kashin, Alexander Alyabyev, Titov, Cavos, Alexey L'vov and others.

An important part in Russian musical life was played by sacred music and the influence of the imperial chapel was widespread. A key figure was Dmitry Bortnyansky, director of the imperial chapel until 1826. He wrote 117 sacred works, including nine for three voices, 29 for four voices, 30 works for double choir, 45 concertos (of which ten are for two choirs) and four hymns and prayers, all subsequently published in 1882 in ten volumes by Tchaikovsky. In his arrangements of traditional sacred *znamenny*, Kievan, Greek and Bulgarian chants, he took a melody and transformed it rhythmically, so that it became symmetrical. His euphonious harmonizations, clearly influenced by Italian models, are often deeply moving.

Bortnyansky also did much to elevate the performance of sacred music, for although Emperor Paul had endeavoured by an edict of 1797 to prevent abuses, the practice of singing excerpts from operatic arias to sacred texts (for example, singing the Priest's bass aria from Spontini's *La vestale* to the words 'We Praise Thee, O God') during the service continued. In 1816 the synod forbade the use of manuscript music and the inclusion of such pieces in the service, allowing only works by Bortnyansky or music approved by him. However, concerts continued to be given and another edict was issued in 1850. Bortnyansky hoped to publish the *znamenny* chant in its original notation but this was never accomplished.

Arrangements of ancient chants were made by another Ukrainian

80. Final scene from an early production of Glinka's 'A Life for the Tsar', first performed in St Petersburg in 1836

attached to the imperial chapel, Pyotr Ivanovich Turchaninov (1779–1856), a pupil of Sarti. He adhered more closely to the original melodies, but his works suffer from an excessive use of parallel 3rds and 6ths. His harmonizations, which include sharps and flats, were permitted by a decree of the synod (dated 18 May 1831) and his music was published in several volumes. Sacred works were also written by Alyabyev, Alexander Egorovich Varlamov, Verstovsky and Vinogradov.

After Bortnyansky's death, Fyodor L'vov was appointed director of the imperial chapel (1826–36), though he was more an administrator than a composer. His son Alexey Fyodorovich L'vov (composer of the Russian national anthem) was a good all-round musician and a skilled violinist. When he succeeded to the post of director (1836–70) he raised the singing to unprecedented heights; indeed, Berlioz was greatly impressed when he heard the choir in 1847. Familiar with west European music (he arranged Pergolesi's *Stabat mater* for choir and orchestra) and influenced by German Romanticism (as is evident from his compositions), L'vov none the less was anxious to restore the ancient chants to their proper rhythm and to make the music subservient to the text. Though he did not entirely succeed in realizing his aims, he assembled a huge body of material and in 1848 published a complete cycle of liturgical chant used through the church year, which became a standard work. In it the music is for four voices arranged in conventional four-part harmony with the chant given to the top voice. The arrangements were made by Lomakin (a skilled composer in his own right) and Vorotnikov, teachers at the imperial chapel who worked under L'vov's guidance. Interestingly, to gain free rhythm, some of the music is written without bar-lines. L'vov's work was influential in establishing the style of what is known as the 'Petersburg School' of sacred composition.

A different approach to the arrangement of sacred chant is found in the work of Glinka and Prince Odoevsky: realizing that the original chants were written diatonically, they thought the harmonization should be diatonic too. As a result of the success of his opera *A Life for the Tsar* (1836), Glinka was invited in 1837 to be a choirmaster of the imperial chapel, where he composed a *Kheruvimskaya* ('Cherubim's Song') for six-part chorus. He was dissatisfied with it, and, having left the chapel, did not return to sacred composition until 1855, with an *Ekteniya pervaya* ('First Litany') and *Da ispravitsya molitva moya* ('Let my Prayer be fulfilled rightly before Thee'), based on Greek chant, for three-part male choir. Both works use diatonic harmonies and have no regular barring. At this time Glinka was under the influence of Sheremetev's choir (conducted by Lomakin), which performed Western sacred music. Convinced that ancient Russian chants could be harmonized in a manner based on the old church modes and not on the European major and minor system, Glinka went to Germany to study with Siegfried Dehn in Berlin; but death put an end to his plans.

Prince Vladimir Odoevsky, one of the most remarkable and influential figures in early nineteenth-century Russian culture, was also concerned with sacred chant and appears to have been the first Russian scholar to draw attention to theoretical writings on the subject. By working on sixteenth- and seventeenth-century manuscripts by Shaydurov, Mezenets and others, he unearthed a great deal of information, some of which he published.

From the beginning of the nineteenth century, concert life began to develop more widely, though it was still centred on St Petersburg and Moscow. Concerts were usually given at Lent, a tradition that persisted for many decades. In the 1830s, concerts became more frequent and more widespread, catering for a larger and more socially diverse audience. Subscription concerts were organized by singers and orchestral musicians to augment their wages. The programmes were unremarkable, and composed of items from the theatrical repertory. Foreign artists continued to visit Russia in ever-increasing numbers; they included John Field, Hummel, Bernhard Romberg, Angelica Catalani, Paganini, Henselt and, later, Clara Wieck, Berlioz and Liszt. Such visits not only demonstrated new instrumental and vocal techniques, but introduced the latest forms of Western music. Several virtuosos, such as Field and Henselt, settled in Russia as teachers.

Musical education was almost entirely in the hands of foreigners, private lessons being given in the houses of the nobility and in the institutes of the privileged classes.[27] Notable among the Moscow and St Petersburg pedagogues were Charles Mayer (1799–1837), himself a pupil of Field, Franz Schoberlechner, Herke and Miller the theoretician. Field not only created a new school of piano playing in Russia (the influence of which was felt in Moscow until the end of the century through his pupil Dubuque) but had great influence on Russian music in general through the work of Glinka.

A special role was played by concerts instituted for charitable purposes, most of which were organized initially by the nobility. Often the performers were of humble origin and these concerts were a means of displaying their talents. Charitable aims brought into being one of the first Russian concert organizations – the St Petersburg Philharmonic Society, founded in 1802. It provided concerts in which emphasis was placed on major choral works by Handel, Haydn and Cherubini, and Mozart's Requiem. Beethoven's *Missa solemnis* was given its première there in 1824.

Towards the middle of the century the demand for concert performances increased. Amateur societies sprang up, at first restricted mostly to the aristocracy, a typical example being the 'Society of

Lovers of Music', inaugurated in the early 1840s; although its
concerts were in open concert halls, admission was available only
through the personal recommendations of members. A particularly
interesting society was known as 'Musical Rehearsals of Students of
the Imperial University'. These amateur 'University Concerts' came
into being on the initiative of a university inspector, A. I. Fitztum von
Ecstedt. The repertory was mostly symphonic music. A good impression of the society's activities is gained from Vladimir Stasov in his
reminiscences:[28]

> In these rehearsals the performers were actual students, former
> students and a number of amateurs, while any missing parts would
> be made up by inviting members of the theatre orchestra (e.g.
> trombones or horns, or a few other wind instruments). The orches-
> tra consisted of 50–60 people, and the conductor was Karl
> Bogdanovich Schubert, an excellent cellist, soloist of the opera
> orchestra of the imperial theatre, a great friend of Fitztum, a fine
> quartet player, and a very kind man. These 'rehearsals' (called
> everywhere 'University Concerts') were held on Sunday mornings,
> beginning at the end of November or the beginning of December
> (sometimes even in October) at 1.00. Usually there were ten in the
> winter in all, though sometimes (but very rarely) there were extra
> ones, and for that – i.e. for ten concerts, one paid only five roubles!
> Although they were amateur concerts, played without rehearsals,
> nevertheless, thanks to the conductor, K. Schubert, and his skill in
> capturing the young people's enthusiasm and cooperation – and
> among them there were some very talented members – the perform-
> ances were not at all bad. But the main thing was that any one
> wishing to get to know orchestral music was given the chance. The
> concerts were accessible to extremely poor people and when I went
> to them (from 1846 to 1856) the great university hall was always full;
> one had to get one's tickets beforehand. Only students were allowed
> in the gallery and they were let in free.

The pieces performed in these concerts were mostly by Haydn,
Mozart and Beethoven, Schubert, Weber and Mendelssohn. Several
of Schumann's compositions received their first Russian performances
there, including his *Manfred* overture. Mention should also be made of
the so-called Pavlovsky Muzykal'ny Vokzal (Pavlovsk Music Hall), a
hall built in 1838 in the outskirts of St Petersburg at which outdoor
concerts were given during the summer as well as entertainments that
attracted a wide spectrum of the populace.

Amateur music-making continued to grow and there are
many accounts of it in the literature of the period. The salon of
Count Mikhail Vielgorsky (1788–1856) and his brother Matvey was
frequented by many visiting celebrities, including Liszt, Schumann,
Clara Wieck, Berlioz and Bernhard Romberg. The Vielgorsky salon

was so much in the centre of St Petersburg musical life that they were given the official right to 'audition' all visiting artists to assess their ability, for which they received a state subsidy of 15,000 roubles a year.[29]

Music-making spread slowly through society. Instrumental music was popular, favourite instruments being the piano, harp, guitar and the *gusli* (a kind of zither). The guitar was used to accompany songs and dances. A key figure in its promulgation was Andrey Sikhra (1773–1850) who arrived in St Petersburg in the early 1820s, gave concerts and was active as a teacher and publisher of guitar journals.

Song played the most important part in amateur and domestic music-making. A number of different genres existed: a favourite was the *bytovoy romans*, a simple sentimental song with piano, harp or guitar accompaniment, often in a minor key and showing the influence of Russian folk or gypsy song. *Romances* of this type were written in substantial numbers by such composers as Alexander Varlamov (1801–48) and Alexander Gurilyov (1803–58), as well as by Alyabyev, Dargomïzhsky and Glinka. Equally popular were the 'Russian songs', in the folk idiom, and histrionic dramatic ballads, such as Verstovsky's *Chornaya shal'* ('The Black Shawl') which, composed in 1823 to Pushkin's text and performed on stage in costume, enjoyed within Russia lasting success.

At a time when music printing in Russia was still in its infancy, a favourite means of popularizing such works was the 'musical album' and almanach, of which many were published in the 1820s and 30s in St Petersburg and Moscow. Whereas the almanachs contained poems, prose and critical articles, together with music supplements in the form of *romances*, songs or vaudeville couplets, the 'musical albums' were even more popular, consisting of vocal and piano pieces, *romances*, 'Russian songs', piano variations on popular folksongs, opera and *romance* melodies and dances for piano, most by native composers. In the absence of any organized system of music publishing, the albums were the most convenient way of propagating music on a wide scale and this method was used by Glinka.

Several publishers in St Petersburg (though mostly foreigners) issued albums composed almost entirely of Western music, in which salon pieces were ranked alongside works by Beethoven, Haydn and Mozart. To give difficult pieces the semblance of simplicity, publishers sometimes resorted to cunning. Thus, in the *Album musicale pour l'année 1828*, published by I. Brief, Beethoven's Rondo in C was included, but to avoid printing the name of the formidable composer, the work was given the disarming title of *Une soirée d'été au bord de la Newa*.

Journals appeared intermittently, and from the beginning of the nineteenth century such publications as *Journal d'airs et duos choisies dans les meilleurs opéras français et italiens donnés au Théâtre de St Pétersburg et arrangés pour pianoforte, Journal pour la guitarre, Severnaya arfa* ('The Northern Harp') and *Zhurnal dlya fortepiano* ('Piano Magazine') were in circulation. In these were printed arrangements of operatic selections, variations, dances and so on.

These enterprises were short-lived, however, and it was not until 1839, with the publication of the musical journal *Nouvelliste*, that the periodical firmly established itself. Indeed, the *Nouvelliste* was in existence until the beginning of the twentieth century. At first it appeared each month in music books containing four or five pieces, but after 1846 the number was increased to ten; N. Bernard, the publisher, added to the musical section a literary one, which up to 1878 was called the 'Literary Supplement'. The journal printed many works (mostly for piano or voice) by Russian composers – Alyabyev, Glinka, Varlamov, Dargomïzhsky and others.

The press played a part in the development of Russian civic musical life.[30] An examination of contemporary newspapers, journals and chronicles reveals the extent to which public awareness of music developed in half a century – 1931 entries in the period 1800–25, 3775 in 1826–40, 5803 in 1841–50. Informative, too, are the number of references to foreign countries or reports received from them, a reflection of influences and changing musical tastes. Thus in the first period we find 17 references to England, 20 to Germany, 20 to Italy and 59 to France. In the second period (1826–40) the figures are 36, 23, 27 and 186; and in the third (1841–50) 62, 30, 33 and 244: while the upper classes may have favoured Italian opera, public interest appears to have been directed more towards France.

The number of entries for each composer or performer is another indication of popular taste. Thus, in the first period the singer Angelica Catalani has pride of place, being allocated 109 major entries, followed by Haydn (93), Rossini (44), Mozart (37), Weber (33), the cellist Bernhard Romberg (20), the French singer Fodor-Mainvielle (19), John Field (18) and Liszt (nine). Of the Russians, most frequently referred to are the composers Daniil Kashin (23) and Alexey Zhilin (fourteen), while the singer Sandunova has twelve entries and Degtyaryov eleven. There are two references to Glinka. In the second period Paganini predominates with 99 entries, followed by the singer Henriette Sontag (76), Mozart (44), Meyerbeer (42), Beethoven (39), Rossini (38), the pianist Belleville-Oury (29), the singer Malibran (26) and the composer Ole Bull (25), while of the Russians Glinka has 62 entries, succeeded by Verstovsky (33) and Alyabyev and Varlamov (both eleven). In the final period Liszt dominates with 132 entries, followed by Berlioz and Rossini (both 74), the singer Rubini (67), Meyerbeer (62), Jenny Lind (55), Mozart (52), the violinist Vieuxtemps (42) and the singer Viardot-García

The Early Romantic Period

(39). Among the Russian composers Glinka has 92 major entries, with A. F. L'vov (28), Verstovsky (21), Dargomïzhsky (20), Varlamov (18) and Anton Rubinstein (14).

Though the standard of musical journalism was not high at this period, the writings of Osip Senkovsky (1800–58) and Vasily Botkin (1810–69) rise above the norm. Prince Odoevsky, as well as being author of critical writings, wrote two Russian musical novels – *Beethoven's Last Quartet* and *Sebastian Bach*. Also noteworthy was Alexander Ulybyshev's three-volume *Nouvelle biographie de Mozart*, one of the first biographies of the composer to be published.

*

We have seen that the role of the court in determining musical life lessened dramatically, though the principal theatres still remained under state control. Foreign culture, manifested by Italian, French and German opera, along with visiting virtuosos, continued to play a significant part in Russian musical life and the role of foreign teachers was invaluable. Though attitudes towards Russian music differed according to social groups, nationalism became increasingly evident in the late 1830s and 1840s, seen particularly in the interest in the first Russian composer of outstanding ability – Mikhail Ivanovich Glinka. Not only was he the first outstanding Russian composer, but his operas and orchestral works served as models for his successors. From his operas *A Life for the Tsar* (1836) and *Ruslan and Lyudmila* (1842) originate the two streams of epic and 'fantastic' opera that were to persist during the nineteenth century and beyond, culminating in such masterpieces as Musorgsky's *Boris Godunov* on the one hand and Rimsky-Korsakov's *The Golden Cockerel* on the other. Glinka's orchestral fantasy *Kamarinskaya* (1848) was also of great influence both orchestrally and in its treatment of folk material. Not without reason did Tchaikovsky claim that it embodied the whole of the subsequent Russian orchestral school, just as the seed of the oak is contained in the acorn.

NOTES

[1] *Lettres du Comte Valentin Esterházy à sa femme 1784–1792* (Paris, 1907), letter dated 'Petersbourg 11 Octobre-30 Septembre 1791', 318–19.

[2] 'Some Particulars Respecting the Manners and Customs of the Russian Peasants', *Aberdeen Magazine* (12 Feb 1789), 65–6.

[3] See R. A. Mooser, *Opéras, intermezzos, ballets, cantates, oratorios, joués en Russie durant le XVIIIe siècle* (Basle, 3/1964), 42.

[4] A score of *Le faucon*, ed. O. Levasheva, was published by Muzyka (Moscow, 1975) and a recording is available (Melodiya C 10–07459 62).

[5] A score of the opera, attributing it to V. A. Pashkevich with the title translated as *Like Life, Like Renown, or The St Petersburg Gostiny Dvor*, ed. Y. Keldysh, was published by Muzyka (Moscow, 1980).

[6] A score, ed. Y. Keldysh, was published by Muzyka (Moscow, 1977); the overture and a chorus are available in a recording (Melodiya D 018241–2).

[7] A recording is available (Melodiya C 10–08765–8).

[8] For a more detailed account of the band, its origins and repertory, see G. R. Seaman, 'The Russian Horn Band', *MMR*, lxxxix (1959), 93–9.

[9] An extraordinary account of life as a member of a horn band, by 'the F sharp of the Russian Imperial Horn Music', appeared in *Harmonicon*, no.xviii (June 1824), 104.

[10] For a fuller discussion of these periodicals see G. R. Seaman, 'An Eighteenth Century Russian Pocket-Book', *Slavonic and East European Review*, lx (1982), 262–72.

[11] See A. Mischakoff, *Khandoshkin and the Beginning of Russian String Music* (Ann Arbor, 1983).

[12] Material on Michael Maddox is from G. R. Seaman, 'Michael Maddox, English Impresario in Eighteenth-Century Russia', *Slavic Themes: Papers from Two Hemispheres: Neuried 1988*, 321–6.

[13] See R. A. Mooser, *Annales de la musique et des musiciens en Russie au XVIIIe siècle*, ii (Geneva, 1951), 168.

[14] *Moskovskie vedomosti* [Moscow gazette] (1780), no. 280; quoted in A. Gozenpud, *Muzykal'ny teatr v Rossii: ot istokov do Glinki* [The music theatre in Russia: from its sources to Glinka's time] (Leningrad, 1959), 96. A *sazhen* is equivalent to 2.13 metres.

[15] Y. D. Khripunov, *Arkhitektura Bol'shogo teatra* [The architecture of the Bol'shoy Theatre] (Moscow, 1955), 16; quoted in Gozenpud, *Muzykal'ny teatr v Rossii*, 97.

[16] N. Roslavleva, *Era of the Russian Ballet* (London, 1966), 29.

[17] Mooser, *Annales*, ii, 292.

[18] See Y. Keldysh, *Russkaya muzyka XVIII veka* [Russian eighteenth-century music] (Moscow, 1965), 116.

[19] *Moskovskie vedomosti* [Moscow gazette] (1781), no. 36; quoted in Mooser, *Annales*, ii, 310.

[20] Roslavleva, *Era of the Russian Ballet*, 29.

[21] Mooser, *Annales*, ii, 292.

[22] See V. Belaiev, 'An English Operatic Manager in Eighteenth Century Russia', *The Dominant* (Jan 1928).

[23] For details of the operas and comedies given from 1782 to 1805 together with the number of annual performances, see O. Chayanova, *Teatr Maddoksa v Moskve, 1776–1805* [The Maddox Theatre in Moscow, 1776–1805] (Moscow, 1927), 222–39.

[24] Mooser, *Annales*, ii, 344.

[25] Ibid, 536.

[26] For details of Italian opera in Russia, see Vol'f, *Khronika peterburgskikh teatrov* [Chronicle of the St Petersburg Theatres] (St Petersburg, 1877–84), pts. 1–2.

[27] M. S. Pevelis, *Istoriya russkoy muzyki* [History of Russian music], i (Moscow and Leningrad, 1940), 222.

[28] V. V. Stasov, *Muzikal'nie vospominaniya* [Musical reminiscences].

[29] See G. R. Seaman, 'Amateur Music-Making in Russia', *ML*, xlvii (1966), 249–59.

[30] *Muzykal'naya bibliografiya russkoy periodicheskoy pechati XIX veka* [Musical bibliography of the Russian nineteenth-century periodical press], compiled by T. Livanova, is a vast collection of 11,509 items, published in Moscow in parts: Part 1 [1801–25] (1960); Part 2 [1826–40] (1963); Part 3 [1841–50] (1966). My figures are taken from this source.

BIBLIOGRAPHICAL NOTE

Historico-political background

For a concise overview of the social, political and historical life of the period, particularly useful is *The Cambridge Encyclopedia of Russia and the Soviet Union* (London, 1982), of which a second edition is in progress. An excellent insight into late eighteenth-century Russia is provided by I. de Madariaga's *Russia in the Age of*

The Early Romantic Period

Catherine the Great (New Haven and London, 1981); valuable information on the succeeding period is found in H. Seton-Watson's *The Russian Empire 1801–1917* (Oxford, 1967).

Literature and the visual arts

The Cambridge Encyclopedia, with its good bibliographical sources, is again of value; special mention should be made of *Literature in the Age of Catherine the Great*, ed. A. G. Cross (Oxford, 1976), and *Nineteenth Century Russian Literature*, ed. J. L. Fennell (London, 1973). G. H. Hamilton's *Art and Architecture of Russia* (Harmondsworth, 2/1975) and T. T. Rice's *A Concise History of Russian Art* (London, 1963) retain their value.

Music

The most comprehensive body of data relating to eighteenth-century Russian music is in R. A. Mooser's *Annales de la musique et des musiciens en Russie au XVIIIe siècle*, 3 vols. (Geneva, 1948–51), *Opéras, intermezzos, ballets, cantates, oratorios, joués en Russie durant le XVIIIe siècle* (Basle, 3/1964) and *Violonistes-compositeurs italiens en Russie au XVIIIe siècle* (Turin and Milan, 1938–50). Mooser did not concern himself with musical analysis but sought to agglomerate a huge mass of historical and biographical material, which in the case of the *Annales* is supplemented with an excellent collection of well-reproduced illustrations.

For a general survey one may consult G. R. Seaman's *History of Russian Music, i: from its Origins to Dargomyzhsky* (Oxford, 1967) which contains comprehensive material on cultural, social and political life, an examination of concert life, Russian folksong and folksong collections and studies of individual composers, with many music examples, substantial bibliographies and assessment of resource materials. Also concerned with the question of music in Russian society are G. R. Seaman's articles 'The First Russian Chamber Music', *Music Review*, xxvi (1965), 177–93; 'Amateur Music-Making in Russia', *ML*, xlvii (1966), 249–59. Excerpts from Count Valentin Esterházy's correspondence, in translation, are in G. R. Seaman, 'A Musical Entertainment', *Russia and the World of the Eighteenth Century: Bloomington 1984*, 651–65. An article on the Russian horn band is in the English journal *Harmonicon*, no.xviii (June 1824), 104. There are articles on individual composers and cities in *Grove 6*.

Important material in Russian on eighteenth-century music includes A. Gozenpud, *Muzykal'ny teatr v Rossii: ot istokov do Glinki* [The musical theatre in Russia: from its sources to Glinka's time] (Leningrad, 1959); T. Livanova, *Russkaya muzykal'naya kul'tura XVIII veka* [Russian musical culture in the eighteenth century], vols.i–ii (Moscow, 1952–3); and Y. Keldysh, *Russkaya muzyka XVIII veka* [Russian eighteenth-century music] (Moscow, 1965). Of value is A. Gozenpud, *Russky operny teatr XIX veka (1836–1856)* [The Russian nineteenth-century opera theatre (1836–56)] (Leningrad, 1969), while for comprehensive details of opera performances one is referred to A. I. Volf, *Khronika Peterburgskikh teatrov s kontsa 1826 do nachala 1855 goda* [Chronicle of the Petersburg Theatres from the end of 1826 to the beginning of 1855], Parts 1–3 (St Petersburg, 1877–84). A major source of information on most aspects of Russian music is T. N. Livanova, *Muzykal'naya bibliografiya russkoy periodicheskoy pechati XIX veka* [Musical bibliography of the Russian nineteenth-century periodical press], Parts 1–3 (Moscow, 1960–66).

Examples of different types of Russian music may be found in S. L. Ginzburg, *Istoriya russkoy muzyki v notnykh obraztsakh* [History of Russian music in printed music examples], vols.i–iii (Leningrad and Moscow, 1940–1952, 2/1968–70). A recent development has been the publication of music by Russian composers before Glinka's time in the series Pamyatniki Russkogo Muzykal'nogo Iskusstva [Monuments of Russian music].

Chapter IX

The USA:
a Quest for Improvement

KATHRYN BUMPASS

Music in early nineteenth-century America displayed considerable variety, though by and large it was not equal in sophistication to that of Europe. It nevertheless had a distinctive character which reflected the goals, attitudes and aspirations of the young nation. An expanding political democracy and corresponding opportunities in commerce soon left their peculiarly American stamp on artistic life which, given so many colonial settlers from religious minorities, was characterized by a perennial quest for moral uplift and for personal and social improvement.

Andrew Jackson, President of the USA from 1829 to 1837, was the living symbol of early nineteenth-century American democratic ideals and free enterprise. Active in law, land speculation, commerce, politics and military service, Jackson made money, lost it, accepted senior political appointments and became a national hero in January 1815, when he soundly defeated the British at New Orleans. He exemplified the American ideal: the self-made man. In American political mythology Jackson is the standard-bearer of the common man and the champion of a dynamic, radical democracy. Of equal importance, however, was his role in economic life. As president, he did much to promote entrepreneurial activity by small businessmen and land holders and in this he was perfectly in tune with the national preoccupation – making money.

Writing in 1836, Francis J. Grund observed:

> Business is the very soul of an American: he pursues it, not as a means of procuring for himself and his family the necessary comforts of life, but as the fountain of all human felicity . . . It is as if all America were but one gigantic workshop, over the entrance of which there is the blazing inscription, 'No admission here, except on business'.[1]

Alongside the burgeoning political and social democracy and the intense pursuit of wealth stood two potent and often interlocking

81. Title-page of the 'Happy Family Polka' (1851) by Francis H. Brown

forces: the emulation of European culture, often referred to as the 'genteel tradition', and the aspiration towards moral improvement. These produced a powerful impetus for reform, in religious life, manners and the arts.

The reformers' zeal played an important role in musical life, but reform must be seen against the background of the variety of music in nineteenth-century America, where the genteel or cultivated tradition existed alongside a native, vernacular tradition. The genteel tradition flourished especially in urban areas; it encompassed vocal and instrumental art music, sentimental song, parlour music for solo piano or other instruments, ballroom dance music, patriotic songs and marches. Its patrons were generally comfortable financially and socially, were literate and aspired to ever-higher status. Many could read music and owned and played instruments. By the 1840s, with music increasingly viewed as a social necessity in middle-class and wealthy homes, this group comprised a large market not only for concerts but also for instrument sellers and sheet-music publishers.

Instrumental music remained largely derivative in style and conception until the appearance of Anthony Philip Heinrich, a Bohemian immigrant who first went to America in 1805 and settled there after 1810. After some time in the east, Heinrich made an exhausting journey from Philadelphia to Pittsburgh on foot, continuing by boat down the Ohio River to Bardstown, Kentucky, on the edge of the American frontier wilderness. There he lived a rustic life in a log cabin and devoted himself to composing chamber music, piano and vocal works and other pieces. He also mounted what is believed to be the first performance in America of a complete Beethoven symphony, probably no.1.[2] In 1820 Heinrich published a collection of his works under the romantic title *The Dawning of Music in Kentucky, or The Pleasures of Harmony in the Solitudes of Nature.* It was praised in 1822 for its 'vigor of thought, variety of ideas, originality of conception, classical correctness, boldness and luxuriance of imagination'.[3] One critic saw in Heinrich nothing less than 'the Beethoven of America'. Heinrich sought to unite, in a uniquely American setting, two central Romantic notions: the pure life of nature and the elevating power of high art. His music not only brought 'culture' to the frontier, it also advocated the ideal of the natural man.

Heinrich dedicated his D major Sonata from *The Dawning of Music in Kentucky* 'to the VIRTUOSOS of the United States' as a ' "firstling" in its kind from the BACKWOODS'. Cast in three movements, it opens 'Alla maniera giusta' with an introduction of 26 bars for voice and piano, though the main body of the sonata is for solo piano. The virtuoso Allegro is somewhat irregular in form and marked by some striking short-term chromatic progressions, the whole nevertheless firmly anchored in the home key of D. The brief Andante is built on a simple melody consisting mainly of pathetic sigh-figures, the basic motifs ornamented by pianistic embellishments in parallel 3rds. This movement opens in D minor and closes on the dominant of B♭ major. The 'Finale alla Pollaca' begins and – surprisingly – ends in B♭ rather than D, and the ending brings a four-bar return of the voice. A certain conventionality in thematic invention and pianistic figuration notwithstanding, Heinrich's sonata is marked by some interesting departures from the norms of harmony and form.

Now famous for his music as well as for his exotic mode of life, Heinrich returned to urban civilization in the early 1820s, spending time in Philadelphia and Boston and touring Europe in 1826–31, 1833–7 and 1856–9. He was acquainted with several major European composers and leading figures in European and American political life, the arts, law and other professions. Even so, he found it difficult to obtain frequent performances of his larger, more elaborate works, especially in the USA, which still suffered from a shortage of highly trained musicians in the first half of the nineteenth century.[4] Heinrich died in relative poverty in 1861.

Opera proved extremely popular among adherents of the genteel tradition. English adaptations of operas by Mozart and Rossini led the way (c1817–1818) and Italian opera, first in English and later in the original language, flourished from the 1820s onwards. New Orleans, with its Gallic heritage, favoured French opera, but Italian opera gained a foothold there in the mid-1830s.

Sentimental song was another staple. Simple in style, it appealed to the amateur singers and pianists for whose homes it was primarily

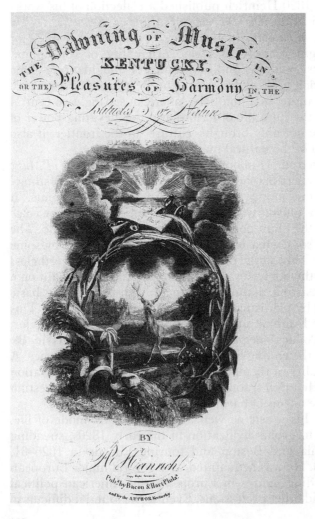

82. Title-page of Anthony Philip Heinrich's 'The Dawning of Music in Kentucky' (1820), a collection of his songs and pieces for piano and violin

83. The Moravian Bishop Jacob van Vleck performing music with girls, probably from the Bethlehem Seminary, of which he was principal: birthday greeting, in watercolour, given to the bishop in 1795

intended. American song of this type was heavily indebted to English models, such as T. Moore's *Irish Melodies*, published between 1808 and 1834, with music arranged and composed by Sir John Stevenson.[5] Moore's *Irish Melodies*, abounding with melancholy and nostalgia, enjoyed enormous popularity in both England and America throughout the nineteenth century. A leading figure in sentimental song was the Englishman Henry Russell, who emigrated to the USA in the mid-1830s. Russell composed numerous songs, varied in character and style, but the best loved were generally the simplest. *The Old Arm Chair*, published in 1840, was enormously popular. It recounts a man's attachment to an old armchair that was his mother's favourite place of repose; the chair serves to recall the mother's tenderness, warmth and piety, and inspires both reverence and deep feeling. The vocal and piano parts are easily within reach of most amateurs and the piece is cast in one of the simplest designs, strophic form. Its content reflects some of the most characteristic and recurrent themes in nineteenth-century American music – 'nostalgia for youth, home, parents, old friends, lost innocence and happiness'.[6]

The music of a small immigrant group, the Moravians, presents a special case in the American cultivated tradition. Unlike other religious groups at the time, the Moravians sanctioned learned music for use in church services and provided the musical training and instruments necessary to perform it. They established communities in Pennsylvania and North Carolina during the eighteenth century and from the beginning imported musical instruments and established *collegia musica*. Benjamin Franklin, who visited their community at Bethlehem, Pennsylvania, in 1756, recalled, 'I was at their Church, where I was entertained with good Musick, the Organ being accompanied with Violins, Hautboys, Flutes, Clarinets, &c'.[7]

The Bethlehem Seminary for girls, in existence since the eighteenth century, put its pupils through a strenuous curriculum in the humanities, theology and music, as well as polite ladies' arts such as needlework and drawing. So great was its reputation that many non-Moravians, including George Washington, sought to have their young female relatives enrolled there. The Salem Boarding School, a similar institution in Winston-Salem, North Carolina, claimed as pupils two eventual presidential wives, Mrs Andrew Jackson and Mrs James K. Polk.

The music cultivated by the Moravians and spread outside their communities by some of their illustrious and socially powerful graduates was rooted in the German and Austrian pre-Classical styles. Among Moravian composers active in the early nineteenth century were Johann Friedrich Peter, Johannes Herbst, Georg Mueller and a host of others who produced substantial amounts of concerted church music. Some also composed secular works, especially chamber music for strings. Peter's six quintets of 1789 are thought to be the first serious chamber pieces composed in the USA. Collections of music used by the Moravians for both sacred and secular purposes include numerous works by European masters as well as Moravian composers. Another unique Moravian contribution was the trombone choir, consisting of treble, alto, tenor and bass trombones, that lent a grand character to public ceremonies. Though the Moravians' immediate influence was limited, their music helped lay foundations for the practice and appreciation of European art music in the new nation.

The so-called vernacular tradition was represented by America's first school of native composers, the New England tunesmiths, including such men as William Billings, Daniel Read and Timothy Swan. Their vigorous sacred music, mostly fuging tunes and anthems, sometimes with rough harmonies and unorthodox progressions, enjoyed great popularity in the late eighteenth and early nineteenth century. Typically, the composers of the First New England School were not full-time musicians but men engaged in trades or business for whom music was both a recreation and an additional business interest: they worked part-time as singing masters, helping to create a market among amateur musicians for their own published collections. William Billings was the best known; born in 1746, he was a tanner who published six music collections between 1770 and 1794 while directing church choirs and singing schools in Boston. Daniel Read of New Haven, Connecticut, though a composer and music publisher, ran a general store and earned his living as a merchant and businessman; a true Yankee entrepreneur, he published six collections between 1785 and 1817. Before long this repertory, intended to help make New Englanders musically literate, itself became the object of another reform movement which sought to replace such rough and 'unscientific' music with hymns and anthems based on European art music.

At the numerous revival meetings spawned by the second religious 'awakening' in America there were varieties of folk hymnody, rooted for the most part in vestiges of British folk music still heard among pockets of mostly non-literate or semi-literate Protestant fundamentalists. This large body of hymns had close stylistic connections with the composed music of the First New England School, and the two were often combined in the same published collections. Extremely popular among some segments of the population during the early and mid-nineteenth century, they proved very durable in later times. Numerous collections of these 'white spirituals', as they came to be called, appeared. But in urban centres, the adherents of the genteel tradition scorned this 'primitive' music sung by uneducated rural people in a coarse style.

Meanwhile, the music of blacks began to be heard. They had their own distinctive music which formed the roots of blues and jazz, but in several urban centres they also participated as patrons and performers of popular and classical music. In the nineteenth century, though, the white population experienced black music mainly in the diluted form of minstrelsy, a type of entertainment designed to parody black characters, mannerisms and music. The earliest performers were whites in blackface, rendering simple music in a rustic or popular style with superficial Afro-American touches: Negro dialect and such folk instruments as the banjo and bones.

Two types of Negro character appeared in the 1820s and 30s, one 'patterned after the southern plantation hand: uncouth, ragged, and jolly', the other 'a ludicrous black replica of the white dandy of Main Street or of New York's Broadway'.[8] One of the most famous characters of minstrelsy was Jim Crow, the creation of Thomas D. 'Daddy' Rice. Legend has it that Rice based his character on the person and mannerisms of a black worker he observed in his travels. Jim Crow was the arch-representative of the plantation Negro, dressed in a 'picturesquely dilapidated' costume, who sang the song that bore his name and accompanied himself with a characteristic dance made up of odd and grotesque gestures. The song *Jim Crow* is a simple, square tune, with the kinds of snappy rhythm often found in

84. The original Jim Crow, created by Thomas D. 'Daddy' Rice: detail of a sheet music cover (c1829)

minstrel tunes. The text is in dialect and runs to twenty verses, many filled with rustic humour and good sense, or with nonsense:

> I den go to de Presiden,
> He ax me wat I do;
> I put de veto on de boot,
> And nullefy de shoe.

The Broadway dandy type of Negro was portrayed most vividly in the character of Zip Coon, later called Dandy Jim. Zip Coon was attired in exaggeratedly fashionable clothes, the most essential item being a blue coat with very long tails; this was the subject of a famous minstrel song, *My Long Tail Blue*, published in New York in the 1830s. The character assumed a kind of pompous dignity and entertained the audience with comments about politics and other topical issues.

The successes in the early 1840s of two troupes, the Virginia Minstrels and Christy's Minstrels, signalled the increased popularity of the fully developed minstrel show. Shows now followed a more standardized format than those of the 1820s and 30s: the first part usually offered inidividual songs, jokes and humorous dialogue; the second, longer part, the olio, was made up of larger acts and dramatic skits and frequently included a burlesque of some grand opera by Rossini, Bellini or a similarly famous composer; the olio concluded with a grand finale uniting all members of the company.

The enormous popularity of minstrelsy was reflected not only in the shows themselves, for which there was always a ready market, but also in the flood of so-called 'plantation songs' or 'Ethiopian melodies' composed from the 1840s. These were modelled on minstrel show tunes in that they employed Negro dialect and adopted a rustic or simple musical style. The most famous American composer to write songs of this kind was Stephen Foster. One of his earliest, *Oh, Susanna*, became a great success from the moment it was published in 1848. The popularity of his early minstrel tunes made Foster decide to devote himself seriously to the 'Ethiopian business', with a view to making the songs more refined. As he wrote to E. P. Christy in 1852:

> I find that by my efforts I have done a great deal to build up a taste for the Ethiopian song among more refined people by making the words suitable to their taste, instead of the trashy and really offensive words which belong to some songs of that order.[9]

The result was a type of 'Ethiopian' song that incorporated many aspects of the popular sentimental song. Foster endowed his black characters with greater humanity, range and power of feeling than other composers of minstrel songs. During the 1850s he increasingly abandoned the use of dialect, catering rather to the most popular emotion of the day: nostalgia. Some songs portrayed slaves so sympathetically that in the 1850s they were occasionally inserted into stage performances of Harriet Beecher Stowe's anti-slavery work, *Uncle Tom's Cabin*.

Just as many different types of music flourished in nineteenth-century America, so different ideals endowed music with various – sometimes contradictory – values. Although much music was intended primarily to entertain, reformers pressed continually for higher standards in musical composition and performance, to improve people's minds and tastes. It is no accident that many of these reformers were either church musicians or clergy. The desire to improve public musical taste also took on a social aspect, for in the USA, as in Europe, the cultivation of art music conferred increased social status.

These ideals are reflected in nineteenth-century journal articles, essays and lectures on music, introductions to music collections and similar sources. One of the more influential music journals was *The Euterpeiad*, published in Boston in the early 1820s. The prospectus, issued on 1 April 1820, announced articles on Beethoven, Handel, Haydn, Corelli and Mozart, theoretical discussions, essays on the music of other nations including non-Western countries, music reviews and concert reviews. The ambitious editor further promised that every third or fourth number 'will contain a fashnable [*sic*] Song, Air with Variations, March, Waltz or Dance, arranged for the Piano

Forte'. *The Euterpeiad* took as its models for musical excellence the art music of western Europe and its more 'scientific' methods of composition and performance. Thus, the report of a performance of sacred music in the Boston area chided the chorus for their old-fashioned practice, typical of the First New England School, of octave-doubling the tenor part, which bore the melody.

Numerous other journals championed 'scientific' qualities. *The Lyre*, of New York, faulted a recently published collection for consecutive 5ths and other awkward progressions. The reviewer lamented the setting of one 'fine old tune, well-known, but here [provided with] a very meagre arrangement, few if any of the chords properly filled up with harmony', clearly a reference to the older practice of incomplete triads. The *Western Messenger*, published by the Western Unitarian Association, felt differently. An article on church music in the first issue (1835) noted that, while music in church was highly desirable for the expression of 'higher and nobler sentiments', it had become too professional and too sophisticated. The author observed that many wealthy and fashionable churches had trained choirs and expensive organs and performed Handel and Haydn in a very professional manner. 'Is this', he asked, 'the object of sacred music? Is it meant to be this cold intellectual art, confined to a few?' Fashionable churches were spending thousands of dollars 'for the sake of having what is called "scientific music" ' to attract large congregations, thus turning divine services into concerts. One writer even upbraided the Boston Handel and Haydn Society, whose recent publications of church music 'have tampered too much with good old tunes, under the pretense of *improving* them'.

The pursuit of 'scientific' music was not confined to churches. The *American Musical Journal* promised 'to furnish the most perfect models by which correctness of taste, and a knowledge of the different schools and masters may be obtained'. Various publications noted the importance of musical attainments for social acceptance and especially for the proper social education of women. *The Euterpeiad* observed, 'In the modern system of female education, this fascinating accomplishment [music] is very generally considered as an indispensable requisite; and the daughters of a large portion of the community, in the middle and upper ranks of life, think themselves neglected if they are not indulged'. Increasingly, middle- and upper-class families gathered after dinner for songs and piano music, especially if there were visitors. Daughters held centre-stage, offering not only pleasant entertainment but also ample opportunity for their charms to be admired.

Music's potential for moral and social improvement and its power to confer social status on both individuals and society assured it of widespread support throughout the century. But the more critically minded had misgivings. As the influential Boston critic John Sullivan Dwight complained in 1845:

> Musical as yet we [in the USA] are not, in the true sense. We have no composers, no great performances in our churches; no well-endowed and thorough academies to train the artist, or to educate the public taste by frequent hearings of the finest compositions, except in a very limited degree. Our concerts are attended more from fashion, it may be, than from real love. Our daughters are taught the piano as an accomplishment, to make them 'ladies,' rather than to inspire their womanhood with that Music which has been termed 'the feminine principle in the Universe'.

Dwight did believe that important starts had been made in the USA in the development of a true musical culture, citing the formation of music societies and singing schools and the import of virtuosos from Europe. But he felt that Americans still had far to go before they truly appreciated music as 'the language of that deeper experience in which all men are most nearly ONE'.

BOSTON

Like most larger American cities, Boston, the hub of intellectual and artistic life in New England, grew rapidly from about 18,000 to over 43,000 by 1820, and twice that number twenty years later.[10] Its generally prosperous population enjoyed a rich theatrical and musical life. The Federal Theater opened its doors for the first time on 4 February 1794. The theatrical performances, following the European custom, included 'musical interludes' of various kinds. A typical early nineteenth-century evening began with Shakespeare's *Macbeth*, then:

> After the play, the favorite song of Crazy Jane, in character, by Miss Field. In the course of the evening, the favorite song of The Twins of Latona, by Mr. Story. The whole to conclude with a Farce. . .called The Spirit of Contradiction. Written by a Gentleman of Cambridge.[11]

The theatre orchestra performed symphonies by Karl Stamitz, Haydn and Dittersdorf, among others, and there were also evenings devoted to concerts, even in the earlier part of the century. Typically for the age, programmes consisted of a pot-pourri of vocal and instrumental works of various types.

The principal leaders of Boston musical life in the early part of the century were Gottlieb and Catherine Graupner.[12] Gottlieb Graupner, of German birth, had served in the electoral band at Hanover. He moved to London some time before 1791 and was reported to have played in the orchestra that gave the first performances of Haydn's London symphonies during the 1791–2 season. About 1795 Graupner went to the USA and played in the City Theater Orchestra in

Charleston, South Carolina. Meanwhile, the English actress and singer Mrs Catherine Hillier had made her American début at the Federal Theater in Boston in December 1794. She too travelled to Charleston, where she performed during the 1795–6 season at the City Theater and married Graupner. The following year the Graupners went to Boston. Gottlieb soon established himself as a performer, teacher and conductor and came to be recognized as the leading professional musician in the city. He became conductor of the Philharmonic Society and a founder of the Musical Academy while Catherine distinguished herself as a 'singing actress' popular with Boston audiences not only because of her vocal prowess, which was universally praised, and her acting, which was apparently less adept, but also through her charm and her eminent respectability.

Another imposing figure in Boston musical life was George K. Jackson, the English-born organist, choirmaster and teacher, who had arrived in the USA in 1796, armed with impressive credentials. His first Boston concert, a lavish event on 29 October 1812 which included choruses and airs from several of Handel's oratorios, delighted the large audience.[13] But he failed to register as an 'alien enemy' during the war of 1812 and had to leave Boston. Jackson was eventually able to return in 1815 and regained much of his influence, notwithstanding his abrasive personality. As a church organist he was notorious for his lack of patience with ministers and congregations.

The two most important musical institutions in early nineteenth-century Boston were the Philharmonic Society and the Boston Handel and Haydn Society devoted to choral music. The Philo-Harmonic Society, as it was originally called, started in October 1809 with both amateur and professional players, many from the Federal Theater orchestra; it was most active from 1817 to 1822, providing concerts of its own as well as in collaboration with the Handel and Haydn Society.[14] The latter, more influential and longer-lived, consisted mainly of amateur musicians; it grew out of earlier singing societies that had their roots in the eighteenth-century singing schools and amateur church choirs. It was thus no accident that it existed 'for the purpose of extending the knowledge and improving the style of performance of church music', nor that nearly all the 46 founding members were drawn from Boston church choirs.[15] Membership was restricted to men, though in time women were invited to rehearsals and participated, as guests, in performances. Most of the original members were solidly middle class: merchants, bank tellers, attorneys, apothecaries, schoolmasters and skilled craftsmen of various kinds.

The Handel and Haydn Society presented its first public performance on Christmas night 1815 – arias and choruses from Haydn's *Creation* and oratorios by Handel. Perhaps the most ambitious undertaking in its early history was a series of three concerts, 1–4 April

1817, in which Handel's *Messiah* and Haydn's *Creation* were performed in their entirety. Some contemporary reports suggest that, from the purely technical point of view, these performances were a bit ragged. But as a moral and spiritual experience, they were edifying. As a member of the audience put it:

> We attend [the Handel and Haydn Society's] performances, not only to be pleased, but to be improved. While the critic in music admires the display of skill, and the mere lover of fine sounds enjoys an exquisite repast, the deaf spirit may be awed with admiration, melted into tenderness, and kindled to praise.[16]

By 1820, the society occupied a leading place in the musical life of Boston. At this point its history is linked with that of Lowell Mason, who was to become one of the most representative figures in nineteenth-century American music.

Mason was born in 1792 near Boston in Medfield, Massachusetts, into a musical family. In 1812, unsure about a career, he went to Savannah, Georgia, where he earned his living as a bank clerk but also pursued his musical interests. He studied with the German-born musician F. L. Abel and became organist and choirmaster at the Independent Presbyterian Church, where he conceived the idea of compiling his own collection of church music.[17]

Rooted in the New England tradition of moral improvement, Mason championed the cause of 'scientific' church music as a way of changing people's tastes and inspiring them to higher things. He looked to European Classical music for inspiration as well as for more specific aid. His own first tunebook was modelled after William Gardiner's collection *Sacred Melodies from Haydn, Mozart and Beethoven, Adapted to the Best English Poets and Appropriated to the Use of the British Church*. Mason outlined his aims to John R. Parker, a Boston friend:

> For several years I have been constantly importing from Europe the best publications of Sacred music and have at the same time been attending to the principles of Thoro'bass and Composition under the direction of an eminent German master [F. L. Abel] – from all the mass thus *collected* I have been constantly *Selecting* . . . [These were now] harmonized according to the modern principles of thorough bass – and I trust every false relation, and every forbidden progression will be avoided.[18]

Mason was concerned not only about church composition but also performance. Shall 'the whole congregation be encouraged to join promiscuously, in this exercise [singing]? – or shall it be committed to a select choir?', he asked rhetorically. He felt that since members of a congregation were inclined to sing in their own way and not 'scientifically', it was 'necessary . . . that in every church there should be a choir of cultivated singers'. The congregation might sing, 'provided they are qualified to do this with propriety and effect'.[19]

Mason's tunebook came to the attention of the Handel and Haydn Society, which published it in 1822 as *The Boston Handel and Haydn Society Collection of Church Music*. Apparently by his own desire, the editor was not named: 'I was then a bank officer in Savannah, and did not want to be known as a musical man'. But his collection became a best-seller, eventually running through 22 editions and selling more than 50,000 copies. Characteristic of Mason's composing and arranging style is his famous *Missionary Hymn* ('From Greenland's Icy Mountains'). The simple melody, in the tenor, is prevailingly triadic and of limited range and the accompanying parts hold little interest. All phrases are four bars long and each begins on the tonic triad in root position. The first three phrases cadence on the dominant, the fourth returns to the tonic. In this almost static harmony, the 'rules' of part-writing and harmonic progression are scrupulously observed.

Following the success of his tunebook and the wide acceptance of his views on church music, Mason was invited to settle in Boston. He returned to his native city in 1827 and took charge of the music in three churches. That year he was elected president of the Handel and Haydn Society, in which capacity he served until 1832. His ultimate goal, however, was universal musical literacy for the American population, an end best served by musical training for children. He began with singing schools in churches, but the numbers of his pupils grew, and in 1832, with other Boston musicians, he founded the Boston Academy of Music; in its first year, it provided free instruction for some 1500 children. At the same time, Mason pressed hard for music in the public schools in accordance with the principles developed by the Swiss pedagogue Johann Heinrich Pestalozzi; in 1838 he was named Superintendent of Music in the Boston public schools.

Mason's career epitomizes the social and musical ideals of nineteenth-century America, but his success was more than financial or even social. He enjoyed a kind of moral authority in music and education that was probably unsurpassed by any other musician of his day and he set an agenda that found widespread approval among educated musicians. It was largely thanks to Mason that the *Boston Musical Gazette*, in its prospectus, could quote the widely held opinion that Boston 'takes the lead of all others in the Union, both in devotion to Music, and in the Institutions for its perpetuation and improvement'.

PHILADELPHIA

Like Boston, Philadelphia, the original capital of the USA, experienced rapid growth in population, from 119,325 in 1820 to 205,580 in 1840.[20] It was founded as a refuge for the Society of Friends, whose members were inclined to view music and other worldly entertainments with suspicion. But the Friends were tolerant of their music-loving fellows, and by the end of the eighteenth century Philadelphia had a healthy musical life, thanks in part to the influx of several influential professionals from abroad. The most important was Alexander Reinagle, who arrived about 1786 and quickly took charge of the city's musical life. Following his departure in 1800, two English immigrants, Benjamin Carr and Raynor Taylor, shared that role. Restrictions imposed during the Revolutionary War had been lifted and the Chestnut Street Theater was the recognized centre of theatrical and much musical activity in Philadelphia. Opened in 1794, with Thomas Wignell and Alexander Reinagle as its first managers, it was modelled on the Theatre Royal in Bath and was considerably more imposing and luxurious than any of the other theatres.[21] Repertory ranged from Shakespeare to ballad operas and all sorts of musical entertainment. In the first decade of the century, some 45 operas or plays with music, sixteen musical farces, six pieces described simply as 'musical entertainments' and various shorter musical numbers used as preludes and interludes were given.[22]

The Musical Fund Society, charitable in its inspiration, was founded in 1820 'for the relief and support of decayed musicians and their families'. It was apparently an offshoot of informal chamber music evenings held in private homes. Two physicians provided medical treatment, free of charge, for needy members and their families and the society financed other charitable activities from the proceeds of its concerts.[23] Both professionals and amateurs performed orchestral, solo vocal and choral music, with emphasis on large-scale sacred works for chorus and orchestra, such as Handel's and Haydn's oratorios. A typical concert, like that of 8 May 1821, offered a mixture of movements from symphonies and concertos, opera overtures, sentimental songs and glees.

By the 1840s the society had begun to branch out musically. On 8 February 1841 it gave the first American production of Mozart's *Die Zauberflöte*, which was also its first operatic undertaking. This was a major musical event of far more than local importance. People came from Boston and New York to it and the *Philadelphia National Gazette* declared that the city had established a new standard for opera in the USA: 'The Public has now had such samples of operatic excellence that mediocrity will no longer answer. What is now done in that way must be done fully and well to command success'. However promising the production may have seemed, and however favourable the response of thoughtful critics, the public still preferred ballad opera. The Musical Fund Society decided, rather than accept musically inferior works of the kind theatre audiences preferred, it would not pursue opera for the time being.[24] Meanwhile, a touring

French opera company based in New Orleans had been well received as early as 1827 and returned annually to Philadelphia until 1842. Moreover, in the 1827–8 season there were performances by Mrs Austin's Company, which gave the American première of Rossini's *La Cenerentola*, and it was Italian opera that finally broke the grip of ballad opera on Philadelphia audiences.

A leading figure in the campaign on behalf of Italian opera was the Philadelphia composer and music critic William Henry Fry. Born into a prominent family, he studied music with the immigrant musician Leopold Meignen. Fry's father, William, founded one of the city's leading newspapers, the *Philadelphia National Gazette*, and in 1836 Fry became its music critic. His devotion to Italian opera showed in his own compositions. His most successful opera, *Leonora*, was first produced on 4 June 1845 and enjoyed performances not only in Philadelphia but also in New York. Its unabashedly Italian style prompted the following from a reviewer for the *New York Express*: 'The opera seems to us a study in the school of Bellini. It is full of delicious, sweet music, but constantly recalls the Sonnambula and Norma. The peculiarities which most strongly distinguish his production are sweetness of melody and lack of dramatic characterization'.[25]

Fry was an important figure in the musical life of Philadelphia, but far more representative was Benjamin Carr. Born in London in 1768, he received his musical education primarily from Samuel Arnold and Charles Wesley and emigrated to the USA with his father and brothers, all of whom became active in music publishing, first in Baltimore and then in other cities.[26] Acutely sensitive to public taste, they offered hit tunes from the best-known ballad operas, sentimental songs and light pieces, as well as sonatas by Haydn, Mozart, Pleyel and Hummel. Benjamin's brother Thomas is thought to have been the first publisher of *The Star-Spangled Banner*. Benjamin, possibly the most enterprising and energetic member of the family, moved to Philadelphia in 1793 but also had business interests in New York. In the late 1790s he was active as a composer, singer, actor and music publisher; his ballad opera *The Archers* (1796) achieved considerable success, and with Reinagle and others he produced concert series in Philadelphia and was among the founders of the Musical Fund Society. Riding the wave of enthusiasm for patriotic songs he published, among other successes, Joseph Hopkinson's *Hail Columbia* for an actor friend whose rendition roused a Philadelphia audience to demand six encores before it joined in singing the chorus. Carr lost no time: it appeared in print two days later with the title 'The New Federal Song'.

One of Carr's biggest successes was his *Federal Overture*, a pot-pourri of favourite patriotic and popular tunes, the most famous of which was *Yankee Doodle*. Heard for the first time on 22 September 1794, it proved so popular that it became a staple of Philadelphia and New York theatrical evenings.[27] After 1800 Carr spent most of his efforts on the publication of music for the church and the home and pedagogical literature. His *Musical Miscellany in Occasional Numbers* appeared at irregular intervals between 1812 and 1825 and included popular music of the English theatre, French music, favourite airs from Italian operas and didactic works.[28]

NEW ORLEANS

New Orleans owed its uniqueness to its extraordinary cultural and racial mix. French, Spanish and Anglo-American elements all contributed special qualities, and New Orleans had the largest black population of any American city in the nineteenth century. The theatre was as important to musical life as it was in other American cities, but public balls enjoyed a special position, since ballroom dancing was not viewed with the same suspicion as it was in cities where Protestant influences prevailed. Balls were held frequently and were widely regarded as nothing less than a social necessity. Moreover, nearly every concert before 1830 had an associated ball, and occasionally a play or an opera was followed by a ball held in the theatre itself.[29] The frequency of balls and the number of competing ballrooms created a shortage of musicians in the early nineteenth century, forcing the New Orleans dancing master Francisqui in 1809 to enlist members of General Wilkinson's military band. Thereafter several ballrooms employed military bands. Another, more expensive, solution was to import musicians from Europe, a practice that began about 1819.

The racial mix in New Orleans provided a special twist to the public balls. As early as 1805, the actor, dancer and entrepreneur Auguste Tessier announced his intention to offer two balls every week 'for free women of color at which all colored men would be excluded', thus marking the beginning of the famous New Orleans 'quadroon balls', attended primarily by coloured women and white men. They were extremely successful, providing more excitement and opportunities for flirtation than the all-white balls. Dances specifically for free blacks resembled those for whites in both their formality and repertory; moreover, slaves as well as free blacks attended (some without their masters' permission).

Income from balls often supported theatres, the more so as New Orleans was the only American city to maintain an opera company continuously except during the Civil War. Before the war the city supported as many as three opera companies at the same time. Naturally the staples of the repertory were operas by French composers. The first New Orleans performance of Rossini's *Il barbiere di Siviglia* was on 4 March 1823, but it was not until the next decade that

Italian opera gained a secure foothold in the city. In 1836 James Caldwell brought an Italian opera company to New Orleans to perform at the St Charles Theater and their first production, Bellini's *Il pirata*, was a resounding success.

New Orleans did not merely patronize opera lavishly at home: it also sent its singers on tour to other parts of the country. Thus in 1827 the impresario John Davis took his company to New York City and in just over two months presented 40 performances before moving on to Philadelphia. Their repertory included Boïeldieu's *La dame blanche* and Weber's *Der Freischütz* (in the bowdlerized French version, *Robin des bois*) and works by Dalayrac, Auber and Isouard. The company toured annually for six years, acquainting audiences in Boston, New York, Philadelphia and Baltimore with the latest French operas. Ironically it was New Orleans, geographically and culturally on the 'exotic periphery' of American society, that introduced to this important body of European music.

Since the late eighteenth century, band music formed an important part of life – not just musical life – in the city. The people of New Orleans were inordinately fond of parades, for which bands were needed. Various military units had their own bands; many of them were organized along ethnic lines and included Spanish, Italian, Swiss, German, Irish, French and American players. Bands routinely paraded on Sundays. Some residents protested about bands 'going about the city early on Sunday mornings, squeaking and rattle-te-banging away . . . and waking everybody'. Ministers and church-goers complained that band music drowned out sacred organ music and sermons. But most people seemed to enjoy these impromptu Sunday concerts. Parades and band music also served to honour the dead, a practice peculiar to New Orleans.

The most distinctive music, though, was that of the blacks. Slaves were permitted to assemble on Sundays before sunset in the Place Congo for singing and dancing. These weekly gatherings attracted many white observers intrigued by music and dancing carried over from African practice. A report published in 1886, but consistent with remarks by earlier witnesses, describes the riveting scene:

> The booming of African drums and blast of huge wooden horns called to the gathering . . . The drummers bestrode the drums; the other musicians sat about them in an arc, cross-legged on the ground . . . The singers almost at the first note are many. At the end of the first line every voice is lifted up. The strain is given the second time with growing spirit . . . [The dancers] swing and bow to the right and left, in slow time to the piercing treble of the Congo women . . . The women clap their hands in time, or standing with arms akimbo receive with faint courtesies and head-liftings the low bows of the men, who deliver them swinging this way and that.[30]

85. *Blacks attending a ball: sheet music cover, 'The Dark Sett', of a collection of Afro-American quadrilles arranged for piano by S. O. Dyer (third edition, 1848)*

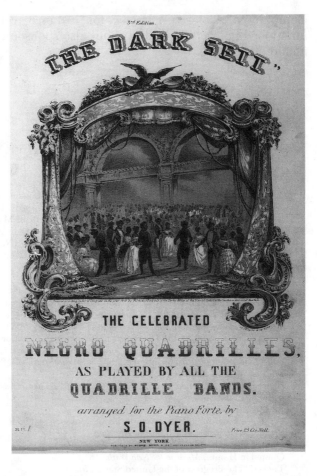

Negro church services exhibited many of these characteristics. In one such service: 'The congregation sang; I think everyone joined . . . and the collective sound was wonderful. Many of the singers kept time with their feet, balancing themselves on each alternately and swinging their bodies accordingly'. The preacher 'raised his voice above all, clapped his hands, and commenced to dance'.[31]

Black musicians also performed at the quadroon and all-white balls. And many slaves, as well as free blacks, attended concerts and operas, most theatres having special galleries for blacks. Free blacks organized separate concerts and opera performances for themselves. The Negro Philharmonic Society, founded in the late 1830s, had over a hundred members; its concerts featured local musicians as well as visiting artists. While the role of blacks in concert music was especially significant in New Orleans, with its large population of slaves and free blacks, it was not unique. The Philadelphia Library

Company of Colored Persons, for instance, established in 1833, functioned not only as a library but also sponsored cultural activities including concerts.[32]

NOTES

[1] Quoted in R. A. Hofstadter, *The American Political Tradition* (New York, 1948), 57.

[2] D. Barron, 'Heinrich, Anthony Philip', *Grove A.*

[3] C. Hamm, *Music in the New World* (New York, 1983), 211.

[4] Barron, op cit.

[5] M. W. Disher, *Victorian Song: from Dive to Drawing Room* (London, 1955), 75.

[6] C. Hamm, *Yesterdays: Popular Songs in America* (New York, 1983), 182.

[7] D. M. McCorkle, 'The Moravian Contribution to American Music', *Notes*, xiii (1955–6), 597–600; this has been an invaluable source of information for the discussion that follows.

[8] H. Nathan, *Dan Emmett and the Rise of Early Negro Minstrelsy* (Norman, Oklahoma. 1962), 52–9. Nathan provides a full account of Jim Crow and Zip Coon, based on contemporary reports.

[9] Quoted in C. Hamm, *Music in the New World*, 240.

[10] Population figures taken from C. A. Pemberton, *Lowell Mason: his Life and Work* (diss., U. of Minnesota, 1971), 17; and G. Tucker, 'The Progress of the United States in Population and Wealth', *Ideology and Power in the Age of Jackson*, ed. E. C. Rozwenc (New York, 1964), 5.

[11] Quoted in H. E. Johnson, *Musical Interludes in Boston, 1795–1830* (New York, 1967), 32.

[12] For a fuller account of the Graupners' activities and reception in Boston, see Johnson, *Musical Interludes*, 166–200, from which the following brief discussion is drawn.

[13] For a more complete discussion, see Johnson, *Musical Interludes*, 80.

[14] Johnson, *Musical Interludes*, 121–52.

[15] H. E. Johnson, *Halleluia, Amen!: the Story of the Handel and Haydn Society of Boston* (Boston, Mass., 1965), 13–14, 33–4.

[16] Johnson, *Halleluia*, 32.

[17] For more biographical information about Mason, see Hamm, *Music in the New World*; Pemberton, *Lowell Mason*; and Johnson, *Halleluia*.

[18] Quoted in Pemberton, *Lowell Mason*, 92–3.

[19] Quoted in Hamm, *Music in the New World*, 165.

[20] Tucker, 'The Progress of the United States', 5.

[21] I. Lowens, 'Benjamin Carr's *Federal Overture* (1794)', *Music and Musicians in Early America* (New York, 1964), 96.

[22] R. D. James, *Cradle of Culture* (Philadelphia, 1957), 127–39.

[23] R. A. Gerson, *Music in Philadelphia* (Westport, Conn., 1970), 56–9.

[24] Gerson, *Music in Philadelphia*, 65–6, 70–71.

[25] Quoted in G. Chase, *America's Music: from the Pilgrims to the Present* (New York, rev. 2/1966), 331.

[26] V. L. Redway, 'The Carrs, American Music Publishers', *MQ*, xviii (1932), 151–60, from which this discussion of Benjamin Carr's activities is drawn.

[27] For the most thorough discussion of this work, see Lowens, 'Benjamin Carr's *Federal Overture*'.

[28] E. R. Meyer, 'Benjamin Carr's *Musical Miscellany*', *Notes*, xxxiii (1976–7), 253–65.

[29] H. A. Kmen, *Music in New Orleans* (Baton Rouge, 1966), 5. I have drawn on this book for much of the information that follows.

[30] Quoted in Chase, *America's Music*, 307–8.

[31] Quoted in Kmen, *Music in New Orleans*, 236.

[32] E. Southern, *The Music of Black Americans: a History* (New York, 1971), 109.

BIBLIOGRAPHICAL NOTE

Music in the USA can scarcely be understood apart from its wider context, especially in the nineteenth century. R. Hofstadter's Pulitzer Prizewinning *Anti-Intellectualism in American Life* (New York, 1963) provides the most succinct and most penetrating account of the themes and attitudes that governed American culture from colonial times until about World War II. Hofstadter skilfully connects American Protestantism, populist politics, reform movements and entrepreneurship to a prevailing anti-intellectualism.

America's Music by G. Chase (Urbana, rev. 3/1987) offers non-technical discussion of American music 'from the Pilgrims to the present' and establishes a cultural setting for each repertory. Chase seeks to account for the peculiarly American features of the more distinctive genres. Similar in aims is C. Hamm's *Music in the New World* (New York, 1983), which includes more technical descriptions of particular pieces; it is strongest on the distinctively American repertories, less inspired in discussion of derivative types. I. Lowens's *Music and Musicians in Early America* (New York, 1964) is a collection of his extremely informative essays dealing with music of the colonial period and early nineteenth century. Though some of the musical discussion is specialized, it should be accessible to the interested lay reader.

The definitive study of early minstrelsy is H. Nathan's *Dan Emmett and the Rise of Early Negro Minstrelsy* (Norman, Oklahoma, 1962). A thorough study of the early master of blackface minstrelsy, this book is written in a lively narrative style. The story of authentic Afro-American music is told in E. Southern's *The Music of Black Americans: a History* (New York, 1971); she has edited a companion volume of selected documents from the period of slavery up to the twentieth century: *Readings in Black American Music* (New York, 1971).

Chapter X

Latin America:
Independence and Nationalism

GERARD BÉHAGUE

At the beginning of the nineteenth century, most Latin American and Spanish Caribbean countries found themselves on the eve of their struggle for independence, which led eventually to political and cultural changes throughout the rest of the century. The preceding era of colonization had seen the transfer, adaptation and reinterpretation of European cultural values and practices. Inevitably, while maintaining its fundamental kinship with Europe, this 'Americanized' or criollo culture also absorbed numerous indigenous traits. The quest for independence in Spanish America and Brazil from about 1810 to 1825 in turn represented the first phase of a broadly based movement of nationalism and democracy that differed ideologically from the American and French revolutions in that the Spanish American criollos continued to depend on the crown and the church to maintain their control of the masses of Indians and blacks. They could, therefore, insist on their right to self-determination while supporting Ferdinand VII at the time of his imprisonment by Napoleon in 1808. Rousseau's social contract may have enjoyed popularity among the leaders of the independence movement, but they tended in practice to favour a more aristocratic political system. In fact, events in Portugal and Brazil led to the establishment of an independent Brazilian monarchy that ruled until 1889.

Class-consciousness remained very strong throughout independent Latin America and greatly influenced musical life during the nineteenth century. The churches, presidential or imperial palaces and aristocratic salons and, increasingly, middle-class bourgeois homes continued to reflect contemporary European practices and tastes, political independence from Europe notwithstanding. And because art music in Latin America was and still is largely based on the European written tradition, it has received most of the attention of historians and sociologists to the detriment of the many musical activities of the less privileged sectors of society, which, because of their essentially oral nature, lack adequate documentation. In the

(a) una chingana (a popular gathering with music and dance)

(b) una tertulia (a colonial soirée with music) at Santiago, 1790
86. Two illustrations from 'Historia física y política de Chile' (Atlas, 1854) by Claudio Gay

absence of any comprehensive social history of Latin American music, one can, therefore, hope at best to point in the right direction.

The strong rural–urban dichotomy characteristic of Latin American societies in the nineteenth century also determined the types of activity and institution that supported musical life in the cities and the provinces. Art music, both sacred and secular, was limited almost exclusively to the major cities, where most composers and performers lived and where musical institutions existed or were gradually becoming established. There, a growing and diverse public stimulated the creation of amateur and professional performing organizations, music schools, theatres and music libraries and the development of a local market for musical instruments and sheet music as well as other publications. Social patterns of music consumption in the nineteenth century remain to be explored in depth but middle-class amateur musicians clearly preferred salon-type music for the piano and for solo voice; and there was a considerable urban market not only for celebrated European pieces but also for local products.

Opera had been implanted in many cities during the eighteenth century and flourished subsequently in most capitals, thanks to European imports as well as a growing number of more or less successful local composers. The aristocracy provided much of the patronage of grand opera, while the lighter genres, such as the *tonadilla escénica*, the *sainete*, the zarzuela and the *teatro de revista*, appealed primarily to popular audiences. Major theatres, conservatories and schools of music and the first orchestras and choral societies received government subsidies in most countries. Government grants also facilitated the European training of promising or socially well-connected composers. In smaller cities the municipal authorities traditionally took pride in their musical organizations and sponsored them as a matter of course. All this was done in the hope of promoting local talent that could contribute to the achievements of civilized urban society as defined by the predominantly European values of the time.

MEXICO

By 1810, when the war of independence began, music in Mexico was no longer focussed on the magnificent achievements of colonial cathedral musicians. The theatre rather than the church supported most musicians and the new middle class gladly paid for the sort of entertainment that only the popular theatre could supply. The *tonadilla escénica*, *sainete* and other comedies with music in turn gave birth to the *sones*, *jarabes* and *canciones*, popular song genres that developed throughout the nineteenth century. The *tonadilla* gave rise to some 60 per cent of genuinely Mexican music.[1] Even church musicians, like Manuel Arenzana, *maestro de capilla* of Puebla Cathedral, devoted themselves to theatre music, as some had done during the colonial period. Arenzana's two-act opera *El extrangero* is reported to have been performed in 1805 at the Coliseo Nuevo, Mexico City's main playhouse, with 'much applause'.[2]

Italian opera came to the fore with the production in 1806 of Paisiello's *Il barbiere di Siviglia* by a Spanish company that included the Italian singer Victorio Rocamora, 'galán de música', whose popularity in Mexico was influential in attracting foreign talent.[3] Paisiello's opera, though, did not escape the much-demanded interludes, consisting of *bailes* and various Mexican dances and *sones*. Efforts were made 'not to lengthen unduly the whole evening's presentation',[4] but the prevailing tastes of theatre-goers tended to assert themselves. Despite the popularity of such events and the excellent salaries paid to the singers (as reported, for example, by the *Diario de México* in 1816), the Coliseo Nuevo went into bankruptcy in 1816, and Italian and Mexican operas were produced regularly thereafter only in the wake of independence.

The composer most in evidence during the revolutionary period and the early phase of Mexican independence was José Mariano Elízaga (1786–1842), a strong advocate of art music and influential champion of music education. In 1824 Elízaga led the effort to organize Mexico's first philharmonic society with an eye to instituting a permanent symphony orchestra, a choir and a conservatory. The latter, the Philharmonic Academy, was, however, short-lived because it lacked the necessary official support. Elízaga's efforts in music education then took the form of two didactic works, *Elementos de música* (1823) and *Principios de la armonía y de la melodía* (1835), intended to remedy what he called 'a disgracefully low level, both in church and in chamber music' in Mexico. It fell to later pedagogues to realize his ideals when socio-economic circumstances proved more favourable. Thus in 1866 the Sociedad Filarmónica Mexicana founded a conservatory that eventually developed into the government-subsidized Conservatorio Nacional de Música, which has been in existence since 1877 and has spawned some of Mexico's most important composers and performers. Its curriculum followed nineteenth-century Italian models so closely that 'the Mexican musical horizon between independence and the close of the Porfirian epoch (1911) was narrowly confined within the world of Italian opera'.[5]

Indeed, opera from Rossini to Verdi, with its many catchy tunes (which influenced the melodic nature of numerous Latin American popular songs) and popular singing stars, dominated musical life, as it did in most major South American cities. Though sponsored primarily by the well-to-do, it appealed no less to the growing mestizo classes, possibly because of their familiarity with the lighter theatrical lyric genres. By contrast, nineteenth-century urban social conditions did not favour the development of regular large audiences for symphonic and chamber music.

Italian opera sung in Italian was introduced in 1827 by the company of Manuel García, a Spaniard; he made his headquarters the Teatro de Las Gallos, inaugurated in 1822 and remodelled in 1825. Filippo Galli's Italian opera company took up residence from 1831 to 1837 and reinforced the Mexican love of Italian opera to the point where the Teatro Principal, formerly the Coliseo Nuevo, began to put on regular seasons. In 1836 Lauro Rossi (1810–85) went to Mexico as director of the orchestra and house composer. This was also the time of the great Italian prima donna Marietta Albini, considered the consummate Norma, and Adela Cesari, whose local rivalries produced a popular 'albinista' group and an aristocratic 'cesarista' following.[6]

By mid-century, Mexican composers were embarking on careers writing Italian opera. Among the better-known were Luis Baca (1826–55), Cenobio Paniagua (1821–82) and Melesio Morales (1838–1908). Their operas to Italian librettos were generally adequate imitations. Paniagua had one considerable if brief success with *Catalina di Guisa* in 1859, and Morales with *Ildegonda*, given its première in 1866 with the most celebrated Mexican diva of the century, Angela Peralta (1845–83), who had a brilliant career in her own country and in Europe, where she was known as 'the Mexican nightingale'. Peralta also starred with the famous Italian tenor Enrico Tamberlik in *Guatimotzín* (1871) by Aniceto Ortega (1823–75), a doctor who was an amateur composer. This opera, which glorified the Aztec prince Cuauhtémoc, was hailed as the 'national' opera *par excellence*, because of its Indian theme; at any rate, it represented the first serious attempt to incorporate into opera some supposedly indigenous native rhythms.[7] Although true Indianism flourished only after the 1910 revolution, the Indian ancestry of Mexican culture was invoked 50 years earlier during the strongly patriotic period that followed the triumph of Juárez against French intervention and the execution of Maximilian.

Inspired no doubt by European models, Mexican piano virtuosos turned their attention to piano arrangements of folk and popular dance tunes and songs well before 1850. The *jarabe*, which became the most popular dance after independence, in particular attracted many salon composers. In 1841 José Antonio Gómez, active in Mexico City, wrote a series of virtuoso variations on the *jarabe* much as Thalberg did on popular opera themes in France. Tomás León followed with the Jarabe Nacional (1860) and eventually Julio Ituarte with *Ecos de México* (c1880), a stylized arrangement of popular material and the first example of the integration of Mexican melodies with a character-istically Mexican style.[8]

CUBA AND PUERTO RICO

In contrast to other Hispanic-American territories, Cuba remained a Spanish colony throughout the nineteenth century but was at the same time one of the most important centres of Spanish American intellectual and artistic activity. It was in Cuba that some of the most characteristic Afro-Caribbean dance music developed, which in turn exerted considerable influence on other popular musical genres in Central and South America. A substantial black population contributed greatly to the island's musical life with many free blacks in early nineteenth-century Havana regarding music as their primary activity, if only because prejudice barred them from many other professions. These Afro-Cuban musicians in particular provided music for dancing. Besides the fashionable Spanish, French and mestizo dances, always in demand at the creole public halls, they performed Cuban dances, such as the *contradanza*, *zapateo*, bolero and *guaracha*, and younger members of the colonial bourgeoisie grew increasingly fond of the rhythmic drive that characterized the music of these bands. In effect, the creolization process of Cuban music led from public dancing-houses to stately homes. In 1856, at a formal grand ball to honour General Concha in Santiago, the aristocratic participants indulged with much zest in dancing a *contradanza* entitled *Tu madre es conga*; its accompaniment included the modified habanera figure known in Cuban popular and folk music as *tresillo* and very common in the *conga* (hence its title).[9] While free blacks made by and large 'white' music, with some idiosyncratic adornment, until the abolition of slavery (1885) traditional Afro-Caribbean music remained confined to slave quarters.

During the first years of the nineteenth century, music teaching and publishing began in earnest in Cuba, first at the Academia de Música (founded in 1814) and, from 1816, also at the Academia de Música S Cecilia. One of the first pieces of music published in Cuba was the contradanza *San Pascual Bailón* (1803). It was followed by examples of other popular musical genres such as the *guaracha* and bolero. As elsewhere, however, salon music dominated sheet-music publishing, just as Italian and French opera dominated the theatres (Teatro Principal, Teatro Tacón, Liceo Artístico y Literario).

From 1832 Havana enjoyed the services of the music teacher and later music publisher, Jean-Frédéric Edelmann, son of the Alsatian composer, harpsichordist and pianist who was guillotined in Paris in 1794. Edelmann had gone to Havana to give a concert and his enthusiastic reception persuaded him to settle there. Among his numerous Cuban students was Robredo Manuel Saumell (1817–70) who, as early as 1839, entertained the idea of writing a national opera that would stress certain aspects of Cuban folklore. But he never followed this up and was at his best in small piano pieces of the *contradanza* type, writing more than 50 exquisite examples. Their 'rhythmic and melodic invention . . . is prodigious',[10] with an extraordinary variety of rhythmic combinations governing the national character of the middle sections in particular. Some of Saumell's rhythmic patterns later became dance formulae. The Cuban *danzón*, as cultivated by urban popular composers (combining the habanera figure with superimposed semiquaver pulsations), appears in several of his *contradanzas*. Indeed, the 'father of the *contradanza*' created a style in which rhythmic interest prevailed in ways quite unlike the virtuoso and superficial salon music of the time.

Puerto Rico, its rather similar culture and ethno-history notwithstanding, did not measure up to Cuba in musical importance. In San Juan, the island's capital and the centre of its artistic life throughout the period under consideration, a municipal theatre was inaugurated in 1832 with the participation of numerous foreign and Puerto Rican musicians, including Adelina Patti, the British tenor William Pearman and Louis Moreau Gottschalk. The first opera written by a Puerto Rican composer on a local subject was *Guarionex* (1856) by Felipe Gutiérrez y Espinosa (1825–99). Piano music represented by far the largest musical production in nineteenth-century Puerto Rico.[11] Particularly significant is the attention given by several piano composers during the second half of the century to the *danza puertorriqueña*, which began to appear with this name in popular compositions of the 1830s; its precise origin has not been determined, but the Cuban *contradanza*, habanera and *guaracha* as well as the Puerto Rican *seis* (a widespread folkdance and song) were obviously influential.

VENEZUELA AND THE ANDEAN NATIONS

During the last quarter of the eighteenth century, the city of Caracas enjoyed a particularly productive phase in the cultivation of religious music, thanks largely to the Academia de Música attached to the congregation of the Oratorio de S Felipe Neri, modelled on the original Italian order, by the priest Pedro Palacios y Sojo (1739–99), the most notable patron of music in Venezuela. Between 1785 and 1800, the group led by the composer Juan Manuel Olivares (1760–97) known as the Escuela de Chacao or Escuela del Padre Sojo consisted of 30 composers and over 150 performers. Among the composers were José Francisco Velásquez (*c*1755–1805), José Antonio Caro de Boesi (*c*1760–1814), Pedro Nolasco Colón (*b c*1750), José Cayetano Carreño (1774–1836), Juan José Landaeta (*c*1780–1812), Lino Gallardo (*c*1775–1814) and last but not least José Angel Lamas (1775–1814). Except for Lamas and Carreño, they were all free mulattos who, as a result of their musical activities, rose to privileged social status.

As for major theatres, the original Coliseo (later renamed Teatro Público) dated from 1784; but it was destroyed in 1812 and a new Coliseo was not available until the 1830s. This was followed by the Teatro Caracas, the Teatro de la Zarzuela and eventually the Teatro Municipal. The first opera by a Venezuelan composer was *Virginia* by José Angel Montero (1839–81), given its première at the Teatro Caracas in 1873. Montero wrote zarzuelas and salon music but, as *maestro de capilla* of Caracas Cathedral, also composed many sacred works. An important nineteenth-century Venezuelan composer was Felipe Larrazábal (1816–73), a lawyer, historian and well-known political figure.[12] He wrote piano and chamber music that reveals skilful treatment of harmony and counterpoint and imaginative melodic writing. Apparently, most of his manuscripts were lost in a shipwreck off the northern coast of France, where he had planned to have several of his historical and musical works published.

For the Colombian capital, with its rich musical past, the republican period opened a new phase typified by the cultivation of European operatic and symphonic repertories and style. Thus, Juan Antonio de Velasco (*d* 1859) organized a series of concerts in Bogotá to promote the Viennese Classicists and arranged operatic music for piano and military bands, while Nicolás Quevedo Rachadell (1803–74) attempted to establish regular concert seasons. Henry Price (1819–63), born and educated in London, settled in Bogotá in 1840 and with Quevedo and others founded the Sociedad Filarmónica (1847), to which a school of music was attached. This was the first step towards the establishment of the Academia Nacional de Música in 1882 by his son, Jorge W. Price (1853–1953). Henry Price left many solo songs and overtures as well as numerous piano pieces, including *Vals al estilo del país* (1843), a stylized *pasillo*, one of Colombia's most widespread folkdances.

In the viceroyalty of Peru, the splendour of colonial musical life had no counterpart during the period of independence. Church music continued to be written but in a secularized, romantic style exemplified by some works by the mulatto José Bernardo Alcedo (1788–1878), composer of the Peruvian national anthem who, however, spent much of his life in Chile. Until mid-century, Peruvian musical life, within the church, the theatre or the home, continued to reflect colonial dependence, in spite of emancipation and the prevailing nationalist sentiment. The search for a true national identity started only later in the century, when Peruvian composers of professional competence turned their attention to folk and popular music. Characteristically, immigrant musicians were the first to deal with Peruvian subject matter, though in the Romantic tradition of collecting folksongs and harmonizing them or rewriting them in accordance with established conventions. This was true, for example, of the Italian Carlo Enrico Pasta (1817–98), who composed the first opera on the story of *Atahualpa* (1877, Lima). In 1868 another Italian, Claudio Rebagliati (1847–1909), wrote *Un 28 de julio en Lima* in honour of the Peruvian independence day, 'A Peruvian Rhapsody', on well-known tunes and street shouts.

Santiago de Chile attempted to establish a solid cultural and artistic life throughout the nineteenth century. Several theatres became available in the 1840s, such as the Teatro de la Universidad, the Teatro de la República and especially the new Teatro Municipal.[13] As early as 1819, efforts had been made to encourage the development of chamber music beyond amateur social gatherings. Regular opera seasons began in 1844, but public concerts had to await the additional patronage of European immigrants in the second half of the century. Even then, however, the Sociedad de Música Clásica and the Sociedad del Cuarteto, founded in 1879 and 1886 respectively, lasted only a few years.

ARGENTINA

Argentina's musical life intensified greatly during the nineteenth century when, as in other South American nations, patriotic and theatre music accompanied important national events. The first half of the century witnessed the creation of new musical associations, especially in the capital of Buenos Aires, but serious music remained concentrated primarily in the churches, opera houses and, to a lesser degree, philharmonic societies. Salon music flourished. Among the musicians associated with Buenos Aires Cathedral during this period, the *maestro de capilla* José Antonio Picasarri (1769–1843) exerted a major influence on the city's musical life, teaching the first Argentine professional musicians, founding music societies and organizing instrumental ensembles. He inaugurated the Escuela de Música y Canto in 1822 under the auspices of the Minister (later President) Rivadavia. He also helped to found the Sociedad Filarmónica (1822), where he gave the first performances of important works, including Beethoven's *Missa solemnis* (1836).

Juan Pedro Esnaola (1808–78), an accomplished pianist and composer, cultivated a Romantic idiom in his songs and symphonic and choral music, including a *Himno a Rosas* extolling the Argentinian dictator. Other well-known Argentine Romantic composers, such as Amancio Alcorta (1805–62) and Juan Bautista Alberdi (1810–84), wrote primarily salon piano pieces, polkas and *contradanzas*. Salon music, which developed especially during the period 1830 to 1850, included dances of European origin with some local adaptations, like the *minué montonero* or *nacional* and fashionable fantasies and variations on operatic arias.

At the same time, the popular tradition of song and poetry of the gaucho (the cowboy of the pampas) began to be explored in Argentina's urban areas. Domingo Sarmiento's *Facundo* (1845), the first major literary work to romanticize the gaucho, describes the various dances and songs of the pampas: the *gato*, *vidalita*, *triste* and others. These were the sources on which the first nationalist composers drew. Since the revolutionary period the gaucho character had symbolized the national folk, but during the Rosas regime (1835–52) the gaucho came to epitomize Argentina herself. It was only natural, therefore, that the music of the payadores (folk-ballad singer-improvisers) and gaucho guitarists should exert a profound influence on composers of nationalistic tendencies.

Opera in Buenos Aires had begun during the eighteenth century with the opening of the Teatro de Operas y Comedias (1757), followed by the Teatro de la Ranchería (1783), which presented *tonadillas* and zarzuelas. Italian opera, however, began to predominate in the 1820s. The Teatro Coliseo, established in 1824, produced Rossini's *Il barbiere di Siviglia* as early as 1825, and the popularity of Italian and French opera and lighter genres was soon such that no fewer than ten theatres opened during the century. In 1854, perhaps as the result of rivalry between an Italian and a French opera troupe, 30 operas were produced in Buenos Aires, half by Italian and half by French composers.

BRAZIL

When Rio de Janeiro became the Brazilian capital in 1763, it also assumed a central role in the musical life of the country. Then, with the transfer of the Portuguese royal family to Rio in 1808, under the threat of the Napoleonic invasion of the Iberian peninsula, it became the hub of the entire, huge Portuguese empire. The career of the mulatto church music composer and priest José Maurício Nunes Garcia (1767–1830) was closely tied to the sojourn in Rio of the prince and subsequent king John VI (until 1821) and the reign of Pedro I. In 1784 José Maurício, as he is generally referred to in Brazil, the most distinguished Brazilian composer of his time, had been among the co-founders of the Brotherhood of St Cecilia, one of the most important professional musical organizations. Seven years later he joined the Brotherhood of São Pedro dos Clérigos. The fact that he was a mulatto does not seem to have been an obstacle to his ordination, which took place in 1792. By the time the Portuguese court arrived, his fame as a composer was well established (he had been appointed *mestre de capela* at Rio Cathedral in 1798). Following the long tradition of the Bragança royal family, John VI was a patron of music and in 1808 appointed José Maurício *mestro de capela* of the royal chapel, for which he wrote no fewer than 39 works in 1809 alone. The city's nobility, in turn, was enchanted with his improvisational skill at the keyboard, which caused Sigismund Neukomm, an Austrian composer and pupil of Haydn who lived in Rio from 1816 to 1821, to call José Maurício 'the foremost improviser in the world'.

The return of John VI and part of the court to Portugal in 1821 diminished the importance of Rio's musical life. Although Pedro I was himself a musician, the years following independence (1822) were not favourable for artistic development. The imperial chapel experienced such a deterioration that its orchestra was dissolved with Pedro I's abdication in 1831. Only in 1843 was the orchestra reinstated, thanks mostly to Francisco Manuel da Silva (1795–1865), composer of both the imperial chamber and the imperial chapel. Remembered today primarily as the composer of the Brazilian national anthem (officially recognized as such only in 1890), he was instrumental in organizing musical life in Rio during the major part of the Second Empire. His most significant project was the foundation of the Rio de Janeiro Conservatory in 1847, which, taken over by the government in the 1850s, established the principle of free music instruction in Brazil. The creation of an annual fellowship for a year of study in Europe benefited a number of younger composers. Da Silva directed the conservatory until his death and contributed substantially to operatic life.

Brazilian opera was dominated in the early nineteenth century by Marcos Portugal (1762–1830), the most famous Portuguese composer of his time, who arrived in Rio in 1811, and, to a lesser extent, by José Maurício, whose opera *Le due gemelle*, written for Queen Maria I's birthday, was first performed at the Teatro Régio in 1809. Rio's other important theatre was the Real Teatro de São João, opened in 1813 but later rebuilt and in 1826 renamed São Pedro de Alcântara. It was a replica of the São Carlos theatre in Lisbon, attesting to Prince John's determination to make Rio the new royal capital. Although the first seasons included works by Marcos Portugal, Italian operas by Salieri, Puccitta, Nicolini, Rossini and others furnished the bulk of the repertory. 1821 saw the first performance of Mozart's *Don Giovanni* at the São João. During the unstable regency era opera performances were suspended until in 1844 the first Brazilian performance of Bellini's *Norma* marked the beginning of the uncontested hegemony of Italian opera, with appearances by some of the most celebrated Italian and French singers. Henceforth, Rio was to enjoy the best of Italian opera, often within only a few years of the European première.

NOTES

[1] V. T. Mendoza, *Panorama de la música tradicional de México* (Mexico City, 1956).
[2] E. de Olavarría y Ferrari, *Reseña histórica del teatro en México* (Mexico City, 1895, 3/1961), 159.
[3] M. Galindo, *Nociones de historia de la música mexicana* (Colima, 1933), 392, gives the date 1809 for that production, but R. Stevenson, *Music in Mexico: a Historical Survey* (New York, 1952), 174, provides the correct date.
[4] *Diario de México* (4 Dec 1806), as quoted and translated in Stevenson, *Music in Mexico*, 174.
[5] Stevenson, *Music in Mexico*, 192.
[6] See G. Carmona, 'Período de la Independencia a la Revolución (1810 a 1910)', in *La música de México*, ed. J. Estrada (Mexico, 1984), iii, 27.
[7] Ibid, 122.
[8] O. Mayer-Serra, *Panorama de la música mexicana desde la independencia hasta la actualidad* (Mexico City, 1941), 126.
[9] See A. Carpentier, *La música en Cuba* (Mexico City, 1946), 141–3.
[10] Ibid, 260.
[11] For detailed information, see R. Stevenson, *A Guide to Caribbean Music History* (Lima, 1975), and C. Dower, *Puerto Rican Music Following the Spanish American War* (Lanham, NY, and London, 1983).
[12] See J. A. Calcaño, *La ciudad y su música* (Caracas, 1958), 311–19.
[13] For specific samples of opera seasons in this theatre, see E. Pereira Salas, *Historia de la música en Chile (1850–1900)* (Santiago, 1957), 155–69.

BIBLIOGRAPHICAL NOTE

Among various historical-cultural sources in English dealing with the period of independence in Latin America in the 1810s, the series of essays *Latin America and the Enlightenment*, ed. A. P. Whitaker (Ithaca, NY, 2/1961) remains informative in relation to philosophical, political and artistic thought. A penetrating cultural history of Brazil is F. J. de Oliveira Vianna's *Evolução do povo brasileiro* (Rio de Janeiro, 4/1956). Various relevant entries are found in the single-volume *Encyclopedia of Latin America*, ed. H. Delpar (New York, 1974).

Biographical information on composers is available in the two-volume dictionary *Música y músicos de Latinoamérica* (Mexico, 1947), compiled by O. Mayer-Serra. Chapter 4 of R. Stevenson's *Music in Mexico: a Historical Survey* (New York, 1952) presents a generous overview of nineteenth-century Mexican music. A good biographical essay on Elízaga is J. C. Romero's *José Mariano Elízaga* (Mexico, 1934). Romero also provides a survey of operatic activity in Mexico since the eighteenth century in *La ópera en Yucatán* (Mexico, 1947). More recently vol.iii, by G. Carmona, of *La música de México*, ed. J. Estrada (Mexico, 1984), details the music history of Mexico from 1810 to 1850 in the first three chapters.

Cuban music and musicians are the subject of special study in A. Carpentier's *La música en Cuba* (Mexico City, 1946) and Puerto Rican music is treated in vol.vii, *La música* by H. Campos-Parsi, of the *Gran enciclopedia de Puerto Rico* (Madrid, 1976). A general survey of music in Caracas is J. A. Calcaño's *La ciudad y su música* (Caracas, 1958) and on theatre and dance music is A. Calzavara's *Historia de la música en Venezuela* (Caracas, 1987). A useful sketch of some aspects of musical life in Caracas at the end of the eighteenth century is provided by W. Guido, *José Angel Lamas y su época* (Caracas, 1981).

Colombian music is briefly surveyed in J. I. P. Escobar's *Historia de la música en Colombia* (Bogotá, 3/1963) and nineteenth-century Peruvian music is the subject of a special chapter by E. Iturriaga and J. C. Estenssoro in *La música en el Perú* (Lima,

The Early Romantic Period

1985). E. Pereira Salas deals in part with early nineteenth-century Chilean music in *Los orígenes del arte musical en Chile* (Santiago, 1941), updated by S. Claro-Valdés and J. U. Blondel in *Historia de la música en Chile* (Santiago, 1974).

Argentine music is studied comprehensively by V. Gesualdo in the first two volumes of *Historia de la música en la Argentina* (Buenos Aires, 1961). An excellent source, with ample documentation, for Rio de Janeiro's music institutions and activities, 1808–65, is A. de Andrade's *Francisco Manuel da Silva e seu tempo*, 2 vols. (Rio de Janeiro, 1967). Also invaluable is R. T. de Lima's *Vida e época de José Maurício* (São Paolo, 1941). L. H. Corrêa de Azevedo provides much information in *150 anos de música no Brasil, 1800–1950* (Rio de Janeiro, 1956). Brazilian salon music in the first half of the nineteenth century is well documented in M. de Andrade, *Modinhas imperiais* (São Paolo, 1930).

Chronology

MUSIC AND MUSICIANS	POLITICS, WAR AND RULERS
1789 *Philadelphia Harmony*, a book of popular American and European sacred music, published. Daniel Gottlob Türk (1750–1813) publishes his *Clavierschule*. For a performance of the oratorio *Hiob* by Carl Ditters von Dittersdorf (1739–99), citizens are first able to buy tickets for the Berlin court opera.	**1789** French Revolution begins with the storming of the Bastille on 14 July; on 4 August, Declaration of the Rights of Man by the new French National Assembly.
1790 *Così fan tutte* by W. A. Mozart (1756–91) given, Vienna. *Euphrosine* by E. N. Méhul (1763–1817), given, Paris. Concert Spirituel, Paris, founded in 1725, closes down.	**1790** Death of Joseph II of Austria; succeeded by Leopold II, Grand Duke of Tuscany.
1791 Mozart's *La clemenza di Tito* given, Prague, and *Die Zauberflöte*, Vienna; he dies (35). First visit to England (–1792) of Joseph Haydn (1732–1809): symphonies nos.93–8. *Lodoïska* by Luigi Cherubini (1760–1842) given, Paris.	
1792 Ludwig van Beethoven (1770–1827) settles in Vienna. *Il matrimonio segreto* by Domenico Cimarosa (1749–1801) given, Vienna. Berlin Singakademie founded by C. F. C. Fasch (1736–1800). Teatro La Fenice, Venice, opens. Annotated music bibliography by J. N. Forkel (1749–1818) published.	**1792** Death of Leopold II of Austria; succeeded by Franz II, the last Holy Roman Emperor. Execution of Louis XVI; French Republic established, with National Convention until 1795. Assassination of Gustavus III of Sweden by dissatisfied nobles; succeeded by Gustavus IV.
	1793 Britain, the United Provinces, Spain, Portugal, Naples, Tuscany and the Holy Roman Empire declare war on France.
1794 Haydn's second visit to England (–1795): symphonies nos. 99–104.	
1795 Beethoven's first two piano concertos performed, Vienna. Paris Conservatoire founded.	**1795** The Directoire in France (–1799).
1796 The first two of Haydn's late masses composed, Vienna.	**1796** Death of Empress Catherine II of Russia; succeeded by Paul I.
1797 Haydn's op.76 string quartets composed. Cherubini's *Médée* given, Paris.	**1797** Death of Friedrich Wilhelm II of Prussia; succeeded by Friedrich Wilhelm III.
1798 Haydn's *The Creation* given, Vienna. Beethoven's op.13 piano sonata ('Pathétique') written. First collected edition of Mozart's works begun. The *Allgemeine musikalische Zeitung*, Leipzig, founded.	**1798** Battle of the Nile; Horatio Nelson plays a leading part in the destruction of the French fleet.
1799 Lithography developed for the printing of music.	**1799** The Consulat in France, with Napoleon Bonaparte as First Consul; the reform of civil law (the *Code Napoléon*) completed 1804.

LITERATURE, PHILOSOPHY, RELIGION	SCIENCE, TECHNOLOGY, DISCOVERY	FINE AND DECORATIVE ARTS, ARCHITECTURE
1789 William Jones (1746–1794) translates the Sanskrit drama *Sakuntala* into English, making Hindu language and literature accessible to Europeans and laying the foundations of comparative philology.	**1789** Antoine Lavoisier (1743–94) produces his first memoir on respiration, *Traité élémentaire de chimie*, laying the foundations for the study of human metabolism. Alessandro Malaspina (1754–1810) explores the north-west coast of America (–1794).	**1789** Francisco Goya y Lucientes (1746–1828) becomes court painter to Charles IV of Spain. The monumental entrance to Edinburgh University built by Robert Adam (1728–92), considered his masterpiece.
1790 N. M. Karamzin (1766–1826) publishes *Letters of a Russian Traveller*, becoming the first Russian writer to gain an international reputation (–1802).		**1791** Thomas Sheraton (1751–1806) publishes *The Cabinet Maker and Upholsterer's Drawing Book*, extensively used both sides of the Atlantic (–1794).
1791 James Boswell (1740–1795) publishes *The Life of Samuel Johnson*. Tom Paine (1740–1809) publishes *The Rights of Man* in reply to Burke's *Reflections on the French Revolution*.	**1794** Erasmus Darwin (1731–1802) publishes *Zoonomia, or The Laws of Organic Life*, primarily pathological but postulating the mutability of species (–1796).	**1792** The Alexander Palace, Tsarkoe Selo, begun by Gianomo Querenghi (1744–1817), a gift from Catherine II to the future Alexander I (–1796).
1794 Ann Radcliffe (1764–1823), leading exponent of the Gothic novel, publishes *The Mysteries of Udolpho*. Johann Gottlieb Fichte (1762–1814), German Idealist philosopher, expounds 'ethical pantheism' in a series of works (–1805).	**1795** Mungo Park (1771–1806) explores West Africa and the River Niger (his *Travels* are published in 1799). James Hutton (1726–97) publishes *Theory of the Earth*, outlining the new science of geology.	**1793** The Louvre opens as the first national art gallery in Europe. **1796** The fantastical Fonthill Abbey in the Gothic style begun by James Wyatt (1746–1813). J. M. W. Turner (1775–1851) exhibits his first work in oils, *Fishermen at Sea*, at the Royal Academy.
1798 First edition of *Lyrical Ballads* by William Wordsworth (1770–1850) and Samuel Taylor Coleridge (1772–1834): the beginning of the Romantic movement in English literature.	**1798** Edward Jenner (1749–1823) publishes his theory of vaccination against smallpox. William Herschel (1738–1822) discovers the infra-red radiation in sunlight.	**1797** Thomas Bewick (1755–1828) publishes *A History of British Birds*, raising the level of the woodcut to new artistic heights (–1804).
1799 Friedrich von Schiller (1759–1805) completes his *Wallenstein* trilogy, his finest drama.		

The Early Romantic Period

MUSIC AND MUSICIANS	POLITICS, WAR AND RULERS
1800 Beethoven's Symphony no.1 performed, Vienna. Cherubini's *Les deux journées* ('The Water Carrier') given, Paris. Carl Czerny makes his public début, Vienna, playing a Mozart concerto.	**1800** Napoleon's army crosses into Italy and defeats the Austrians at Marengo; France in control of Italy. The French also defeat the Austrians at Hochstedt and Hohenlinden.
1801 Haydn's *The Seasons* performed Vienna. Cimarosa dies, Venice (51).	**1801** Peace between France and Austria marks the passing of the Holy Roman Empire, after 1000 years; Franz II renounces the Imperial Dignity in 1806 and becomes Emperor Franz I of Austria. Assassination of Tsar Paul I of Russia; succeeded by his son Alexander I. Danish action against British shipping provokes the Battle of Copenhagen, another victory for Nelson.
1802 John Field (1782–1837) settles in St Petersburg. Muzio Clementi (1752–1832) publishes his three large-scale piano sonatas, op. 40; he embarks on eight years of travel. The earliest pocket scores (of symphonies by Haydn) are published. St Petersburg Philharmonic Society founded.	**1802** Peace of Amiens between Britain and France: a temporary peace. Napoleon Bonaparte becomes President of the Italian Republic and first Consul of France for life; annexes Elba, Piedmont, Parma and Piacenza.
1803 Beethoven's Symphony no.3 ('Eroica') composed. *Peter Schmoll* by Carl Maria von Weber (1786–1826) given, Augsburg. Haydn leaves his last string quintet unfinished.	**1803** Abolition of Holy Roman Empire ecclesiastical states and free cities; German states reconstituted as Confederation of the Rhine, under French and Russian influence. In America, Ohio becomes a state of the Union, and the USA buys Louisiana and New Orleans from France.
	1804 Napoleon crowned Emperor Napoleon I by Pope Pius VII in Paris.
1805 Beethoven's *Fidelio* (first version) given, Vienna. Nicolò Paganini (1782–1840) composes his 24 Caprices op.1.	**1805** 21 October: Battle of Trafalgar, where Lord Nelson's inspired action against the French and Spanish fleets ensure British naval supremacy for 100 years. December: Russian and Austrian armies defeated by Napoleon at Austerlitz; Austria forced to give up the Tyrol, Bavaria, Baden, Württemberg and possessions in Dalmatia and Italy.
1806 Beethoven's symphony no. 4, Violin Concerto and Appassionata Sonata composed.	**1806** Napoleon creates his brothers Joseph King of Naples and Louis King of Holland (in 1807, Jerome King of Westphalia). France defeats Prussia at Jena and Napoleon occupies Berlin; continental ports closed to British ships to cripple the economy.

LITERATURE, PHILOSOPHY, RELIGION	SCIENCE, TECHNOLOGY, DISCOVERY	FINE AND DECORATIVE ARTS, ARCHITECTURE
1800 Mme de Staël (1766–1817) publishes *De la littérature*, treating it as a product of social history and environment.	**1800** The invention of the electric battery or Voltaic cell by Alessandro Volta (1745–1827) enables research on electrolysis by Davy, Faraday and others.	**1800** Jacques Louis David (1748–1825), a central figure of neo-classicism, paints his exemplary work of heroic official art, *Napoléon au Grand St Bernard*, and his *Mme Récamier*.
	1801 Karl Gauss (1777–1855) publishes his *Disquisitiones arithmeticae*, establishing the theories of cyclotomy and arithmetical forms, and begins his calcuations on the orbit of Ceres, just discovered by G. Piazzi.	**1802** J.-N.-L. Durand (1796–1834) publishes *Précis et leçons d'architecture* (–1809).
1802 François, Vicomte de Chateaubriand (1768–1848), publishes *Génie du christianisme*, a defence of Catholic Christianity against the rationalist philosophers.	**1803** *Essai de statique chimique* by Claude Berthollet (1748–1822), arguing that the focus of chemical affinity must be proportional to the masses of the reacting substances.	**1803** John Crome (1768–1821) founds the Norwich Society of Artists, with John Sell Cotman (1782–1842) as Vice-President (1806). Henry Raeburn (1756–1823), the leading portrait painter in Scotland, paints *The Macnab*.
1803 Sunday School Union founded.		
1804 Schiller's *Wilhelm Tell* written. Immanuel Kant (*b*1724) dies.	**1804** Thomas Telford (1757–1834) begins the construction of the Caledonian Canal (–1847).	**1804** Antoine Jean Gros (1771–1835), Napoleon's official war artist, paints *Plague at Jaffa*.
	1805 Publication of *Voyage aux régions équinoxiales* by Alexander von Humboldt (1769–1859) and Aimé Bonplaud, a study of the geology, botany, economics and inhabitants of Spanish America (–1834).	**1805** Turner paints *The Shipwreck*, the culmination of a new Romantic approach to landscape. Antonio Canova (1757–1822) begins *Venus Victrix*, a marble portrait of Napoleon's sister Pauline Borghese.
1805 Walter Scott (1771–1832) publishes *The Lay of the Last Minstrel*, one of his highly influential long poems.		
	1806 Humphrey Davy (1778–1829) proposes theories of electrolysis and voltaic action and gives the first important electrical explanation of chemical reactivity (*Elements of Chemical Philosophy*, 1812).	**1806** Charles Percier (1764–1838) and P.-F.-L. Fontaine (1762–1853), chief architects to Napoleon, build the Arc du Carousel, crowned by four bronze horses looted from Venice.

MUSIC AND MUSICIANS	POLITICS, WAR AND RULERS
1807 *La vestale* by Gasparo Spontini (1774–1851) given, Paris.	**1807** Treaty of Tilsit: Napoleon meets Tsar Alexander I and Friedrich Wilhelm III of Prussia, who cedes possessions west of the Elbe and Polish lands to form a Duchy of Warsaw under the King of Saxony. Abolition of the slave trade in the British Empire through the efforts of William Wilberforce (1759–1833); existing slaves not freed until 1843.
1808 Beethoven's Symphonies nos.5 and 6 performed, Vienna. Gesellschaft der Musikfreunde founded, Vienna. The publishing house of Ricordi founded, Milan.	**1808** French army occupies Rome. France invades Spain, ousting Charles IV; Joseph Bonaparte becomes King of Spain and Joachim Murat takes his place in Naples.
1809 Spontini's *Fernand Cortez* given, Paris. Haydn dies, Vienna (77).	**1809** Arthur Wellesley defeats the French at Oporto, forcing them to retreat from Portugal, and then at Talavera (created Viscount Wellington, Duke in 1813). Franz I of Austria, with British aid, declares war on France but is defeated and Vienna is taken by Napoleon; Prince Metternich becomes Chief Minister of Austria.
	1810 The annexation of Oldenburg by Napoleon violates the Treaty of Tilsit and alienates Alexander I. Napoleon marries Marie-Louise of Austria.
1811 Beethoven's Fifth Piano Concerto performed Leipzig. Weber's *Abu Hassan* given, Munich. Damper pedals for the piano invented.	**1811** Prince of Wales becomes Prince Regent for the ill George III. Luddites begin destroying machines in England.
1812 Field's first nocturnes published, Moscow.	**1812** The Duke of Wellington advances through Spain, taking Madrid after the battle of Salamanca. Invasion of Russia by Napoleon, who defeats the Russians at Smolensk and Borodino and occupies Moscow; the retreat from Moscow is a disaster for the French army.

LITERATURE, PHILOSOPHY, RELIGION	SCIENCE, TECHNOLOGY, DISCOVERY	FINE AND DECORATIVE ARTS, ARCHITECTURE
1807 Benjamin Constant (1767–1830) writes *Adolphe*, a novel of psychological analysis. Jacob Friedrich Fries (1773–1843) publishes *Neue oder anthropologische Kritik der Vernunft*, offering a basis of psychological analysis for Kant's critical theory. Lamb's *Tales from Shakespeare* published.	**1807** Robert Fulton (1765–1815) convinces Americans and Europeans of the future of the steamboat with the sailing of his *Clermont* on the Hudson River; the first steam warship, *USS Fulton*, was built in 1815.	**1807** A. D. Zakharov (1761–1811) begins the New Admiralty in St Petersburg.
1808 Johann Wolfgang von Goethe (1749–1832) publishes the first part of *Faust*.		**1808** P. Runge (1777–1810), German Romantic, paints two versions of *Morning*, trying to express cosmic harmony through the symbolism of colour, form and numbers. Pierre Paul Prud'hon (1758–1823) paints *The Rape of Psyche*. Caspar David Friedrich (1774–1840), the leading German Romantic, paints *The Cross in the Mountains*, which caused controversy for its use of landscape in this context.
1809 Washington Irving (1783–1859) publishes the burlesque *A History of New York* under the pseudonym 'Knickerbocker'. Publication of lectures by August Wilhelm von Schegel (1767–1845), leader of the new Romantic criticism and translator of Shakespeare, *Über dramatische Kunst und Literatur* (–1811).	**1809** *Observations on the Geology of the United States* by William McClure (1763–1840): the first in English.	
	1811 Charles Bell (1774–1842) publishes *Idea of a New Anatomy of the Brain*, establishing that different parts of the brain serve different functions.	**1809** Johann Friedrich Overbeck (1789–1869) and Franz Pforr (1788–1812) found the Nazarenes, or Lukasbrüder, in Rome, turning to primitives for inspiration to revive German religious painting.
1810 Mme de Staël's *De l'Allemagne* published, opening up French literature to German ideas. Heinrich von Kleist (1777–1811) publishes *Kätchen von Heilbronn*.	**1812** George Cuvier (1769–1832) publishes *Recherches sur les ossements fossides des quadrupèdes*, laying the foundations of modern palaeontology. Pierre Laplace (1749–1827) publishes *Théorie analytique des probabilités*, the basis of most subsequent work in probability theory. Johann Burckhardt (1749–1827), Swiss orientalist, arrives in Cairo, travels up the Nile, discovers the Great Temple at Abu Simbel and makes the pilgrimage to Mecca (–1815).	**1810** Richard Westmacott (1775–1856), neo-classical sculptor, begins work on the tomb of Charles James Fox at Westminster Abbey.
1811 Publication of *Sense and Sensibility* by Jane Austen (1775–1817).		**1811** Sir John Soane (1753–1837), English architect, designs Dulwich Art Gallery.
1812 Lord Byron (1788–1824) publishes the first two cantos of *Childe Harold's Pilgrimage*.		

MUSIC AND MUSICIANS	POLITICS, WAR AND RULERS
1813 *Tancredi* and *L'italiana in Algeri* by Gioachino Rossini (1792–1868) given, Venice. The Nonet by Louis Spohr (1784–1859) composed. The Philharmonic Society of London founded. Weber appointed opera director in Prague (–1816). A.-E.-M. Grétry dies, Paris (72).	**1813** Wellington drives the French out of Spain; the British army crosses the Pyrenees into France (October). Napoleon defeated at Leipzig by allied armies (October); Confederation of the Rhine and Kingdom of Westphalia dissolved. The Austrians defeat the French at Valsamo and regain a foothold in Italy.
1814 Final version of Beethoven's *Fidelio* given, Vienna. Valves applied to brass instruments, enabling them to play chromatically.	**1814** Abdication of Napoleon at Fontainebleau (April) and banishment to Elba; Louis XVIII (brother of Louis XVI) becomes king and France recognizes 1792 frontiers. Formal opening of Congress of Vienna. Russia hands over Saxony to Prussia, in opposition to Austria, the German states and France.
1815 Franz Schubert (1797–1818) begins a period of prolific song composition (*c*100 a year to 1817). Rossini settles in Naples as artistic director of S Carlo theatre, to concentrate on serious opera (e.g. *Otello*, 1816; *Armida*, 1817). J. N. Maelzel invents the metronome.	**1815** Napoleon breaks his exile and lands in France (March); Wellington and Blücher defeat him at Waterloo and he is banished to St Helena (dies there, 1820). Under final act of Congress of Vienna (June), map of Europe redrawn and 38 German states become the German Confederation.
1816 Rossini's *Il barbiere di Siviglia* given, Rome. Spohr's *Faust* given, Prague; his violin concerto in the form of a vocal scene composed. Paisiello dies, Naples (76).	**1816** Brazil becomes an independent empire under John, Prince Regent of Portugal (full independence, 1822). Indiana admitted to the Union as a state (followed in 1817 by Mississippi, 1818 Illinois, 1819 Alabama and Florida).
1817 Weber appointed Royal Saxon Kapellmeister, Dresden. Part I of Clementi's *Gradus ad Parnassum* published. Méhul dies, Paris (54).	
1818 Beethoven's Piano Sonata in B flat op. 106 ('Hammerklavier') composed.	**1818** Death of Charles XIII of Sweden; succeeded by Jean Baptiste Bernadotte (1763–1844) as Charles XIV, founding a new dynasty which still reigns. Simon Bolivar (1783–1830) declares Venezuela independent.
1819 Schubert's 'Trout' Quintet composed.	**1819** 'Peterloo' massacre in Manchester: 11 killed and over 400 wounded – the worst incident of repression in the political and industrial unrest after the Napoleonic wars. Bolivar becomes President of the Republic of Colombia.

LITERATURE, PHILOSOPHY, RELIGION	SCIENCE, TECHNOLOGY, DISCOVERY	FINE AND DECORATIVE ARTS, ARCHITECTURE
1813 Percy Bysshe Shelley (1792–1822) completes *Queen Mab*, a visionary, ideological poem which reveals him as heir to the French and British revolutionary intellectuals.	**1814** George Stephenson (1781–1848) constructs the first effective steam locomotive, the *Blücher*.	**1814** Goya paints *The Shootings of 3 May 1808*.
1814 Publication of *Waverley* by Scott, establishing the form of the historical novel.	**1815** Jean Lamarck (1744–1829) publishes *Histoire naturelle des animaux sans vertèbres*, propounding four 'laws' for evolution. William Smith (1767–1839) publishes the first geological map, *A Delineation of the State of England and Wales*. Miner's safety lamp invented by Humphrey Davy.	**1815** John Nash (1752–1835) redesigns the Royal Pavilion, Brighton, in a mixture of styles (–1823).
1815 E. T. A. Hoffmann (1776–1822) writes *Elixire des Teufels*.		**1816** Lord Elgin sells to the nation the sculptures from the Parthenon in Athens and others he has acquired from the Turks in 1801–3. Benjamin West (1738–1820), the first American painter to achieve an international reputation, paints *Christ Healing the Sick* for the Pennsylvania hospital. John Martin (1789–1854) completes his *Joshua Commanding the Sun to Stand Still*.
1816 Pierre-Jean de Beranger (1780–1857) publishes the first of his *Chansons*. Count Leopardi (1798–1837), the greatest Italian Romantic poet, begins his *Canti*.	**1816** John McAdam (1756–1836) publishes *Remarks on the Present System of Road Making*; most main roads in Europe were built on his principles.	
1817 Coleridge publishes his *Biographia literaria*, a major work of poetic criticism and philosophy. Georg Wilhelm Friedrich Hegel (1770–1831) publishes *Encyclopaedie der philosophischen Wissenschaft der Logik*, an attempt to encompass all human knowledge.	**1818** Friedrich Bessel (1784–1864) publishes *Fundamenta astronomiae*, codifying and reducing *c*4000 star places based on the work of James Bradley (1729) and inaugurating a new era of practical astronomy. First Arctic voyage of John Ross (1777–1856), to search for the North-West Passage.	**1817** Sir Francis Chantrey (1781–1841) designs the monument for the Robinson children in Lichfield Cathedral, admired for its naturalism and simplicity.
1818 John Keats (1795–1821), publishes *Endymion*. Mary Wollstonecraft Shelley (1797–1851) writes *Frankenstein*.		**1818** William Blake (1757–1827), artist, poet and philosopher, begins engravings for *The Book of Job* and later *The Divine Commedy*.
1819 Arthur Schopenhauer (1788–1860) publishes *Die Welt als Wille und Vorstellung*, one of the chief anti-Christian systems of 19th-century Germany.	**1819** One of the greatest 19th-century chemists, Jons Berzelius (1779–1848), publishes his *Essay on Chemical Proportions*, linking electrochemistry with atomic theory. Discovery of rich platinum deposits in the Urals.	**1819** Théodore Géricault (1791–1824) exhibits his most famous painting, *The Raft of the Medusa*, based on a recent disaster; his work had enormous influence, notably on Delacroix.

MUSIC AND MUSICIANS	POLITICS, WAR AND RULERS
1820 First use (Spohr later claimed) of the conductor's baton, at the Philharmonic Society concerts, London. Metal piano frames first used. The brass band movement begins, in Britain and the USA, in the 1820s.	**1820** Frankfurt Diet sanctions the Carlsbad Decrees: freedom of the press abolished, universities placed under state supervision, revolutionary and liberal movements to be suppressed in Germany. Death of George III; succeeded by George IV, Regent since 1811. Missouri enters the Union as a free state (Maine as a slave state, 1821). Revolts crushed in Spain, Naples and Portugal.
1821 Weber's *Der Freischütz* given, Berlin. Beethoven's last two piano sonatas, opp. 110–11, composed. Felix Mendelssohn (1809–47) taken to meet Goethe.	
1822 Schubert's Symphony no. 8, in B minor ('Unfinished') written. Royal Academy of Music founded, London.	**1821** Peru declares independence from Spain, followed by Guatamala, Panama and Santo Domingo.
1823 Beethoven begins the composition of his late string quartets (–1826). Spohr's *Jessonda* given, Kassel.	**1822** Start of the Greek War of Independence after 1821 uprising against the Turks and Turkish atrocities at Chois. Byron dies fighting for the Greeks in 1824.
1824 Beethoven's Symphony no.9 (Choral) performed, Vienna; his *Missa solemnis* performed, St Petersburg. *Il crociato in Egitto* by Giacomo Meyerbeer (1793–1864) given, Venice. Schubert composes *Die schöne Müllerin*. Rossini becomes director of the Théâtre-Italien, Paris.	**1823** The Monroe doctrine closes 'American continents to colonial settlements by non-American Powers' and excludes 'European Powers from all interference in the political affairs of the American Republics'.
1825 Schubert composes his 'Great C major' Symphony. *La dame blanche* by Adrien Boieldieu (1775–1834) given, Paris. Johann Strauss the elder forms his own orchestra, Vienna. The first Italian opera given in New York. Cast iron piano frames patented.	**1824** Death of Louis XVIII; succeeded by the reactionary Charles X.
	1825 Death of Ferdinand of Naples; succeeded by Francis I. Death of Maximilian I of Bavaria; succeeded by his son Louis I. The Hungarian Diet reopens after 13 years and Franz I agrees to triennial meetings. Death of Tsar Alexander I; succeeded by younger son, Nicholas I. Decembrist Rising demanding a representative assembly easily crushed.
1826 Weber's *Oberon* given, London; he dies there (39). Mendelssohn writes his overture *A Midsummer Night's Dream*.	
1827 Schubert composes *Winterreise* and two piano trios. Franz Liszt (1811–86) settles in Paris. F.-J. Fétis founds *La revue musicale*. Beethoven dies, Vienna (57).	
1828 Schubert composes String Quintet in C and his last three piano sonatas; he dies, Vienna (31). *La muette de Portici*, a grand opera on a revolutionary theme by D.-F.-E. Auber (1782–1871), given, Paris. *Der Vampyr* by Heinrich Marschner (1795–1861) given, Leipzig. G. Baini's Palestrina biography published.	**1827** Battle of Navarino, the last major one under sail: Russian, French and British squadron destroys the Turkish and Egyptian fleets.
1829 Rossini's *Guillaume Tell* given, Paris. Mendelssohn conducts the first performance since Bach's time of his *St Matthew Passion*, Berlin.	**1829** Peace of Adrianople: Turkey agrees to recognize the independence of Greece, the Danubian provinces and Serbia; Russia obtains land south of the Caucasus.

LITERATURE, PHILOSOPHY, RELIGION	SCIENCE, TECHNOLOGY, DISCOVERY	FINE AND DECORATIVE ARTS, ARCHITECTURE
1820 Alphonse de Lamartine (1780–1869) publishes *Méditations, poétiques et religieuses*. **1821** *The Spy* published by James Fennimore Cooper (1789–1851) Friedrich Schleiermacher (1768–1834) publishes *Der christliche Glaube* (defining religion as the feeling of absolute dependence which finds its expression in monotheism). **1823** Alexander Pushkin (1799–1837) begins his greatest and most sophisiticated work, *Eugene Onegin* (–1831). **1824** Leopold von Ranke (1795–1886) publishes *Geschichte der roman und german Völker von 1494–1535*, the foundation of modern historiography. **1825** Alessandro Manzoni (1758–1873) begins work on *I promessi sposi*, a landmark in the establishment of literary Italian. **1827** John Darby (1800–82) breaks from the Church of England and soon founds the Plymouth Brethren. Heinrich Heine (1797–1856) publishes *Buch der Lieder*, containing some of his greatest lyric poems. **1827** Honoré de Balzac (1799–1850) publishes the first of his 91 works of *Comédie humaine*, an attempt to depict contemporary French society in fiction. **1829** Passing of the Catholic Emancipation Act, enabling Roman Catholics to hold public office in Britain.	**1821** Augustin Fresnel (1788–1827) formulates the law of double refraction. **1823** Discovery of Lake Chad, Central Africa, by Walter Oudrey (1790–1824). **1825** Stephenson's Darlington and Stockton Railway, the first to employ locomotive traction and to carry both freight and passengers. **1826** Niels Abel (1802–29), Norwegian mathematician, publishes *Mémoire sur une propriété remarquable*, leading to equation theory and elliptic functions. **1827** André Ampère (1775–1836) publishes his greatest work, *Mémoire sur la théorie mathématique des phénomènes électro-dynamique*, describing the laws of action of electric currents. **1827** Georg Ohm (1789–1854) publishes his theory of electricity, Ohm's Law, in *Die galvanische Kette*, defining the relationship between resistance and current. John James Audubon (1785–1851) publishes *Birds of America*. Josef Ressel (1793–1857), Austrian engineer, takes out a patent on the screw propeller for steamships. **1829** Stephenson's locomotive *Rocket* wins trials for the Liverpool and Manchester railway.	**1821** John Constable (1776–1837) paints *The Hay Wain*; he profoundly influenced French Romantic landscape artists and eventually the Impressionists. **1823** Karl Friedrich Schinkel (1781–1841), the greatest German architect of the early 19th century, works on the Altes Museum in Berlin, a Greek Revival work. **1824** Jean-Auguste Dominique Ingres (1780–1867) exhibits *Vow of Louis XIII* in Paris and is acclaimed as the leader of the opposition to the new Romanticism of such as Delacroix. Foundation of the National Gallery, London; the present building, designed by William Wilkins (1778–1839), was opened in 1838. **1825** Thomas Cole (1801–48), American Romantic painter, founds the Hudson River School with T. Doughty and Asher B. Durand. T. Hamilton (1784–1858) begins his masterpiece, the Royal High School in Edinburgh in Greek Revival style. **1826** The US National Academy of Design founded, with Samuel Morse (1791–1872) its first president.

The Early Romantic Period

MUSIC AND MUSICIANS	POLITICS, WAR AND RULERS
1830 *Symphonie fantastique* by Hector Berlioz (1803–69) composed. Mikhail Glinka (1804–57) goes to study in Italy. A. B. Marx is appointed professor of music at Berlin University.	**1830** Death of George IV; succeeded by his brother William IV. July Revolution in France; abdication of Charles X and election of Louis Philippe as king under a constitutional charter. Revolution in Belgium against union with Holland (since 1815); Leopold of Saxe-Coburg becomes king of a neutral Belgium.
1831 *La sonnambula* and *Norma* by Vincenzo Bellini (1801–35) are given, Milan. Meyerbeer's *Robert le diable* is given, Paris. Robert Schumann (1810–56) composes his early piano music. Fryderyk Chopin (1810–49) settles in Paris.	**1831** Revolutionary outbreaks in Modena, Parma and the Papal States, suppressed by Austria.
1832 *L'elisir d'amore* by Gaetano Donizetti (1797–1848) given, Milan. Theobald Boehm builds his first flute using a revolutionary system of fingering.	**1832** The Great Reform Bill in Britain extends the franchise from half to one million. Metternich's Six Articles passed to maintain despotic government within the German confederation. Giuseppe Mazzini (1805–72) founds 'La Giovine Italia' with aim of national independence.
1833 Mendelssohn composes his Italian Symphony. *Gustave III* by Auber. Chopin's first set of piano studies published. *Le ménéstrel* founded, Paris.	**1833** Death of Ferdinand VII of Spain; succeeded by his daughter Isabella II (declared of age, 1843).
1834 Liszt composes *Harmonies poétiques et religieuses*. Berlioz composes *Harold in Italy*. First issue of the *Neue Zeitschrift für Musik* published, Leipzig, edited by Schumann.	
1835 Donizetti's *Lucia di Lammermoor* given, Naples. *La juive* by Fromental Halévy (1799–1862) given, Paris. Schumann's *Carnaval* composed. Mendelssohn appointed conductor of the Leipzig Gewandhaus Orchestra. Joseph Mainzer founds a free singing class in Paris. Bellini dies, near Paris (33).	**1835** Death of Franz I of Austria; succeeded by his son Ferdinand I.
1836 Glinka's *A Life for the Tsar* given, St Petersburg. Meyerbeer's *Les Huguenots* given, Paris.	
1837 Berlioz composes his *Grande messe des morts*. Liszt composes his *24 grands études*. *Zar und Zimmermann* by Albert Lortzing (1801–51) given, Leipzig. Richard Wagner (1813–83) appointed musical director in Riga. Field dies, Moscow (54). J. N. Hummel dies, Weimar (58).	**1837** Death of William IV. Succeeded by his niece Victoria in Britain, but in Hanover (under Salic law) by Ernst August, Duke of Cumberland (Victoria marries Prince Albert of Saxe-Coburg-Gotha, 1840).
1838 Schumann composes *Kinderszenen* and *Kreisleriana*. First known piano recital series given, by Ignaz Moscheles, in London. Donizetti settles in Paris.	**1838** Austrians evacuate most of the Papal States. People's Charter issued by Chartists.
1839 Chopin composes his Piano Sonata in B flat minor.	**1839** Opium war between Britain and China; Hong Kong taken.

LITERATURE, PHILOSOPHY, RELIGION	SCIENCE, TECHNOLOGY, DISCOVERY	FINE AND DECORATIVE ARTS, ARCHITECTURE
1830 Foundation of the Church of Jesus Christ of the Latter-Day Saints in New York by Joseph Smith (1805–1844). Stendhal (1788–1842) publishes *Le rouge et le noire*. First performance, in Paris, of *Hernani* by Victor Hugo (1802–85)	**1830** Charles Lyell (1797–1875) publishes *Principles of Geology*, which greatly influenced Darwin.	**1830** Eugène Delacroix (1798–1863) paints *Liberty leading the People*, celebrating the July Revolution; its mixture of realism and allegory ensured his position as leader of the French Romantic movement.
1831 Franz Grillparzer (1791–1872) Austrian dramatist, writes *Des Meeres und der Liebe Wellen*.	**1831** Michael Faraday (1791–1867) discovers electromagnetic induction. Circumnavigation by Charles Darwin.	**1831** Franz Klenze (1784–1864) begins *Valhalla*, near Regensburg, a copy of the Parthenon in honour of German heroes. Paul Delaroche (1797–1856) paints one of his most famous works, *The Little Princes in the Tower*.
1832 George Sand (1804–76) publishes *Indiana*, first of her portrayals of the struggles of individual women against social constraints.	**1832** Completion of the first continental railway, from Budweis to Linz. The chemist J. von Liebig (1803–73) and Wöhler discover the 'benzoyl radical', a cluster of atoms (C_7H_5O) that remains unchanged through a series of transformations.	**1832** Antoine-Louis Barye (1796–1875) creates the bronze *Lion Crushing a Serpent*, its violent movement and tense posture influenced by Romanticism.
1833 John Keble (1792–1866) starts the Oxford Movement, which aimed at restoring 17th-century Anglican High Church ideals. Alfred Tennyson (1809–92) begins *In Memoriam*.	**1833** Thomas Graham (1790–1857) publishes *On the Law of the Diffusion of Gases*, by which the specific gravity of gases could be determined.	**1833** Francois Rude (1784–1855) begins his famous patriotic high relief to complete the Arc de Triomphe.
1835 David Friedrich Strauss (1808–74) writes *Leben Jesu*, denying the historical foundation of super-natural elements in the gospels.	**1834** John Herschel (1792–1871) conducts astronomical observations of the southern hemisphere. Charles Babbage (1792–1871) invents the principle of the analytical engine, forerunner of the computer.	**1836** Charles Barry (1795–1860) wins the competition for the new Houses of Parliament in London, built 1839–52. Peter von Cornelius (1783–1867) works on frescoes in the Ludwigskirche, Munich.
1836 Nikolay Gogol (1809–52) writes *The Government Inspector*. Charles Dickens (1812–70) begins his literary career with *Sketches by 'Boz'* and invents Mr Pickwick.	**1837** Louis Daguerre (1787–1851) invents the daguerreotype, the first practicable process of photography.	**1837** Edward Landseer (1802–73), Queen Victoria's favourite artist, paints *The Old Shepherd's Chief Mourner*. Théodore Rousseau (1812–67), central figure of the Barbizon landscape school and pioneer of open-air painting, paints his *Avenue of Chestnut Trees*.
1839 Mikhail Lermontov (1814–41) writes his prose masterpiece, *A Hero of Our Times*. Edgar Allan Poe (1809–49) writes *Tales of the Grotesque and Arabesque*, including 'Fall of the House of Usher'.	**1838** The steamship *Great Western*, built by Isambard Brunel (1806–59), crosses the Atlantic in 15 days. **1839** William Henry Fox Talbot (1800–77) produces a photographic negative.	

The Early Romantic Period

MUSIC AND MUSICIANS	POLITICS, WAR AND RULERS
1840 Schumann, after marrying Clara Wieck, composes over a hundred songs (including the *Frauenliebe und -leben* and *Dichterliebe* cycles). Donizetti's *La fille du régiment* and *La favorite* given, Paris. Paganini dies, Nice (57).	**1840** Death of Friederich Wilhelm III of Prussia; succeeded by his son Friederich Wilhelm IV.
1841 Liszt composes his *Réminiscences de Norma* for piano. Schumann's 'symphonic year'. John Hullah opens his singing school for schoolmasters, London.	
1842 Wagner's *Rienzi* given, Dresden. Verdi's *Nabucco* given, Milan. Glinka's *Ruslan and Lyudmila* given, St Petersburg. Mendelssohn's Scottish Symphony composed. The *Sinfonie sérieuse* and *Sinfonie capricieuse* of Franz Berwald (1796–1868) composed. Schumann's Piano Quintet and other chamber works composed. The 'Classical Chamber Concerts' of Sterndale Bennett begin, London. Meyerbeer is appointed General-musikdirektor, Berlin. Cherubini dies, Paris (81).	
1843 Wagner's *Der fliegende Holländer* given, Dresden; he is appointed joint Kapellmeister there. Donizetti's *Don Pasquale* given, Paris. Berlioz's treatise on orchestration published. Leipzig Conservatory opens, with Mendelssohn its first director.	**1843** Abolition of slavery in India.
1844 Mendelssohn's Violin Concerto composed. *Hunyadi László*, by Ferenc Erkel (1810–93), the foundation of Hungarian national opera, given, Pest. Liszt's connection with the Weimar court (to produce many of his major works) begins. *The Musical Times* founded, London.	**1844** Factory Act in Britain regulates the working hours of women and children.
1845 Wagner's *Tannhäuser* given, Dresden. Schumann's Piano Concerto written. The first chamber music concerts with analytical notes, the Musical Union, begin, London.	**1846** Irish Potato Famine; Robert Peel repeals the Corn Laws in Britain.
1846 Mendelssohn's *Elijah* performed, Birmingham. Berlioz's *La damnation de Faust* performed, Paris. Adolphe Sax develops the saxophone family.	**1847** Lajos Kossuth (1802–94) elected a member of the Hungarian Diet.
1847 Verdi's *Macbeth* given, Florence.	**1848** Year of revolutions: uprisings in Sicily, Paris, Vienna (3), Venice, Berlin, Milan, Parma, Papal States, Warsaw, Prague; all suppressed except Paris, constitution granted in Prussia. Abdication of Ferdinand I of Austria; succeeded by his nephew Franz Joseph (until 1916). Abdication of Louis Philippe and French Republic proclaimed (February); Louis Napoleon, nephew of Napoleon I, becomes President (December).
1848 Glinka's *Kamarinskaya*, central to Russian nationalist music, composed. *Halka* by Stanisław Moniuszko (1819–72), the foundation of Polish national opera, given concert performance, Vilnius. Wagner flees to Weimar to escape arrest. Donizetti dies, Bergamo (50).	

LITERATURE, PHILOSOPHY, RELIGION	SCIENCE, TECHNOLOGY, DISCOVERY	FINE AND DECORATIVE ARTS, ARCHITECTURE
1841 John Henry Newman (1801–90) advocates a Roman Catholic interpretation of the 39 Articles, causing controversy in the Church of England. L. A. Feuerbach (1804–72) argues in his *Wesen des Christentums* that Christianity is an illusion. Henry Longfellow (1806–73) publishes *Ballads and Other Poems*. **1843** John Stuart Mill (1806–73) publishes *A System of Logic*, stressing the importance of inductive methods while giving deduction its proper share (his *Principles of Political Economy* appeared in 1848). **1847** Charlotte Brontë (1816–55) publishes *Jane Eyre* and Emily Brontë (1818–48) *Wuthering Heights*, William Makepeace Thackeray (1811–63) publishes *Vanity Fair*. **1848** Alexandre Dumas *fils* (1824–95) writes the novel *La Dame àux Camélias*, which he later dramatized. Elizabeth Gaskell (1810–65) writes *Mary Barton*, whose cast of working-class characters and setting in industrial Manchester were new. Anne Brontë publishes *The Tenant of Wildfell Hall*.	**1841** James Prescott Joule (1818–89) publishes *On the Production of Heat by Voltaic Electricity*. **1842** Julius Robert von Mayer (1814–78) publishes his paper *Bemerkungen uber die Krafte der unbelebten Natur*, propounding the first law of thermodynamics, on the conservation of energy. John C. Fremont (1813–90) explores the Oregon trail reaching California. Crawford W. Long (1815–78), US physician, uses ether to produce surgical anaesthesia. **1844** Samuel Morse (1791–1872) sends his first coded message over his 40-mile telegraph line from Washington to Baltimore. **1845** Alexander von Humboldt (1769–1859) publishes the first book of the *Kosmos*, describing and illustrating the history of the physical world. Sir John Franklin (1786–1847) leads an expedition to discover the north-west passage. **1846** Discovery of Neptune by John Galle. **1847** Sir James Simpson (1811–70) first uses chloroform as an anaesthetic. **1848** Richard Owen (1804–92) publishes *The Archetype and Homologies of the Vertebrate Skeleton*.	**1843** John Ruskin publishes the first of five volumes, *Modern Painters*. **1844** Turner paints *Rain, Steam and Speed*, a forerunner of Impressionism. Théodore Chassériau (1819–56), Ingres's most gifted pupil, decorates the Cour des Comptes in the Palais d'Orsay, Paris, with allegorical scenes of *Peace* and *War* (now destroyed). **1847** Thomas Couture (1815–79), French historical and portrait painter, exhibits *The Romans of the Decadence*. Gottfried Semper (1803–79), the most important German architect of the mid-19th century, builds his last building in Dresden, the Picture Gallery, in Italian Renaissance style. **1848** Jean François Millet (1814–75) paints *The Winnower*, the first of his scenes of rustic life in which he emphasized its serious and melancholy aspects. The Pre-Raphaelite Brotherhood founded in England by Holman Hunt (1827–1910), John Millais (1829–96) and Dante Gabriel Rossetti (1828–82), who aimed to recapture the sincerity and simplicity of early Italian paintings.

Index

Page numbers in *italics* refer to captions to illustrations.

Abel, C. F., 206
Abel, F. L., 271
Ablesimov, Alexander, 238
Abraham (arranger), 64, 65
Académie des Beaux-Arts, 46
a cappella movement, 12
Adam, Adolphe, *Giselle*, 54
Adelaide, Queen of Britain, 223
Adlung (Kantor), 115, 119
advertising, *see* publicity
aesthetics, 6–7, 8, 11–12, 23–8, 89–90,
        267–9
African music, *see* black music
Agoult, Countess Marie d', 67, *68*
Agricola, Johann Friedrich, 109
Aguado, Alexandre Marie, 43
Ah, ça ira!, 34, 35, 65
Alberdi, Juan Bautista, 288
Alberghi, Ignazio, 124
Albini, Marietta, 284
Albrechtsberger, Johann Georg, 86, 89
Alcedo, José Bernardo, 287
Alcorta, Amancio, 288
Alkan, Charles-Valentin, 69
Allgemeine musikalische Zeitung
    history, 10, 103, 150, 155–6
    quoted, 110, 118, 127, 133, 136
Allgemeiner musikalischer Anzeiger, 103
Alyabyev, Alexander, 249, 251, 254, 255
amateurs, 42, 214, 241, 254, 260–61, 282
    composers, 264–5
    journals and, 156
    performances by, 93, 109, 116n11, 252–3
American Music Journal, 268
'ancient' music, devotees of, 202, 203, 207,
        208;
    see also early music *and under* London
        (Concerts of Ancient Music)
Anderson, Lucy, 215
'antique' instruments, 37, *38*
Arenzana, Manuel, 283
arias, 100, 207, 211
    transposition of, 124

Arnault, Antoine-Vincent, 47
Arnold, Samuel, 274
arrangements, 64, 65, 89, 93, 255
    for military band, 132, 133
Artaria (music publishers), 103
Assen, Benedictus van, *206*
Athenaeum, 218
Auber, Daniel-François-Esprit, 46, 50, 56, 57,
        76, 136, 148, 220, 276
    Le cheval de bronze, 51
    Fra Diavolo, 51, 115
    Gustavus III, 230
    Le maçon, 51
    Manon Lescaut, 56
    La muette de Portici, 8, *9*, 13, 53, 114–15
audiences, 29
    behaviour, 164–6, 179–82, 207
    demands on, 10
    satire on attitudes of, 60–61
Austin, Mrs, 274
Ayrton, William, 213, 218, 221

Baca, Luis, 284
Bach, C. P. E., 109, 154
Bach, J. C., 206
Bach, J. S., 150
    biography of, 155
    novel about, 256
    publications of works, 154
    'revival' of, 12, 152, 209
    used as model, 59
    Goldberg Variations, 103
    St Matthew Passion, 12, 118
Bacon, Richard Mackenzie, 213, 218
Bähr, (Franz) Josef, 110
Baillot, Pierre, 33, 64–5, 71, 72, 91
Baini, Giuseppe, 12
ballet, 54, *55*, 204, 246
Ballochino (opera director), 104
balls, 123–4, 130–31, 179, *180*, 275, 277,
        277
bands, 33, 37, *38*, 132–4, 276
Barbaja, Domenico, 93, 102, 182

Barbier-Walbonne, Mme, 60
Bärmann, Heinrich, 124
Barnett, John, 228
Baroque music
  used as model, 59
  see also 'ancient' music *and* early music
Bartleman, James, 211
Batiste, Edouard, 59
Beauharnais, Eugène de, 19
Beaumarchais, Pierre-Augustin, 1–3
Beer, Herz, 128
Beer, Jakob Liebmann, *see* Meyerbeer,
  Giacomo
Beethoven, Johann van, 3
Beethoven, Ludwig van, 3–5, 8, 16, 26, 39, *68*,
    85–6, *87*, 88–9, 93–5, 103, 156,
    174n16, 255, 267
  Berlioz and, 73, 75
  chamber music, 91–2
  concerts, 92–5
  copyright, views on, 6
  Hoffmann and, 10
  influence, 218
  Liszt and, 69
  London and, 95, 211, 213, 215–16, *215*
  novel about, 256
  orchestration, 20–21
  overtures, 25–6
  performances of works by, 10, 19, 42, 44, 61,
    67, 71, 72, 73, 95, 97, 100, 115, 116,
    117, 118, 122, 126, 127, 134, 136, 148,
    151, 152, 211, 213, 215, *215*, 223, 252,
    253, 261, 288
  publications of music by, 254
  Wagner and, 19, 30, 148
  works, arrangements of, 271, 272
  An die ferne Geliebte, 25
  bagatelles, 90
  Battle Symphony, 5, *5*, 95, 122
  Choral Fantasia, 92–3, 127
  Christus am Oelberge, 122
  concertos, 211
  Coriolan, 84
  Diabelli Variations, 103
  Egmont, 5
  Fidelio, *3*, 4, 49, 146, 221
  Missa solemnis, 95, 252, 288
  Piano Concerto no.3, 215
  Piano Concerto no.4, 92, 215
  Piano Concerto no.5, 5, 215
  piano sonatas, 67
  Prometheus, 89, 127
  Rondo in C, 254
  Die Ruinen von Athen, 12–13
  Septet, 89
  string quartets, 91, 92, 118
  symphonies, arrangements of, 133, 134
  Symphony no. 1, 61, 89, 151
  Symphony no. 2, 115
  Symphony no. 3 ('Eroica'), 20, 21, 39n16,
    61, 72, 89, 92, 126, 151, 213
  Symphony no. 5, 20, 21, 61, 92, 151, 211, 213
  Symphony no. 6 ('Pastoral'), 92, 117, 126,
    213
  Symphony no. 7, 213
  Symphony no. 9, 20, 73, 95, 100, 136, 149,
    152, 215, *215*, 216
  Die Weihe des Hauses, 215
Belgium, 8, *9*
Belinsky, Vissarion Grigorievich, 246
Belleville-Oury, Anna Caroline, 255
Bellini, Vincenzo, 23, 51, 56, 148, 175, 176,
    186, 266
  Hexameron on themes from, 125
  influence, 274
  orchestration, 186
  performances of works by, 56, 148, 220, 266,
    276, 290
  politics, 192
  vocal writing, 171, 186
  I Capuleti e i Montecchi, 189
  Norma, 29, 30, 171, 186, 189n29, 194–5,
    230, 290; works based on, 67, 68–9
  Il pirata, 188, *188*, 276
  I puritani, 56, 115, 185, 186, 188
  La sonnambula, 56, 115, 172, 186, 188
Benda, Ernst Friedrich, 109
Benda, Franz, 109
Benda, Georg, 109
Benedict, Julius, 30, 230
benefit concerts, *see under* concerts
Bennett, William Sterndale, 228–9
Béranger, Pierre-Jean de, 42, 44, 57
Berezovsky, Maxim Sonzontovich, 239
Bériot, Charles- Auguste de, 125, 215
Berlin
  cathedral, and choir, 120, 121, 127
  concerts spirituels, 109
  Corsica House, 109
  court/Sanssouci, 127–8
  English House, 109
  Euterpe Orchestral Society, 111, 134
  Hofkapelle, 109–10, 111–12, 115, 116,
    117, 120, 121, 134, 135
  Hofoper, 110, 111, 112–14
  Hôtel de Paris, 116
  Konzerte für Kenner und Liebhaber, 109
  Liedertafel, 120, 143
  Musikalische Assemblée, 109
  Musikübende Gesellschaft, 109
  Nationaltheater, 110, 111
  Opera, 101, 122
  orchestral school, 117
  Philharmonic Society, 119
  Residenztheater, 114–15
  Schauspielhaus, *114*, *122*
  Singakademie, 118–19, *119*, 120, 143
  Singverein, 119
  Society of Musicians, 127
  Stern'sche Gesangverein, 121

The Early Romantic Period

Berliner musikalische Zeitung, 111, 117
Berlioz, Hector, 10, 14, 16, 19, 28, 39, 43, 44,
    54, 63, 73–8, *74, 75*, 255
  and development of symphonic poem, 25
  and Russia, 251, 253, 255
  concerts, 75–7, *75*, 104
  instrumentation, 23
  journalism, 11, 76
  Liszt and, 69
  London and, 225, 231
  on Berlin, 109
  on Italy, 166, 181
  on Méhul, 49
  performances of works by, 54, 74, 77–8,
    255
  Wagner and, 148
  Béatrice et Bénédict, 77
  Benvenuto Cellini, 54, 74–5, *74*, 229
  La damnation de Faust, 30, 59, 76, 104
  L'enfance du Christ, 49, 77
  Grande messe des morts, 20, 58–9, 75
  Harold en Italie, 25, 75
  Lélio, 74
  Les nuits d'été, 58
  Roméo et Juliette, 30, 75, 76, 104
  songs, 57–8
  Symphonie fantastique, 25, 28, 73–4, 75
  Symphonie funèbre et triomphale, 59, 75
  Les troyens, 77–8
  Traité de l'instrumentation, 22–3, 73
Bernard, N., 255
Bertati, Giovanni, 168
Berton, Henri-Montan, 34, 57
Best, Anthony, *21*
Best, Mary Ellen, *21*
Bethlehem Seminary, *263*, 264
Beutler, Herr, 132
Bianchi, Francesco, 169, 205
Billings, William, 264–5
Billington, Elizabeth, 205
Bilse, Benjamin, 135
biographies, 155, 256
Bishop, Anna, 221
Bishop, Henry, 213, 220, 221, 225
Bizet, Georges, 56
black music, 265, 267, 276–8, 285
black people, 275, 276–8, *277*, 285, 286–7,
    289
Blangini, Joseph, 57
Bliesener brothers, 116
Bliesener (clarinettist), 115
blues, 265
Blume (singer), 133
Blyma, Franz Xaver, 248
Boccaccio, Giovanni, 239
Boccherini, Luigi, 64, 71
Bochsa, Nicolas, 217, 221
Bocquillon, Guillaume (Wilhelm), 44, 57
Boëly, Alexandre, 59
Boesi, José Antonio Caro de, 286–7

Bogotá
  Academia Nacional de Música, 287
  Sociedad Filarmónica, 287
Bohrer, Herr, 114
Boieldieu, François-Adrien, 49–50, 57, 62,
    73, 132
  in St Petersburg, 248
  La dame blanche, 50, 276
  Jean de Paris, 111, 144
Bologna, Accademia Filarmonica, 163, 239
Bonaparte, Jérome, 4, 85
Bonaparte, Joseph, 19
Bonaparte, Louis-Napoleon, *see* Napoleon III
Bonaparte, Napoleon, *see* Napoleon I
Bondini, Pasquale, 150
Boosey, Thomas, 229
Borra, Giulio, *193*
Bortnyansky, Dmitry, 239, 241, 249
Boston
  Boston Academy of Music, 272
  Federal Theater, 269, 270
  Handel and Haydn Society, 270–1, 272
  Musical Academy, 270
  Philharmonic Society, 270
  Boston Musical Gazette, 272
Botkin, Vasily, 256
Braham, John, 205, 215
Brahms, Johannes, 28, 63, 79, 100, 105
Brambilla, Giovanni, 84–5
Branchu, Caroline, 50
brass instruments, 22, *24*, 37, *38*, 53, 240, *240*,
    264
Breitkopf, Bernhard Christoph, 155
Breitkopf, Bernhard Theodor, 242
Breitkopf, Christoph Gottlob, 154
Breitkopf, Johann Gottlob Immanuel, 153–4
Breitkopf & Härtel, 6, 10, 103, 150, 153–4
Brendel, Franz, 90, 156
Brenndel, Franz, 90, 156
Brenglas, Adam, *126*
Bridgetower, George, 207
Brief, I., 254
Broadwood (piano-makers), 229
Brockhaus (publishers), 155
Brown, Francis, H., *259*
Brubi, Antonio, 37
Bruckner, Anton, 89, 105
Brühl, Karl von, 112, 122
Brussels, 8, *9*
buccin, 37, *38*
Buenos Aires
  cathedral, 288
  Escuala de Música y Canto, 288
  Sociedad Filarmónica, 288
  Teatro Coliseo, 289
  Teatro de la Ranchería, 289
  Teatro de Operas y Comedias, 289
Bull, Ole, 255
Bülow, Hans von, 112
Bunn, Alfred, 230
Bureau de Musique (publishers), 154

Index

Burghersh, Lord, 216, 217
Burgmüller, Frederick, 55
Burke, Edmund, 192
Burney, Charles, 213
Byron, George Gordon, Lord, 68, 75, 184,
    186

Caecilian movement, 102–3
Caldwell, James, 276
Calkin, James, 228
Callcott, John Wall, 209–10, 210
Cannabich, Christian, 115
Canobbio, Carlo, 241
Canthal (conductor), 135
Caracas
    Academia de Música, 286
    Coliseo/Teatro Publico, 287
    Teatro Caracas, 287
    Teatro de la Zarzuela, 287
    Teatro Municipal, 287
Carmagnole, La, 34
Carr, Benjamin, 273, 274–5
Carr, Thomas, 274
Carreño, José Cayetano, 286
Casper, Johann Ludwig, 129, 130
Castelli, J. F., 103
Casti, Giambattista, 169
Castil-Blaze, 53–4
castratos, 167, 187, 188–9
Catalani, Angelica, 112, 124, 252, 255
Catel, Charles, 18, 33, 34, 47, 61
Catherine II (the Great), Empress of Russia,
    236, 238–9
Cavaillé-Coll, Aristide, 59
Cavos, Catterino, 247, 248, 249
celebrations/ceremonies, 40, 41; see also
    festivals
censorship/censors
    in England, 202, 210, 220, 221, 230–1
    in France, 42, 44, 46–7
    in Italy, 169, 175, 182, 192
Cesari, Adela, 284
chamber music, 20, 21, 64–5, 70–2, 89,
    91–2, 264
    concerts of, 91–2, 116, 117, 118, 125, 225
chant, 59, 249–52
Chappell, Samuel, 229
Charles Felix, King of Sardinia, 162
Charles III, King of Naples, 160
Chateaubriand, Francois René, Vicomte de,
    3, 51
Chelard, Hippolyte-André-Baptiste, 221
Chénier, M.-J., 47
Cherubini, Luigi, 39, 47, 49, 61
    and Paris Conservatoire, 33, 41, 46, 61
    Berlioz and, 78
    in London, 211, 213
    influence, 49, 51
    performances of works by, 72, 97, 115, 247,
        252

politics, 4, 34, 39, 41, 49
Ali Baba, 115
Les deux journées, 49, 144, 244
Lodoïska, 48, 49, 127, 144
Marche religieuse, 58
Médée, 48, 48, 49
Requiem, 59, 119
sacred works, 58, 59
songs, 57
string quartets, 64, 71
Symphony in D, 63
children, 37, 44, 207, 228
Chopin, Fryderyk, 8, 16, 22, 26, 65, 66,
    69–70, 70, 90, 129
    Bellini compared to, 186
    Liszt and, 69
    London and, 231
    piano concertos, 100
    piano sonatas, 22
Chorley, Henry, 218
Choron, Alexandre, 12, 41, 43, 59
choruses/choirs, 104, 112, 132–3, 270
    benefits for, 122
    boys', 99
    concerts by, 118–21, 127
    in Latin America, 282, 283
    in London, 208
    in Vienna, 93
    male, 97, 120–1, 208
Christy, E. P., 267
    Minstrels, 266
Cicéri, Pierre-Luc-Charles, 53
Cimarosa, Domenico, 40, 169, 205, 238
    church music, 190
    Il matrimonio segreto, 169, 170, 244
    Gli Orazi e i Curiazi, 167
clarinet, 21–2, 23
class, 55
    and appreciation of music, 6–7
    and participation in music, 44, 214
    and subject matter of opera, 49
    audiences', 43–4, 73, 93, 111, 135, 179,
        202, 203, 209, 223, 225, 226
    in Austria, 85–6
    in Berlin, 110–11
    in Latin America, 280–2, 283–4
    in Vienna, 93
    Liszt and, 67–8
'classical'/'classics' of music, early uses of
    term, 10, 202, 203
Clementi, Muzio, 10, 88, 154, 207, 213, 218,
    229
Clementi (piano-makers), 10
Clementi (publishers), 6, 229
Cocks, Robert, 229
Colbran, Isabella, 182
Collin, Heinrich Joseph von, 84, 103
Colón, Pedro Nolasco, 286–7
Colonne, Edouard, 77
Comelli, Adele, 188

311

composers
  conditions, 177
  Latin American, grants for, 282
  players rather than singers, 207
  speed of work on operas, 176–7, 190, 195
  training, 175–6
concertos, 207, 210–11, 225, 232
concerts, 7–8, 44
  benefit, 43, 95, 121–4, 125, 206–8,
    219–20, 252
  Berlioz's, 75–7, *76*, 104
  finances, 60, 75, 76, 93, 111, 121–2, 124,
    207–8
  in Berlin, 109–12, 115–30, 132–7
  in Dresden, 143
  in houses, 95, 97, 109, 128–30
  in Latin America, *281*, 287, 288
  in Leipzig, 143–4, 151–3
  in London, 95, 120, 202–3, 204–9, *209*,
    210–13, 214–16, *215*, 218–20, *220*,
    222, 223–6, *224*, *227*, 229–30, 231–2
  in Paris, 60–2, *62*, 71–3, 76, 77, 226
  in Russia, 252–4
  in USA, 269, 275, 277–8
  in Vienna, 88, 89, 91–7, 99–102, 104
  length, 207, 212
  private, 202, 218–19
  promenade, 226, *227*
  repertory, 10, 60, 62–4, 93–7, 99–102, 115–
    16, 118–20, 121–2, 127, 133–5, 207,
    210–11, 212, *215*, 223–6, 231–2, 269
  restrictions on audiences, 202, 210
  Schubert's, 95, 96
  subscription, 72–3, 111, 115, 116, 119, 151,
    202, 208, 210
  ticket prices, 73, 111, 124, 134, 151, 202,
    207, 210, 219, 223, 226
conducting, 19–20, 212–13, 225, 229
Conradi, August, 134
Conservatoire National Supérieur de
  Musique, *see* Paris, Conservatoire
contests, 88
Cooke, Thomas S., 228
copyright, 6, 191, 195
Corelli, Arcangelo, 202, 208, 267
Corelli, Jean, *55*
Corri, Philip Anthony, 210
Costa, Michael, 230, 231
Cramer, François, 210
Cramer, John Baptist, 207, 210, 213, 218, 229
Cramer, William, 206, 207, 210
Cramer (piano-makers), 229
criticism, 96, 213, 216, 218–19, 228, 229, 255,
  256, 261, 267–9; *see also* journals
Crotch, William, 217
Cruikshank, George, *203*
Cuba
  Academia de Música, 285
  Academia de Música S Cecilia, 285
Czerny, Carl, 66, 93

Dalayrac, Nicolas-Marie, 39, 276
Dance, William, 210
dancing, 16–18, *17*, 93, *101*, 123–4, 130–1,
    130, 179, *180*, 275, 276, 277, *277*, *281*, 285
Dancla, Charles, 71
Danhauser, Josef, *68*
Danton, Georges Jacques, 35
Danzi, Franz, 119–20
Da Ponte, Lorenzo, 205
Dargomïzhsky, Alexander Sergeyevich, 246,
    249, 254, 255, 256
Dauprat, Louis François, 72
David, Félicien, 44, 73, 75–6
  Le désert, 13, 59, 75
  Lalla-Roukh, 76
  Le perle du Brésil, 76
David, Ferdinand, 152
David, Giovanni, 189n29
Davïdov, Stepan Ivanovich, 248
Davis, John, 276
Davison, James William, 218, 228
Debussy, Claude, 58, 79
Degtyaryov, Stepan Anikiyevich, 239, 241,
    246, 255
Dehn, Siegfried, 89
Delacroix, Eugène, 44, *69*, *77*
Della Maria, Pierre, 49
Démachy, P. A., *36*
Dessauer, Josef, 100
Deutsche Allgemeine Zeitung, 155
Devienne, François, 60, 61
Devrient, Eduard, 112, 129, 130
Devrient, Wilhelmine, *see* Schröder-Devrient,
    Wilhelmine
Diabelli, Anton, 6, 103
Dibdin, Charles, 205
Dittersdorf, Carl Ditters von, 269
Dixmerie, Nicolas-Bricaire de la, 39
Doche, Joseph, 57
Doebbelin, C. T., 110
Döhler, Theodor von, 125
Doles, Johann Friedrich, 151
Dolgoruky, Prince, 243
Donizetti, Gaetano, 23, 44, 56, 102, 115, 175,
    176, 186, 189, 190–1, 196, 220
  and Naples, 163
  Rossini and, 174
  politics, 192
  Anna Bolena, 56
  Dom Sébastien, 53
  Don Pasquale, 191
  Don Sebastiano, 102
  L'elisir d'amore, 191
  La favorite, 53
  Linda di Chamonix, 102
  Lucia di Lammermoor, 29, 184, 189, 191
  Lucrezia Borgia, 182, 191
  Maria di Rohan, 102, *102*
  Maria Stuarda, *183*
  Les martyrs, 53

Donzelli, Domenico, 189n29, 215
Dorn, Heinrich, 130
Dotzauer, Johann Friedrich, 148
Dresden
    Dreyssigsche Singakademie, 143
    Hofkapelle, 142, 143
    Hofoper, 142–3
    Hoftheater, 143, *143, 149*
    Liederkreis, 142
    Liedertafel, 143
    Opera, 144–9
    Theater auf dem Linckeschen Bade, 142
    Tonkünstlerverein, 143
Dreyschock, Alexander, 125
Du Mont, Henri, 59
Dubois, Théodore, 46
Dubyansky, Fëdor, 241, 242
Duchambge, Pauline, 57
Dumas, Alexandre (the elder), *68*
Duparc, Henri, 58
Duport, J. P., J. L., 110
Duprez, Gilbert-Louis, 54, 189
Dussek, Jan Ladislav, 65, 127, 154, 203, 218
Dutch Academy, 12
Duvernoy, Frédéric Nicolas, 33, 60, 62, 63–4
Dwight, John Sullivan, 269
Dyer, S. O., *277*

early music
    performances of, 12, *12*, 97, 152, 202, 208, 226
    publications of, 97, 154, 155, 209
    studies of, 12
    used in churches, 59, 102–3
    see also 'ancient' music
Ecstedt, A. I. Fitztum von, 253
Edelmann, Jean-Frédéric (the elder), 285
Edelmann, Jean-Frédéric (the younger), 285
education, musical, 18–19, 33, 117, 118, 161, 175–6
    for working-class children, 226–8
    in Berlin, 117, 118
    in Latin America, 282, 283, 285, 290
    in London, 213–14, 216–17, 226–8
    in Russia, 252
    in USA, 262, 264, 268, 272
Egyptian melodies, 13
electricity, 4
Elízaga, José Mariano, 283
Elleviou, Jean, 48
Elsler, Fanny, 95, 102
Eltz, Josef, *85*
Emerson, Ralph Waldo, 20
Engel, G., 137
Engel (conductor), 135
Erard (piano makers), 65
Erdödy, Countess Marie von, 86
Ernst, Heinrich Wilhelm, 125
Esnaola, Juan Pedro, 288
Esterházy, Count Valentin, 236, 239

'Ethiopian songs', 267
Eunicke, Johanna, 112, 115
Euterpeiad, The, 267–8
exoticism, 12–13
Eybler, Joseph, 102, 103

Falcon, Cornélie, 53
Fasch, Carl Friedrich Christian, 118
Fauré, Gabriel, 58, 59, 79
Fechner, Mme (pianist), 128
festivals
    music, 7, 96–7
    revolutionary, 35–7, *36, 38,* 59
Fétis, François-Joseph, 12, 64, 67
Field, John, 10, 207, 252, 255
Fink, Gottfried Wilhelm, 136
Fischer, Joseph, 112, 115
Flemming (composer), 117
Florence, Teatro Pergola, *185*
flute, 21
Focosi, A., *165*
Fodor-Mainvielle, Joséphine, 255
folk music, 131, 239, 247, 287–8
Fomin, Evstigney Ipatovich, 238, 239–40
Forkel, Johann Nikolaus, 155
Foster, Stephen, 20, 267
Fragonard, Alexandre Evariste, *14*
France
    revolution of 1789, 32, 46, 110
    revolution of 1830, 20, 42
    revolution of 1848, 44–5
    see also Paris
Franck, César, 25, 59, 79
Franklin, Benjamin, 264
Frezzolini, Erminia, 248
Friedrich, Caspar David, *27*
Fröhlich, Josephine, *94*
Fry, William, 274
Fry, William Henry, 274
Fürstenau, Anton Bernhard, 148

Gade, Niels, 135
Gail, Sophie, 57
Gallardo, Lino, 286–7
Galletti, Andrea, 244
Galli, Filippo, 189, 284
Galuppi, Baldassare, 238, 239, 240
Ganz brothers, 117–18
Garat, Pierre-Jean, 57, 60
Garcia, José Maurício Nunes, 289–90
García, Manuel (the elder), 30, 51, 284
    family, 30
García, Pauline, *see* Viardot-García, Pauline
Gardiner, William, 271
gas lights, 4
Gautherot, Mme, 203
Gautier, Théophile, 58
Gaveaux, Pierre, 35, 49

Gay, Claudio, *281*
Geiger, A., *90*, *101*
Geminiani, Francesco, 202, 208
Gern, Georg, 120
Gerstenberg, Johann Daniel, 242
Geyer, Floduard, 120–1
Gilbert, W. S., 190
Giornale musicale del Teatro Italiano di St Petroburgo, 241–2
glees, 217
Glinka, Mikhail Ivanovich, 239, 246, *247*, 249, 251–2, 254, 255, 256
    A Life for the Tsar, 20, 248, *250*
    Ruslan and Lyudmila, 248
Gluck, Christoph Willibald von, 33, 50, 51, 73, 114, 132
    Berlioz and, 78
    operas described as revolutionary, 1
    Rossini and, 147
    Wagner and, 148
    Alceste, 112, 148, 164
    Armide, 148
    Iphigénie en Aulide, 148
    Iphigénie en Tauride, 47
Goethe, J. W. von, *6*, 7, 73, *77*, *96*, 119, 141
Gogol, Nikolay Vasilyevich, 246
Gómez, José Antonio, 183
Gossec, François-Joseph, 18, 33, 34, 37, 41, 61, 62, 63
    Marche lugubre, 61
    Offrande à la liberté, 47
    Père de l'univers, 37
Gottlieb, Johann, 109
Gottschalk, Louis Moreau, 286
Götzenburger, Jakob, *12*
Gounod, Charles, 56, 59, 79
    Faust, 30
    Roméo et Juliette, 30
Gozzi, Carlo, 185
grands motets, 32–3, 38
Granville, J. J., *45*
Graun, Carl Heinrich, 109
    Der Tod Jesu, 109, 118
Graupner, Catherine, 269, 270
Graupner, Gottlieb, 269–70
Greatorex, William, 208
Gregorian chant, *see* chant
Grétry, André-Ernest-Modeste, 47, 50, 246
    Les deux avares, 244
    Richard Coeur-de-lion, 47
Griboedov, Alexander Sergeyevich, 245
Griesbach, John Henry, 228
Grillparzer, Franz, 84, 86, *94*
Grisi, Carlotta, *55*
Grisi, Giulia, 51
Gross (cellist), 110
Grund, Francis J., 259
Guardasoni, Domenico, 150
Guasco (singer), *102*

Guglielmi, Pietro Alessandro, 169
Guhr, Karl, 221
Guilmant, Alexandre, 59
guitar, 254
Gungl, Josef, 134–5
Gurilyov, Alexander, 254
Gutiérrez y Espinosa, Felipe, 286
Gyrowetz, Adalbert, 95

Haak (violinist), 110
Habeneck, François-Antoine, 8, 19, 42, 61, 62, 72–3, 74–6
Halévy, Fromental, 44, 115, 196
    La juive, 29, 53, 55, 196
Handel, George Frideric, 99, 103, 202, 216, 267
    performances of works by, 96–7, 152, 208, 223, 252, 268, 270–1, 273
    Alexander's Feast, 118
    Belshazzar, *98*, 118
    Israel in Egypt, 118
    Jephtha, 118
    Joshua, 118
    Judas Maccabeus, 118, 129
    Messiah, 118, 120, 129, 271
    Samson, 127
    Semele, 129
    Solomon, 118
    Te Deum, 127
Hanslick, Eduard, 15, 90, 97, 100, 101–2, 104
Hansmann (organist), 119
Harmonicon, 218, 220
harmony, 21–2, 169
harpsichords, 226
Harrison, Samuel, 211
Härtel, Gottfried Christoph, 154, 156; *see also* Breitkopf & Härtel
Hasenclever, J. P., *129*
Haslinger, Tobias, 103
Hasse, Johann Adolf, 142
Hauptmann, Moritz, 89
Hausmann (cellist), 110
Hawes, William, 229
Haydn, Joseph, 33, 86, 99, 103, 203, 216, 255, 267, 290
    arrangements of works by, 133, 271, 272
    Barbaja and, 182
    in London, 206, 207, 207–8
    influence, 218
    Mayr and, 169
    performances of works by, 2, 60, 62, 71, 72, 97, 101, 116, 118, 122, 134, 136, 151, 152, 223, 241, 252, 253, 255, 268, 269, 270–71, 273
    publications of works by, 153, 154, 254, 274
    Rossini and, 174
    The Creation, 101, 118, 122, 151, 271
    masses, 119–20
    The Seasons, 101, 118, 151
    string quartets, 64

Hegel, G. W. F., 4
Heine, Heinrich, 11
Heinrich, Anthony Philip, 261–2, *262*
Heller, Stephen, 65
Hensel, Fanny, *see* Mendelssohn, Fanny
Henselt, Adolf von, 252
Herbst, Johannes, 264
Herke (teacher), 252
Hérold, Ferdinand, 50, 51
Herz, Henri, 8, 15, 65, 67
Hexameron on themes from Bellini, 125
Hiller, Ferdinand, 65, 129
Hiller, Johann Adam, 150, 151, 153
Hillier, Catherine (Catherine Graupner), 269,
    270
Himmel, Friedrich, 111, 144
Hoffmann, E. T. A., 7, 10, 12, 89, 91, 114, 120,
    156
    Undine, 114
Hoffmeister, Franz Anton, 89, 154
Hoffmeister & Kühnel (publishers), 150
Holst, Fräulein von, 132
Hopkinson, Joseph, 274
horn bands, 240, *240*
Horsley, Charles Edward, 228
Hugo, Victor, 44, 45, 54, *68*, 75, 186, 191
    Hernani, 44, *45*
    Les misérables, 44
    Le roi s'amuse, 182
Hullah, John, 226–8
Hummel, Johann Nepomuk, 65, 86, 221,
    252
    concerts, 99, 207, 215, 219–20, 252
    performances of works by, 211
    publications of works by, 274
    Septet, 89
Hünerfürst (conductor), 135
Hünten, Franz, 8, 15
hymns, 265, 272
    see also revolutionary hymns

Iffland, August Wilhelm, 111, 112
impresarios, 182, 242
improvisation, contests in, 88
Indy, Vincent d', 59
Institut National de Musique, *see* Paris,
    Conservatoire
instrument-making, 22, *24*, 37, 42, 44, 229
instrumentalists, *see* string playing *and*
    wind playing; *see also* education
instrumentation, *see* orchestration
Isabey, Jean Baptiste, *14*
Isouard, Nicolas (Nicolò), 49, 276
    Cendrillon, 144
Ituarte, Julio, 284–5

Jackson, Andrew, 259
Jackson, George K., 270
Jadin, Louis, 57, 65
Janet, G., *52*

Janiewicz, Felix, 207
jazz, 165
Jeitteles, Alois, 25
Jews, 15–16, 99, 128, 216
Jewson, Frederick Bowen, 228
'Jim Crow', 265–6, *266*
Joachim, Joseph, *125*, 129, 130
Joseph II, Holy Roman Emperor, 4, 84,
    143
Joséphine, Empress, 51
journalism/journals, 8, 10, 11, 15, 44, 103,
    105, 111, 123, 150, 153, 155–6, 183,
    213, 218, 241–2, 254–5, 267–8
Jullien, Louis, 226, *227*, 231

Kalkbrenner, Friedrich, 65, 67, 71,
    211
Kanne, Franz August, 103
Karamzin, Nikolay Mikhailovich, 245
Kashin, Daniil, 249, 255
Kastner, Jean-George, 22
Kauer, Ferdinand, 144
Kemble, Adelaide, 230
Kenner, Josef, *91*
Khandoshkin, Ivan Yevstafyevich, 242
Khmel'nitsky (writer), 247
Khripunov, Yury, 243
Kiesewetter, Christoph Gottfried, 214
Kiesewetter, Raphael Georg, 12, 97
Kind, Friedrich, 99
Kinsky, Prince Ferdinand Bonaventura, 5
Klein, Bernhard, 120, 128, 129
Klein, Elisabeth, 128
Klein, Lili, 128
Klopstock, Friedrich Gottlieb, 7, 88
Knyazhnin, Jakov, 240
Knyvett, Charles, 211
Koch, Heinrich Gottfried, 150
Körner, Th., 127
Kovalëva, Praskov'ya, 241
Kozłowski, Józef, 241
Kraisil, Ludwig, *94*
Kreutzer, Konradin, *Nachtlager von Granada*,
    99
Kreutzer, Rodolphe, 34, 47, 62
    Lodoïska, 48
    violin concertos, 115, 116, 127
Kroll, Josef, 134, 135, 136, 137
Krylov, Ivan Andreyevich, 245
Kühnel, Ambrosius, 154
Kullak, Theodor, 128
Küstner, Karl Theodor von, 115

Laade (conductor), 135
Lablache, Luigi, 51, 189
Lacépède, Etienne de, 63
Lachner, Franz, *94*
Lafermière (librettist), 239
Lamas, José Angel, 286
Lamennais, Félicité de, 44

Lamoureux, Charles, 77
Lanari, Alessandro, 182
Landaeta, Juan José, 286–7
Lanner, Joseph, 16, 97, 99, 100, 103–4
Laporte, Pierre, 221–3, 230
Larrazábal, Felipe, 287
Laube, Heinrich, 155
Le Brun (horn player), 110
Lecerf (conductor), 127
Lefèvre, Xavier, 62, 63–4
Leidel (conductor), 132
Leipzig, 101, 103
   Conservatory, 153, 230
   Gewandhaus, *153*
   Gewandhaus concerts, 149, 151–3, *154*,
     155
   Gewandhaus Quartet, 151
   Grosses Concert, 151
   Liedertafel, 150
   Musikausübende Gesellschaft, 151
   Singakademie, 150
   Stadttheater, 150–51
   Thomaskirche, 150, 151
Leipziger Allgemeine Zeitung, 155
Leipziger Lesegesellschaft, 155
Leipziger Zeitung, 155
Lemmens, Jacques-Nicolas, 59
Lemoine, Gustave, 57
Léon, Tomás, 284
Lepsius, Elisabeth, 128
Lepsius, Richard, 128
Lermontov, Mikhail Yuryevich, 246
Lessing, Gotthold Ephraim, 7, 141
Lesueur, Eustache, *34*
Le Sueur, Jean-François, 18, 33, 34, 40, 41,
    47, 49, 58, 73
   La caverne, 48
   La mort d'Adam, 50
   Ossian, 50
   sacred works, 58, 59
   Le triomphe de Trajan, 50
Lichnowsky, Prince Carl von, 86
Liebig, Karl, 135, 137
lieder, 25–6, 27, 92, 100
lighting, 4
Lind, Jenny, *11*, 30, 97, 112, 125, 128, 129,
    154, 231, 255
Lipinski, Carl, 148
Liszt, Cosima, 67
Liszt, Franz, 10, *22*, 65, 66, 67–9, *68*, 78, 228,
    253, 255
   and class, 67–8
   and education, 44
   and London, 231, 232
   Berlioz and, 25
   Chopin and, 69
   concerts, 125, *126*, 129, 214–15, 226
   journalism, 11, 67, 68
   Années de pèlerinage, 68
   Ce qu'on entend sur la montagne, 25

Harmonies poétiques et religieuses, 68
Lyon, 67–8
Paraphrase on themes from *Norma*, 68–9
piano concertos, 100
Piano Sonata in B minor, 22
Les préludes, 25
literature, 7, 54, 73, 84–5, 89–90, 141, 184,
    191, 245–7
   as entertainment in 'soirées', 127
   novels about music, 256
lithography, 4
Litolff, Henry, 130
Lobe, J. C., 147, 148n8
Lobkowitz, Prince F. J. von, 5, 92
Locatelli, Pietro Antonio, 242
Loiseau, Louis-Luc, 50
Lomakin, Gavriil Yakimovich, 251
Lomonosov, Mikhail Vasilyevich, 245
London, 95, 201
   Almack Rooms, 206
   Argyll Rooms, 206
   Chapel Royal, 208
   Concerts d'Hiver, 226
   Concerts of Ancient Music (Ancient
    Concerts), 206, 208, 211, 216, 217, 223,
    229
   Covent Garden Theatre, 202, 203, *203*, 205,
    206, *206*, 213, 220, 221, 223, 226, *227*,
    230–1
   Crown and Anchor Tavern, 206, 210
   Drury Lane Theatre, 202, 203, 205, 206,
    220, 221, 223, 226, 231
   Exeter Hall, 216, 226
   Hanover Square Rooms, 206, *224*
   King's Theatre (Her Majesty's Theatre),
    203, 204, *204*, 206, 213, *220*, 221–23,
    222, 230, 231
   Philharmonic Society, 19, 20, 210–13,
    214–16, *215, 221, 223, 224*, 225,
    229–30, 231–2
   Professional Concerts, 206–7, 210, 211
   Royal Academy of Music, 217, 221, 228
   royal court, 208–9, 223
   Royal Society of Musicians, 214
   Sacred Harmonic Society, 216, 226, 231
   St James's Palace, 208–9
   St Paul's Cathedral choir, 209
   Vocal Concerts, 211
   Westminster Abbey, and choir, 208, 216
   Willis Rooms, 206
Lortzing, Albert, 123, 135, 150–1
   Die beiden Schützen, 151
   Der Wildschütz, 151
   Zar und Zimmermann, 20, 115, 151
Louis-Philippe, King of France, 42–3,
    59
Lucas, Charles, 228
Lully, Jean-Baptiste, 41
Lumley, Benjamin, 223, 230–1
Lütke, L. E., *114*

L'vov, Alexey Fyodorovich, 249, 251, 256
L'vov, Fyodor, 251
L'vov, N. A., 239
Lyre, The, 268
Lyser, Johann Peter Theodor, *87*

Macfarren, George Alexander, 228
Maclise, Daniel, *220*
Maddox, Michael, 242, 243, 244–5
Maelzel, Johann Nepomuk, 4
Magazin muzkal'nykh uveseleniy, 242
Mahler, Gustav, 27
Mainzer, Joseph, 226–8
Malibran, Maria, 51
Manfredini, Vincenzo, 238
Manfroce, Nicola, 167, 169n13
Manns, August, 135
Mantius, Eduard, 112
Manzoni, A., 191
Mara, Gertud Elisabeth, 124n33
Marcello, Benedetto, 208
Mareš, Jan Antonín, 240
Mario, Giovanni Matteo, 248
market forces and music, 6, 8–10, 43
Marschner, Heinrich
    Hans Heiling, 114, 115
    Der Templer und die Jüdin, 115
    Der Vampyr, 150
Marseillaise, La, 34–5, *34*, 37, 47
Martín y Soler, Vicente, 205
Martini, Giovanni Battista (Padre), 163,
    189–90, 239, 246
Marx, Adolph Bernhard, 129
Marx, Pauline, 112, 148
Mason, Lowell, 271–2
Massenet, Jules, 56
Matinsky, Mikhail, 238, 239
Matthäi, August, 151
Maurício, José, 289–90
Mayer, Charles, 252
Mayr, Johann Simon, 169, 174, 175
    Medea in Corinto, 167–9
meaning in music, 7, 23–6, 28
Mechanics' Institutes, 228
Méhul, Etienne-Nicolas, 38, 40, 47, 49, 57, 61
    and Paris Conservatoire, 18, 61
    Berlioz and, 78
    performances of works by, 97, 115, 132
    politics, 4, 34
    La caverne, 48
    Chant du départ, 35
    Héléna, 144
    Horatius Coclès, 47
    L'irato, 244
    Le jeune Henri, 63
    Joseph, 49, 144
    Joseph in Aegypten, 112
    symphonies, 63
    Uthal, 49

Meignen, Leopold, 274
Meissonnier, Jean-Antoine, 57
Menageot, F.-G., *13*
Mendelssohn, Abraham, 128, 129–30
Mendelssohn, Fanny, 130
Mendelssohn, Felix, 7, 10, 19, 129–30, *152*
    and early music, 12, 118, 152
    and London, 225, 229–30, 231–2
    concerts, 7–8, 151–3, 215, 225
    conducting, 225
    on meaning in music, 7
    painting, *25*
    performances of works by, 71, 101, 119, 120,
        133, 134, 152, *154*, 253
    Schumann on, 15–16
    Sterndale Bennett and, 228
    teaching, 152
    Die beiden Pädagogen, 130
    chamber music, 20
    Fingal's Cave, 25
    Die Heimkehr aus der Fremde, 130
    Meerestille und glückliche Fahrt, 133
    Der Onkel aus Boston, 130
    piano concertos, 152
    St Paul, 15, 20, 101, 152
    Songs Without Words, 7
    Symphony no. 3 ('Scottish'), 152
    Symphony no. 4 ('Italian'), *25*
    Violin Concerto, 152
    Die wandernden Komödianten, 130
Mendelssohn, Leah (Leah Salomon),
    129–30
Menzel, Adolph, *125*
Mercadante, Saverio, 56, 186–7
Metastasio, Pietro, 84–5, 166–7
metronome, 4
Metternich, Prince Klemens, 67
Mexico/Mexico City
    Coliseo Nuevo/Teatro Principale, 283, 284
    Conservatorio Nacional de Música, 283
    Philharmonic Academy, 283
    Sociedad Filarmónica Mexicana, 283
    Teatro de Las Gallos, 284
Meyer, H. J., 135–6
Meyer, Léopold de, 65
Meyer (conductor), 135
Meyerbeer, Giacomo, 13–15, 39, 51, 53, 56,
    76, 127, 128, 129, 148, 196, 255
    and education, 44
    Berlioz and, 75
    instrumentation, 23
    performances of works by, 51, *52*, 53, 112,
        114, 115, 133, 148, 220, 221, 247–8,
        255
    Wagner and, 14, 39, 53, 148
    L'africaine, 78
    Il crociato in Egitto, 51
    Emma di Resburgo, 112, 145
    Ein Feldlager in Schlesien, 114, 133
    Das Hoffest von Ferrara, 114

Meyerbeer, Giacomo *cont'd*
　Les Huguenots, 13, 14–15, 20, 30, 53, 54, 196, 226
　Le prophète, *14, 52*, 54–5, 78, 196
　Robert le diable, 14, 29, 53, 54, 115, 147, 221, 247–8
Milan
　musical education in, 19, 175–6
　La Scala, 102, 162, 163, *165, 171*, 176, *180, 183*, 195
Milder-Hauptmann, Anna, 112, 129
military bands, 132–4
Miller (theorist), 252
'minstrelsy', 265–7
Mitterwurzer, Anton, 148
Molitor, Simon, 97
Momigny, Jérôme-Joseph de, 59
Monpou, Hippolyte, 57
Monsigny, Pierre-Alexandre, 244, 246
Montero, José, 287
Monteverdi, Claudio, 176
Moore, T., 263
Morales, Melesio, 284
Moralt, Georg, 128
Moralt, Joseph, 128
Morelli, Francesco, 244
Morichelli, Anna, 60
Morlacchi, Francesco, 146–7, 148
　Tebaldo e Isolina, 146
Moscheles, Ignaz, 16–18, 93, 129, 153, 215, 216
　and London, 16–18, 215, 216, 229–30
　conducting, 216, 225
　historical concerts, 226
　performances of works by, 125
Moscow
　Petrovsky Theatre, 243–4, 245
　Vauxhall Theatre, 244
　Znamenka Theatre, 243
Mosel, Ignaz von, 103
Möser, Carl, 110, 111, 115, 116–18, 124
Mozart, Leopold, 18
Mozart, Wolfgang Amadeus, 25, 86, 88, 103, 163, 169, 203, 207, 216, 255, 267
　arrangements of works by, 133, 271, 272
　Barbaja and, 182
　biography of, 256
　concerts commemorating, 93
　influence, 218
　Lortzing and, 151
　Mayr and, 169
　Paer and, 147
　performances of works by, 51, 61, 71, 72, 97, 99, 112, *113*, 114, 115, 116, 118, 119–20, 121, 127, 129, 134, 136, 144, 150, 152, 209, 211, 213, 215, 221, 223–5, 244, 252, 253, 255, 262, 273, 290
　publications of works by, 154–5, 254, 274
　Rossini and, 174

　La clemenza di Tito, 167
　concertos, 211, 215
　Così fan tutte, 112
　Don Giovanni, 14, *15*, 51, 99, 144, 150, 213, 290
　Die Entführung aus dem Serail, 144
　Idomeneo, 167, 188
　masses, 119–20
　Le nozze di Figaro, 150, 170, 213
　Requiem, 87, 118, 120, 121, 252
　Symphonies nos. 39–41, 61, 116
　Die Zauberflöte, 87, *113*, 114, 144, 221, 244, 273
Mudie, Thomas, 228
Mueller, Georg, 264
Müller brothers, 125
Musard, Philippe, 226
Musical Library, 218
Musical Times, 218
Musical World, 218
music festivals, 7, 96–7
musicians
　actions by, 221, 230
　demands on, 10
　employment, 33, 70, 214, 217
　numbers of professional, 110
　pay and conditions, 72, 112, 126, 214, 219, 241
　pensions, 112, 116
　training, *see* education
　see also orchestral musicians, singers, string playing *and* wind playing
music instruction books, 242

Nabholz, J. C., *240*
Naples
　musical education in, 19, 161, 163, 175
　royal theatres, 182
　San Carlo Theatre, 162, 163, 164, 176, 182
Napoleon I, 4, 5, 8, 18–19, 40–1, 50–1, 110
　and Italy, 160–1, 174
　and Saxony, 141, 142
Napoleon III, 45
national anthems, 8, 34, 251, 287, 290
National Guard (France), 33
nationalism
　in art, 141
　in English music journals, 218
　in Latin America, 280, 284
　Russian, 256
　Verdi's operas and, 191–3
Naumann, Johann Gottlieb, 127
Neate, Charles, 210, 213, 215, 228
Negro music, 265, 267
Neidhart, A. H., 133
Neue Berliner Musik zeitung, 123
Neue Berliner musikalische Zeitung, 127
Neue Zeitschrift für Musik, 8, 150, 156
Neukomm, Sigismund von, 88, 290

New Musical Fund (England), 214
New Orleans
  Negro Philharmonic Society, 277
  St Charles Theater, 276
Nichelmann, Christoph, 109
Nicolai, Otto, 93, 99, 100–01, 165–6
  Die lustigen Weiber von Windsor, 100–01,
  114
Nicolai family, 128
Nicolini, Guiseppe, 290
Nicolò, *see* Isouard, Nicolas
Niedermeyer, Louis, 59
Nixon, John, 205
Norma, see under Bellini, Vincenzo
Norwich Mercury, 213
Nourrit, Adolphe, 30, 53, 54
Nouvelliste, 255
Novello, Vincent, 209, 229
novels about music, 256

Odoevsky, Price Vladimir, 251, 252,
  256
Offenbach, Jacques, 45, 78–9
Olivares, Juan Manuel, 286–7
Onslow, Georges, 71
opera, 28–30, 87–8
  and politics, 8, *9*, 13, 46–8, 55–6, 91, 104,
    151, 169, 181, 191–3
  and revolutionary hymns, 39
  arrangements from, 64, 65
  controversies over, 16
  costumes, *13*
  finances, 181, 182, 195, 204–5
  forms, 170, 173–4, 187
  in Berlin, 109–10, 112–15, *113*,
    114
  in Dresden, 142–3
  in Italy, 160, 162, 163, 164–75, 176–89,
    190–7
  in Latin America, 282, 283–4, 288, 289,
    290
  in Leipzig, 149–51
  in London, 203–4, 213, 217, 220–3,
    230–1
  in Paris, 46–56
  in Russia, 238, 241, 242–5, 247–9,
    250
  in USA, 262, 273–4, 275–6
  in Vienna, 90–1, 97–9, 102, 104
  opéra-comique, 48–50
  realism in, 14
  rehearsal, 195
  spoken dialogue in, 48, 49
  status, 45–6
  subject matter, 13–14, 29, 39, 48–9, 54–5,
    172, 182, 184, 186, 187, 196
  ticket prices, 43, 177–9, *203*
  types, 20
  voices used, 187–9
operatic fantasies, 65, 67

oratorios, 101, 103, 161, 206, *206*, 226
orchestral musicians, 19–20
  action by, 221
  benefits for, 122
  deputizing, 209, 214
  entry to profession, 213–14
  pay and conditions, 72, 112, 126, 135, 204,
    208–9, 211–12, 214
  pensions, 116
  training, 175, 214
orchestras
  in Berlin, 110, 111–12, 116, 117, 126–7,
    131, 134
  in Dresden, 148
  in Latin America, 282, 283
  in Leipzig, 151, *155*
  in London, 204, *205*, 208, 211–13, 214, 221,
    224, 229
  in Naples, 163
  in Paris, 61, 72–3
  in Russia, 241, 245, 253
  in theatres, 46
  in USA, 269–70
  in Vienna, 91, 93
  leadership/conducting, 19–20, 61, 212–13,
    214, 225, 229
orchestration, 14, 20–21, 22–3, 100, 169,
  174, 184–5, 240
organs, 59
ornamentation, 207
Ortega, Aniceto, 284
d'Ortigue, Joseph, 59
Oury, Anna Caroline, 255
overtures, 25–6, 63
Ozi, Etienne, 33, 63–4

Pacini, Giovanni, 176, 187
Paer, Ferdinando, 41, 44, 51, 146–7
  Camilla, 146–7
  I fuorusciti di Firenze, 146
  Leonora, 146
  Sargino, 146
Paganini, Nicolò, 15, 44, 65, *68*, 95, 96, 124,
  129, 252, 255
  Berlioz and, 75
  and publicity, 11, 97
  London concerts, 219–20, *220*, 221
pageants, 50
Paisiello, Giovanni, 40, 41, 51, 169, 205, 238,
  246
  Il barbiere di Siviglia, 238, 244, 283
  Nina, 172
  Il re Teodoro in Venezia, 169
Palacios y Sojo, Pedro, 286
Palestrina, Giovanni Pierluigi da, 12,
  189
Palschau, Johann Gottfried Wilhelm, 242
Paniagua, Cenobio, 284
Panseron, Auguste, 57
Pantaleoni (singer), 125

The Early Romantic Period

Paris
 Chapelle (Royale), 32, 33, 41, 43, 58
 Concert de la Loge Olympique, 60
 'Concerts de la rue de Cléry', 61, 62
 Concert Spirituel, 33, 60, 100, 151
 Conservatoire, 18, 33, 41, 46, 62, 72, 76
  concerts in, 61–2, *62*, 72–3, 76
 Ecole de Musique de la Garde Nationale,
  18
 Ecole Royale de Chant, 18, 33,
 Institut de Musique Religieuse Classique,
  12, 41, 43
 musical education in, 18 (*see also*
  Conservatoire)
 Notre Dame, 32–3, 58, 59
 Nouvelle Société Philharmonique, 77
 Opéra, 33, 42, 43–4, 47, 48, 50–1, 52, *52*,
  74–5, 78, 79
  concerts spirituels, 72
  finance, 43, 50, 53
 Opéra-Comique, 47–8, 51, 56, 60
 Opéra-National, 56
 population, 4, 201
 Salle des Italiens, 47
 Salle Pleyel, *71*
 Théâtre de la Porte-St-Martin, 46
 Théâtre Favart, 48
 Théâtre Feydeau (Théâtre de Monsieur),
  47–8, *48*, 60–1
 Théâtre-Italien, 42, 43, 51, 56
 Théâtre-Lyrique, 56, 78
Parthey, Gustav, 129
Parthey, Hans, 128
Parthey, Lili, 128
Pasdeloup, Jules, 77
Pashkevich, Vasily, 239
Pasta, Carlo Enrico, 288
Pasta, Giuditta, 43, 51, 169, 181, 215,
 248
Patti, Adelina, 286
Pearman, William, 286
pensions, 209, 214, 245
Peralta, Angela, 284
Pergolesi, Giovanni Battista, 251
periodicals, *see* journals
Peter, Johann Friedrich, 264
Peters, Carl Friedrich, 154
Peters (publishers), 144, 154–5
Petipa, Lucien, *55*
Petrov, Osip Afanasevich, 248
Philadelphia
 Chestnut Street Theatre, 273
 Musical Fund Society, 273, 274
 population, 272
Philadelphia National Gazette, 273, 274
Philidor, François-André Danican, 39,
 244
Phillips, Henry, 215
Phillips, William Lovell, 228
philosophy, 89–90

piano music, 65–70, 96, 284–5, 286
 in concerts, 99–100
piano playing, 207, 252
pianos, 22, 65, 229
Picasarri, José Antonio, 288
Piccinni, Niccolò, 50, 172
Pisarev (writer), 247
Pividor, G., *178*
Pixis, Johann Peter, 65, 67
plainchant, 59, 249–52
'plantation songs', 267
Pleyel, Camille, 211
Pleyel, Ignace, 34, 63, 64, 206, 274
Pleyel (piano makers), 65
Pohlenz, Christian August, 151
Poland, 8
politics
 male choirs and, 97
 music and, 141, 149
 opera and, *see under* opera
Popov, M., 238
population, 4, 42, 110, 201, 272
Portugal, Marcos, 290
Potter, Cipriani, 215, 218, 228
Práč, Jan Bohumir, 239
Prague, 101
Price, Henry, 287
Price, Jorge W., 287
printing, 4, 153
programme music, 25–6, 65, 90
progress, idea of, 3
publicity, 10, 67, 95, 208, 219
publishing, 153, 155–6, 213, 245
 contracts, 6, 70
 music, 6, 10, 34, 42, 44, 57, 89, 103, 144,
  153–5, 229, 242, 254–5, 274, 285
 of concertos, 207
 of early music, 97, 154, 155, 209
 of operas, 46
Puccitta, Vincenzo, 290
Puget, Löisa, 57
Pugin, Augustus Charles, *204*
Pushkin, Alexander, 245–6, 254

Quantz, Johann Joachim, 18
Quarenghi, G., *237*
Quarterly Musical Magazine and Review, 213,
 216, 218–19

Raaff, Anton, 187–8
Rachadell, Nicolás Quevedo, 287
Radziwill, Prince Maciej, 119
Rameau, Jean-Philippe, 33, 39
Rastrelli, Bartolomeo Francesco, *237*
Read, Daniel, 264, 265
Rebagliati, Claudio, 288
Reckers, Johannes, *23*
recordings, 169n13, 239nn4,6
rehearsal, 193; *see also* orchestras, leadership/
 conducting

Reicha, Antoine, 18
Reichardt, Johann Friedrich, 5, 25, 84, 86, 88,
    92–3, 109
Reimers, Carl, *155*
Reinagle, Alexander, 273, 274
Reinhardt (clarinettist), 114
Reissiger, Carl Gottlieb, 115
religious music, 12, 29–30, 58–9, 102–3,
    119–20, 209–10
  in Berlin, 119–20
  in concerts, 231
  in England, 209–10
  in France, 29–30, 41, 58–9
  in Italy, 161, 189–90
  in Latin America, 286
  in Russia, 249–52
  in USA, 263–4, 265, 268, 271–2, 277
Rellstab, Johann Karl Friedrich, 109
Rellstab, Ludwig, 118, 134
Renaissance music, *12*, 59
  performances of, 97, 208
  used as model, 59
Reveil du peuple, Le, 35
revolutionary songs and hymns, 34–5, *34*, 37,
    38, 39–40, 42, 47, 48
revolutions, 1–4, 8, 97
  of 1848, 44–5, 104–5, 110, 123, 167, 192,
    193, *194*, 196
  see also under France
Rice, Thomas D., 265–6, *266*
Richardson, Samuel, 172
Riemann, Hugo, 89
Ries, Ferdinand, 19–20, 95, 211, 213
Ries, Hubert, 118
Rietz, Eduard, 129
Rietz, Julius, *155*
Righini, Vincenzo, 111, 115, 119
Rio de Janeiro
  Conservatory, 290
  Real Teatro de São João/São Pedro de
    Alcântara, 290
  Teatro Regio, 290
riots, 8, *9*, 13, 166, *203*, 230
Risorgimento, 191–2
Ritter, Georg Wenzel, 110
Ritz, Eduard, 119
Robespierre, M. F. M. I. de, 37
Rocamora, Victorio, 283
Rochlitz, Johann Friedrich, 91, 156
Rode, A., 127
Rode, Pierre, 33
Rolla, Anton, 148
Romagnési, Antoine, 57
romances, 56–8, 247, 254
Romani, Felice, 185
Romanticism, 6–7, 11, 16, 26, *27*, 28,
    44
  and folksong, 287–8
  Beethoven and, 89
  Heinrich and, 261

literary, 54
London and, 231–2
musical scholarship and, 12
opera and, 147, 183–6, 191
politics and, 192
Russians and, 245–6, 251
Vienna and, 89–90, 101
Romberg, A., 127
Romberg, Bernhard, 252, 253, 255
Ronconi, Giorgio, *102*, 248
Rossi, Gaetano, 147
Rossi, Lauro, 284
Rossini, Gioachino, 44, 51, 54, *68*, 73, 147,
    166, *168*, 169, 170–1, 172–3, 174–5,
    186, 190, 220, 255
  and Naples, 163
  arrangements of works by, 93, 266
  influence, 51, 166, 183, 187, 190, 196
  Meyerbeer and, 145
  Morlacchi and, 147
  orchestration, 184–5
  performances of works by, 19, 73, 97, 114,
    136, 148, 182, 255, 262, 275, 283, 289,
    290
  politics, 192
  popularity, 13, 42, 51, 86, 95, 97, 103
  Schumann on, 8
  Il barbiere di Siviglia, 112, 172, 213, 275,
    289
  La Cenerentola, 172, 274
  Le comte Ory, 51
  La donna del lago, 51, 184
  Elisabetta, regina d'Inghilterra, 112
  La gazza ladra, 112, 172
  Guillaume Tell, 51–3, 115, 196, 230
  L'italiana in Algeri, 86, 114, 170, 173, 190
  Mosè in Egitto, 171, 174, 192
  Otello, 112, 189n29
  Semiramide, 51, 93, 170, 171, *171*, 181, 189
  Stabat mater, 190
  Tancredi, 86, 112, 173
  Il turco in Italia, 185
  Il viaggio a Reims, 51
Roubaud, B., *74*
Rouget de Lisle, Claude-Joseph, 34
  La Marseillaise, 34–5, *34*, 37, 47
Rousseau, Jean-Jacques, 86, 167, 280
  Le devin du village, 238
Rowlandson, Thomas, *204*
Royal Society of Musicians (England), 214
Rubini, Giovanni Battista, 51, 188, *188*, 248,
    255
Rubinstein, Anton, 256
Rudolph, Archduke of Austria, 95
Rungenhagen (composer), 119
Russell, Henry, 263

Sacchini, Antonio, 50, 205
Sack, Johann Philipp, 109

The Early Romantic Period

St Petersburg
  Bol'shoy Theatre, 246
  The Hermitage, 236, *237*, 238
  imperial chapel, 249–51
  Pavlovsk Music Hall, 253
  university concerts, 253
Saint-Saëns, Camille, 79
Saint-Simonians, 44
Salieri, Antonio, 50, 86, 87, 88, 246, 290
  Der Rauchfangkehrer, 88
  La Scuola de' gelosi, 244
  Tarare, 1–3
Salomon, Charles K., 228
Salomon, J. P., 206, 207, 211
salon music, 217, 282, 285, 288–9
salons, 128–30, 216, 218, 253–4
Salvi, Lorenzo, 248
Sand, George, *68*, *69*
Sandunova, Elizaveta, 245, 255
Sanquirico, Alessandro, *171*, *183*
Santiago de Chile
  Sociedad del Cuarteto, 288
  Sociedad de Música Clásica, 288
  Teatro de la Républica, 288
  Teatro de la Universidad, 288
  Teatro Municipal, 288
Santley, Charles, 166
Sarmiento, Domingo, 289
Sarrette, Bernard, 18, 33, 37, 41
Sarti, Giuseppe, 205, 238, 240–1, 251
  Le gelosie villane, 169
Saumell, Robredo Manuel, 285–6
Sax, Adolphe, *24*, 53
Saxony, 141–2
saxophone, 22, *24*
Scarlatti, Alessandro, 161
Schade, C. F., 109
Schebest, Agnes, 148
Schemelli, Georg Christian, 153
Schicht, Johann Gottfried, 151
Schikaneder, Emanuel, 87
Schiller, J. C. F. von, 7, 141, 191
Schimon, Ferdinand, *146*
Schinkel, Karl Friedrich, *113*, 114, *114*, *122*
Schlesinger, A. M., 130
Schlesinger, Maurice, 6
Schmidt, Johann, 89
Schneider, Friedrich, 119
Schneider, Georg Abraham, 116, 132–3
Schneider, Julius, 119, 120
Schoberlechner, Franz, 252
Schoenberg, Arnold, 27
scholarship, musical, 12, 89; *see also* early
  music
Schöller, J. C., *90*, *101*
Scholze, Johann Sigismund (Sperontes), 153
schools, 118, 127; *see also* education
Schott (publisher), 6
Schröder-Devrient, Wilhelmine, 112, 132,
  144, 148

Schubert, Ferdinand, 104
Schubert, Franz, 16, 26, 86, 90, *91*, *94*, 95–6,
  103, 104
  concerts, 95, 96
  performances of works by, 10, 95–6, 225,
    253
  publication of works by, 103
  Schubertiads, *94*, 95
  chamber music, 20, 21, 95, 96
  Das Dörfchen, 95
  Erlkönig, 95, *96*
  Gesang der Geister über dem Wasser, 95
  lieder, 25–6, 27, 57, 95, *96*
  Octet, 89, 95
  piano music, 90, 96
  piano trios, 95
  Die schöne Müllerin, 26, 27
  string quartets, 95, 96
  String Quintet in C, 21
  Symphony no. 8 in B minor ('Unfinished'),
    21, 26–7
  Symphony no. 9 ('Great C major'), 10, 21,
    135, 152–3, 231–2
  'Trout' Quintet, 21
Schubert, Karl Bogdanovich, 253
Schultz, Johann Philipp Christian, 151
Schulz, Josephine, 130
Schulze-Kilitschky, Josephine, 112
Schumann, Clara, *see* Wieck, Clara
Schumann, Robert, 8, 10, 11, 16, 26, 27, 28,
  67, 89, 129, 253
  and London, 225, 231
  and *Neue Zeitschrift für Musik*, 156
  and Sterndale Bennett, 228
  criticism and journalism, 8, 13–16, 30, 67,
    156, 228
  on Mendelssohn, 15–16
  on Meyerbeer, 13–15
  performances of works by, 253
  chamber music, 20
  Manfred overture, 253
  Das Paradies und die Peri, 119, 152
  Piano Concerto, 100
  piano pieces, 90
  Symphony no. 1, 26, 27, 152
  Symphony no. 2, 152
  Symphony no. 4, 152
Schuppanzigh, Ignaz, *91*, 95
Schwind, Moritz von, *91*
Scio, Julie Angélique, 48
Scott, Walter, 54, 184, 186, 192
Scribe, Eugène, 13, 14, 53
Sechter, Simon, 89
Seconda, Joseph, 142
Seidel, Friedrich Ludwig, 116
Seidler, Caroline, 112
Seidler (violinist), 110
Selivanovsky (publisher), 242
Semper, Gottfried, 143, *143*
Senefelder, Aloys, 4

Senkovsky, Osip, 256
serfs, 241
Seyfried, Ignaz von, 93, 103
Seyler, Abel, 150
Shakespeare, William, 73, 75, 191
    Hamlet, 213
    Verdi compared to, 196
Shakhovskoy (writer), 247
Shaw, George Bernard, 183, 197
Sheremetev, Count, 241, 246, 251
Shestakova, Lyudmila, *247*
Shirreff, Jane, 230
Signale für die musikalische Welt, 123, 133, 150,
    156
Sikhra, Andrey, 254
Silva, Francisco Manuel da, 290
singers, 112, 167, 207
    action by, 230
    fees, 181, 193, 203–4, 243
    technique, 30, 54, 99, 161, 171, 188, 189
    training, 18, 19
    voices favoured, 187–9
singing, mass, *34*, 35; *see also* choruses/choirs
Singspiel, 20
Smart, George, 213, 216, 221, 225
Smithson, Harriet, 28, 76
Society of British Musicians, 218
Sokolovsky, Mikhail, 238
song cycles, 25–6, 27
songs, 56–8, 242, 247, 254, 262–3, 267
    revolutionary, 34–5, *34*, 37, 39–40, 42, 48
    satirical, 60–61
    see also lieder
Sonnleithner, Leopold von, 95, 105
Sonntag, Nina, 221
Sontag, Henriette, 97, 114, 128, 255
Sperontes, 153
Spieloper, 20
spirituals, 265
Spohr, Louis, 124, 129, 214
    and conducting, 19–20, 225
    performances of works by, 215
    Faust, 115, 117
    Jessonda, 114, 144, 150
    Die Kreuzfahrer, 115
    Septet, 89
Spontini, Gaspare, 39, 51, 112, 117, 122, 221
    Berlioz and, 78
    music used in church, 249
    performances of works by, *13*, 73, 112, *113*,
        114, 117, 132, 148, 247, 249
    Rossini and, 147
    Agnes von Hohenstaufen, 114
    Fernand Cortez, *13*, 51, 112
    Olimpie/Olympia, 51, *113*, 114, 117
    La vestale, 29, 51, 112, 148, 249
Spontini Foundation, 122
Stadler, Maximilian, 103
Stamitz, Johann, 33
Stamitz, Karl, 269

Stasov, Vladimir, 253
Steibelt, Daniel, 47, 65, 88, 207
Stendhal (Henri Beyle), 51, 165, 169
Stern, Julius, 135
Stevenson, John, 263
Stifter, Adalbert, 84
Stockhausen, Margarethe, 215
Storace, Nancy, 205
Storace, Stephen, 205
Stowe, Harriet Beecher, 267
Strauss, Johann (the elder), 16–18, 93, 97, 99,
    100, *101*, 103–4, 134, 135
string instruments, 22
string playing, 19, *21*, 72, 110, 112, 207, 244
string quartets, 64–5, 71, 91–2
    concerts of, 116, 117, 118, 125, 136
Stümer (singer), 130
style, 62–3, 169
    descriptions of, 202, 203
subsidies, government, 181, 182, 193, 282
Süe, Eugène, 54
suffrage, 42, 45
Sullivan, Arthur, 190
Sulzer, Salomon, 99
Süssmayr, Franz Xaver, 86–7
Swan, Timothy, 264
symphonic poems, 25–6
symphonies, 63
symphonies concertantes, 63–4
Szymanowska, Maria, 215

Tadolini, Eugenia, *102*
Tamberlik, Enrico, 248, 284
Tamburini, Antonio, 230, 248
taste, 49, 93, 97, 103–4, 207, 211, 214, 223,
    255–6, 267
    distrust of new/modern music, 136, 216,
        225
Taubert, Wilhelm, 111
Tausch (composer), 115
Taylor, Raynor, 273
Tchaikovsky, Pyotr Il'yich, 249
technology, 4
Teplov, Grigory, 241
Tessier, Auguste, 275
Thalberg, Sigismond, 65, 66–9, *66*, 99–100,
    228, 284
    Fantasy and Variations on themes from
        Norma, 67, 68
Thalheim, Jenny, 128
theatre
    in France, 46
    in Italy, 162, 163, 177–9
    in Latin America, 282, 285
    in London, 213
    in Paris, 39, 41, 43, 46
    in Russia, 244, 246–7, 249
    in USA, 269–70, 273
    music for, 46, 126
theorists, 89

The Early Romantic Period

Thibaut, A. F. J., 11, *12*
Thomas, Ambroise, 46
Tichatschek, Joseph, 112, 148
ticket prices, *see under* concerts *and under*
    opera
Tieck, Ludwig, 91, 142
Times, The, 219
timpani, 229
Tischbein, J. H. W., *6*
titles (of pieces of music), 90
Titov, Alexey Nikolayev, 248, 249
Titov, N. S., 242
Tomášek, Václav, 90, 96
tone poems, 25–6
Traetta, Tommaso, 238
training, *see* education
Trollope, Frances, 99
trombone choirs, 264
Truhn, Hieronymus Friedrich, 136
tuba curva, 37, *38*
Tucholsky, Kurt, 97
Tuczek, Leopoldine, 112, 128
Tulou, Jean-Louis, 72
Turchaninov, Pyotr Ivanovich, 251

Urusov, Prince, 242, 243
USA constitution, 4
  and Mendelssohn, 101

Vaccai, Nicola, 187
Valentino (conductor), 72
valves, 22, *24*
variations, 65, 103, 284
Varlamov, Alexander Egorovich, 251, 254,
    255, 256
Varnhagen, Karl, 128
Varnhagen, Rahel, 128
vaudeville, 247, 249
Velasco, Juan Antonio de, 287
Velásquez, José Francisco, 286–7
Velluti, Giovanni Battista, 147, 167
Venice
  La Fenice, 164, *171*, 177, *178*, 181, *195*
  music schools, 175
  orphanages, 161
  San Carlo, 193
Verdi, Giuseppe, 8, 79, 175, 186, 187, 189,
    190, 191–3, 195–6, 197, 283
  orchestration, 185
  politics, 192–3
  vocal writing, 171–2
  Aida, 51
  Un ballo in maschera, 189n28
  La battaglia di Legnano, 193
  Don Carlos, 79
  Ernani, 104, 191–2
  Falstaff, 191
  La forza del destino, 195
  Un giorno di regno, 191
  I Lombardi alla prima crociata, 191, 192, 193

Macbeth, 182, 184, *185*, 186, 191–2
Nabucco, 8, 171–2, 191–3
Rigoletto, 182, 186, *194*, 195–6
Simon Boccanegra, 195
La traviata, 172, 174, 195–6
Il trovatore, 173, 187, 189, 195
Les vêpres siciliennes, 79
verismo, 197
Véron, Louis, 43–4, 53
Verstovsky, Alexey Nikoayevich, 248–9, 251,
    254, 255, 256
Vestris, Lucia Elizabeth, 215
Viala, Agricola, 47
Viardot-Garcia, Pauline, 112, 125, 128, 132,
    248, 255
Victoria, Queen of Britain, 215
Vielgorsky, Count Mikhail, 253
Vienna
  Conservatory, 99
  dance halls, *17*
  Gesellschaft der adeligen Damen, 95
  Gesellschaft der Musikfreunde, 93, 100,
    104, 105
  Grosser Redoutensaal, 100
  Kärntnertortheater, *3*, 93, 95, 99, 102, *102*,
    104
  Musikverein, 91
  National Singspiel, 143
  Nationatheater, 104
  philharmonic concerts, 100–01
  population, 201
  St Stephen's Cathedral, 99
  synagogue, 99
  Theater an der Wien, *90*, 104
  Winterreitschule, 97, *98*
Vierne, Louis, 59
Vieuxtemps, Henry, 255
Viezzoli, G., 187n26
Villoteau, Guillaume, 13
Vinogradov, M. A., 251
Viotti, Giovanni Battista, 60, 62–3,
    203
Virginia Minstrels, 266
Vleck, Jacob van, *263*
Vogl, Johann Michael, *94*
Vogler, Georg Michel (Abbé), 119–20
Voltaire, F. M. Arouet de, 35, 37, 39,
    184
Vorišek, Jan Hugo, 96
Vorobëva, Anna Yaklovlevna, 248
Vorontsov, Count, 242
Vorotnikov (composer), 251

Wackenroder, W. H., 16, 89
Wagner, Cosima, 67
Wagner, Richard, 44, 79, 89, 90, 99, 185, 186
  and Dresden Opera, 148–9
  Beethoven and, 19, 30, 148
  Berlioz and, 75
  Meyerbeer and, 14, 39, 53, 148

Wagner, Richard, *cont'd*
  Weber and, 148
  influences, 14, 149
  on Méhul, 49
  politics, 15, 16
  Der fliegende Holländer, 115, 147, 148–9
  Lohengrin, 29, 149, 164
  Die Meistersinger, 14
  Rienzi, 14, 39, 133, 148–9, *149*
  Tannhäuser, 29, 39, 79, 148–9
  Tristan und Isolde, 184
Waldmüller, Ferdinand Georg, *85, 94*
waltzes, 16–18, 93, 97
Warren, James, *152*
Washington, George, 264
Weber, Bernhard Anselm, 122
Weber, Carl Maria von, 16, 89, 129, *145*, 186,
    220, 255
  and Dresden Opera, 143–7
  in England, 219, 221
  influence, 14, 249
  novel, *Tonkünsters Leben*, 147
  on Méhul, 49
  performances of music by, 53–4, 73, 97,
      112, 114, 117, 127, 130, 132, 134, 145,
      150, 215, 220–1, 247, 253, 255, 276
  politics, 8
  views on music, 7
  Wagner and, 148
  Abu Hassan, 112
  Euryanthe, 97–9, 114, 144–5, 147
  Der Freischütz, *28–9*, 29, 49, 53–4, 99, 114,
      114, 144, 147, 150, 184, 220–1, 247,
      276
  Oberon, 114, 117, 130, 221
  Silvana, 112
  songs for four voices, 127
Weigl, Joseph, 87
  Die Schweizerfamilie, 87, 144
  Das Waisenhaus, 87, 144

Weller (conductor), 132, 133
Wesley, Charles, 274
Wesley, Samuel, 209
Western Messenger, The, 268
Westphalia, 4
Westrop, Henry, 228
Wieck, Clara (Clara Schumann), 8, 28, 102,
    124–5, *125*, 129, 253
Wiener Allgemeine musikalische Zeitung, 103
Wieprecht, Wilhelm, 111, 120–1, 133–4,
    137
Wignell, Thomas, 273
Wilhem (Bocquillon, Guillaume), 44, 57
William IV of Britain, 223
wind instruments, 22, *23*, *24*, 37, *38*
wind playing, 18, 19, *23*, 61, 110, 112, 179–81,
    207, 214
Winter, Peter von, 87
Wolf, Hugo, 90
women
  composers, 57
  in audiences, 43, 151, 179
  in choirs, 270
  instrumentalists, 207, 214
  London Philharmonic Society and, 212
  restrictions on, 43
Würst, Richard, 134

Zagoskin, Mikhail Nikoleyevich, 245
Zaneboni, Joseph, 244
Zeitung für die elegante Welt, 155
Zelter, Carl Friedrich, 117, 119, 120,
    129
Zeno, Apostolo, 84–5
Zhilin, Alexey, 255
Zhukovsky, Vasily Andreyevich, 245
Zimmermann (violinist), 118
'Zip Coon', 266
znamenny chant, 249
Zumsteeg, Johann Rudolf, 25